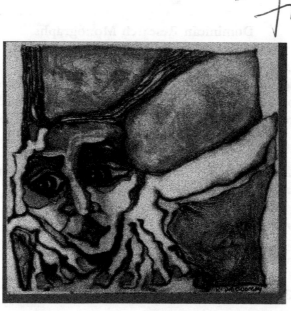

DOCUMENTS OF DISSIDENCE

SELECTED WRITINGS BY DOMINICAN WOMEN

Compilation, Bibliography and Introduction
by
Daisy Cocco De Filippis

D1398965

CUNY DOMINICAN STUDIES INSTITUTE
Foundational Documents Series

Dominican Research Monographs

Foundation Documents Series, one of the publication series of the CUNY Dominican Studies Institute, seeks to disseminate knowledge of the Dominican experience in the United States, the Dominican Republic, and elsewhere. Generally, the texts published in the series will have been generated by archival recovery projects sponsored by the CUNY Dominican Studies Institute.

Title: Documents of Dissidence: Selected Writings by Dominican Women
Compilation, bibliography and introduction: Daisy Cocco De Filippis
Cover Design: Raquel Paiewonsky
Publications Consultant: Jennifer Radtke

ISBN: 0-9676741-2-3

Credits: This publication has been made possible in part by the support of the Office of Organized Research, the City University of New York. Special thanks to Dr. Louise Mirrer, Vice Chancellor for Academic Affairs, and Ernesto Malavé, Director of University Budget.

The CUNY Dominican Studies Institute at City College is an organized research unit of the City University of New York approved by the Board of Trustees of the University on February 22, 1994. City College, Hostos Community College, and the central administration of CUNY, with the support of the Dominican community in New York, have led the effort that created the CUNY Dominican Studies Institute.

For information on the series or on the overall research agenda of the Institute, you may reach us at:

The CUNY Dominican Studies Institute
The City College of New York
North Academic Center, Room 4-107
New York, NY 10031
Tel: (212) 650-7496
Fax: (212) 650-7489
e-mail: dsi@phantom.cct.ccny.cuny.edu

Table of Contents

DEDICATION

For las señoritas Violeta Rodríguez del Prado, Anita Fiallo, Cristinita Fiallo, Margarita Contín y Aybar and Consuelo Nivar, and for don Babá Henríquez and la Srta. de la Cuesta and the faculty and staff of the "Instituto Escuela" in Santo Domingo in the 1950's

Alma mater

Un rinconcito de ensueño,
una fuente de alegría,
donde moran como en cuentos,
amor y sabiduría,

sol que con paz y cariño,
vas derramando tu luz,
en nuestras mentes de niños,
eso eres tú, eres tú.

Instituto, Instituto Escuela,
yo te ofrezco, agradecida mi canción.
Eres parte de mi tierra quisqueyana,
y eres parte de mi tierno corazón.

Y aunque pase mucho tiempo al recordarte,
en mi pecho, sentiré, honda emoción.
Y aunque pase mucho tiempo al recordarte,
en mi pecho, sentiré, honda emoción.

From the age of five until I was eleven years old, I was privileged to attend a very unique school. Created by some of the more progressive intellectuals in Santo Domingo in the early 1950's, the "Instituto Escuela" became a refuge for many children from the indoctrination on behalf of Trujillo's regime which was passed off as curriculum in many of our institutions of learning at the time.

A co-educational school, the "Instituto Escuela" implemented many theories about a secular and scientific education for both boys and girls, proposed by Eugenio María de Hostos and Salomé Ureña de Henríquez during the last two decades of the nineteenth century. Reading Mercedes Laura Aguiar's personal account of daily activities at Salomé Ureña de Henríquez's "Instituto de Señoritas" brought me a deep sense of recognition, for at the "Instituto Escuela" we were exposed to a similarly comprehensive curriculum and many of the same pedagogical practices. At the "Instituto Escuela," however, instruction was given to a student population made up of boys and girls who also enjoyed co-educational sports, singing and dancing, which included folk songs from many parts of the world.

We benefited from a sense of continuity in the history of pedagogy in the Dominican Republic, illustrated by the choice of strategies and instruments used to teach us. For example, there was a time of the day devoted to agility of thinking, which included movements forward and backward in mathematical operations, described and solved orally, much as don Pancho (Francisco Henríquez y Carvajal, Salomé Ureña's husband) had implemented at the "Instituto de Señoritas." Even today my recollections of using the same microscope that Salómé Ureña de Henríquez displayed proudly on her desk at the "Instituto de Señoritas" are of particular poignancy and beauty. The culture of learning, the concept of accountability and the value of striving for excellence were also replicated, and just like Salomé Ureña's pupils had done, we were required to bring home our report cards every Friday! I can tell you that at times this practice was responsible for unhappy week-ends for some of us.

During my last stay in Santo Domingo, I passed by the Calle Hermanos Deligne, and was reminded of the Instituto's recent history of closings and openings. At that time, I whispered a quiet prayer for its future. By writing these words, I honor the memory of my early teachers, individuals who instilled in me a sense of wonderment and inquiry and of civic responsibility. I also hope to remember the quiet heroism displayed every day by many teachers throughout the world.

Con agradecimiento
D.C.D.F.

ACKNOWLEDGMENTS

I acknowledge the effort, good will and talent of the authors whose works have been selected for inclusion in this anthology, as I thank Margaret A. Ballantyne for her able translation of ten of the documents included in this publication. The impactful and telling illustration of the book cover is the talented, generous and solidary work of Raquel Paiewonsky.

Various institutions lent their support to this project: York College of The City University of New York granted me a "Fellowship Leave" for the academic year 1996-97 and the Rockefeller Foundation a visiting scholar fellowship at the CUNY Dominican Studies Institute at City College (1996-97) which allowed me to dedicate a good part of my time during the spring of 1997 to the completion of this project. A small grant from the Faculty Development Committee for Sponsored Programs at York College supported in part the preparation of this manuscript.

It pleases me to mention individuals without whose support this project would not be possible: Chiqui Vicioso, Emelda Ramos, Bonnie Lander, Neicy Zeller, Ylonka Nacidit-Perdomo, Jean Weissman, Ida Hernández Caamaño, Myrna Guerrero, Altagracia Pou, Franklin Gutiérrez, Frank Moya Pons, Silvio Torres-Saillant, Jennifer Radtke, David Koteles and my colleagues on staff at the "Archivo Nacional" in Santo Domingo.

Finally, as always, I thank Nunzio De Filippis, my husband and mi compañero of the last thirty-five years, for his generous and constant support.

D.C.D.F.

PREFACE

After first reading in the early 1990s the pamphlet *Historia de una mujer* (A Woman's Story), published in 1849 by the Dominican folk poet, political activist and ideologue Manuela Aybar Rodríguez, it dawned on us at the then nascent CUNY Dominican Studies Institute that the widespread absence of Dominican names from Latin American and Caribbean collections of women's writings had hardly anything to do with whether or not Dominican women had spoken up in writing about their deepest yearnings and their views of the world. The absence seemed to correspond rather to the overall marginality that plagued the study of things Dominican in Latin American studies programs in most colleges and universities throughout the United States. It was the recognition of that predicament which led to the creation of the Dominican Institute as a research unit of the City University of New York devoted to the production and dissemination of knowledge on the experience of Dominicans before and after the great exodus which has led to the formation of a Dominican diaspora with branches in the United States, the Caribbean, some parts of Latin America, and Europe. Since its inception, the Dominican Institute has tackled several intellectual gaps by publishing volumes that lay crucial foundations in the process of documenting the Dominican experience so as to make its study more feasible than it was less than a decade ago. *Documents of Dissidence*, edited and translated by Dominican literary scholar Dr. Daisy Cocco De Filippis, is a meaningful milestone in that process.

Conceived initially in early 1994, when we were fortunate to elicit the interest of Dr. De Filippis in assuming responsibility for compiling the volume, the project leading to the present publication has been several years in the making. The delay had to do with a combination of factors: the sheer difficulty of selecting, translating, and editing the numerous texts herein included, the limited ability of the Dominican Institute to finance projects of this magnitude, and the multiple instructional, organizational, and scholarly commitments of the compiler. But, temporary obstacles aside, at no point did we harbor the slightest doubt as to the importance of the project. We never wavered from the conviction that the compilation, as prepared by the expert hand of Dr. De Filippis, would contribute to bringing the voices of Dominican women within hearing range of the Latin Americanists and Caribbeanists who at present dominate a good portion of the discussion of feminism and gender issues. Following the publication of *Documents of Dissidence*, our peers in Latino studies and Caribbean studies courses or scholarly colloquia will necessarily find it less easy to justify persisting in their common exclusion of Dominican voices from discussion of the positions women have taken in and outside the sphere of the written text.

Finally, the publication of this volume marks the culmination of nearly a decade of (in our view) mutually enriching collaboration between the Dominican Institute and Dr. De Filippis. We have been fortunate to host her as a frequent speaker at our events, and on several occasions have followed her bidding in the organization of literary panels and readings, especially those involving women writers from the Dominican Republic. We have regularly co-sponsored conferences she has organized at York

College and have invariably supported the Caribbean women writers symposia she has coordinated at Hunter College. The Dominican Institute supported Dr. De Filippis' effort as founding president of the Dominican Studies Association and had the privilege of hosting her for one academic year as one of our first Rockefeller Foundation Humanities Fellowships resident scholars. Dr. De Filippis is the editor of "La literatura dominicana al final del siglo: Diálogo entre la tierra natal y la diáspora," the text of one of the issues in our Dominican Studies Working Papers series. Our recognition of the value of her work as an estimable pioneer in the current development of Dominican studies no doubt has caused us to place a greater demand on her energy and time than might seem considerate. We would like *Documents of Dissidence* to serve as a tribute to that collaboration, which we hope has been as beneficial to her as it has been to us.

Dr. Silvio Torres-Saillant
Director
CUNY Dominican Studies Institute

INTRODUCTION

Listening for the Sweet Sound of Their Own Words:
Reflections on the Dominican Feminine Essay

Gathered around you, like butterflies fluttering around a lamp giving out a very bright light, our souls hanging on your every word, our spirits transported with the fragrant emanations of your superior soul, united by the sacred bond of your affection, under the powerful spell of the sweet accent of your divine word, how pleasant were those hours of relaxation! How tender the beat of hearts who received from your soul the candid host of duty and truth and goodness, in the sanctuary of the intimacy of your affections!

— Mercedes Laura Aguiar, "Meseniana"

The only affectation some men cannot forgive in women is that of being talented.
— Abigaíl Mejía Soliere, *Ideario feminista*

Something does not add up. If by the mere chance of carrying out as our first obligation the act of independent creation, we forget the patriarchal surroundings which marginalize us, silence comes. It is against that environment, defeating the same, that we ought to circumscribe the diffusion or acceptance of the literature created by women.

— Carmen Imbert-Brugal, "La varona intelectual".

Nevertheless, April gave birth to a presence we must not forget: A public, militant female presence that escaped, on certain occasions, all the restrictions of a patriarchal culture which relegates women, permanently, to a secondary status. This presence faced death and all the other risks, in the same way that it faced the minutia of daily life.

— Margarita Cordero, *Mujeres de abril*, tr. Margaret A. Ballantyne

INTRODUCTORY REMARKS:

I begin these introductory remarks by evoking and listening to the sweet and bittersweet echoes of women who speak to us through time and space; women whose essays I literally "chased" during the better part of the last decade of work. In the pages of this book, I have gathered moments of tenacious daring and achievement, of great aspirations and inconsolable losses and disillusionments, but ultimately of plans for the future of women in the Dominican Republic. These writings cover the passing of almost one hundred and fifty years in the life of Dominican women. They speak of personal concerns and public struggles, and they represent in their individuality and collectivity a powerful and affirming contradiction to the official control of Dominican thought by men.

In her illustration for *Documents of Dissidence*, Raquel Paiewonsky ably captures the essence of the book. Her depiction of a woman pulling out her hair as she emerges from a rock, speaks clearly of moving away from tradition to new beginnings and of the painful and yet liberating experience this movement represents. The image of individuals pulling their hair to symbolize death and transformation appears in western culture as early as the eighth century B.C., as part of a transition from art depicting animals to the artistic representation of the human body. Our ancestors discovering themselves, and for the first time, perhaps, aware of their bodies, were learning to reproduce it in art. This is why at that time complete bodies were seldom depicted. Charioteers' bodies, for example, were painted hidden behind the shields they were carrying. (Griffiths Pedley: 116)

In a sense, Raquel Paiewonsky's portrayal of this new Dominican woman, coming out of the rock, emerging from behind the shield that has protected her as well as obscured her existence, has much in common with the essays selected for this publication. In choosing these works, I paid special attention to the inclusion of voices representative of different fields of endeavor and of diverse cultural, racial and class backgrounds. These essays serve to illustrate different stages in the lives of Dominican women in the process and struggle to set themselves free and to come out and show themselves as whole and intelligent beings. Their writings speak of vibrant and engaged human beings who contribute to the creation of culture and to the recording and keeping alive the contribution of women to all aspects of the Dominican experience.

A. THE ESSAY AND DOMINICAN ANTHOLOGIES:

The process has not been easy as recent events continue to illustrate. I can refer specifically to the publication in 1996 in the Dominican Republic of *Dos siglos de literatura dominicana*, a two-volume anthology of prose edited by José Alcántara Almánzar. In general, in his selection of writers to be included in the anthology, Alcántara Almánzar continued a trajectory of exclusion and the resulting shutting out of the voice of women from the public sphere. Of the thirty essayists included in the anthology only two were women: Flérida de Nolasco and Camila Henríquez Ureña.

In his introduction, Alcántara Almánzar points out that

> *In this section texts of great thematic diversity have been gathered which, seen as a whole, offer a panorama of Dominican thought during the xix and the xx centuries, its evolution, characteristics and theoretical leanings, and the manner in which our writers have approached the complex problems of the nation in order to explain them, or to point out the ways by which, in their opinion, Dominican society ought to evolve. (22)*

If we are guided by the opinions expressed above or by the selection of writings by women included in Almánzar's anthology, we need not conjecture as to the kind of role the editor understands women have played in pointing "out the ways by which Dominican society ought to evolve" and in the expression and formation of national identity. Firstly, his selection of essays is by itself a portrayal of an evolution which in its greater part appears to reserve limited spaces for the presence and contribution of representatives of more than half of the Dominican population (the feminine gender) and in the last instance, for the representatives or spokespersons for the interests of the majority of Dominican people (less privileged classes and those individuals who identify themselves as persons of color).

In fact, in the "thematic diversity " Alcántara Almánzar announces in his introduction we could question the inclusion of cultural diversity, a topic of debate in other areas of the Spanish speaking world, as Amaryll Chanady indicates in the introduction to the collection of essays *Latin American Identity and the Construction of Difference*:

> *At the same time that the nation is constructed, it is deconstructed by the successive, and always complementary and substitutive interpretations whose incompleteness and constant succession and mutual contradictions demonstrate the inexistence of any originary center: its space is "internally marked by cultural difference and the*

heterogeneous histories of contending peoples, antagonistic authorities and tense cultural locations."

Homi Bhabha in Chanady: x

If we stop for a moment to consider the epistemological implications of their introductory pronouncements and selection of materials, we may arrive at the conclusion that anthologies such as Alcántara Almánzar's appear to have failed in their stated purpose to present a national trajectory. The scarce representation of "cultural differences and heterogeneous histories" convert the selection of editors such as Alcántara Almánzar in a canon representative of one community, "imagined", to use the term coined by Benedict Anderson, by one sector of society. I propose here that we consider the concept of a Dominican nation from the perspective of more than one community. In that case, what would be the space/place alloted for voices such as the ones chosen by our colleague?

Another effort to create an anthology of the Dominican essay presents an even more lamentable portrait. I am thinking of the introduction and selection of texts by Margarita Vallejo de Paredes in Volume IV (Speeches, Biographies and Essays) of her *Antología literaria dominicana*. In the three hundred and three pages of this volume, where the work of forty-seven authors is included, there is only one woman author: Salomé Ureña de Henríquez. And of those three hundred and three pages only two pages are reserved for the presentation of the contribution by women. Vallejo de Paredes presents the section on speeches where Ureña is included with the following:

This section encompasses the extensive field of oratory. Men need to express themselves. That unavoidable activity in their lives is carried out by means of signs, which are presented in different forms: gestures, colors, representations, etc. One must also include here words, be they oral or written. (3)

Among the questions that these comments oblige us to formulate, I point out one: if the term "men" is used in an inclusive manner (to mean men and women), why isn't there a better representation of women? Surely this does not indicate a lack of women writers in the Dominican Republic. I notice here— disheartened, because it is so egregious— the exclusion of the numerous speeches made by Ercilia Pepín (1884-1939), who had been Mrs. Vallejo de Paredes' own teacher and whose biography Mrs. Vallejo de Paredes herself published in 1990. This is the same Ercilia Pepín whose speeches, supported by scientific data and rigorous research, planted the seeds of Dominican feminism. Interested individuals have easy access these days to Pepín's discursos in William Galván's 1986 publication of an anthology to commemorate the centennial of her birth. This is also the same Ercilia Pepín whose concept of national sovereignty and of fatherland was heard with strong and brilliant accents in a series of speeches which began to resonate throughout the nation barely forty days after the North American invasion of 1916. And finally, this is the same Ercilia Pepín who raised her voice and lowered the flag in her school to protest Trujillo's abuses. She paid the price for speaking out by losing the directorship of the beloved school she had fought so hard to build. Didn't Pepín have the need to express herself, and don't her words in fact have something to contribute to the anthologies of Vallejo de Paredes and Alcántara Almánzar about the articulation of a Dominican nation? Pepín is not an isolated case, as the selection included in the present anthology demonstrates.

B.   HISTORY AND MANIFESTATIONS OF THE ESSAY IN SPANISH AMERICA AND THE SPANISH SPEAKING CARIBBEAN:

The examples cited above oblige us to reflect on the history of the genre and its affiliation and identification with the masculine gender in the Caribbean and Latin America. In these lands, the essay has served dominant classes quite well, and I would dare to fix its antecedents in the documents of the conquest, for example, the *Diario* kept by Cristóbal Colón, the sermons included in de las Casas' *Breve historia* or *Las cartas de relación* by Hernán Cortés. These writings in their different manifestations (chronicles, letters of information, brief histories, etc.) served different functions, among them to annotate and record, but also to persuade, convince, disguise, distort and establish hierarchies of power and personal versions of a/some moment/s in history. It suffices to remember the various accounts written by chroniclers of the conquest of Mexico. As such they served as a useful compass in the demarcation of a new cartography.

The contemporary essay in Spanish America also traces its origins to the peninsular heritage of the humanists, Antonio de Guevara and Juan Luis Vives, to cite a couple of names who contribute to the anchoring of masculine authority in the genre. But there are essays that can guide the creation of new cartographies, born of the independence movements and of the formation of the concept of the Spanish American nation. Among them, we note the writings by Bolívar, Bello, Sarmiento, Rodó, Martí and others. (Meyer 1-9) A look at more traditional studies of the essay in Spanish America, for example, the volumes of Leopoldo Zea (*Fuentes de la cultura latinoamericana*) and of Martin S. Stabb (*In Quest of Identity: Patterns in the Spanish American Essay of Ideas, 1890-1960*) present a more complete spectrum of the canon for the genre Stabb has called the "essay of ideas".

Nevertheless, the essay of ideas is but one of the manifestations of the genre in our lands. There are others. Another history of the essay could be traced, parallel to that created by men, and written by women. In her valuable article "'Don't Interrupt Me': The Gender Essay as Conversation and Countercannon," Mary Louise Pratt explains the complexities in the formation of a canon for the Latin American essay. Pratt names the so-called essay of ideas the criollo essay, and she defines the word criollo as designating a class of Latin Americans who identify themselves as descendants of Europeans and who make up, for the most part, the ruling and elite class in almost all the countries in the region. According to Pratt, this type is the spinal chord of the essay canon, and the statue of Rodin, "The Thinker", its representation par excellence since it encapsulates the self-definition of these authors as the owners of the monopoly of thought. (Pratt in Meyer: 10-25)

In his introduction to *The Dissenting Voice: The New Essay of Spanish America. 1960-1985*, Martin S. Stabb points out the great variety of styles in essays written in the last few decades, indicating that

> *This no-man's land of 'essayistic' writing—collage testimonials, diaries, poetic prose, and other hybrid forms—cannot be ignored simply because it does not fit easily into well-established formal categories. (1)*

And although Stabb pays minimal attention to the essay written by women (the work of Rosario Castellanos, for example, is discussed briefly only in the context of its relationship with the essays written by Octavio Paz), his monograph is a true cornucopia of the contemporary essay written by well-known male authors. I point to some of the strategies illustrated in Stabb's volume in the chapter titled "Toward a new essay": the essay as poem (Octavio Paz' *El mono gramático* and Julio Cortázar's *Prosa del observatorio*); the essay as literary transgression (Gabriel Zaid's *Cómo leer en bicicleta*, Alejandro Rossi's *Manual del distraído* and Salvador Elizondo's *El grafógrafo*); the essay as collage (Julio Cortázar's *Ultimo Round* and Augusto Monterroso's *Lo demás es silencio*); the essay as a play on the authorial voice (Julio Cortázar's *Historias de cronopios y famas* and Jorge Ibargüengoitia's *Viajes en la América ignota*) [94-125] To this panorama we could add the essay as a workbook for idiots exemplified in the political satire by Plinio Apuleyo Mendoza and others which circulated widely in 1996.

It is interesting to note the phraseology used by Stabb, "no man's land" to refer to the more hybrid manifestations of the contemporary essay in Spanish America. Pratts, on her end, explains that the criollo essay, written in book form, or as polemic, journalism or speech and dealing with the issue of identity on the national, hemispheric or continental level, was considered, as they called it in the west, "a no woman's land". The choice of terms made by these critics in which land serves as the metaphor for a genre which has evolved into two excluding dicotomies, the version for males and the version for females, is not gratuitous. These comparisons serve to illustrate how closely the essay is tied to the public representation, the definition and the demarcation of peoples and national territories. We begin to understand then that the essay by its very definition (non-fiction) and its mission (to persuade) became the instrument par excellence for the public articulation of the interests of one class, in particular, the elite criollo class. This is why other voices and perspectives who usually are not attributed authority to persuade, define, convince and change are not considered weighty enough to find a place in the anthologies used to support the creation of canons and the continuity of *historias oficiales de la literatura.*

C. CARIBBEAN AND SPANISH AMERICAN WOMEN WRITERS AND THE ESSAY:

But, have women not written essays of ideas? Let us remember some examples which belie this categorization, among them: Manuela Gorriti's *Panorama de la vida*; Clorinda Matto de Turner's *Cuatro conferencias sobre América del Sur*; Mercedes Cabello de *Carbonera's La influencia de las Bellas Letras en el progreso moral y material de los pueblos*; Gabriela Mistral's *Recados: Cantando a Chile*; Luisa Capetillo's *La humanidad en el futuro*; Magda Portal's *América latina frente al imperialismo.* (Pratt in Meyer: 10-25) The answer is evident but we might want to consider a couple of examples to illustrate the point.

In her essay "The Letter as a Feminine Literary Expression", Camila Henríquez Ureña (1894-1973) chooses four women authors whose correspondence serves as the barometer, expression and answer to the historical moment they lived. Among them we find two writers whose names should head the history of the essay in the Spanish language: Santa Teresa de Jesús (1515-1582) and Sor Juana Inés de La Cruz (1648-1695). I will briefly point out some of the characteristics of Sor Juana's essay "La respuesta a sor Filotea." Josefina Ludmer has coined the phrase *Las tretas del débil* to describe Sor Juana's strategy (to affirm that we accept what we transgress in the very process of transgressing it). Sor Juana's wit, sharpness of intellect, intellectual subversion and affirmation of her right as a woman to live the life of the intellect serve today as the example to emulate for women essayists in our culture.

We find another singular example in the case of María de las Mercedes Santa Cruz y Montalvo, the countess of Merlin (1789-1852), born in Cuba but raised in France. The countess of Merlin visited Havana in 1840. Between 1840 and 1841 she published an account of her visit which appeared in three volumes entitled *Viaje a la Habana.* On a personal level, her writings are a voyage of self-discovery while at the public level they create an opportunity to strengthen her social position in France and to defend the interests of her class in Cuba by proposing the importation of Europeans to the island. What is interesting and daring about this essay is that it represents one of the first instances in which women come from behind their gated windows to enter a public conversation about politics, which in her case, took place in three places since her memoirs were published in Cuba, Spain and France. Claire Emilie Martin has written an excellent essay about this interesting character which is titled "Slavery in the Spanish Colonies," which I consulted for the preparation of these introductory remarks. [Martin in Meyer: 37-46]

Despite a constant participation and contribution of women to the essay in Spanish America, Pratt points out in her monograph already cited that the criollo essay has been used to create canons which exclude other manifestations of the genre. It is not redundant to repeat here that this is why with the passing of time and after the "excavation" of so many works written by women even up to our days canonized texts continue to represent the vast majority of essays published in anthologies. These collections ignore the evidence that women produce a substantive contribution to the criollo essay and an exceptional corpus in what Pratts has called the gender essay.

The term "gender essay" serves to denote a series of texts whose central theme has been the status and the reality of women in society. By nature it is a dissident text which insists in changing a monologue and turning it into a dialogue that would negate men's cultural and historical monopoly. (Pratt in Meyer: 15-18) Among the manifestations of the gender essay, we can point to:

1. The historical catalogue: An enumeration of the names of women who contributed to society and history. These texts are designed to show that women have been agents of history, a role denied them in the *historias oficiales.* Some examples in this category include: Soledad Acosta de Samper, *La mujer en la sociedad moderna* (1895); Clorinda Matto de Turner, *Las obreras del pensamiento* (1895); and Angeles Mendieta Alatorres, *La mujer en la revolución mexicana* (1961).

2. The analytical commentary on the social and spiritual condition of women. In this manifesta-

xii Daisy Cocco De Filippis

tion of the genre, women challenge men in what they considered a "man's land": thought. Some examples in this category include: Sor Juana Inés de la Cruz, "La respuesta a sor Filotea" (1691); Juana Manso, *Emancipación moral de la mujer* (1858); Gertrudis Gómez de Avellaneda, *La mujer* (1860); Victoria Ocampo, *La mujer y su expresión* (1936); Camila Henríquez Ureña, *Feminismo* (1937); Abigaíl Mejía, *Ideario feminista* (1939); Alicia Moreau de Justo, *Socialismo y la mujer* (1946); Rosario Castellanos, *Mujer que sabe latín...* (1973). (Pratt in Meyer:15-18)

D. DOMINICAN WOMEN ESSAYISTS:

The essay written by women in the Dominican Republic has been dissident in its vast majority and presents a parallel history, a dialogue which at times appears to be with deaf men, about the condition, position and participation of women in Dominican society. For the purposes of this essay and because we must begin to build on some structure, I propose a Dominican feminine essayistic tradition which consists of four manifestations:

1. The essay as bridge from the private to the public sphere;
2. The essay as recovery of history;
3. The essay as demythification and construction of women's own identity;
4. The essay as expression of cultural research.

There is also diversity in the use of language and in the tone of the narrative, which I summarize in four styles: 1. defiant, openly militant; 2. double-voiced; 3. poetic or evocative; 4. scientific or objective.

1. The Essay as a Bridge from the Private to the Public Sphere:

a. Political Dissidence:

When, to give an account of the political intrigues that she almost paid for with her life, Manuela Aybar o Rodríguez (1790?-1852) decided to write, publish and disseminate her "Story of a Woman," she laid the first stone in the history of the Dominican feminine essay. Manuela Aybar, "the Deaconess" picked up a pen and a hand-cranked press to disseminate her writings, poems and political diatribes, among masons and all other interested parties. A follower of Santana, Aybar persevered in her political position even when she put at risk her own life, and she managed by her own efforts to leave a record of her active and public participation in the political intrigues of the nation.

Her essay represents the first instance of a Dominican woman facing down the authorities to express her own opinion and to dissent with the "official story." In this category we may also include some of the speeches given by Ercilia Pepín (1884-1939) and Abigaíl Mejía (1895-1941), among others.

b. Political Activism:

Born a little later but definitely convinced of the importance of the role she was to play in Dominican political life, in the articulation of the future nation and the narrative of its inception, Rosa Duarte (1819-1888) bequeaths her notes on the life of her brother Juan Pablo Duarte, one of the trinitarios, and leader of the independence movement of 1844. In her correspondence, Rosa Duarte expresses her preoccupation with the preservation of Duarte's papers and she addresses herself to distinguished figures of her day to secure their assistance in this quest, among them, Federico Henríquez y Carvajal.

Although Rosa Duarte seems to write her letters from an understanding that women must guard against appearing too daring (she signs her letters with both her sister Francisca's and her own name), in moments when she comments on the deterioration of the political situation of her country she almost inadvertently switches to the "I" form affirming her conscience as a woman who fights for the life of the mind. In this category we may also include some of the chapters of *Monseñor de Meriño, íntimo* by Amelia Francasci (1850-1941) and some of the contributions of Petronila Angélica Gómez (1883-1971) to the journal *Fémina*, among others.

c. Formal Education and Political Education:

Salomé Ureña de Henríquez (1850-1897) was one of the earliest and most distinguished women teachers. A poet, consecrated in the altar of the great ones in the nineteenth century, Salomé Ureña de Henríquez, nevertheless, dedicated a great deal of her time to educational reform and to the education of women. This was an effort for which she paid dearly. Unfortunately, few samples of her prose writing have been preserved. In this collection we gather two speeches given at crucial moments: The first is the farewell speech for Hostos, her partner in lay, positivista reform of Dominican education; the second is her farewell speech as she stepped down as director of the "Escuela Normal de Señoritas", whose doors would soon close down. Formal education and political education are common topics in the writings by Dominican women. From a large number of authors, we may include the essays by Ercilia Pepín (1884-1939), Evangelina Rodríguez (1880-1947), María Josefa Gómez (1892-1971), Camila Henríquez Ureña (1894-1973), Magali Pineda (1940?), Clara Báez (1945?), Chiqui Vicioso (1948), Lusitania Martínez (1945), Carmen Imbert Brugal (1954) and Angela Hernández (1956).

2. The Essay as Recovery of History:

a. Catalogues:

The historical catalogue presents one of the better examples of how women have tried to give evidence of their role as agents of history. In this category we highlight the essays by Dominican feminists included in Petronila Angélica Gómez' *Mi contribución a la historia del feminismo dominicano*, Abigaíl Mejía's *Ideario feminista* and Livia Veloz' *Historia del feminismo dominicano*. Including essays, lists, copies of letters, poems etc., these publications give evidence and portray vividly the process and the struggles of the Dominican suffrage movement, its achievements and political and personal disappointments.

b. "Tallying and Billing":

With her *De críticos y creadoras*, Angela Hernández (1956) began the process of making Dominican editors "give an account" of the exclusion of the work by creative women. Arming herself with exact calculations, Hernández constructs an essay of great strength and persuasion and in the process she manages to give a tour de force of the world of exclusions resulting from the assignation of roles and obligations on the female gender. The last decade has seen the publication of many other essays of "tallying and billing" among them *Mujeres de abril* by Margarita Cordero (1947?), "Hacia una narrativa femenina en la literatura dominicana" by Emelda Ramos (1948), "Mujer, arte y marginalización" by Myrna Guerrero Villalona (1951), and "Imagen de la mujer en los textos de historia dominicana" by Margarita Paiewonsky (1960), all included in this anthology.

c. Evocations:

With her "Meseniana", written on the occasion of the death of her teacher Salomé Ureña de Henríquez, Mercedes Laura Aguiar (1872-1958) gives us one of the first examples of the essay as a poetic evocation, photograph colored by reminiscence and the passing of time, which is designed to leave for posterity the memory of a shared experience. In this case, it is the experience of sharing affection and knowledge with a group of women who knew themselves to be priviledged in having the opportunity to receive a scientific education. A most approriate reminiscence of a teacher who was also a poet, Aguiar's words gather for us the beauty, feeling and pain of a lost time. In this same vein, we may recognize some of the essays written by Virginia Elena Ortea (1866-1903) and in our days the evocations written by Ida Hernández Caamaño (1949) and Leyda Veras (1946).

d. Portrait of Customs:

In her more than two thousand articles written for the newspapers and in her numerous volumes of essays, Aida Bonnelly de Díaz (1925?) has recorded customs and traditions that have begun to change with the passing of time. A commentarist of great subtlety, her writings reflect a delicate balance between traditions and her experience as a woman. The use of the double-voice has in Aida Bonnelly de Díaz one of its best practitioners Among other writers of this genre, we may include the work of Edna Garrido de Boggs (1913?) and of Consuelo Oliver Vda. Germán (1920?).

e. Biographical Sketches and Studies of Other Writers or Artists:

The essay on the life and work of a creative woman began with the publication of Abigaíl Mejía's articles on the art of Adriana Billini and the life and works of Amelia Francasci. Since then we have had a series of studies which in the last two decades have turned into, besides being an introduction of the biography, a new reading of their work or approach to their art. Among contemporary Dominicans, we may include Chiqui Vicioso's essays, published in the early eighties, the first to offer a feminist reading of the literature written by Salomé Ureña de Henríquez, Carmen Natalia and Aida Cartagena Portalatín. Other writers: Jeannette Miller (on Celeste Woss y Gil); Daisy Cocco De Filippis (on Delia Weber, Aída Cartagena Portalatín, Julia Alvarez and Chiqui Vicioso, among others); Ylonka Nacidit-Perdomo (on Delia Weber and Hilma Contreras).

3. The Essay As Demythification and Construction of Identity:

a. Attributions to Gender:

There is no one like the combative Ercilia Pepín (1884-1939) to belie the image of women as inferior or incapable of assuming the responsibilities of employment and participation in the social, cultural and political life of the nation. Among other writers whose essays reflect on women's construction of their own identity, we may include the work of Abigaíl Mejía (1895-1941), Camila Henríquez Ureña (1894-1973), Delia Weber (1900-1982), Carmen Imbert-Brugal (1954), Chiqui Vicioso (1948), Daisy Cocco De Filippis (1949), Ylonka Nacidit-Perdomo (1955), and others.

b. Racial Identity:

Among the mythifications Dominican womanhood has undergone are the denominations of "trigueña" (golden like wheat) or "india" (indigenous woman). At first in her poetry and later in her essays, Aida Cartagena Portalatín (1918-1994) expresses in strong, almost irate terms, the need to know, to accept and to pay attention to the African roots of Dominican culture and identity. In her collection of essays *Culturas africanas: rebeldes con causa*, Cartagena Portalatín expresses in a very personal manner the dilemma of a mulatto intellectual in different parts of the world. Among other essays dealing with the topic of woman and African cultures, we may include the work of Celsa Albert Batista (1944) and the work of the women in "Casa por la Identidad de Mujeres Afro," among them Luisa América Diclo (1954?).

4. The Essay as Expression of Research on Culture:

Camila Henríquez Ureña (1894-1973), Flérida [García] de Nolasco (1891-1976), María Ugarte (1914) and Marianne de Tolentino (1930?) have distinguished themselves in the field of cultural research. Their essays are of an interdisciplinary nature and reflect solid erudition. Among other younger writers with an academic training, we may include the work of Jeannette Miller (1944), Celsa Albert Batista (1944?), Chiqui Vicioso (1948), Daisy Cocco De Filippis (1949) and Soledad Alvarez (1950), among many others.

SOME FINAL COMMENTS:

The publication of the essays selected here represents an effort to bring about systemic change through recording the participation of women as agents of culture and history. I conclude with an invitation to scholars to continue the work begun with this first effort. Nothing would please me more than to have others point to omissions in the selection of authors or categories, presented here only as a point of departure for the creation of a history of the thought of Dominican women. Given the circumstances, I wish to affirm that with this publication as with my other anthological efforts, I am not proposing the creation of feminine canons but the inclusion of the work of women in all aspects of Dominican cultural life. We are still far from reconstructing our history and therefore this volume cannot be presented as complete or perfect. It is simply a fragment of a history that at different times some of us women will have to rewrite and often repeat, until we begin to feel in our own lives the impact of the sweet accent of our own words, included as an integral part of our readings, and shaped, to remember Eugenio María de Hostos and Camila Henríquez Ureña's words, by the product of our science (intellect) and conscience.

> Daisy Cocco De Filippis
> Rockefeller Fellow
> CUNY Dominican Studies Institute
> Spring 1997

BIBLIOGRAPHY OF WORKS CONSULTED

Alcántara Almánzar, José. *Dos siglos de literatura dominicana. V. X* (Prose). Santo Domingo: Publicación de la Secretaría de Educación y Bellas Artes, Cultos, 1996.

Anderson, Benedict. *Imagined Communities: Reflections on the Origin and Spread of Nationalism.* London and New York: Verso, 1991.

Avilés Blonda, Máximo (prólogo). *Muestra de ensayo generación del'48.* Santo Domingo: Comisión Permanente de la Feria del Libro, 1988.

Chanady, Amaryll, ed. *Latin American Identity and Constructions of Difference.* Minneapolis: University of Minnesota Press, 1994.

Earle, Peter G., and Robert G. Mead Jr. *Historia del ensayo hispanoamericano. Mexico*:Ediciones de Andrea, 1973.

Galván, William. *Antología de la obra de Ercilia Pepín.* Santo Domingo: Editora de la UASD, 1986.

Griffiths Pedley, John. *Greek Art and Archaeology.* New Jersey: Prentice Hall, 1993.

Henríquez Ureña, Camila. "La carta como forma de expresión literaria" in *Feminismo y otros temas sobre la mujer en la sociedad.* Santo Domingo: Taller, 1985. 85-140.

Ludmer, Josefina. "Tricks of the Weak" in *Feminist Perspectives on Sor Juana Inés de la Cruz,* ed. Stephanie Merrim. Detroit: Wayne State University Press, 1991. 86-93.

Mendoza, Plinio Apuleyo et al. *Manual del perfecto idiota latinoamericano.* Barcelona: Plaza & Janés, 1996.

Meyer, Doris, ed. *Reinterpreting the Spanish American Essay.Women Writers of the 19th and 20th Centuries.* Austin, Texas:University of Texas Press, 1995.

Ripoll, Carlos, ed. *Conciencia intelectual de América: Antología del ensayo hispanoamericano.* New York: Las Américas, 1966.

Stabb, Martin S. *The Dissenting Voice: The New Essay of Spanish America, 1960-1985.* Austin, Texas: University of Texas Press, 1994.

—————. *In Quest of Identity: Patterns in the Spanish American Essay of Ideas, 1890-1960.* Chapel Hill: University of North Carolina Press, 1967.

Sommer, Doris. *Foundational Fictions: The National Romances of Latin America*. Berkeley: University of California Press, 1990.

Vallejo de Paredes, Margarita. *Antología literaria dominicana, vol. 4* Santo Domingo: INTEC, 1981.

Zea, Leopoldo, compiler. *Fuentes de la cultura latinoamericana II*. Mexico: Fondo de Cultura Económica, 1993.

PART I: AUTHORS

(In chronological order, by author's date of birth)

MANUELA AYBAR O RODRIGUEZ

San Juan de la Maguana, 1790-1852

There is very little information available about the life and works of Manuela Aybar or Rodríguez, or la Deana (1790-1852) as she is known, except for her own comments in "Story of a Woman." La Deana's autobiographical piece is a seminal essay on the condition of women in Dominican society. Careful to couch her comments within the constraints society imposed on women, la Deana, nevertheless, sketches a life quite free of the expectations placed on women by Hispanic culture in general, and, in particular, in the Dominican Republic of her time.

Doña Manuela is known as la Deana because as the unmarried godchild of Dean José Gabriel de Aybar with whom she lived, her involvement in politics and community affairs far exceeded the norm. As a spinster, la Deana might have been expected to play a more active and supportive role in the church (vestir santos, perhaps). Instead, she occupied herself as a contractor of masons working on the reconstruction of historical buildings.

Convention might also require her to be more genteel, less willing to speak about her own illegitimacy and modest financial circumstances. Instead, la Deana wears these traits as badges of honor, being careful to explain that her circumstances are no different than those of many others in her community, including her foe, the contemporary president of the newly formed republic, Jiménez.

"Story of a Woman" is an essay constructed with irony and subterfuge. La Deana goes to great pains to explain that she is a woman without political aspirations on behalf of her own relations (and, since she is a woman, of course, she has no political aspirations of her own). Yet she keeps a hand-cranked press at home that is used to reproduce her verses, mostly political, pro-Santana and anti-Jiménez. These verses are distributed two-fold to anyone requesting a copy, and distributed generously among the working class (the stone masons, for example).

Despite her efforts, however, her literary contribution has not been preserved for posterity, with the exception of a few poems. These pieces, generally of poor literary quality, nevertheless, serve to present a portrait of her fascination with politics, as the verses included in "Story of a Woman" illustrate. These verses were written in honor of Santana, on the occasion of the defeat of the Haitian invasion of 1849. Politics were complicated and volatile in those days. Pedro Santana and his brother were part of the cattle raising, landowning conservative faction. A man who by means of cajoling and violence rose to the presidency of the newly formed republic and who stood in stark contrast to the liberal ideals of the Trinitarios, Santana's name is written in dark ink in the sad pages of the post-independence to restauración history of the Dominican Republic. Santana's involvement culminated with the infamous annexation of the Dominican Republic to Spain.

La Deana's involvement, consequently, was not an innocent past time. Rodríguez Demorizi points out that "her bastardly compositions contributed, considerably, to foment the political partisanship so ill-fated in the Republic." (*Poesía popular dominicana*: 207). As discussed at length in the last twenty years by critics such as Francine Masiello, family unity was more than a metaphor in the early years after independence movements in many countries in Latin America. In fact, powerful families exerted a great deal of political power, many times creating alliances between their interests and those of the fatherland. The work of La Deana exemplifies the extension of the metaphor family-order-welfare of the nation into the compadrismo and caudillismo that constitute the mal-estar of many of our Latin American nations even today.

Manuela Aybar, as she herself indicates in her "Story of a Woman," did not have much of an opportunity to study. Nevertheless, la Deana, an illegitimate daughter, a woman of limited economic resources and even less literary talent, found a role in life other than wife. Beyond her lack luster and mediocre literature, Manuela Aybar o Rodríguez comes to us as an example of a woman of independent spirit. La Deana is not only a spinster but one who is of a happy disposition, content with her civil status and conscious of the value of the written word, though a disquieting character for the reader of our day.

La Deana died a littler over a year after the 1850 publication of her "Story of a Woman," without having managed (despite the tauntings and efforts described in her essay) to become either a martyr in the cause of the "mother fatherland" or a victim of political literary defiance. She died in 1852 at a time when the nation was beginning to realize the effects of a political instability that would last for many years to come.

SELECTED BIBLIOGRAPHY:

Story of a Woman. Santo Domingo: Imprenta Nacional, 1849. 14 p. (essay)

STORY OF A WOMAN

(Dedicated to Mr. Jonathan Elliot, U.S. Commercial Attaché)

To you noble American
I dedicate my story
retained in my memory
written by my hand;
And understand that if at the hands
of a Cuban you received such an offense
you should know yourself beloved
by those you have protected,
for noble is your suffering
and strong is your defense.

It will be for the ink of others to narrate the happenings that preceded, and caused the unique story I want to tell and to bequeath to posterity; although it will be necessary to touch upon them, once in a while, because of their tie to my story.

In the long stretch of my life, already a sexagenarian, favored by fortune since I saw the light of day; beloved by my kin and appreciated by strangers, I can truthfully say that with the exception of those calamities that afflict all living beings—illnesses, deaths of dear ones, etc.— and those that are inevitable and common to all, such as political occurrences, I have never had to suffer, nor to fear that anything would disturb my repose. Without a child, siblings, or relatives for whom I would harbor ambitions of employment, to me all forms of government are fine; nevertheless, I venture to say that if it were left up to me (although women don't hold personal views on such things) I would always choose a fair form of government, dedicated only to the welfare of the community, the progress of the nation, etc. instead of a government that fosters disorder and anarchy. Since I have no suit to bring to bear, no treaties nor contracts to sign with any person born, the Courts are as if non-existent to me. I have been far from thinking that the day would come when I would find myself persecuted and trampled by the rulers of my country, and that the presidency of Mr. Manuel Jiménez, my blood-relation, would create such an impact in the story of my life.

Perhaps there might be someone who upon reading my inarticulate and poorly written story would stop when he sees that I say that Mr. Jiménez is my blood-relation, and so that he sees the truth in my words I will say in passing that the Aybar Sánchez y González Mederos family is one and the same and although I may not descend from a legitimate branch, I believe that this will not make Mr. Jiménez have more González blood than I have of the Aybar's; and even more so since his mother and I were not only relatives but point by point equal in our birth.

Another relationship beside the aforementioned also ties me to Mr. Jiménez, that although it may not be a family tie, it is at the very least a certain affinity of origins, that is to say: orejano is a name given here to all those who have been born outside of the walls of the capital city, and who do not receive an education to suit their rank. I to my sorrow was born in San Juan de la Maguana, and as far as education is concerned, it was a miracle I was taught to write because in those days there was a law that ordered that young girls not be taught, to prevent note writing to their young men. Mr. Jiménez was born and spent the first years of his childhood in a town called Ballamo, in the island of Cuba. As far as his education I will limit myself to say that I met him as a petit enfant d'eglise. However, let us get down to business and proceed with my story: because of my acquaintance with masons working for the state, and with the majority of those from my town, since the division was made, I had the habit or I imposed upon myself the duty, of going once in a while to visit them wherever they would be working in the reconstruction project; they would be able to attest to the nature of my visits.

After the Haitians in their last invasion, because of unwise decisions made by Mr. Jiménez, had managed to proceed ninety leagues into Dominican territory; Azua having been lost, the army disseminated, families on the run, and the enemy marching on to the Capital; after the constant efforts of the National Congress having defeated President Jiménez' opposition, ordered and sent General Santana to head an army no longer existing in the south, spirits defeated were rebuilt, the families in San Cristobal, San Carlos and some in Baní returned to their home, and the run away soldiers ran to unite themselves with their Chief, he who had in the past led them to victory.

I who was one of many in whom hope was reborn, closed myself at home and wrote some verses as the following: 12 of April:

> REFRAIN
> Illustrious leader,
> swiftly galloping,
> to save the nation
> from horrendous yoke.
>
> Run, Santana,

Run, our leader,
Victory waits
for you alone.
If many families
are on the rebound
they yearn for your presence
in bitter pain.

The children are dying
the sun is drowning
mothers are shouting
poor wretched ones.

All of the army
has fled afar
while the enemy
marches on with pride.

Newly born Camilo
don your swift sword
let the bitter battle
come to an end.

Challenge Soulouque
dare his troop
for you are followed
by thirty groups

Come on, challenge him,
let the battle begin,
for victory already calls
you her only son.

Also the armies
swell with national pride
for they are following
Santana's might.

And the poor enemy,
wretchedly daring,
upon hearing your name,
withdraws with shame.

Despite the not-to-be-believed efforts of Jiménez and his supporters, they were not able to prevent Santana from positioning himself to contain the enemy; whether by having the soldiers coming from the east retreat, or by firing on others, or by denying Santana the fire arms he requested for the few who followed him. But Santana managed to bring together 856 men, who, full of enthusiasm, offered to die beside him. The 21 of April finally arrived and Santana after a hard-fought two-day campaign on the border Ocoa managed to undo the plans of his enemies and to bring them to complete defeat. But, who would believe it! this happy occurrence, applauded with happiness by the people, so enraged Jiménez that he ordered imperiously to have removed from his sight the spoils of victory taken from his very own enemies.

The first news of the campaign came on Sunday, and the second news, of victory secured and the Haitian army defeated, came on Monday afternoon, and the following day I was tempted to compose some verses you will find at the end of this manuscript.

Since during the first days at every and any moment someone would come to ask me for a copy of these verses, tired of writing them out, and having at home a hand-cranked printing press, I typed in my poem, and got out more than two hundred copies, and to each person who requested one I would give three or four copies. I knew well how little Jiménez and his supporters liked this praise of SANTANA, and I was pleased to see them squirm over my poetry; but not even remotely could I think that it would be a crime that merited a death penalty, to reduce to verses, the public and heroic deeds of the immortal SANTANA; because neither I nor any Dominican, in the entire territory of the island, could imagine that Jiménez, eaten alive by shameful envy, would exercise the barbarism of declaring war on the General and army that rescued the nation from a Haitian invasion.

Some days later, remembering the workmen, I went to the Fort of St. Michael where they were working, taking with me, of course, four or five copies of my poem to give to those I was better acquainted with, and not finding them there because they had been taken to build a circle of a cannon in Fort Charity, other friends asked me for copies and I gave them out, and those for whom I had taken the poems in the first place, later came over my house to request them.

Five or six days later, namely: the tenth of May, having a need to speak to a mason from my town about some beams I had offered him, not finding him at home, I went to the Fort called Santiago or Palo Hincado, and there another worker asked me for a copy of the poem, and I gave it to him. I returned home, ran four more copies, and in the afternoon I went to the Fort and from there I called him out and gave these to him. He went up and gave them out among his co-workers, they pasted one in the porter's lodge and there they read it and re-read it until they had memorized it.

Mr. Mauricio de Silva, the foreman of Public Works, took one away from one of the workers and by Juan Barriento, saw to it that Mr. Jiménez got a hold of the poem. On Friday the eleventh of the month, Jiménez himself went to the Fort quite upset; he spoke, he formulated theories, etc. and not satisfied with having given orders that I not be allowed to visit there, he went to the Conde and ordered that a guard be posted at the entrance of the Fort. No sooner had he left to go home when some of the same workers ran to inform me of this development, but for the moment I was not concerned; nevertheless, since everyone and I were witnessing the moving of canons, the unstopping vigilance of the troops, and other hostile maneuvers, I began to be somewhat intimidated, and I locked myself at home, waiting to see where this thing would explode. At eight in the evening, I already knew I was not safe at home, and Mr. Francisco Javier Abreu was so kind to send his son to offer me his house, a home where the Commercial Attaché of the U.S. lived. I spent a sleepless night, not daring to leave the house, for fear of finding a group of soldiers, but at four in the morning I ventured out in the company of a woman who worked for me, and went to await the light of day in a hut in front of Mr. Abreu's house, where I entered after they had opened the house. The generous Mr. Elliot and the Abreu ladies received me with such kindness that in a few hours I had recovered from the unpleasantness of the previous night.

It was not eight in the morning of the twelfth when an assistant showed up with four soldiers to take me to jail, and not finding me at home, tried to find out my whereabouts and how I had left. Sunday afternoon, they prepared an edict to declare SANTANA a traitor to the Motherland. Jiménez' agents were shouting in every corner of town: "Long live Jiménez." They also said, "Death to the traitor and Doña Manuela la Diana!" For two straight days two assistants went looking for me and they even tried to ambush me in the house next to Mr. Abreu's where I had gone by the backyard to see my friend.

My cause began to be discussed: my sentence should have been four bullets, because it was necessary (as my judges would say) to make an example of me, to teach a lesson to the evil ones who like me had committed the crime of saying that SANTANA defeated the Haitian army at Carreras.

Had Jiménez managed to pull me out of my safe heaven, surely not even with one foot in the gallows would I have betrayed the feelings of my heart; and even there I would have said what I said before, say now and will say later, that is: if a woman is allowed to appreciate the merit of an honorable man, I would say: that PEDRO SANTANA appears to deserve occupying a place in the pages of the History of the World and that Dominicans ought to take pride in having their soil produce such a man; just as in the old days they knew to take pride in having a Morlas, a Mezniel. The world has produced many Hannibals and Scipions; but in my opinion, no other SANTANA. Those individuals had disciplined, well-provided for, well-dressed, well-fed, well-paid, well-armed armies, etc. They had experienced generals, artillery, engineers, etc. and what did SANTANA have? Without a military strategy, an orderly army, artillery, and with a handful of men, lacking discipline, hungry, naked, and perhaps with only a machete as armament, he has been capable more than once of facing and defeating completely an army of half-beast men, well-provided for and well-disciplined, and with leaders at the head, who if they do not proceed willingly, make them move on by virtue of the rod. If to say this is a crime, and it is to attempt against the government, Mr. Jiménez set the example in a proclamation of lies he had published, with boxes, music and many cheers, saying that: Duverge had won, he had victory, defeated the enemy and saved the country: no, by golly I remember it now, the crime was to say that SANTANA had done this, the only target of envious bullets. But since the National Congress, just judges of civil valor, has conferred upon him the glorious title of FREEDOM FIGHTER FOR THE MOTHER FATHERLAND and I as of now say no thank you, for the employment they might wish to give me, based on how hard and long I have suffered. But I, thanks to the charity of God, need nothing, neither now nor ever, and had Mr. Jiménez been able to catch me, there in the calabooze even if with charcoal I would have written on the wall these other verses:

> In prison I find myself
> I feel no sadness
> for I am not the first
> nor do I stop being myself
> even if I go there, to Havana

> I have honorable kin
> In Puerto Rico, some lawyers
> and a little something to take;
> because as a true Aybar
> I never threw dice

And when having concluded the trial they would have taken me by the almond tree; eyes that saw your departure, because to anticipate what was coming and in the event I was caught, when I left my house I took with me a key (and it was not fake) to open the doors and disappear like the witches. I would have liked to have asked Mr. Jiménez why, through the past six years when he was Minister of War, he did not go to the forts to ask what I was doing there? I would surely have answered what Augustus said to Primus' defender when he asked imperiously: who called you here? The welfare of the nation, answered Augustus, and who knows if I could have challenged his service to the nation; because although I am an old woman, I have not lost my memory, and I remember quite well the night of the 27 of February, when Martin Giron and his six Spanish soldiers surrendered the door to the Conde. Mr. Jiménez got on his little horse and rode to Monte Plata, fleeing from the fire; and it was lucky he remained there a couple of days, because, had he presided over the surrender, who knows if we would have come out of that presidency as we came out of this one, with good sense thrown to the wind (although to our good fortune, SANTANA showed up then, to take us out of the mess). Meanwhile Jiménez was whiling away the time in Monte Plata, with his ounces of gold in his pockets, so that in the event he lost, he would be able to repeat what he did in Azua, run for his life; I was here working in the fort of San Anton, not physically because I do not have the strength to carry rocks, but with my purse. Later on when Mr. Jacinto Concha went from house to house collecting signatures, to make him general, I went from house to house to collect royal palm tissues to shelter our poor soldiers in comfort. I did other things that I do not mention because they are long in telling, while Mr. General spent his time seeing to it that the canons and the bullets would keep out SANTANA, when like now, he returned victorious from the border.

From then on, I dare say, and even swear, that Mr. Jiménez has not seen any more war, though he is Minister of War, than the one he waged against all those who like me, had to find shelter in consular flags; and no more bullets than the ones he had fired at SANTANA and all the brave men who were with him.

It remains for me to tell, by way of conclusion, that I did not place the poem in its proper place to avoid a repetition of the same occurrences because since I was sure that I would fall into Mr. Jiménez' hands, of course, I planned to write it; and if there is someone who does not like it, let him go to Curazao, because I have made up my mind to spend the rest of my days writing poetry. I also would like to warn you that I don't plan on dying before I reach the age of my grandparents, which was more or less ninety years of age.

DECIMA

> SANTANA, noble hero,
> Dominican Napoleon,
> confused and defeated Haitians
> at your feet in a pool of blood

Glory is yours,
you have destroyed the invader
the high honor is yours,
the world is full of your fame
and your countryland proclaims you
Illustrious Freedom Fighter.

If once Spain had
its don Rodrigo, the Cid,
his valor is now eclipsed
by our noble SANTANA

If Souloque was defeated
by ONE of our countrymen
he must, of course, be known
as our Dominican Napoleon.

Ocoa, you were the witness,
of our victory from tyranny,
where SANTANA defeated
and confused the Haitian army.

With a heart of iron
without David's arm
there at your feet another giant
defeated in bloody battle.

Victorious, the Haitians,
might have settled here
But after Jiménez's flight
Victory was yours to have.

Solely guided and armored
by your bravery and your pride
where there was none, you created hope
to defeat and destroy the intruder.

Defeated our enemy lies,
your army infused with valor
at one they proclaim and cry
yours is all honor

Envy worked long and hard
and irony fills his voice
and Jiménez trembles to see
yours, the people's clamor.

And to reward your dedication
the Legislative Body
decrees and orders it said
that you are the Nation's Freedom Fighter

Signed: A Dominican Woman

ROSA DUARTE
Santo Domingo, Rep. Dom. 1819-Caracas, Venezuela, 1888

A sister of Juan Pablo Duarte, Rosa Duarte dedicated her life to the support of the lofty ideals behind the Dominican independence movement and the creation of the new nation. A woman of convictions, she preferred to stay in exile with her family rather than remaining in a Santo Domingo that had turned its back on her brother and his ideals. Her *Apuntes* preserves for posterity the biography of her illustrious brother and the historical moment she lived.

Both the selections included here, a fragment from *Apuntes* and a letter, point to her keen sense of the importance of recording history and of her role as participant, thinking person, chronicler and preserver of historical "truth" and her family's role in the creation of an independent nation.

SELECTED BIBLIOGRAPHY:

Apuntes de Rosa Duarte, archivo y versos de Juan Pablo Duarte, edited and annotated by E. Rodríguez Demorizi, C. Larrazábal Blanco and V. Alfau Durán. Santo Domingo: Secretaría de Estado de Educación, Bellas Artes y Cultos, 1994.

SELECTION FROM *Apuntes*

Caracas, April 22, 1888

Mr. Emiliano Tejera
Santo Domingo

Esteemed Friend:

We are exceedingly grateful for your affectionate greetings and the sincere manifestations of affection and esteem with which our fellow citizens were pleased to honor us on the 27th of February, regretting infinitely that the courteous compliments of our friend Mr. José María Pichardo were received by us on the twenty-third of last month past seven o'clock in the evening, because the distinguished administrator Mr. Rafael Cedillo was kept by his many occupations from coming to see us.

In your gracious missive you tell us "that if we have documents that would confirm past events, we ought to publish them"; since we handed over to the Commission in this city the venerable remains of our brother, we have been sending out original documents, and also copies of the originals that we lent in this city to Dr. Ponce de León to whom we have written two times to claim them, and since we have not received any answer to the letters we have written to him, we have recently sent to our friend Federico Henríquez y Carvajal a letter authorizing him to claim in our name before Mr. Santiago Ponce de León the original documents we gave him in this city in the form of a loan.

In months past we gathered for our friend F.H.Carvajal several documents, among them letters from the as unfortunate as we are Juan Isidro Pérez, and a handwritten notebook, where we have copied letters and official documents that vindicate the honor of our venerable Father, and brothers, but in order to authenticate the identity of those copies, we need to have Mr. P. de León return the originals. When I remember what has passed and I look at the present of my unhappy fatherland, and that to cap all our misfortunes, those who by their own decorum ought to raise their voice remain mute, I tell myself: when you least expect it, people degenerate, this is not a reproof to that country of mine, they are not to blame, we are particularly to blame because instead of ambling errantly we should have returned to die by our flag, but for us it is all over; it has all disappeared. If we were only to be consoled by the knowledge that our country far from going backwards moves forward, we would say: we have not lost all, because we have a fatherland, which tomorrow we would see in the chariot of progress moving at the vanguard with her sister countries in the Americas.

With regret we tell you that we are informed about the deplorable situation the country is undergoing and that a great part of our fellow countrymen are to blame, and all to what purpose? Because they go abroad, and are dazzled by tinsel and whitewashed sepulchers, inhabited by demons at home and angels in society, and when they return to the land that gave them their being they do nothing more than to look for money, to come to have a good time, when what the ingrates do abroad is to exhibit their nullity.

Excuse us from taxing your attention, and please be kind enough to give our affectionate respect to your wife and family and to the right Reverend Don Apolinar whom we always remember with affection and you, believe in the unchanging affection of your country women and friends who wish you health and happiness.

Rosa and Francisca Duarte

Notes for the History of the Island of Santo Domingo and for the Biography of the Dominican General Juan Pablo Duarte y Diez

In the year 1813, the 26 of January, in the city of Santo Domingo was born the General Juan Pablo Duarte y Diez. His parents were Mr. Juan José Duarte, a Spaniard born in the city of Seville, and his respected wife Manuela Diez, born in the city of Santo Domingo, the Capital of the Island formerly known as Hispaniola. His godparents of baptism were Mr. Luiz Méndez, and his respected wife Vicenta de la Cueva. It was generally believed that one of his godparents had been his holiness the Archbishop Don Tomás de Portes; he was by affection, for his godchildren were others among Duarte's siblings. His family belonged to the best of societies and they were esteemed by their own folk and by all others. When he was quite young, his mother taught him the alphabet. Mrs. Montilla, a close friend of his mother's, wanted to be the one to teach him to read. His mother accepted this friendly offering, and with the help of said lady he was able to read by the age of six, and to recite by memory the catechism: his parents decided then to put him in a school for boys. The maid who cared for him and loved him with adoration put the pen in his hands to avoid the teacher's rod. The teacher praised him quite a bit because his first assignment did not need corrections. From that school he moved on to Mr. Manuel Aybar's, a well-versed individual whose students were ahead of all others. His great dedication always earned him the affection and esteem of his teachers who would present him before other pupils as a model of dedication and good behavior. In that school he was always first monitor, a distinction his classmates saw without envy, for they loved him because of his sweet and affable nature. Whatever limited knowledge he acquired was due to his love of learning. (When the presbyter Dr. José Antonio de Bonillas spoke of how Duarte had a facility for understanding everything, the presbyter Dr. Gutiérrez replied: Duarte possesses a natural talent. Had he been born in Europe, at that age he would be a scholar.) I repeat that the limited knowledge he acquired was due to his love of learning, stimulated by the laudable purpose of educating himself to be able to free his fatherland; he was unfortunate to find when he arrived at the age of reason that his fatherland was weeping under the ominous domination of the Haitians. The Haitian government closed down the illustrious university allowing only some schools to remain open where they taught what was barely necessary for the limited commerce available at that time, and later on by the end of the darkest of reigns it allowed a public school where French was taught. In Mr. Manuel Aybar's school he learned to read, to write, Castilian grammar, arithmetic and bookkeeping.

With Monsieur Bruat he studied French, and later on English with Mr. Groot. In order to please him his father sent him to travel with a friend to North America planning to go from there to Europe. In New York, he continued learning English, and he began to study world geography with Mr. W. Davis who gave lessons at home; from the North he moved to England, from England to France. He landed in le Havre, and continued directly to Paris, where he perfected his French. From France he went to Spain by way of Bayonne. Barcelona was the last city he visited in Spain and his point of departure for America; at his arrival in Puerto Rico he found a ship which moved him immediately to Saint Thomas and from there to Santo Domingo where he was received with great joy by his parents and relatives, and his faithful friends from childhood, his classmates. Among those who went to congratulate his parents for the felicitous return was Sr. Dr. Manuel Maria Valverde (father) a good and esteemed friend of the family. After embracing him, the Doctor asked him what had caught his attention and pleased him the most in his travels. He answered him: "The laws and freedoms of Barcelona, laws and freedoms I hope we will give our fatherland some day." His words were received with enthusiasm by the young people around him. Dr. Valverde, himself moved by his words told him: "In such a noble undertaking you can count on me," (an offer the dignified and illustrious patriot met religiously). As a reward Santana sent him into exile with his worthy family. Since his return to the fatherland Duarte did not think of anything other than to educate himself and to gather followers. He was of a delicate constitution, which made him look younger than he was. People named the revolution the Revolution of the Young Men, for beside the majority of those participating being of a young age, the one who led them did not look quite eighteen years of age!

(Fragment)

Translation by Daisy Cocco De Filippis

SALOME UREÑA DE HENRIQUEZ
Santo Domingo, 1850-1897

Salomé Ureña was born on the 21 of October of 1850. Her parents were Gregoria Diez y León and Nicolás Ureña de Mendoza. In his introduction to the 1920 edition of her selected poems, her son, the distinguished intellectual Pedro Henríquez Ureña, tells us that during her childhood she did not attend school other than for the first letters, the only ones opened to women then; [her mother taught her to read] but her father, a discrete poet and lawyer with a good reputation, who held positions in the Senate and the Judicial System, gave her the best literary education that could be had in those days: the reading of the classics of the Spanish language was fundamental in her preparation. Wise teachings and wise readings forged the intellect of this woman who became one of the most distinguished figures in the history of literature and education in the Dominican Republic.

For many years Salomé Ureña de Henríquez was the only feminine presence in our literary history. She enjoys a critical acceptance seldom granted to women writers in the Dominican Republic. From her early years as a writer, she has occupied a favored place in Dominican literary circles and has won the general approval of critics outside of the island. In 1878, at the age of twenty-eight, the Dominican people awarded her a medal, funded by the public. And although she never left her native soil, she was a member of honor in a number of literary societies in and outside of her country, among them, "Amigos del país" in Santo Domingo, "Fe en el porvenir" in Puerto Plata, "El Liceo de Puerto Príncipe" in Cuba and "Alegría" in Venezuela. At her death in 1997 she was one of the most respected poets in the country not only because of her literary production but also because of her complete commitment and dedication to the struggle to create a better society where women would have an integral role to play.

Her daughter Camila Henríquez Ureña shows us a life and work which were at times difficult,

> *In my mother's day, when she founded the first secondary school for women in her country, in collaboration with the wise maestro Eugenio María de Hostos, she was harshly censured for wanting to take women from the protected bosom of their home and from the ignorance which was imposed on them as a virtue inherent to their sex. (Ideas pedagógicas de Hostos: 2)*

I have included here some speeches and letters which serve to illustrate Salomé Ureña de Henríquez' idealism and her disillusionment as educator, her preoccupations as a mother and her disenchantment as a wife: public and private lives where the situation is often precarious and heartaches are plentiful.

SELECTED BIBLIOGRAPHY:

Poesía. Santo Domingo: Imprenta de García Hermanos, Sociedad Literaria "Amigos del país", 1880. xv-214 p. Unsigned biography by José Lamarche and prologue by Fernando A. de Meriño.

Poesías. Madrid: Tipografías Europa, 1920. 142 p. Selected and with a prologue by Pedro Henríquez Ureña.

Poesías completas. Ciudad Trujillo: Secretaría de Estado y Bellas Artes, Colección Biblioteca Dominicana, vol. IV, serie I, 1950. 351 p.; 5ta. ed. Santo Domingo: Secretaría de Educación Bellas Artes y Cultos, 1975; 6ta. ed. Santo Domingo: Publicación de la ONAP, 1985; 7ma. ed. Santo Domingo: Publicación de la ONAP, Feria del Libro Dominicano, 1988; 9na. ed. Santo Domingo: ONAP, 1992; 10ma. ed. Santo Domingo: Publicación de la Comisión Permanente de la Feria del Libro, 1997.

Poesías escogidas. Ciudad Trujillo: Librería Dominicana, Julio D. Postigo, Colección Pensamiento Dominicano No. 19, 1960. 188 p.

Cantos a la patria. Santo Domingo: Publicaciones América, nd, np.

Poesía completa. Santo Domingo: Fundación Corripio, Biblioteca de Clásicos Dominicanos VII, 1989. 299 p.

Anacaona. Santo Domingo: Publicaciones América, Colección Parnaso Dominicano, nd. 94 p.

Words*

*From the Director of the "Instituto de Señoritas" on the second investiture of her
pupils, in the Escuela Normal de Santo Domingo, December of 1888.*

I have come to fulfill a sacred duty, to pay only in the slightest of degrees a debt of immense gratitude. Oh! even if I were to bring to extremes an inexhaustible flow of recognition, this debt would not be satisfied completely.

I speak, ladies and gentlemen, of the debt contracted with the Director of the Normal School, with the sincere and conscientious innovator of the rational method of modern teaching in Dominican society. **

I saw him appear bringing as his retinue the rays of new ideas, of redeeming ideas, of ideas about contemporary civilization, and I, who have always yearned, who yearn still, who will yearn while there is a breath in me, for the moral and material growth of my country, clapped my hands with joy and waited. But the more precious portion of this youth in whose hands the future has been placed did not participate in this development of light and conscience. Woman, mother, needed to fortify herself with the possession of truth and moral science, so that she could prepare and strengthen in turn, by means of the art she alone possesses, the conscience of future generations. I proposed then, although with weakened strength, to collaborate with the magnanimous labor, and, encouraged by the generous companion of my life, whose ideal is the triumph of goodness, of virtue and of science, I undertook the difficult task. I do not wish to know if ignorance has regaled me with the insults of its enmity. Voices of encouragement were raised to give me strength in the task, among them that of this very

---

* Published for the first time in Revista de Educación, No. 17, March 31, 1933, p. 58. Taken from Salomé Ureña, *Poesía completa*, ed. Jaime A. Viñas Román; prologue by Joaquín Balaguer, 6th. ed. Santo Domingo: Publicaciones ONAP, 1985.

** Ureña de Henríquez refers to the Puerto Rican writer and educator, Eugenio María de Hostos. D.C.D.F.

same doctrinarian who has taken particular pleasure in applauding my work and crowning the triumph of my selfless efforts.

But, alas, he—always quick to offer support on behalf of noble ideas and to contribute to the achievement of all work for the betterment of society, of the light and the progress that begins to take place whenever he is around, ill-judged, because he has been misunderstood, fights— against the unleashed elements of an unjust opposition; and fatigued from the long and harsh combat, although firm and serene of conscience, leaves us to go on to appease his spirit in another sphere of the wider horizons of intellectual life. But what is so strange about it? That is usually the harvest gathered by the producers of goodness. Such is humanity at times: it reserves for the reformers, for the civilizers, hemlock and the cross.

And so, I told my disciples, let us place a drop of honey in his goblet of sorrows: let us take to him, as a token of our gratitude and our farewell, the new fruit of our labors, so that he may consecrate it with his words of love. And here you find us fulfilling a sacred duty. Our presence in this place is the expression of our vote of thanks and our farewell.

Oh! I adore this fatherland where my parents were born, where I came to the world, where I have seen the light of existence shine on my children, and you arrived with the inducements of goodness, and, enamored of its beauty and prescient of its higher destiny for the future, you wished to thrust it into the civilizing current of ideas. Be blessed! I will not forget the noble persistence with which you gave yourself to the task of dignifying it in its place as a free nation.

You are leaving us; the seed you leave in the furrow will sprout and the fruits of the future will be fertilized in the sap of your pedagogical doctrines.

Farewell! When in the quiet hours that await you under another sky, a bitter thought pulsating the name of my fatherland comes to your mind, think that there are also friendly hearts who remember, and grateful souls who bless you.

------◆◆◆------

Words*
*From the Director of the Instituto de Señoritas at the last investiture of her students
in the Escuela Normal de Santo Domingo, December 1893.*

Here we are for the third time consecrating, under the auspices of the Normal School, new priestesses in the apostolate of teaching. These feasts of the spirit already seem common place when only yesterday women in our country were denied all aspirations outside of the limits of home and family.

This teaching institution opened its doors, the exclusive privilege of men, and boys had the space and guidance to develop their reason and to transform themselves a bit at a time into conscientious professors, capable of directing themselves and of vigorously developing the minds of children. No longer will the education of childhood be trusted to the first intruder, without skills for the high min-

---

* Published for the first time in *Revista de Educación*, No. 17, 31 of March 1933, p. 60. taken from Salomé Ureña, *Poesías completas.* ed. Jaime A. Viñas Román, prólogo, Joaquín Balaguer, 6th ed. (Santo Domingo: Publicaciones ONAP, 1985).

istry, without scientific knowledge, without a plan, without a purpose in this work of light and conscience, in this work that generates the great destinies of the future. From today onward boys will have in each teacher a mentor, a guide for the development of their faculties, for the expansion of their spirits.

And how can we tolerate it! The intellect of girls, the intellect of women, the intellect of mothers, will it grope in darkness when their companions live in full light? How unjust! What an imbalance in that home where the boy can give lessons to his mother! It is not possible, it is not possible! Let us also prepare that extremely important half of humanity, mentors and guides to expand their minds and prepare them to direct and to encourage the tender beings that nature entrusts to them and who would then regard them with twice as much love and veneration. Let us prepare them to collaborate intelligently in the social reform that begins with the development of consciousness.

But where? And how? Here is the problem that twelve years ago I attempted to resolve, and on whose behalf I have sacrificed my rest and not a small portion of my health.

Oh! That center which was created exclusively for men will open its door to us when we call to demand equal rights for women. That is what I said, that is what we said; and, working indefatigably, in accordance to our strength, we called humbly, and the generous educator* whose effigy hangs above our heads, assists us mutely but eloquently, in the continuation of our work, the eminent educator, listened engrossed and pleased to our demands; and the doors of the Normal School opened joyously and we entered amid the applause of joy, to anoint for the ministering of new ideas feminine foreheads as well.

Here we are again and again, and our presence no longer appears strange nor our boldness daring. Thank you!

But, alas! exhausted by the struggle, without resources, without means of any kind to persevere with shoulder to the wheel, being claimed by the holy duty of the education of my children, a duty that demands completely all the energies of my spirit, I seal, with this last proof of the arduous labor, the work begun twelve years ago.

It pleases me to see that it has not been fruitless, since its reputation grew until it became deserving of national recognition by unanimous vote, and that the Instituto de Señoritas was raised by decree to the category of Normal School for Women Teachers, and that the women professors who have their degrees from the Normal School of Santo Domingo find themselves recruited with zeal either to give lessons to families and institutions of education, or by other regions in the Republic, a calling they have not answered up to now because of the difficulties entailed in the change of residency.

It suffices me, ladies and gentlemen, with intimate satisfaction, to see the change that has been gradually taking place in the education of Dominican women; and if there is any glory to be had, I claim it completely for those who have collaborated with me in the realization of this work. For my life's companion, without whose generous effort and fecund labor it would not have begun or borne its first fruits; for professors Dubeau, Prud'homme, Zafra, and Federico Henríquez, who lent their efficient efforts in the first exams of the institute; for those very same young women professors, who, without remuneration, with exemplary dedication, have been carrying the burden for this past six years; for those who have generously contributed with their personal donations to give one more year

---

*   She refers to Eugenio María de Hostos. D.C.D.F.

to a dying institution, and finally for the Normal School and its distinguished founder, without whose valuable support the Instituto de Señoritas would not have achieved its purpose or crowned its toil.

From Salomé Ureña de Henríquez to Francisco Henríquez y Carvajal*

March 9, 1888

Pancho:

Today I have had the always pleasant surprise, but this time mixed with bitterness, of receiving an unexpected letter from you. With what anxiety I grabbed it to find out about your welfare and to quiet down my heartaches! But, alas!, it brings with it the seal of your anguish which has come to double my own. When your voice full of encouragement speaks to my hopes and encourages me with advice and prescriptions that ought to place our children out of harm from infectious illnesses, then I too lift my spirit and I am inspired with the confidence born of your words. But your accent today is like a ray of intimidation! If one of your children dies you are also to die. Then, what will the poor mother say who struggles alone, anguished, desperate at the slightest menace raised against her children? And if after all her sacrifices, after all of her solicitude, she could not keep death from taking away from her a piece of her soul, would she have reserved for her, too, the still more formidable misfortune of losing the support of her home, the savior of the loved ones that would remain? Oh! by God, if we are exposed to so much to obtain a title from Paris, turn your back without hesitation and return to the bosom of your orphaned home where your wife and children bemoan your absence.

I take care and watch over them with so much solicitude, I am anguished so by any simple cold I detect, that I am advised by all to moderate my fears if I am not to put in danger my own life, by deteriorating my health. But you assure me that the croup is always transmitted by contagion, and I take such excessive care of them that they will not be contaminated. In addition, after the Martínez and Dujaric cases, there is calm again; and that a case occur every three or four months ought not to surprise us, because always in the course of a year we have not lacked three or four cases to lament. You must give me courage if you are determined to continue studying as duty and responsibility contracted demand. We continue in good health, and not even Sillano has had a relapse; but you tell me to get rid of any cold that comes up and I do not know the means to obtain that result. Catarr and a cough they have had. They cough still once in a while without my having had much success in getting rid of it despite my efforts and expenses. Almost all the children have suffered the same, and I believe that until springtime it will not disappear completely. We have gone through a fatal winter, as I have no memory of having seen since I can remember illnesses. Let us wait two or three months and if there is no change, we will decide if it is necessary for you to come or that I go, however great the sacrifices we might need to make. Meanwhile, try without fatiguing yourself unduly to fulfill all the requirements of your program that would be difficult to complete here, and leave all that is not an indispensable requirement for graduation, and that you can complete here at a restful pace. Do not kill yourself, but finish soon.

---

* From Familia Henríquez Ureña, *Epistolario*. Vol. I Santo Domingo: Secretaría de Estado de Educación, Bellas Artes y Cultos, 1996, pp. 41-42.

De Salomé Ureña de Henríquez a Francisco Henríquez y Carvajal

Puerto Plata, August 18, 1896

Pancho:

Your ability to place yourself on the altar and me at the footstool is admirable. When I informed you of Camila's recent weakness of health, I did not know in what form you wrote; but what is certain is that it became clear to me that you believed the person did not meet her responsibilities at my side. I could not be but surprised by this, because I had neither told you a word to that effect nor did I believe that you would dare to make such observations. I would have been incapable of putting myself in the position of telling you such trifles, but when I saw her somewhat preoccupied about what you wrote to her, I believed it opportune to explain to you the state of affairs making you see that my behavior tends always to remove any painful thought that would occur to her on this matter and requesting on your part that you would not make any observation. Now it turns out that I am intolerant and have filled her with concern.

As far as you are concerned, I already know from very sad experiences that you believe everyone to be good because you agree with everything. I, unfortunately, believe differently and I call what is good, good and what is bad, bad. A servant is bad? Well, out he goes! He is good? Well, I treat him with affection and consideration. And if she is a woman and is too close to me and I frequently make her the victim of my nerves? Well, that also passes; because goodness triumphs and a balance is reestablished. Already today I am not irritated with Regina. Why? Because that depended on circumstances; of the change of address in bad conditions, in the case of a woman who is ill, of Camila's poor health, of the same indisposition I was feeling, and many, many other things. She remembered that I had treated her well when she arrived and waited until my irritability passed. The few good servants who have come to the house never leave me; on the contrary, they feel respect and affection for me. Marcos would not be guided by anyone but me. Francisco wrote to me after he left the house to tell me that he was at my disposal in whatever I needed, that if it were because of me he would never have left. Tomás, who was a good servant, was considerate until the end and came to say good-bye before he left. José, José would have followed me to Siberia but...in his ignorance he considered leaving more appropriate than protesting. So there you see, my little child, I am forced to make you see my worth so that I may remain by your side, because I am not willing to lower myself.

The "Intimate" written by Leonor, consoles and dignifies me. No intolerant person can inspire affection so pure, so noble, so altruistic. My son Pedro tells me: "Mother: What expression shall I find to express my affection for you? I have cried a great deal while reading the last paragraph of your letter." Oh, to feel oneself cuddled by that music from heaven is something else. Let me dream and be quiet with your nonsense. I live full of affection and I am happy when I feel myself cuddled by love.

I am forwarding the notes from the Faches so that you make me a double draft I need, because I do not know what am I expected to do or say.

Camila believes that everything she sees is sent by Maria. She saw some shoes that the shoemaker brought and she asked me if they were sent by Maria; I answered affirmatively, and then as if gathering her remembrances, she said: "Do you remember Nanando who played her piano?" What memory the child has!

I am losing my mind over money. During the first month I spent twice as much as you indicated. You can see how much the accounts I sent you were, without minor expenses that could not be detailed. All the money you left and sent is reduced to $675, and after spending $200 at least in many things that are not household expenses and paying some debts that you yourself left me, you now expect me to live three months, when I am not the only one who manages the money. I'd already managed not to receive the change, but now it turns out that I do not know how much is spent. You have willed things to be this way and must send money in abundance, because I am not responsible for how it is spent. What I have done is count, and I assure you that after having paid the rent, I was terrified. Not even if you add a lot will it make it to the date you indicate in your tally.

It is necessary that you understand that with the order of things you have wanted to establish, it is not possible to live with as little money as we had thought. Besides the increase in which expenses, which is not much different from Santo Domingo except for the horses, it turns out that we had not thought about paying the dress maker or the drug store, which has left me stumbling when I have to buy medicines, and that is often. Camila's flour costs $15 a dozen. We may spend somewhat less on milk and plantains, but there are many things which are more expensive here than in the Capital.

Translations by Daisy Cocco De Filippis

AMELIA FRANCASCI
(Amelia Francisca de Marchena y Sánchez de Leyba)
Santo Domingo, 1850-1941

The first Dominican woman novelist was born in Santo Domingo of a father from a Hispanic-Dutch sefardi background (de Marchena) and of a Dominican mother (Sánchez). She was the fourth in a family of nine children. She married Rafael Leyba. The couple did not have any children. For many years she ran from her back rooms a store in the front of her home, and in her ninety-one years of life she enjoyed the friendship and trust of many politicians and intellectuals.

With the encouragement of Meriño and her family, Francasci began to publish in the newspapers of her day, *El eco de la opinión* founded by Francisco Gregorio Billini, the literary Mondays of the *Listín Diario* and in *La cuna de América*. Her first novel, *Madre culpable* (1893), a Dominican version of the *folletines* in vogue in Spain during the second half of the nineteenth century, appeared in installments in the *Listín Diario*. It was so popular in her day that it became one of the few books to see two editions by 1911 in the Dominican Republic.

Her neat, perceptive and subtle prose finds a good vehicle in the publication of *Monseñor de Meriño, íntimo*, where—besides drawing a portrait of one of the most public figures of her day and presenting life and political upheavals in the fin de siecle Dominican Republic and early twentieth century —it gives us a public portrayal of a period in the life of a woman who spent most of her life behind the curtains of her drawing room. The selection included here illustrates a less than common marriage for her times (Francasci's) and the political influence wielded by this extraordinary woman.

SELECTED BIBLIOGRAPHY

Madre culpable: novela original. Santo Domingo: Imprenta de García Hermanos, 1893. 342 p.

Recuerdos e impresiones. Santo Domingo: Imprenta de García Hermanos, 1901. 125 p.

Historia de una novela. Santo Domingo: Imprenta de García Hermanos, 1901. 60 p.

Francisca Martinoff: Drama íntimo. Santo Domingo: Imprenta de García Hermanos, 1901. 235 p.

Cierzo en primavera: historias cortas. Santo Domingo: Imprenta la Cuna de América, 1902. 171 p.

Monseñor Meriño, íntimo. Santo Domingo: Imprenta La Cuna América, 1925. 416 p. 2da. ed. *Colección* Pensamiento Dominicano No. 53, 1975.

Capítulo XL*

General Heureaux, the president of the republic, was killed. That event produced a delirious

---

* Selected from *Monseñor de Meriño, íntimo*. 2da. ed. Santo Domingo: Colección Pensamiento Dominicano, No. 53, 1975.

rejoicing in the nation. It had a very strange effect on me. Yes! The disappearance of that nefarious man, made me feel the great sense of relief others were experiencing, free forever from the horrendous weight his existence meant.

But there was, in the midst of it all a feeling that saddened me. I would think with regret: Why should such a man, gifted by God with exceptional qualities for his condition, have become so corrupt as to become the scourge of his poor fatherland, so needy of men like himself, but endowed with virtue? Why, instead of using his natural intelligence for good—his mind so clear, his able and political nature, his undeniable military valor and other qualities—why would he make himself hated so profoundly because of his wickedness and frightening vices?

I was lamenting it for the sake of the beloved country when I became convinced of the certainty of his death. In an impulse of pious Christian charity, I implored God for the soul of the reprobate, imitating without knowing it a saintly woman, one of the dead, a woman of sublime virtue whom he sacrificed by torturing her husband in such a cruel manner that he took his own life! I speak of the noble widow of the general Eugenio Generoso de Marchena, in Las Clavellinas (Azua) in 1894, father of Dr. Pedro E. de Marchena, Miguel Angel, Adelaida de López Penha, a cousin of mine, executed by Lilís and whose death caused me profound grief.

But at the same time I would ask God for mercy for the deceased monster, I invoked it with fervor and from the most intimate part of my soul so that he would favor me, so that he would enlighten me in the patriotic enterprise I was about to undertake, not thinking for an instant even in my literary projects.

Immediately, filled with valor and hope, I entered the combat.

From the first moment I saw Don Emiliano[1] by my side. All I did was call, and he came hastily.

He as much as I was animated by our patriotic ardor. We understood each other perfectly. My attitude did not surprise him. He found it as natural as I found the zeal with which I was assisted by him.

His practical advice was precious to me; my inspirations served him to orient himself many times. I say it again; we understood each other perfectly.

I was able to admire his great generosity. I found his patriotism to be great and so unaffected.

In that sense—and with all justice I was in spirit with my unforgettable absentee,[2] whose return was now possible—I lived anxiously awaiting.

My labor was productive, assisted by don Emiliano. And delicate too. It had to be. The political situation was not very clear. Pessimists judged it to be chaotic. But we had faith. I found it in my collaborator, he believed in himself and counted on my enthusiasm. We both had placed our hope in the God of the republic who had always saved her from greater calamities and we acted accordingly with spirit.

The government of the old regime, with vice-president general Wenceslao Figuereo as the legitimate president after president Heureaux's death, continued to exist, though in truth it was only the skeleton of a government, nothing more. But it was always to be feared.

And there were two revolutionary factions in existence; the one in the Cibao, headed by those who put an end to the existence of the tyrant, empowered by the popularity it enjoyed because of this

1   She refers to Emiliano Tejera. D.C.D.F.
2   She refers to Archbishop Arturo de Meriño. D.C.D.F.

liberating act, up in arms and ready to defend itself against the remains of the former government; the other, the one represented by my friend A[3], the godchild of Monseñor de Meriño, fervently devoted to me and deserving of all my esteem. That faction favored only the interests of don Juan Isidro Jimenes and was not willing to work for anyone but him.

Before Heureaux's death, both groups were in agreement; united by the enterprise of overthrowing the terrible dictator; but that violent act of justice; the exclusive work of the cibaeños and executed by special circumstances, changed the situation for the revolutionaries among themselves. The jimenistas feared that those on route to the city to lay siege and bring down president Figuereo, would not be disposed to recognize Jimenes as the supreme chief of the opposition. They came surrounded by a popular aura, acclaim in all corners, while the chief of the jiménistas found himself relegated to Nassau after the failure of his expedition against Lilís; would they want to accept him thus defeated? Were they not made conceited by their triumph? It was difficult to know it, because communications were intercepted and it was dangerous to try to bridge the differences between the rebels.

My friend A, suffering great anxiety over the responsibilities he had assumed, was often at my home consulting me or recommending something important to my efficient intervention. He was very suspicious of the government and needed to exercise great prudence.

I appealed to don Emiliano and we both joined efforts in the patriotic deed of uniting the factions and avoiding with that union a double civil war. I found emissaries to whom I could communicate my enthusiastic ardor who would become engaged in bringing key issues to light. They were so bent on doing this that they succeeded in it. And it came to be known, with all certainty, that those from the Cibao continued to be loyal to their original pledge and that they were becoming ready to recognize Jimenes as candidate for the Presidency of the Republic. This gave me great satisfaction. One could work with certainty and counting on success. The manifest in which the declarations of the chiefs of the Cibao were contained, was brought to my hands by my nephew Héctor de Marchena, son of Eugenio, father to Sara, and grandfather to María Isabel. I say incorrectly, my nephew; for he was as a favored son, almost from my childhood, at a time when still a young girl, I played the role of mother in my family.

Tía Amelia was a divinity for her favorite nephew. He exposed himself to danger for my sake, but also because a patriotic chord hummed in his heart. With others as enthusiastic as he was, in that solemn hour, he formed a band that went out late at night, in search of a certain printing shop where clandestinely they could reproduce quantities of the manifest and distribute it throughout the sleeping city. When they found it, I had at my disposal a number of flyers that I myself distributed, employing humble subordinates like the famous Ruperta[4] of the scene with Monseñor de Meriño, and a poor bricklayer, who was as attached to me as she was and who would volunteer for everything for my sake and to serve me. The two poor creatures, with the greatest of care, set the pages to flight in unknown neighborhoods and suburbs until they became popular even in the most hidden corners of the city.

We still needed to know don Juan Isidro Jimenes' intentions. It was still dangerous to communicate with him in Nassau. We had no information about his thoughts on the situation and if he counted with resources for the friends who were were struggling to push his candidacy. A telegram was sent to him, signed by my husband to please my friend A., and to assist me in my work of nation-

3 A is not identified in the book. DCDF

4 Ruperta was Francasci's maid.

al reconstruction. In it, he was advised of everything and was asked for information about his own situation and about his intentions.

And now I must say here that of all my syrtes, and among the most devoted to me was my husband. He gave me free reign of my actions because he enjoyed seeing me in full activity and exercising my better faculties. He had complete confidence in me and was convinced that I would never hurt him in any way! He was seduced by the noble character of all my undertakings. He simply admired me, as much as he respected me. He found it natural for others to love me exceptionally because he loved me in the same manner, and so he did not become confused by the demonstrations of affection that I received as tributes no matter how exaggerated they might appear. I was very grateful to him for his great estimation toward me and I can assure you that it contributed greatly to maintain harmony in our home. I would not have been able to tolerate the least sign of suspicion, so loyal and sincere was I. Freedom was indispensable for me, but my good sense knew where to set the limits. If my husband did not examine my actions, if he left me in full freedom to receive my dearest friends at home alone, in exchange I authorized him to open my mail, to answer many letters for me, and I gave him an account of everything. If I kept anything from him it was for the sake of sparing suffering or mortification. He was also free as far as I was concerned. I always respected him in everything and, in my systematic effort not to displease him, I would go to the extent of not granting entrance in our home to anyone, including relatives of mine, who was not to his liking.

In that manner we got along, although our temperaments were far from being alike. And our marriage lasted.

Chapter XLI

Don Juan Isidro Jimenes answered our telegram. He was pleased with everything and would be coming to the country with resources. That last affirmation had as its outcome an almost ferment of enthusiasm for him. The economic situation of the country was so awful! The coffers of the national treasure were empty and many difficulties were bound to come up, even in triumph, because of the lack of funds. The news spread causing almost general happiness.

What remained to be done was to force Manolao[5] to resign passively. I played a brilliant part in this matter. And I laugh as I say it because it was such easy work.

Manolao did not have any fondness for the presidency. Rich and independent, after the death of Heuraux who controlled him, he preferred to live quietly rather than sustain a struggle for power. I had friends close to him who served him as advisers and to whom he listened. From the beginning I tried to make myself heard by them, insinuating to them the idea of the resignation of the president. I insisted about it continuously. At times I was listened to closely; at others I was answered that he could just as well keep the power for the period required by the Constitution, which was not for very long. Impatient and fearful, I would get to the point of threatening, in the name of the revolutionaries, although without revealing that I was one of them. I would say that I had heard that were he to resist them there would be retaliations. This was effective in planting fear in the soul of the prudent successor to Lilís. Pressure exerted by those means had an effect. President Figuereo resigned.

I found out later on that the illustrious don Manuel de Jesús Galván and don Federico

---

5 Manolao was a nickname for President Figuereo. D.C.D.F.

Henríquez y Carvajal, also illustrious and a noble friend of mine, were called upon to serve by the president, and, without agreement between themselves, declined that favor separately, because they were so advised by their conscience as patriots, allowing Manolao to understand that resignation was the most expeditious action and that it would show more dignity in moments of such trascendence.

And there must have been many in those memorable days who felt their patriotic fibers moved and who, forgetting mean spirited interests, thought only of the welfare of the country. All difficulties had been overcome. There was no government, only a sham that was brought down on the 30 of August by a mob of happy and energetic young men who, as a fanciful masquerade, went into the streets throwing rocks and shouting: "Let revolution live! Down with the traitors!" A provisional government was immediately set up. My friend "A" was part of it. The troops from the Cibao were getting ready to make their triumphal entrance in the city. Informed, Jimenes immediately began to make plans to leave Nassau for Santo Domingo.

I was sick from September 1. I had fallen ill after the excitement of the struggle, worn out by exhaustion, because not everything had been a bed of roses in that battle. I had days of great tribulation; hours of painful anxiety. We were told that I had been denounced; that we had spies near our home; that my friend "A" had been identified as a conspirator and threatened with imprisonment again. Don Emiliano came to see us at dawn and my friend in the late hours of the night. My husband and I would stay awake while the neighborhood slept or had not awakened yet, in order to receive them. The same with my nephew Héctor.

When we were assured that friends of general Manolao would advise him to resist and that troops were being made ready to combat the killers of Lilís and jail and shackles and passports awaited those denounced as conspirators, my disquiet grew painful. I had only one solace when those threats reached me: Let don Emiliano come! He would decide and with me he would examine our situation and, with all lucidity and calm, he would calculate the pros and cons of each and almost always he calmed me down.

"Don't torment yourself so, Amelia," he would repeatedly tell me. "Let us hope all will be fixed." I wanted to have faith. And I had it in him; I had it in my enthusiasm and with it, I managed to communicate it to others. The others believed in me and relied on me for everything. Especially because of my influence over don Emiliano, who was a key figure for them and who, probably, without me, would not have served them the way he did by my side. I was their link to the jimenistas. And, according to him, he had too little acquaintance with the revolutionaries from the Cibao at the time to be as useful to them as he proved to be with my agency.

My collaboration must have been invaluable through all of it.

———•◦•———

Nevertheless, a short while later all had been forgotten. On that occasion more so than in others I received copper in exchange for the gold in my heart which I would give away, according to the psychologist friend of mine who knew the world and its people well!

-It is of little consequence to me.

I was contented with the illusion in my heart to find the days that followed beautiful:

It seemed to me I was swimming in an ocean full of light; that in the skies of the republic there began to rise a resplendent sun; that that sun would shine on forever and that all would be peace, concord and felicity for the Dominican family; that an era of true progress would open up shortly for us;

that all would be divine.

Delicious chimeras! How quickly they vanished!

The afternoon in which the liberator hero (as general Ramón Cáceres was called) and his compatriots entered the capital, while joy overflowed and all was festivity and cries of victory around me, I from my bed, from my bedroom, followed the movements outside, congratulating myself as well on behalf of the country.

A bi-partisan government was formed to prepare for elections to take place a short while thereafter. Jimenes was the candidate for the presidency; general Horacio Vásquez, the chief of the cibaeños, for the vice-presidency. Everything appeared to have turned into perfect harmony all inspired by the best patriotic sentiments. Thus I believed it in my sincerity; thus was expected by my eager soul.

Although I began to find myself relegated; that no attention was being paid to my person, I was satisfied so long as the best interests of the fatherland prospered; that they were being attended to and defended with love.

Translation by Daisy Cocco De Filippis

MERCEDES LAURA AGUIAR
Santo Domingo 1872-1958

Mercedes Laura Aguiar belonged to the first group of women teachers to graduate from Salomé Ureña's Instituto de Señoritas and at barely fifteen she was also the youngest. She dedicated her life to teaching, a labor which began as soon as she graduated, supporting the work of Salomé Ureña de Henríquez at the Women's Normal School until its closing because of its founder's illness and exhaustion. Aguiar continued her work in 1896 when the school opened its doors again under the name Instituto Salomé Ureña.

A fighter for women's rights, she was the founding member and secretary of the patriotic society "Rosa Duarte," the Junta Patriótica de Damas, secretary and president for two periods of the Club "Nosotras," and a founding member of "Acción Feminista Dominicana."

I have included a fragment of a paper titled "Salomé Ureña's Educational Labor" from a rich and varied collection of Aguiar's writings edited by her own disciples in keeping with what Aguiar attempted to do in her own writing: to honor her teacher. In these pages we hear first-hand recollections of the founding of the Instituto de Señoritas, a description of the general outcry and protest over the establishment of the school and Aguiar's own vehement defense of Salomé Ureña's religious and moral standards

Selected Bibliography:

Discursos y páginas literarias 1872-1958. Prologue by Argentina Montás. Santo Domingo: Editora del Caribe, 1972. 131 p. (Loving remembrance of her disciples on the day of her centenary, 16 of February of 1972)

Salomé Ureña's Educational Labor

Paper presented by Prof. Mercedes Laura Aguiar, in the week of celebrations at the Escuela Normal de Señoritas in honor of the hundredth anniversary of the birth of the illustrious poetess and educator

Respected School Authorities:

Out of gratitude, love and duty, I could not decline the honor of the invitation made by this worthy committee to speak of the work of the educator Salomé Ureña de Henríquez and about the life of the "Instituto de Señoritas" in whose bosom my reason and conscience were formed.

I have tried to condense and to abbreviate this work, which by its nature, is quite extensive.

But...if, in spite of my efforts, I start to tire your attention and exhaust your interest in my words, I ask you most vehemently for the favor of your benevolence to listen to the dissertation of this old teacher, "Salomé Ureña de Henríquez in her position as Educator."

In Santo Domingo, this First City of the Americas and capital of the Dominican Republic, was born Salomé Ureña on the 21st day of October of 1850 in the "Isabel la Católica" Street, then "Calle del Comercio".

The house, now number 84, is next to the one where Juan Pablo Duarte, our illustrious founding father and glorious founder of our Republic, was born.

The daughter of don Nicolás Ureña de Mendoza, notable jurist and elegant national poet, and doña Gregoria Díaz y León de Ureña, she was the pampered child of her parents, her aunt, Ms. Ana Díaz, and Ramona, her only sister.

With the warmth of her deeply-felt mother's love, that respectable and respected matron, simple and good-natured, left engraved forever excellent virtues in her daughter, and as a holy relic, the Christian faith, a rich treasure that Salomé kept in her heart as a precious legacy she never destroyed. Because, according to her own words, she never tried to uncover the unquestionable veil that covers the sacred mysteries of our Holy Religion.

And so she proved it to be. Not a single thought, nor a word alone, did she express, that would make pale the light of that beautiful beacon that orients us, and fills us with strength to reach the safe port in the boundless sea of life, in the terrible struggles of the spirit, in the doubts that so many times disturb the peace of our conscience.

By special devotion, every Saturday as an adolescent she would go to the Church of the Lady of Our Mercies to hear the mass offered in honor of the Patroness of the Republic. And so intense was that devotion that after one of her beloved son's, Pedro, serious illnesses, she made an offering of silver and gold shackles to the Redemptor of Captives as a thanksgiving for his health. This votive offering is kept in the Treasure of our Holy Basilica, and each year for her holidays, I myself place them in the hand of the venerated Image of the Lady of Our Mercies.

Because of the Christian teachings of her saintly mother, she would go with her sister Ramona to hear mass every Sunday, and more than once she exhorted us like a solicitous mother to practice this precept "which is so beautiful", as she would tell us.

The love of her mother filled her heart with joy, and she loved her so, she revered her so much, that in sweet song of filial tenderness she says:

> Hear my voice: the lyre
> wanted happily to sing for you,
> and in the language of harmony,
> weak the inspiration, Oh Mother of mine,
> words worthy of your affection
> it could not find.

She moved with her mother and with her sister in the home of her grandparents at the age of ten. There, in No. 56 of the street "19 de marzo", at the corner of "Callejón de la Cruz", she lived and flourished.

That "Callejón" is now the street that bears the enlightened name of "Salomé Ureña".

Her father guided her education, bright promise of the future with love and care, and it seems that he perceived the soul of the fatherland to be innate in her bright poetic inspiration, that as a guiding angel with its wings of love it protected her. Day by day, the doting daughter would go to her father's house at 37 Mercedes Street to enjoy his sweet company and receive his wise teachings.

In the yard, showing off its flowers in a perpetual spring, was a magnolia rose bush, the author's favorite flower. Before going up to her father's study, Salomé would gather fresh magnolias, and as she placed a sweet kiss of filial love on his forehead, she put them in the vase that adorned his desk.

The memory of that room moved her heart filled with pure and delicate tenderness, like noble and sublime ideals.

Father of mine! That cry from the soul, that her lyre translates filled with notes of grief, paints an intense filial love and describes the vast emptiness left in her soul by the absence of the beloved being that gave her life and cultivated her intelligence. By the time death took him away from her, the Poetess was already famous. As our illustrious countryman César Nicolás Penson indicates in the Hymn dedicated to her memory, in the wings of Fame, her name was already flying:

> from the Antillean Corinne
> from the Gulf to the Andean heights
> from one to another Sea

If the echo of that name, resounded in foreign lands, if they came from alien places anxious to meet her, the intellectual, the cultivators of letters, renown poets setting foot on Dominican soil, her countryfolk lived proud of that lyre that vibrated with sublime arpegios whether in "Intimas Páginas," (Intimate Pages) or in the songs of "Shadows" and "Bitterness of Light," or in the hope and faith in the beautiful and bright Future of her "adored gentle Quisqueya".

<hr />

The Cultural Society "Amigos del País" (Friends of the Country), which later became the Ateneo, founded and made up of young people of relevant moral qualities, of dedicated love of letters or anything to do with culture and the exaltation of the Fatherland, admired and valued the extraordinary worth of the distinguished poetess, of the enlightened countrywoman.

In well deserved homage, the country awarded her the symbolic Medalla de Honor (Medal of Honor), and a national collection published the first edition of her poems, richly framed with a prologue by our eminent sacred orator, Fernando Arturo de Meriño, who wanted to be near to her, to listen to her, and to share her sublime ideals for the future and the glory of the Fatherland.

Among that pleyade, that beautiful representation of masculine intellectuality, was the young Francisco Henríquez y Carvajal, Pancho, as he was called familiarly; a prominent member of that cultural circle. He became the most assiduous visitor of the poetess, who in her desire to acquire new scientific knowledge, to ground, expand and deepen the knowledge already acquired, was studying under the supervision of don Pancho, who had become her teacher and mentor.

As Don Pancho himself told us, she turned the knowledge received into very well written works, and in such a manner she grew even to supercede her Teacher in precision of ideas, always expressed with clarity, demonstrating a complete mastery of the topics discussed.

Attracted no doubt by the talent, modesty, genius, sweetness and simplicity of that flower of purity who was hiding her virtue and charm within the beautiful foliage of the maternal home, his heart burst with a luminous sparkle that became a brilliant flame of love. Lit, as a votive lamp, that flame which enlightened the heart of Quisqueya's Muse as well, marked their way with dazzling light and on the 11th of February of 1880, blessed by God, they united forever their names, their lives, their ideals of goodness and progress for society. Those souls were predestined to fuse into one and to make of their home, formed under the shelter of Faith, Love and Virtue, a paradise of happiness, of ideals and of successes, for the good of Dominican society, the Fatherland she loved so intensely and that he knew, one day, he would defend with love, bravery and dignity.

They made a sweet nest of love in the house that is number 25 Hostos Street today.

There, with the memory of her husband, absent while visiting the countryside, her lyre created "Verpertina" when

> from the breeze of the afternoon
> to the soft prodding, with gentle air,
> the plantain in its leaves seeks balance

Mr. Hostos, the great pedagogue, founder of Objective and Rational Teaching in our Fatherland was among us, and the Normal School was already open, founded and superbly guided by him. The Maestro, who had found in don Pancho one of his most apt and efficient collaborators, approached the poetess wanting to know her and to strengthen the ties of friendship with the muse that with her glory would elevate the Dominican Parnassus.

But his admiration grew more and more when he found in her not only the sweet singer of the Ozama, who in verses of sublime inspiration gave soul to the "Song of Her Songs," but also the strong woman, the mind that climbs haughtily, searching for a wider horizon, for something that the Fatherland anxiously needed.

He listened to her thoughts about glory and progress, then touched the dreams that would caress her forehead, and his piercing eye saw the truth:

> Oh, women have within them
> despite vice and its poison,
> treasures of the earth,
> seeds of greatness and goodness

Treasure of virtues, intelligent and understanding, that Dominican woman was called upon to be "Propelling Force" who "would remove the stagnant plant" from the fatherland; and in her hours of wakefulness, in the rest of the night, her restless mind would persist, in the realization of her beautiful ideal that she would see converted in living and tangible reality.

Mr. Hostos, a man of extraordinary talent, of iron will, of great soul and noble sentiments, was surprised by the firm basis of the difficult problem posed by her, and filled with enthusiasm for that steel-strong spirit, for the creative force of that mind, for the intense love of fatherland overflowing her heart, he offered his loyal and firm collaboration to that "noble heroine of supreme redemption."

Perhaps it was that beautiful project behind the happy couple's return to the family home of "19 de marzo" street.

"There she lived and flourished" and there she wanted to plant the fecund seed that her benevolent hand cultivated with such love.

In her mother's house, her aunt, Ana Díaz, or Nana operated an "escuelita" (little school). There we learned to read and write to whatever extent possible; to do basic operations of arithmetic, catechism, Christian Doctrine and manual labor. These were taught by Manina (as we familiarly called Doña Gregoria, the sweet mother of the Poetess-Educator). Don Pancho taught Arithmetic, and it is difficult to find such young students who would know the multiplication table so firmly, by jumps, straight or backwards, without ever making a mistake. Memé, the loving nickname we used to give Salomé, went to our classroom daily, and Valentina Díaz, a cousin who lived with her as a sibling, would assist Nana in her work teaching first letters.

A day in July, of the year 1881, Nana told us to tell our parents or tutors in her name that the school would close on the 31, because she was very fatigued. Her long years prevented her from continuing to work, and she had nothing else to teach us. Upon feeling the impact of the sad announcement, some hid their faces in their hands, while tears of grief ran on their cheeks; others, more sentimental, were weeping, anguished.

Informed of what was going on, Memé and don Pancho came over, to witness the scene created by the children.

"But...Nana, what is going on with these girls?" she said sweetly. Don Pancho, listening to Nana's tale with the frank smile he was known for, told us, "It is natural that this should cause you sadness, leaving the school and saying good-bye to your friends. But...I think THAT THE LION IS NOT AS FIERCE AS HE IS PAINTED. After vacation, you will come back to study, in this same house, in a school that Salomé will open and whose Principal she will be."

Post Nubila Febus!

The sun comes out after the clouds...The tempest had passed and tears had become smiles.

On the 31 of July, the pupils embraced Manina, Nana and Valentina, and happily we left the little school where we had received our first lessons.

Nana blushed. In an angry tone our teacher told us, "SO IT WAS ALL A SHOW...Since you are going to Salomé's school you are not sad to leave us, but happy, flying as if you were butterflies."

The sun, bright with light, would not take long in tearing down the thick clouds...

Plans for the beautiful intellectual edifice had been traced.

Men of goodwill, the masons were also ready for the extraordinary labor. Generous hands brought the material needed, and enthusiasm grew from the beginning, full of faith, love and hope, for the work that would culminate in the success of Dominican Women, symbolized in six adolescents, forged by the warmth of the wishes of that heroic woman, who with sublime abnegation pledged the first offerings of her effort and love to the Fatherland. Success crowned all of their steps, taken with perseverance and without a feint heart.

The Honorable City Council of the capital city assigned a sum to help support the establishment. The High Board of Studies offered enthusiastic support without reservations. Generous hands, such as those of the gentleman don Maximiliano Grullón, opened wide to help cover the indispensable expenses. A falange of enthusiastic young men, without interest in personal gain, sacrificed some of their precious time to transmit their knowledge to the little girls who tomorrow, with their success, would reward the abnegation of that Woman, who sacrificed her repose and the ineffable sweetness of her home, for the betterment of the fatherland, which was the life of her life, soul of her soul, song of love and of heroism, in the chords of her immortal lyre.

On the 16th of October of the year 1881, a letter circulated with the signature of Salomé Ureña de Henríquez, announcing to the parents of the girls from Nana's "La escuelita" and to a good number of heads of households that on the upcoming November 3, the doors would open for the "Instituto de Señoritas," a school to be directed by her, and that would operate according to the Plan for Objective and Rational Teaching implemented by Mr. Hostos, in the Normal School.

Attached to it was the program of studies and the schedule: from 8 to 11 in the mornings, and from 1 to 4 during the afternoons. On Saturdays it would be open only in the morning to offer lessons on Morality, Good Manners, Holy Scriptures, reading and recitations.

While many received the letter with pleasure and sympathy, many others energetically protested.

The winds of ignorance, of slander and of egoism, blew strongly, and raised a dust storm of infamy. How could it be possible that parents allow their daughters to walk the streets all day? How outrageous, to yank them out of their homes to give them lessons that were only suitable for males!... There would no longer be daughters or wives or mothers dedicated to the home, but haughty women, ignorant of the duties suitable to their condition and sex.

Thoughtless and daring as it was, this reaction ignored that the noble founder of the "Instituto de Señoritas" was a model of industriousness, of affection, of noble sentiments, of modesty and virtue, in society and at home. They forgot in their mad confusion, that Salomé Ureña de Henríquez was a valuable guarantee for their daughters, invulnerable shield, who would defend the honor of childhood, of adolescence and of youth, in the noble apostolate that she was about to practice under guard of her crystal clear virtue. She held high, as a banner of success in teaching Letters and Sciences, the purity of her conscience, the powerful brake of morality, healthy and fecund, and the rich treasure of Christian faith. Meanwhile, even if the wind hissed and the sea howled, the falange stood its ground, ready for battle, and to challenge the storm.

The unforgettable November 3, 1881 finally arrived. At 8 in the morning the founding students were already in the main room in the family home at the "19 de marzo" street: The group of the unforgettable Nana: Ana Josefa Puello, the dean; Leonor M. Feltz, Luiza Ozema and Eva María Pellerano, Altagracia Frier, Altagracia Henríquez Bello, Mercedes Echenique, and Mercedes Laura Aguiar, the youngest in the group. With us were registered: Carmela, Filomena and Amelia Grullón, daughters of don Maximiliano, the noble protector of the "Instituto de Señoritas," Emilia C. de Elena, Adelina Henríquez and Altagracia Henríquez Perdomo. A week later, Catalina F. Pou and Carmen Julia Henríquez Perdomo joined us.

Our entrance was moving. All of our hearts were beating furiously.

Two rows of oak desks; at one extreme, between both rows, the great desk of our teacher, who was seated behind it, in a swivel armchair. On the desk: a celestial globe and an earthly one, a strange apparatus, very attractive, that resembled the planetary system. A small handlebar made the spheres that appeared to be the planets turn around the one representing the sun. Saturn and of Jupiter, of course, were not missing their rings, neither was Venus without its beauty and shine, the beautiful "star of the shephard". The small microscope—which fascinated us and now belongs to Miss Consuelo Nivar, current Director of the Instituto-Escuela, given to that dedicated teacher by Pedro Henríquez Ureña—an abacus, a box of figures and geometric bodies, and a big bell, completed the effects. The walls were decorated with a map of the island of Santo Domingo, maps of the Continents, Anatomical drawings, big botannical and zoological prints, and posters with the seven primary colors. On one side, in front of the pupils, next to the blackboard, a compass, a pointer, an eraser and some sticks of chalk.

The workers, ready for work, were there. To the right of doña Salomé, was don Pancho. To the left, on the first tier, don Federico, the beloved centenarian teacher, distributed on one side and the other: don José Dubeau, don Emilio Prud'Homme, don José Pantaleón Castillo, don José Santiago de Castro, don César Nicolás Penson, Ms. Valentina Díaz and don Carlos Alberto Zafra, the youngest in the daring falange.

Salomé Ureña de Henríquez's fine fingers pressed the button of the bell with the same firmness they had pressed the lyre, and the sonorous echo filled the air in the imposing classroom. Majestic, simply dressed in white, with that paleness that rendered her face the color of ivory, filled with sweetness and emotion, she stood up. And as if a magical cord had moved us, the entire teaching body rose and trembling, on our feet, we were, also, her students.

Don Pancho went up to the board and with a firm hand and clear handwriting, wrote:

FIAT LUX!...

And later, she dictated the beautiful and heavenly salutation to one of the girls :

GLORY BE TO GOD IN THE HEAVENS AND PEACE ON EARTH TO MEN OF GOOD WILL

The traces of the white chalk on the dark board, simulated the rays of a brilliant light that would break, triumphant, the shadows of ignorance.

Sweet moment of supreme emotion!

How you have remained engraved with permanent characters in the souls of those who then sang among the flowers, to the light of a resplendent sun, the triumphant hosanna of joy; and today, among the shadows, among the thorns, we sing a melancholic hymn of love and remembrance...! Our director, with words that made her lips tremble with emotion, not with her soul of poetess, but with her soul as patriot, explained to us the meaning of those beautiful words that were still shining on the blackboard. The "Instituto de Señoritas" had been solemnly opened!

In a family environment, life in the school was filled with tenderness, instruction and enchantment, although the rules within its walls were subject to inviolable discipline. Morality came up at each instant in the classes as well as habits of education without it being necessary to wait for Saturday, the day set aside for such lessons.

Another letter invited the Honorable City Council, the members of the Superior Board of Studies, the fathers and tutors of students, and whomever would like to witness the FIRST EXAMS that would take place from the 20 to the 23 of December inclusive of mornings and afternoons, according to the schedule followed by the "Instituto".

The audience was splendid, and the students' performances were highly satisfactory, in writing and in reading, with explanations and answers to questions about what we had read. In arithmetic, knowledge of operations, knowledge and use of the abacus, and extraordinary agility in mental calculations. In geometry, knowledge of lines, figures and bodies.

The lessons were completely objective. We did not use a text during the tests. Attention, observation, intuition and induction, with an exceptional interest on the part of teachers and pupils alike, brought success to these first examinations. The attendees, invited to participate in the exams, had abstained at first, but before the clarity and the good disposition of the examinees, they decided to ask us questions, always inspiring confidence in us.

There were some funny moments: it was said that Miss Echenique had distinguished herself for her walks. Smiling, with the pointer at hand, she would go to the blackboard or from the map, answering questions, until she would approach the examining Jury. Another of the younger pupils, while speaking of the Discovery of America, of the trip of circumnavigation, of Sebastian El Cano, said "pilato" because of a "lapsus linguae." She noticed the smile of her listeners, not of mockery but of friendliness, and immediately full of vivacity, she corrected herself: "I said "a" instead of "o" but I know very well that Pilatos was he who washed his hands to make believe he was not to blame for the death of Christ; and PILOTO is the sailor, who guides the ships with his compass. And I also know," she said stressing her words, "that El Cano was the pilot for Magellan."

An applause rewarded the youthful explanation of the young examinee.

On the 23, the exams finished, the Jury withdrew, surprised, filled with true satisfaction, and effusively congratulated the Director, the teachers, and the small group of students of the "Instituto de Señoritas" who in fifty days had rendered such extraordinary and splendid labor!

One afternoon we were talking in a friendly manner with the unforgettable Teacher, and it occurred to us to tell her: "Madam, why haven't you written since the Instituto was founded?"

She looked at us sadly and answered sweetly: "It is not the Institute. You are not the cause of my silence. My grief for the Fatherland, its retrocessions, its flaws, does not allow me to raise my voice... You still cannot understand how much the Fatherland is loved, and how that sublime love fills all our being... May God grant that my lyre, mute at the moment, break out in trills tomorrow, for my disciples and for the Fatherland."

(Fragment)

Translation by Daisy Cocco De Filippis

EVANGELINA RODRIGUEZ PEROZO
Higüey 1880-San Pedro de Macorís 1947

The first Dominican woman doctor, Evangelina Rodríguez born in Higüey on November 10, 1880 and raised in San Pedro de Macorís, graduated as Normal Teacher in 1902 and was appointed Principal of the Escuela Normal de Señoritas in 1907. She received her university degree in Medicine (Licenciatura) in 1908 and presented her thesis, entitled *Niños con excitación cerebral* (Mentally Disturbed Children) in 1911. She studied and received her degree as gynecologist-obstetrician in Paris (1921-25).

Antonio Zaglul's detailed biography underlines the support she received from such luminaries as José Ramón López and the Deligne brothers as well as the harsh criticism and opposition she had to endure as a black woman from a poor background trying to carve out a place for herself in the field of medicine. She died of schizophrenia in 1947.

Unfortunately, much of her later more polemical writing has not been preserved. I include the first chapter of her first published book *Granos de polen* where we have a glimpse of her capacity for reasoning through an argument and for asserting her point of view in one of the more unique interpretations of love we may come across.

SELECTED BIBLIOGRAPHY:

Granos de polen. San Pedro de Macorís: np, 1915. 170 p. (Essay)

Le Guerisseur: Cuento chino bíblico de moral social. La Vega: Tipografía El Progreso, 19 p. (Short Story)

Zaglul, Antonio. *Despreciada en la vida y olvidada en la muerte: Evangelina Rodríguez Perozo*. Santo Domingo: np, 1980.

CHAPTER I *

Most poets, I will not say thinkers because these are nothing more than poets, agree in their assessment of childhood as the most beautiful stage in one's life. I am not with them on this. The beauty of children is only relative: it comes from nothing more than the immaculate harmony of physical form, in the tight plasticity of the skin, in its innocent chastity. Beauty is nothing more than perfection, and what is perfect would have to be that which is more complete.

The soul of children is pliable like mud still to be modeled. Therefore, I cannot conceive of beauty at that age. Other poets say that the most beautiful stage in one's life (especially in women) is adolescence from age fifteen to sixteen. Plenitude in spring, preamble for summer. I am not with them on this either. Such beauty is like a child's, also relative. This is the indecisive moment of form. Here

---

* From *Granos de polen*. San Pedro de Macorís: s.n., 1915.

is when all will take definitive possession. Now is when all will take a normal tonality. Everything is bigger, more open than in childhood, but in the form of a sketch. This is the step from chrysalis to butterfly. Its wings, wet and titillating, cannot contain themselves. Neither does she know where she is to take flight, nor on what corolla she is to libate. Perhaps she would land on some poisonous wings.

This is the moment in which the mother can use her skills. Like the artist, it is the moment to fix definitively the colors and to give her the last brush strokes. The expert gardener must apply with mastery the cutting of the hedges. This age is not beautiful either, because there cannot be beauty in disorder and disharmony. Reasoning, an organizing and hierarchic faculty, has not set in yet.

In my opinion, the most beautiful stage in life is that of summer, where almost all is complete, where the molding of the physiological form has been completed (the first to be formed and the first to be deformed). And as a natural consequence the psychological one has also been completed. It is the moment prior to procreation, when life prepares itself to give life. The moment of maternity is sublime for every female whose heart beats in Creation! Where, before a new life, all the potential for the life of an organism is concentrated in one organ. Where an entire organism is moved (especially in the superior woman of the species) by a breaking which is more than human, divine, because the design of procreation is divine in Nature, because it has the harmonic coherence of a world of ideas in the brain, and a world of affections in the heart, because it feels itself invaded by something new and ignores what makes her divine! She feels it so and so she expresses it. Let us hear what our laureate poetess doña Salomé Ureña de Henríquez says when her first child is born: The heavens opened up, and he descended to the home in harmony, the angel that my dreams had foreseen, etc.

At this moment my mind is risen, and while risen it descends the abyss, it is rendered nothing, it falls apart and since it is impotent to conceive, there will be no brush nor quill that would provide a means to express the supersublime moment when it palpitated in the breast of eternal Creation! Immense gestation that could not but be an abortion: the Chaos! to complete at a later point its formation.

Even in beings without an active life there is beauty in maternity. Observe plants. Pay attention to a rose bush in its moment of bloom, and you would say that there is truth in the expression of one of our poets when he says: if plants had feeling and expression, they would sing at their moment of bloom!

It is here, at this moment, when I believe love exists for the first time. It is an indescribable feeling in women, a cooing in birds, heat in plants. It is heat, because life is movement, and where it cannot be active it transforms itself into radiations of heat. If you do not believe this, place your hand near flower buds which are opening up, especially those in the family of the cicada* and you will feel an almost burning temperature.

Water plants shoot up their blooms outside of the water in search of heat from the atmosphere, and they open up like an explosion.

As I said before, that is what I translate as love. I am too physiological to believe in what the poets describe: what they describe is what I call a preamble to love, that is Platonism.

Platonic love is nothing more than the vaporization of feeling forged by the vehement heat of passion, which will condense as soon as there is a cooling off period.

* Such as the Candle of the Virgin, or the Sacred Heart of Jesus, etc. (Varieties offered by the author). D.C.D.F.

Song, cooing, warbling in birds, quaking of the zephyr in flowers so pollen may penetrate its stigma, music, poetry, feeling of art, a kiss in man!

Powerful attraction between the opposites of an infinite Nature, made finite by pleasure, to make itself more infinite after the grief of death.

True love is nothing more than a feeling of esteem of our own being: one loves a child because it is the parting or the partitioning of oneself, in whom one continues to live in future generations through time, like the acorns of an oak tree go on to reproduce the woods after it has been cut down. Parents love their children good or bad, because they are their own being in physiological continuation. So too I must also love my book good or bad, because it is the childbirth of my spirit and a means by which I might find psychological continuity. Young mothers: since your love rests on reproduction as the continuation of your being, clearly, you would not want to see yourselves reproduced poorly. It is there where you should place your mother's pride, not so that you are admired in a more complete work.

The ancients, especially Aristotle, used to say that "education ought to begin in infancy, before birth" and they were not wrong. In man one must form first the animal and later on the super animal. If the stable laws of the universe, harmony and life lie in strength, let us not forget strength, which is physiological vigor in the animal species and frondosity in plants. Do not neglect your own vigor, which is that of your offsprings, since we know by now that the weak do not succeed in life. Those who are not sufficiently expert in this field of knowledge because their home had not provided for them sufficiently, can find it in learned books such as those in hygiene, especially those dealing with women in their delicate state and with infantile hygiene.

I hope then that the first kisses, manifestation of tenderness for your luxuriant blooms of flesh, may be the prelude to the baptismal dew of morality with which you will anoint them later on. Let it be so! so that it will be sanctioned by Those Above, and the dove of the Holy Spirit cast its blessings on you.

Translation by Daisy Cocco De Filippis

PETRONILA ANGELICA GOMEZ
Santo Domingo 1883-1971

Petronila Angélica Gómez was born in the San Miguel section of Santo Domingo on January 31, 1883 and died destitute and blind in the Home for the Aged of Saint Francis of Assisi on September 1, 1971.

She studied at the Normal School of Santo Domingo where she received the title of Normal Tutor (1911) and Normal Teacher for Secondary Education (1915). She directed the first co-educational school, Escuela Mixta de San Pedro de Macorís, from 1908 until 1919, when she purchased the Kindergarten that was ran by Mercedes Amiama Gómez and her daughters.

She carved herself a place in history as a fighter for the implementation of feminist principles. In his writings about women's contributions, Julio Jaime Julia points out that "neglected as the pioneer and precursor of the national feminist movement, the time has come to rescue her meritorious contribution as founder and supporter for a period of seventeen years of the journal *Fémina*, founded in San Pedro de Macorís on the 15 of February* of 1922." (45-46) Her lifetime commitment not only to feminist causes but to civic activities on behalf of the nation, was bought at the price of whatever financial stability she might have secured for herself.

I have selected a number of speeches that are not only representative of the early contribution Petronila Angélica Gómez made to the national feminist movement but also illustrate her nobility of spirit, her solidarity with women's causes and her difficult economic situation. Gómez' feminism much in keeping with definitions offered throughout the Caribbean and Latin America at the time, however, defined as "latin feminism," calls for women's rights in order to maintain the balance and happiness of the home: the place for women. Gómez embraced the traditional platform of the Liga de Mujeres Iberoamericanas which called for a feminism that would bring together educated Spanish speaking women.

Selected Bibliography:

Contribución para la historia del feminismo dominicano. Ciudad Trujillo: Editorial Librería Dominicana, 1952. (Essay)

Influencia de la mujer en Iberoamérica. Ciudad Trujillo: Editora del Caribe, 1954. (Essay)

Julia, Julio Jaime. *Haz de luces*. Santo Domingo: CIPAF, 1990.

---

* Other documents indicate that the founding took place on the 15th of July. D.C.D.F.

WORDS**

by our director, Miss Petronila Angélica Gómez,
to close the cultural session, celebrated in
honor of the journal Fémina, on its first
anniversary on the 15th day of July of 1923.

Ladies and Gentlemen;

Dear Sisters:

Before proceeding to the closing of this pleasant ceremony that has filled with perfume this ambience, I wish to express to you briefly what my heart has felt, filled with satisfaction and grateful for the many kindnesses you have bestowed on us.

A sublime cause has compelled us to come together today in this beautiful venue where everything seems lighter, happier, more beautiful!

Grateful emanations have fallen from the calyx of the white lilies, to come to anoint our hearts beating today with gratitude and affection.

It is the fifteenth of July!

Today is the first anniversary of the dawn of the first issue of our journal *Fémina,* born poor of fortune but rich in enthusiasm, rich in good will and rich in the desire to do right by the sex it extols.

And upon its birth, good fortune wanted to plant flowers on its way, to find two self-sacrificing companions and committed fighters: Consuelo Montalvo de Frías and María Angelis de Canino, two branches that open their arms from the same trunk, to form a pedestal where the goddess of perseverance rests proudly.

Ladies and Gentlemen: It is with great satisfaction that I indicate to you that in the time our humble journal has spent in laborious life, there has not been one solitary moment of hesitation, nor has disenchantment taken shelter in the soul of my companions. From its first issue, it appeared resolute to give life to an idea, determined to accomplish the lofty mission it had imposed on itself.

It has not stopped for a moment to look at the thorns on its way, and comforted by the life-giving fire of will, it continues on its serene course, confident of the success, that places before it today a crown of laurels.

Today, gathered in this poetic mansion, twice illuminated by the torch of intelligence, what satisfaction has my spirit felt to hear how the verb of the fecund don Justiniano Ma. Bobea overflows in harmony, the crisp ditirambs of Pedro E. Pérez, the beauty made rhythm by Ligio Vizardi, the warm phrases of don Lucas Espinal, the comforting words of Godofredo Canino and don Moisés de Soto, and the suggestive recitations that have filled the ambiance, other melodious lips, like notes taken from an ideal music!

How to reciprocate such sympathy, such delicacy of spirit, such generosity? Well, by gathering all of the flowers of the garden of our spirit, flowers that carry with them the essence of our gratitude and our affection, and bringing our hearts together, like three gallant lilies, into one gentle lily, and

---

** Selections from *Contribución para la historia del feminismo dominicano.* Ciudad Trujillo: Editorial Librería Dominicana, 1952

offer it amiably to the cultured ladies and the noble gentlemen congregated here in this unforgettable evening of happiness!

For my dear companions, Mrs. de Canino and de Frías, who have known how to give me this lofty proof of friendship, I formulate my wishes so that torrents of light and prosperity might pour on them. And for my special friends Mr.Godofredo and Mrs. María de Canino, to whose benevolence the effectivity and splendor of this cultural activity is owed, I sing a hymn of consideration and gratitude, and I raise my wishes for a long and happy life, for their good fortune, and honor and prestige of civilization in the Antilles.

I have spoken.

———◦•◦———

TO SAVE INFANCY

Paper read by our director, at the Meeting of the Press,
that took place on the Sala de Gobernación Civil on the
night of the 24 of April last, with regard to the infantile
mortality that is dwindling the Dominican population.

Convinced of the importance underlying our coming together, my expression this moment is that of a citizen of the Republic in my triple positions as conscientious community member, teacher and journalist.

Before anything else, my congratulations to Dr. Evangelina Rodríguez, for whom highly sounding adjectives are redundant, for the success with which she begins the constructive labor she has imposed on herself since her return from Lutece.

Existence places many demands on man, but among the many preoccupations human beings are constantly shaken by, there are problems which must be noticed much more so than others, because there are problems on whose solution depends the future of the world.

And that is one: Infantile mortality, terrifyingly has called the attention of conscientious journalists, who have rang a call of alarm in more than one occasion.

But theory is not enough in this case. It is necessary to find a remedy and a practical action is required that would proceed effectively to ward off the apparent epidemic that threatens the extermination of the race.

The plan pointed out by Dr. Evangelina Rodríguez in her insightful conference is the more positive one, since it is geared toward cutting down at the root this terrible scourge on infancy. Therefore, every conscientious person and in whose heart beats a feeling of goodness, must unite he/himrself with Dr. Rodríguez and cooperate with her on the humanitarian task of saving childhood.

This is not a trifling matter. It is important to make a commitment with love, good-will and decisiveness. It is not sufficient to express an idea. Practice must persevere. In this case, the spirit of cooperation must be law among men and women, imposed for its own sake, to confederate wills and to put into practice the transcendental question of the defense of the life of infancy.

And I say transcendental, because in each child that is saved an individual good deed and a collective one will be done at the same time. Infancy is to be saved not only for its own sake but because what is also involved is the salvation of the race, population, society and fatherland.

It is well known that our governments, unfortunately, are not inclined to protect from its inception this type of deeds. It is well known that politics absorbs the thought and activities of men, but fortunately there remains this other half of the human race, that although political influence is reflected indirectly at times on her, she is not seeking for guarantees in politics, but in the mission for which she has been brought on this earth. There remains, (and I speak now in my capacity as Representative of the Liga Internacional de Mujeres Iberoamericanas), there remains, yes, the feminine element, who is disposed, in her capabilities and aptitudes, to face the problem on whose solution depends the future of the world.

It is especially for women who are supposed to approach the crib to fulfill their mission, since every being that sees the light of this world, be it man or woman, needs special protection, so that their development is complete and they can fend for themselves, and lend to others the benefit of their existence.

"A healthy mind in a healthy body," said a wise pedagogue. Give life to children, give them robustness and their souls would match their bodies, healthy souls, that is to say useful members of their families and society.

Let us do then, members of the press a serious campaign in defense of the work, to ward off infantile mortality, and will thus contribute to the task that Dr. Rodríguez so generously has imposed on herself.

Meanwhile, I offer her a sister's embrace because she dreams as I do of a free and strong Republic, and of the building of solid bases on which to build a future for society.

1923

FEMINISM

It pleases us today to dissert with our amiable readers about the meaning of the word "Feminism" so often discussed these days.

This word means SOCIAL EVOLUTION OF WOMEN. Its goal to improve the social condition of women is not a new problem since already it has spread and been solved in all civilized countries in the globe.

But we ought to know also, that feminism is not organized or interpreted in equal manner in all countries, from which it can be inferred, that its practice is much varied, adapting and interpreting itself according to what circumstances have dictated in societies in the different countries where this credo has been given special attention.

Thus we have that while feminism in other races works principally so that women participate in political decisions, the feminism of the latin race struggles, and this is its primordial aspiration, so that women are emancipated civilly, and have a position in the organization of society which constitutes the happiness of the home and the fatherland. And it also works so that those rights and customs which have been deprived to them, to favor men, can be recognized and broadened. This situation is such an abnormality that rather than uniting, can bring about the loss of balance and the dissolution even of the necessary stability to sustain marriage.

Latin feminism conserves women essentially as women, within the home, educating their children and sharing with their partner preoccupations and happinesses, assisting them as brothers and compatriots in all that is within their power, in harmony with their character and condition as women, and assuring the true constitutive peace of the home.

As patriots and as citizens women send to the State, from their home, their concepts, opinions and votes, when they deem it necessary, cooperating in this way to the political welfare of their country, with the only motive that from that well-being would follow the betterment of a society in which their partner and them are integral elements.

The feminism of latin women is not planning to carry a rifle, nor does it have ambitions to manage the reigns of government, as women think, that if it is true that women are not physically prepared for this task, it is no less true that men in any case have never been nor will they be physically or morally prepared for the government of the home.

On the other hand, latin women place the greatest emphasis in their lives on the charm of always keeping alive the flame of love, nourished by that natural affinity that when not manifest in its full intensity, is reflected in the diverse and attractive shades of sympathy.

Interpreting and putting into practice feminism from this logical point of view, men see in women not the enemy burning with desire for freedom, because they find their eternal yoke in the duties of the home, but see in them the lover, companion and advisor, a friend and defender, women in their stead finding in men, the advisors and guides needed to protect and defend them [women].

Based on its development and practice of its General Principles, whose work we are rather familiar with, this is how feminism is interpreted by the Liga Internacional de Mujeres Ibéricas e Hispanoamericanas, and we dare affirm that is the reason this Institution counts day by day, not only with the following of all the women of the race, but also with the sympathy and approval of many illustrious men who praise the work of an association whose goals, narrowing the ties of iberian-american fraternity, dignifies women, lifting their moral condition to the level required by the moral necessities of men, in the field of societies that aspire to a legitimate well-being and a well-understood civilization.

Here is, immediately following the program happily conceived by its Founder, Elena Arizmendi, and put to practice in all countries where this laudable institution operates:

WHAT ARE THE LEGITIMATE ACTIVITIES OF
THE LEAGUE OF IBERIAN-AMERICAN WOMEN?

1. Social activities that serve to achieve the narrowing of the ties between educated hispanic women. This can be easily achieved with spiritual communication.

2. To suggest educational programs that serve to prepare women for the fulfillment of their role as daughters, wives, mothers and citizens.

3. To work for feminine organizations, of a social nature, already existing and those to be established, to form a firm base of moral support, mutual trust and solidarity of ideas.

4. To work so that the progress of our women, which each day reaches greater development, is known outside of our countries.

Every individual without distinction of sex, to the best of their ability, must make an effort to honor their sex and race. This idea of a conduct that meets with the exigencies of our intellectual dignity and morality is designated as the image of this League of Spanish speaking women, which already counts with representatives in many Spanish American countries.

(Fragment)

Translation by Daisy Cocco De Filippis

ERCILIA PEPIN
Santiago 1884-1939

Ercilia Pepín was an educator, writer, feminist, patriot, a woman whose capacity to learn and whose intellectual curiosity brought her to a life dedicated to study, teaching and feminist and political militancy. At the age of fifteen, Ercilia Pepín was appointed Director of the Escuela de Niñas de Nibaje. This appointment was made although she had not met all of the practical and academic requirements for her degree as Normal Teacher in the Escuela Normal de Señoritas, due to its closing in 1900. It was not until 1913 when Pepín had the opportunity to take her exams and graduate with honors.

Pepín was a life-long learner, taking independent courses over the years with the teachers Ricardo Ramírez and Salvador Cucurrullo. In 1908 she was appointed teacher in Mathematics, Physics and Natural Sciences at the Colegio Superior de Señoritas, where she was the only one to teach subjects which normally would have been assigned to four different teachers.

From 1911 she began an active campaign in centers and civic associations to advance the cause of patriotism. Her speech "Juan Pablo Duarte y Eugenio María de Hostos," read only forty days after the North American invasion of 1916, gives evidence of her altruism and courage. Her speeches in support of educational opportunities and the suffrage for women are early examples of Dominican feminism; an activity she sustained throughout her life. Among her many undertakings on behalf of women, we note that in 1928 she founded the Junta Provincial de la Acción Cultural Feminista in Santiago.

Her courageous spirit, her solidarity and love for her motherland, however, would cost her the position as the Director of her school when she protested the death of one of the many teachers who were beginning to be assassinated by the Trujillo regime.

Selected Bibliography

Juan Pablo Duarte y Eugenio María de Hostos. Santiago de los Caballeros, Rep. Dom.: Imprenta La Información, 1917. 2p.

Por la patria y por la escuela. Santiago de los Caballeros, Rep. Dom.: Imprenta de J.M. Vila Morel, 1920. 8 p.

Arboles y madres. Santiago de los Caballeros, Rep. Dom.: Imprenta La Información, 1926. 10 p.

Mi homenaje a las madres. Santiago de los Caballeros, Rep. Dom.: Imprenta La Información, 1929. 8 p.

Ante el ara de la escuela. Santiago de los Caballeros, Rep. Dom.: Imprenta L.H. Cruz, 1929. 8 p.

Feminismo. Santiago de los Caballeros, Rep. Dom.: Tipografía El Diario, 1930. 49 p.

Diversas consideraciones relativas a la evolución intelectual y jurídica de la mujer dominicana en los últi- mos cinco lustros. Santiago de los Caballeros, Rep. Dom.: Imprenta La Información, 1930. 14 p.

Mi homenaje a los héroes y mártires de La Barranquita. Santiago de los Caballeros, Rep. Dom.: Imprenta La Información, 1930. 8 p.

Antología. Selección y notas de William Galván. Santo Domingo: Editora Universitaria UASD, 1986. 97 p.

Speech Given at the Normal School of Santiago, 16 August 1911 on the Occassion The Investiture of a Number of Men and Women Teachers

The solemnity of this act of its own merit, on such a day and time in our fatherland and the exceptional circumstance of having a woman, with the political and social standing she has been grant- ed, who is to speak to all in her position as a teacher... places in my psyche much evangelical enthusi- asm at this very moment, having to ask the almighty for some of the divine grace always granted to those who speak or work in the name of goodness and of virtue. And...before the majesty of the day we are about to consecrate, let it be legitimate to exclaim: what is the motherland?

Here lies, in synthesis, my moral concept of the motherland. Man, in his unavoidable tendency to be sociable, extends himself into families, people, races, defining at last that total immensity that covers the Universe in the name of humanity!

When any part of humanity is placed in determined territories, in which tradition engraves its own seal throughout the centuries to found its interests, then to establish a material and moral world, then organizes to realize in time its destiny, whether it be called geographically, a nation; politically, a state; morally, a motherland!

We, that is, our people, tied to the Archipelago of the Antilles in an island flattered eternally by the genesic action of the mysterious streams of the Mexican Gulf; under the powerful auspices of that intense Sun of fires and ponderous energies. Amid the forestry of our palm trees; by the love of our rivers and in the pleasant shadow of our mountains, we constitute the Dominican motherland, with the sacred heritage of our grandparents, dead and praised by the epic legend; with our great vices and virtues and with all that makes up the tight countenance of all the homes who share the precious brotherhood, the limitless plenitude of the conquered territory!

We; you; all who read, study and learn in the alphabet of the sciences, as all those who till the land, those who plow the seas with the tricolor flag on the high mast of the national vessels, "Those Who Speak and Live Well," as the master once said...we make up a new motherland. Within the molds of the old motherland: that is, on the dorsum of the geographical motherland, we build the bases for a moral motherland in counterposition to those who disassociate themselves and in opposition to and in perpetual fight with the useless drones of the National Beehive!

Because true civic patriotism lives in the hearts of educated people, as the Polish heart lives in the cities of Poland tied not by the avarice that Austria, Germany and Russia are tying up...As the Italian spirit lives in the city of the Italia Irredenta, still subjugated by the Austrians...as the French

---

*   Selections from *Antología.* Selección y notas de William Galván. Santo Domingo: Editora Universitaria UASD, 1986.

spirit lives, after one long century, in the hearts of the Canadians that England dominates; thus, thus lives the true concept of a moral motherland, in the soul of those who know that ignorance enslaves even more than they are being slaved and have been slaved by the oppressors of all times...

And...only through a true national evolution can the high ideals of moral vindication of these societies fly high, unearthing prejudices, superstitions and selfishness and vanity suitable only to the Middle Ages. And only by making the judicial and social entity that is called woman a true human builder, can the motherland, in a fair fight with education, constitute ideal homes that would solve the intricate algebraic problem of the national existence. Because the motherland is a wide home...and it is from the particular home, and from the common home which is also denominated city and further along Province, that the whole State, the whole Nation and the whole Motherland will become great and be saved!...

Now then...if a retrospective look is taken towards the socio-political horizon of all ages, we would see that, together with the solemn proclamation of the rights of men of the French Convention. The most imminent law experts and sociologists have also struggled for the laws, prestige and dignity of women. Thus triumphs Catherine II in Russia from the times of Peter the Great. Municipal voting is granted to women by all of the people of superior cultures in old Europe and the North American States, and women govern in some cities. From its municipalities, she creates hospices; she develops institutions. She is a Teacher; she wears the manly gown of civil law; she practices law. While in obsolete countries, incapable of reacting, she is condemned to the category of a pariah, and thus lives reduced to the narrow environment of the home, deprived of all of her rights as a citizen.

The time has come for Dominican legislators, inspired by the true laws of Democracy, to grant to Dominican women the privileges that the Public Law is already granting, to that precious moral entity in whose womb lives the seed of all wonderment, from whence have come to light the redemptors of all of people; as from the center of the earth, the seed of goodness; the majestic tree of abundance of fruits and with them the florescence of all of the irises and the prosperity of all.

And....it might surprise you, perhaps, that from the lips of a woman would spring such truths to caress the public.

Oh!...The men who pulled Cicero's tongue because it was a treasure of eloquence no longer exist!

Let truth shine eternally, even in the ballads of the simple folk!...Let nothing be hidden from the woman who is educated to do universal battle!

No more irrational mysticisms!...let the verb of pure light shine brightly and incessantly on every lip and let it be an index of a national radio antenna from whence emanate the waves of goodness in an eternal dynamic movement towards the light!...towards the light!...so that the eternal night that threatens to envelope us with its tragic coat might evaporate and spill into the interior caverns where it must reside, while the iris of prosperity is lighted, and an immense parabola of love stretches from heart to heart without any flaw in its continuity among the great souls!

Now...you, the graduates; with your right hand held high! ...with your eye set in the direction of the Infinite...repeat with me the teachings of liberal nations: "Go everywhere and spread the Word!

Speech Given on the Occasion of the Investiture of Men and Women Normal Teachers
Santiago, August 16, 1915

Ladies and Gentlemen:

Those of you old enough to know about my dreams of progress for the motherland, those who have heard me rave on days such as this one of intense happiness and beautiful hopes for the intellectual redemption of Dominican women, it is certain, that seeing me here you would not find it strange to hear once again my repeated theme, since it is only by the constant falling of the drop of water that a dent is made in the hard, immovable, impassive rock. And this is why, ladies and gentlemen, that I—from this august temple built today as a tribune of patriotism, that is light of science, that is light of the preaching of the noble apostolate of teaching, that is also divine light, take such interest in having my well- intentioned though humble, never arrogant, voice heard. And this is why from the heart of this city of gentlemen*, a woman, breaking the old molds of error, rises above the madness of ignorance, to prove that women, as a selective half of the human composite, must and can join the ranks of duty to fight arm-in-arm near man, as an equal, psychologically, biologically, sociologically and juridically for the achievement of the Law of the Ideal for humanity instilled in our souls by the teaching of the Republic's sorely missed Apostle of teaching of reason, Eugenio M. de Hostos. To be, at this moment, before a beautiful group of graduating young women and men, I cannot hide my high spiritual satisfaction since I am well aware of the quality of the stones that are solidly buttressing the wide foundations of the new Motherland.

Each of these young men and women that you see here—clean forehead, serene countenance, with bright eyes looking toward the future—is a new soldier in a Legion of Honor. To them, together with love, the arms for battle have just been granted and...at the foot of the sacred Flag of February, all of the graduates together with you and me before the holy altar, will extend their right hand, their soul up high, their spirit at peace and a prayer on their lips, shaking with emotion, to swear by the manes of our heroes, to go forth and preach the Word!

In an overflowing spirit of duty, they will go to bring the good news of the civilizing alphabet to those who ignore the sublime work of instruction in the darkness of prejudices and superstitions where they have lived as irresponsible machines and livestock. Hand in hand, they will go to the conquest of new days of light that the anguished Motherland requires; and as messenger pigeons of the flood bring the biblical olive branch, all will bring to every home the pure phrase of peace and love until the rainbow of legal peace extends forever, as an immense parabola, above all those who live in the Motherland and for the Motherland!

II

As far as the work of women is concerned, we are pleased to record what has been preached since the days of the French Convention and, further more, from the times of Catherine the Second and Elizabeth the Catholic, the most authorized spokespersons on Public Law, in support of the project of educating women, struggling to break the medieval molds that narrowed the enormous social and moral force that women represent, to answer the call of the great work of universal progress.

---

* She alludes to Santiago de los Caballeros. D.C.D.F.

In the first place, we have to realize that under any sociological aspect it is a grave error to consider collective existence only through the lens of the point of view of men, when women represent a larger number of the human component than men, especially in Europe and in the United States of America.

That is the normal rule of normal cultures, according to the sociological statistics published by Dr. A.F. Weber of Columbia University.

In Cuba, Jamaica, Puerto Rico and the Islands of the Bahamas, because of the anomaly of male immigration, a slight difference in favor of the number of men is observed, in particular in Cuba where it is barely 3%.

But the constant biological principle leads to a serious, powerful predominance of the number of women, more marked as the general prosperity of each country increases.

In Boston, statistics for 1885 yield numbers in excess of 18,000 for women. In Germany, for each 1000 men there are 1040 women. In England it reaches 1064 women per 1000 men, and so forth throughout civilized countries.

Professor Karen Bucher, while studying this curious development, postulates a biological theory which affirms that in the population of all cities there is a marked tendency to produce an excess number of women over men; society being the human block made up of men and women that tends, as a unit, to the general progress of all. The grave error of considering women—the majority of the composite—a useless burden to the cooperating forces of contributors—without doubt its best element—is easily reached by some. But let it be clearly understood that this only happens in countries whose culture is not complete, those immersed in the prejudices of the Middle Ages.

In fact, in the early eighteenth century, Europe began the colossal movement towards the reinvindication of women, in which the prestige of being the first goes to Russia who with Peter the Great and Catherine the Second, gave to the entire world the noble example of emancipating at the same time women and slaves.

That great feminist movement was immediately picked up in the brilliant revolution of the English colonies, perhaps more social than political, because of the transcendence of its impact on universal civilization.

And this is why, even today, in Russia and the United States, women have more access to culture, more freedom and more prestige to the point that Russian women and North American women are personally worth more than Russian men or North American men, respectively.

Lastly, the immortal French Revolution gathered the aspirations of the feminist movement. The illustrious Condorcet supported the Rights of Women, which was defended by two colossal scholarly talents: Turgot and Stuart-Mill, who carried on the light of thought of Erasmus, Rousseau, Hostos, Saint Catherine and Novicow with their capacity for reason and conscience. Already that movement in support of women has entered the field of Public Positive Right, which is why, today, women have the vote in municipal elections in Austria, Russia, England, Ireland, in France in the Tribunals of Commerce, Austria and the 22 states of the American Union.

I have not wanted nor pretended to evoke the process of world evolution in which women have begun to expand their sphere of action and behaviors, with increasing suitable perfection, in all and for all, with men who preceded them in diverse social activities. No, I have had enough of women having the freedom of easy access to all professions of an artistic nature, some of which suit women better than men, without excluding certain positions and services of a political-administrative sort.

There always will be, ladies and gentlemen, some services and public offices reserved exclusively for men because of their better suitability and adaptation to the masculine sex and to those circumstances closed to the feminine sex.

On the other hand, it is also evident to me that our country of eternal trials and errors and continuous ups and downs in the sense of the progress of culture, still does not have a clear concept of the feminist theories and their cristalization in a good number of countries in Europe and America. But the waterdrop erodes the ground through the sheer force of continuously hitting it, and I meet my double responsibility to reason and conscience, to patriotism, when I insist one and another day in advocating in favor of the noble course that has served as the theme, divine theme, of this speech of mine.

Enter, you women, with a firm step, in the field of the civic struggle of the teaching profession and—having placed your heart and your will in the lofty endeavor of strengthening and exalting the value and qualities of women, and their aptitude to reach the heights of learning and to exercise the greatest possible number of their activities, persevere in your effort until you can crown it with triumph in the altar of the Motherland and of Dominican womanhood.

May the light of knowledge and duty illuminate the road and guide you to your desired goal. Santiago, August 16, 1915.

<hr />

Apostles and Summits. Peace. Unity and Harmony. Motherland. Home. Family.
Juan Pablo Duarte and Eugenio María de Hostos
Speech Given in the Salons of "Sociedad Literaria Amantes de la Luz"
January 12, 1917

Ladies and Gentlemen:

This simple speech must be presented to the audience on a day, hour and circumstance like today's—as an offering of civic love—made of the highest ideals in the apostolate on behalf of the Motherland which means for the sake of peace, home and family.

When I say Motherland, it is expedient to begin to instill in the minds of today's youth, the true concept of three mutually constituting terms, like a mathematical equation, having correspondences among themselves and gaining intensity in their differences until they become a harmonious whole: The Country, the Nation and the Motherland.

Motherland, that is: a moral concept. Nation, that is: a lawful term. Country, that is: a geographical denotation of the whole where the Family lives.

That is why, when speaking of the Motherland, it behooves us to consider all that the Motherland is, ought to be and shall be for the Family.

The Motherland of civilized man can no longer be the wide pampas of the pampean where the colt and the tiger live free, nor the Patagonia of the savage, nor the property of the indian. The Motherland of the present and that of the world to come must be something else: a wide Home, ruled by a severe and august Code of Social Morality, without ferocious indians, or untamed Patagonians, nor uncontrollable pampeans.

Today, the citizen of all Motherlands must begin to love the city, the cradle of civic conscience, since CIVITAS was the point of departure for civilizations, from the Great Rome to our days.

We must have a clear notion of CIVITAS and, with it and by it, of the CITIZEN, product of CIVIC CONSCIENCE. Because without the love for the city, the love for the Motherland is almost a myth.

Let us begin with the neighborhoods where the family home of our grandparents serves as a nest.

By the tower of the temple whose bells tolled for happiness at our baptism. By the aging tree that gave shelter to our first childhood games.

By the side of the river from whence we could see from afar the oceanic vision of infinite seas.

Let us begin there, in the NEIGHBORHOOD and the CITY, where there is a seat for the municipality until we can conceive—in essence and possibilities—the harmonious conjunction of the MUNICIPALITIES and the PROVINCES whose fusion or bridging creates the MOTHERLAND itself.

Because the beliefs of the young will never be drawn out—bringing to a restless mind, in the first place, a concept of the universal—without first setting foot solidly on the pedestal of the very land from whence we can see the infinite from afar...

Motherland is not only a resounding three syllable word that comes out of our breast in one shout, just like God is not only a monosyllable with which in all languages the Great Being is designated. God is the Great All synthesized in one monosyllable. Motherland, also, is a deity and mother in the synthesis of three words, mother like the Nature that the God-Pan nourishes in eternal generation, through eternity.

Motherland and nation in constant rise for power. Economic power, intellectual power, and moral strength, on the basis of the Rights of the Home and the Family.

Such is the Motherland in the yearnings of the civic-minded moralist.

Peace and Motherland run corollary, because without peace the conception of the Motherland—like the Home—also becomes a myth.

And in the grain lofts of the Home, the rich wheat. Because without a blessed wheat, our daily bread does not nourish the Home, and the "struggle for survival" brings Man each day closer to the Beast that nests in all of us.

Without Peace—Judicial Peace—anarchy is understood—implacable hydra-transformed in an infinite legion of gnawing rodents that begin by undermining the bases of social structure, to continue their destructive task under the ruins.

Our mother must raise their hands high to secure the union and harmony of the Dominican Family. The workers of the nation, must wave their spade up high, those gladiators whose plow elevates the Motherland; our very own energetic youth, eager for Science, must speak out and work to achieve harmony, under whose loving aegis a thousand tasks urgently needed may be accomplished so that the Nation can boast one day of BEING a Free, Sovereign, Independent, Humanistic, Civilized State, all in one.

Because without peace, union, and true and effective harmony, Freedom—the guardian angel of educated people—folds its wings, and "National Sovereignty", instead of residing in the "Cosmic Force" the Apostle Hostos would speak to us about, becomes the implacable fury in the soul of the masses. Oh!...how we want National Sovereignty always to live in the soul of the People, but not in the soul of the masses.

About judicial peace—I repeat it again—that Apostle of Reason and Law, who passed under our sky as a radiant star leaving streams of light, would speak to us in biblical apothegms.

Hostos, the Apostle, the Apostle Hostos: that is the epithet most fitting to the true condition of the Antillean Socrates to whose death, we, ourselves—it must be confessed— contributed with the excesses of our Family.

When an attempt was made to fit his head in the narrow bier-which was filled with dove- winged ideas of that other Cicero, whose tongue the enemies of conscience would have liked to cut off, the coffin stretched out its walls and from its dark bottom a sort of splendor emanated. It was the Human Aura of that great soul reflecting—even after the flesh had died—its beacon!...

Not everyone saw the prism of the ray of that light.

Those who had been his enlightened disciples noticed it. Those who knew not his "Social Morality", were not touched by the sacred fire of the new Pentecost.

But his "Sermon on the Mount",— the new "Sermon on the Orchard"—was heard everywhere and it is still heard through the ages, until the Credo of a new Religion takes shape: Humanism.

Because Hostos the Apostle gave-like all Christs-his Bible of Love for Humanity, working only for one sector, but for all that is Human.

He cried for Poland; he bled for Cuba; he sobbed for Puerto Rico; he raised a thunderous voice in protest for the Human rights denied to the Chinese people; he would rise magnificently letting his voice be heard in the Capitol in Washington, defending the inalienable rights of the indigenous people of the Americas; he went to the Andes and to the beaches in the Pacific and raised his Lesson of Love loftier still than the Andes themselves. He did not cross Panama where Bolivar in 1822 had wanted to congregate—"like a hen her chicks"—all these peoples, to build the foundations strong and solid of true Pan-Americanism; but the opening of the "Throat of Darien" prevailed and it augured what could be called in brief The Aquarium Divorce of History, and the very same "Caribbean Sea" in our beloved Antilles became what the "Mediterranean" had been in other times.

Hostos followed the same road as Magellan to get to Chile and he was shipwrecked much later—after his trip of circumnavigation as Apostle had ended—upon touching the sharp rocks of our beaches.

Here the hands of his disciples have preserved the remains of his shipwreck, surviving the catastrophe, rising above the waves of passion. With character and strength, some souls raise the pure white flag he always raised.

And those consecrated by his hands continued the "Pilgrimage of Bayoan." Some will die perhaps like Dante died, on strange shores, while they go about meeting their duty as evangelists in other lands.

We, too, must accomplish our mission. To give the daily bread of instruction to those who hunger without expecting a present reward, but in the expectation for a great future that the God of Nations reserves for the Motherland.

As Duarte gave his platonic soul to the "Trinitaria" and was fallen later—as "The Hero of Ayacucho"—at the bottom of the daring Andean pyramid, there the Father of the Motherland also went to fall. Because the sacrificed ones must always fall in the Calvary. To such a Christ, such a Golgotha.

The proud eagles do not die by submerging themselves in the swamps. The eagles fall wounded from the summits. Since already the condors and the eagles fall lifeless, the coarse flesh can well move on to form part of the pile in the atomic concurrence of living humus that the vegetable claims for itself, the immaculate soul floating over the same pines that the humus has turned into giants toward the radiant zenith like a wing.

The Bolivian flag of the South American Right is still held up over the Andes by Bolivar, San Martin and Sucre.

The flag of the redemptive Dominican cross still rises over the "Tina", fastened to its high staff—as a lightening rod—vigorously sustained by the giant spirit of Juan Pablo Duarte.

Above the Blue Mountains, George Washington upholds the colossal North American insignia. And thus they discuss still from North to South and above the equalizing Equator their inalienable rights.

Outstretched hands form a chain of love, Washington from the North, Bolivar from the South and Marti, Hostos and Duarte from the Antillean archipelago. They all ask for the democratic stabilization of the nations they created, restored or freed. Not one has ceded nor will he ever cede his Right nor has he dragged his glorious flag, in spite of trampled rights. Because the rights of this or that other country might be trampled, but the sacrosanct Right would always waive its white flag.

And Dominican women must teach this concept calmly to their children in that Great Classroom of Their Home.

Dominican women are—and ought to be—Soothsayers and Prophetesses of the Motherland. Women must give the child, who they nourish with their lacteous juice, unwavering rations of love for the Motherland, because at this time the Motherland needs the participation of the birds in the multiplication of the seeds, of the bee in its pollinating mission, so that the honey and the honeycombs multiply and existence become less bitter.

And Dominican women must become bees. They must go from flower to flower, from orchard to orchard, from villa to villa, always pollinating and spreading the essence of their soul with the "Sursum Corda" vibrating in their virginal pink lips.

Women the pacifists. Women the educators. The creators of exemplary homes: mending and sewing up again always in the sanctuary of the Home the tricolors of our flag.

Women were those who basted the Crossed Flag with love. It was much later that Men of heart assured with their blood—arm to arm—the weak stitches, making them shine forever, the red of the redemptive blood, in the quarters that form exact corners, with the white cross, symbolizing peace, and in geometric conjunction with the blue squares that symbolize the infinite.

And Man-citizen—in a manly way—must struggle in a constant manner, to save the Right of the Free Motherland by the strengthening of Democratic Institutions, in eternal bee—like labor on behalf of the Motherland Beehive. Absent the savage ires of unfortunate hordes. Absent gestures of vile hatred or unhealthy passion. Rather as an example of the priesthood of august teaching of lofty lessons. We are armed with the serenity of the stoics, going to the bonfire, displaying, with the smile brought about by faith, an immaculate flag.

(Selection)

Translation by Daisy Cocco De Filippis

FLÉRIDA [GARCIA] DE NOLASCO
Santo Domingo 1891-1976

A Doctor in Philosophy and Letters from the Universidad Autónoma de Santo Domingo, Flérida de Nolasco dedicated herself from a young age to the study and research of music, history and folklore.

Although Nolasco could have been considered part of the establishment and her writings for the most part fell within the parameters of conventional academic studies, I am including a fragment of one chapter of her essay on colonial history because its sympathetic and humane treatment of the indigenous people serves as a contrast to some of the texts circulating at the time.

Selected Bibliography

La poesía folklórica en Santo Domingo. Santiago de los Caballeros, Rep. Dom.: El Diario, 1946. 367 p. (Essay)

Rutas de nuestra poesía. Ciudad Trujillo: Impresora Dominicana, 1953. 155 p. (Essay)

Santo Domingo en el folklore universal. Ciudad Trujillo: Impresora Dominicana, 1956. (Essay)

Santa Teresa de Jesús a través de sus obras. Ciudad Trujillo: Impresora Dominicana, 1959. 195 p. (Essay)

La Catedral de Santo Domingo, Primada de América. Santo Domingo: Editora Caribe, 1965. 63 p. (Essay)

Domingo Moreno Jimenes. 3rd. ed. Santo Domingo: Julio D. Postigo e hijos, editores, Colección Pensamiento Dominicano, 1970. 187 p. (Essay)

Clamor de justicia en la Española 1502-1795. Santo Domingo: Impresora del Caribe, 1971. 236 p. (Essay)

Luminarias en vela. Santo Domingo: Editora del Caribe, 1974. 158 p. (Essay)

Días de la colonia. Santo Domingo: Editora del Caribe, 1974. (Essay)

Mi testimonio. Santo Domingo: Editora del Caribe, 1975. 239 p. (Essay)

Cuadros del evangelio. Santiago, Rep. Dom.: Editorial El Diario, s.f. 134 p. (Essay)

The Mother Island*

October 10, 1492. The sailors were losing confidence. They had begun to lose faith. They mutiny. They give in to their desperation. They want to force the great luminary to return to Spain. Columbus exhorts them to keep the faith and continue to hope. "No Complaints, no dejection, no protests will do you any good."

---

* Selection from *Clamor de justicia en la española 1502-1795*. Santo Domingo: Impresora del Caribe, 1971. 236 p.

And the crew calmed down. That night, when they finished singing the Salve Regina that they sang each evening at twilight, the Admiral felt certain that they were near land. As night closed in around them they saw St. Elmos's fire, and, apprehensive, they mumbled many litanies and other prayers.

The next day, new signs: in the sky, flying birds; on the sea, green branches; there in the distance, a light which announced the nearness of man. The twelfth: Land! The prophesy had been fulfilled.

*

The great visionary is painted by the pen of Bartolomé de Las Casas as a man "of agreeable presence, tall, well-built, and with a noble and majestic countenance; his face was neither full nor drawn, and had a somewhat ruddy complexion, dotted with freckles; his nose was aquiline, his cheekbones well-defined, his animated eyes light grey in color, and his expression was full of authority. His hair, blonde at one time, had turned prematurely gray; so that by the time he reached thirty years of age it was completely white. He dressed and ate with utmost simplicity; he was eloquent but without affectation, and his religious devotion was outstanding."

*

The Peruvian historian Luis de Ulloa, tells us this about his predilection for the Island of Hispaniola:

> In the middle of the discovered lands, like the sun surrounded by the planets, the Island was, to him, sacred; the mother island, the cradle, the Island of the pre-discovery, the island, pedestal of his glory, theatre of his misfortune; the place which saw him defeated, but also victorious; the Island of Hispaniola, which remained faithful to its date with his robust faith and unyielding hope.

First to describe the beauty and the natural treasures of our unfortunate Island, which seems to have inherited the afflictions of the post-discovery from the fervent Discoverer because if there has been helplessness and pain, it has been ours.

It is the blessed Island of God; "it has some of the most beautiful plains of the world. A very verdant island, where even the water is a joy to look at. The interior has many great valleys and fields whose beauty is a marvelous sight: all the trees are lush and covered with fruit, and all the meadows are flowering. At night birds sing softly, and crickets and frogs are heard. And those valleys, and those sweet-watered rivers, and those lands are ready for bread, for livestock of all kinds, and for orchards and for all the things in this world that man can ask for. The high mountains, which seem to reach the heavens, are all covered with trees. These hills and mountains, these plains and fields, these lands, which are all so beautiful and lushly bountiful, are meant for planting and seeding, and also for building villages and towns.

*

And how costly it was for the Great Admiral to abandon Isabella, because "it seems that man never wanted to leave there: the sweet, delicious breezes, the marvelously scented trees, pine groves, honey combs, six or eight different kinds of palms . .. Hispaniola is to be seen, and once seen, is never to be left; beauty of the highest order."

Pedro Mártir de Anglería, with a poet's fervor, used to say:

"It seems to me that the Indians of Hispaniola (a place he never went) are happier than the citizens of the great Roman Empire, because they are living in the true Golden Age: naked from head to toe, without clothes or the bother of finery; without the vile trafficking in money, with neither currency nor the means for buying or selling, without that source of misery which is wealth; knowing no scarcity, with no laws to unjustly limit or curb them; with no calumnious judges who know how to invent crimes, with no books to teach them what is better left unknown; without demands, without anxieties, content with this prodigious natural world, they are happy because they live without any worries about the future."

*

Santo Domingo, Hispaniola ... "My Hispaniola", as the great Admiral called it. There would be heard, for the first time, the voice of the confraternity that would deny the rights of conquest, that would proclaim the equality of all men, that would repeat untiringly and with growing and daring compassion and love that all men are born free. From there would depart holy missionaries who would bring the name of Christ to the newly discovered world.

*

Santo Domingo, Hispaniola....From its beaches we have seen depart the reckless adventurers who sail forth on uncharted seas. Towards glory? Towards death? Hernán Cortés, he of the great deed, who facing possible death, sang folk songs; Ojeda, who dazzled the Catholic Queen with his extreme maneuvers; the courtesan Nicuesa, that gallant troubadour, famous guitar player, who left on Hispaniola a wave of pleasant memories of an elegant singer of love serenades, of an incomparable jouster, highly skilled horseman who could make his Andalusian mare dance; and who one day, dreaming of greater glories, departed for the conquest of the continent. His adventure did not allow him to return. No one knew for certain the kind of death he endured.

*

The Conquerors, hard men, men of iron with souls of steel, they never wanted to bring recent arrivals from Spain with them; they wanted men tanned by suffering, men who know great hungers, great dangers, great loneliness and longings, and the innumerable and imminent dangers of land and sea;... men of Hispaniola.

*

—1502—

A member of the same expedition which brings Nicolás de Ovando, Commandant Major of the Military Order of Alcántara to the island of Hispaniola as its Governor, is the licentiate Bartolomé de las Casas, graduate of the University of Seville in Latin and Humanities.

His dream of coming to these recently discovered lands was mere whim. His uncle Francisco de Peñalosa and his father Pedro de Las Casas, a modest merchant who came with two brothers, are residents of the city of Santo Domingo, Primate of the New World. They came on the second voyage of Admiral Christopher Columbus. The uncle, a military man, was in charge of troops during the voyage, and after spending three years here, he returned to Spain. They were not people of note.

*

Nicolás de Ovando and Bartolomé de Las Casas.... they find themselves on opposite sides. Ovando, a man who appreciated order and discipline, will not hesitate to construct entire blocks of stone houses on well-planned streets. He does not pardon disorderly conduct among Spaniards, nor drunkenness, nor disputes. Those who go against the established order are invited to leave the island, and if the guilty find themselves short of funds, he happily lends them the money to cover all expenses incurred on the return voyage. He asks the King not to permit the arrival of blacks because they are arrogant and disobedient. If they do not love him, how much less will they fear him?

When the colonization began, Spain sent convicts to do hard labor in the New World as punishment. But now the situation is changed. If before, the punishment was to bring someone here, now the punishment is to send them back. They reaped a good harvest here, without any expenses or efforts of any type. The hands of slaves would mine the gold. They, the owners, would no longer attempt to mine themselves, since of the three thousand who came out with the Commandant Major, one thousand died trying to excavate gold themselves from the mines at Haina. From that point on, only Indians would do this death-dealing labor, since it doesn't matter if they die.

*

In Seville a group of scholars and young students is part of the court of the Archbishop Diego Suárez de Deza, Order of Preachers. Antonio Montesinos, one of these youths and a friend of Las Casas, is brought into the group. It was then that Suárez de Deza founded the College of Saint Thomas, and among the founders was Reynaldo Montesinos, Antonio's brother. Restless souls, they heatedly debate and deny the incapacity for faith attributed to the natives of the Indies.

Las Casas learns Latin with the renowned Nebrija; and he came to be as fluent in it as he was in the vernacular.

*

Bartolomé was nineteen years old when he saw some Taino Indians in Spain; they had been brought there by the Great Admiral when he returned from his first voyage. Later, his father, coming from his first stay in the Indies, brought him the gift of an adolescent Indian, a curiosity which he would return to Hispaniola a few years later, at the express wish of the Catholic Queen and on the advice of Cardinal Cisneros.

It does not seem that these strange beings left any impression on the young Bartolomé de Las Casas; no mark that would cause him to become interested in these creatures who had appeared, as new as their new land, as nothing more than material to be studied. There was no emotional stirring in him, nor transcendental reflection. There was no foreshadowing of his most noble destiny, and so, to move to action he had to wait for "his hour", which had not yet come.

We usually grope along the journey of life, often times not knowing where our destiny is. And the goal that is reached, or the distance required is not a wonder but a surprise, forgetful as we are that the possibilities of man are nothing more than the possibilities of God.

*

The Indians are in Jaragua celebrating the Commandant Major, whose peacekeeping methods end in mass death. An implacable governor who founded towns and anihilated Indians, he will continue ahead with his hardened heart and cold soul.

No sooner did the Catholic Queen die, who had recommended that the Indians be treated as Castillians, than they took away their miserable pay, making them legal slaves. Men, women, and children began to work without any recompense but a meager food ration.

The only bit of Christianity about Governor Ovando, Commandant Major of the Military Order of Alcántara, was the cross he wore on his chest, to which he raised his impious hand so that the massacre would begin. It was the agreed-upon signal. A hand on the cross...

Anacaona, along with three hundred maidens, was there, having sung and danced the areito for solemn occasions, to celebrate the new Governor. Anacaona... condemned to an infamous and exemplary death. The city of Santo Domingo watched her die on the gallows.

1509. Don Diego Columbus has arrived with his wife Doña María of Toledo. They bear the rank of Viceroys of Hispaniola. The second Admiral goes directly to the Fortaleza, and finds nothing but servants in its precincts.Governor Nicolás de Ovando had left for the city of Santiago, where he relaxed in the coolness of its ever verdant fields and the laughter of its river, the Yaque, and the flowery moss of its hills. He had left the Fortaleza under the charge of his nephew, whose introduction was greeted with harsh words by an uncle who never left carelessness unpunished. A fleeting dislike was forgotten with a tasteful and discreet banquet offered in honor of the Viceroys.

A play was staged. The upright citizens promenaded through the place. The Royal Treasurer, all the royal officials, the Vice-queen's ladies-in-waiting who had arrived with her, maidens about to be married... Who would divert their attention from the joyful flattery, from wondering if there were any tears, if there were lashings, if there would have to be a duel?

*

Since 1503 Queen Isabella the Catholic had asked Pope Julius II to build churches on the island of Hispaniola, since there numbered 17 towns there. But, these towns did not have stable populations, because the gold seekers (those whom Las Casas, with his caustic words, would so often refer to as "executioners"), abandoned Hispaniola once the mines and the Indians who worked them were both completely spent, and moved to nearby islands, or went off to discover new lands and new seas. And so, when Julius II constructed the first churches for this firstborn of the Colonization, the towns chosen were already deserted, abandoned by their transitory populations.

Those brave adventurers were just passing through on their journeys to uncharted seas and lands, where so often death awaited them. Ambitious, romantic and cruel, they exposed themselves to imminent dangers, always ready to continue their route towards dreamed of treasures, toward wherever there could be found a cavern or mountain of precious stones or where some magic fortune-teller knew the secret of eternal life.

Gold, the gold they were so ambitious for, was not always a vain illusion, but rather very real riches, which often vanished from hands eager for possession but not always wise in spending it. They enjoyed the moment and for the first time took pleasure in this world. May God forgive them ahead of time and men forget their deeds: The next life did not matter now. They gave themselves completely to the enjoyment of the moment. (Fragment)

Translation by Margaret A. Ballantyne

LIVIA VELOZ
Santo Domingo, 1892-1980

Poet, educator, feminist, Livia Veloz studied in her early years in the school for young ladies of Bobadilla and later at the Institute created by Salomé Ureña de Henríquez. During her eighty-nine years of life, Veloz participated actively in diverse organizations. She was a founding member of the Club Nosotras and secretary during the presidency of Abigaíl Mejía of the organization Acción Feminista Dominicana. Besides three books of poems, she published two readers for elementary school. Her novel, *La más chiquita*, received honorable mention in a Contest for Unpublished Manuscripts of Latin American Novels, sponsored by the publishing house of Farrar and Rinehart in New York. This novel was published posthumously with the title *Ojos entreabiertos* (1992).

We have selected some fragments from her *Historia del feminismo en la República Dominicana* (Honorable Mention, Secretary of Education, 1975), to illustrate the early history of Acción Feminista Dominicana. As the selected readings underline, the organization was the outgrowth of the cultural club "Nosotras", and as such, its ranks were integrated by educated, usually middle-class or wealthy women. Acción Feminista Dominicana proposed many and very lofty goals. Sadly, by 1942, converted into the feminine wing of the Partido Dominicano, Trujillo's party, these lofty goals had been reduced to a replica of the education of young women described in Veloz' introductory piece: clubs for sewing, mending, cooking, etc.

Selected Bibliography

Preludios sentimentales. Santo Domingo: Imprenta La Cuna de América, 1929. 36 p. (Poetry)

Acordes. Santo Domingo: Imprenta Gómez, 1936. 45 p.   (Poetry)

Transparencias. Madrid: Escuela Nueva, 1971. 79 p. Premio Salomé Ureña 1964. (Poetry)

Historia del feminismo en la República Dominicana. Santo Domingo: Secretaría de Estado de Educación, Bellas Artes y Cultos, 1977. 46 p. (Essay)

Ojos entreabiertos. Santo Domingo: Publicación de la Biblioteca Nacional, 1992. 134 p. (Novel)

FRAGMENT from *Historia del Feminismo en la República Dominicana*
Introduction

When we consider the true state of serfdom in which Dominican women lived and the back-wardness in every sense that surrounded them in the first years of the present century, we cannot but go back a little to take stock of the circumstances that rendered them almost useless beings.

As far as education is concerned, it is natural for the daughters of wealthy or middle class parents to receive an education adequate to the period and their social and economic condition. This was the minority of women; but the majority, the daughters and women of the working class, the poor class, could not count on any possibilities. The small ones would go to the school in their neighborhood; they would learn to read and write poorly and to do some manual labors at the same time that they would receive some notions of catechism.

Once grown up, life would change for them completely. They had to work: some doing housekeeping, others knitting or embroidering for pay; a great number of them by washing and ironing someone else's clothes and doing some other jobs of a domestic nature.

The better prepared ones, those who had managed to study in secondary schools, lived by teaching.

In those days one could not even dream of a young lady working in a public or private office. That was inconceivable.

There was not a father who would consent to the social and cultural development of his daughters.

For women there was only one road, once they had reached legal age: marriage.

And to get married was also a difficult task. Customs of the time did not allow a suitor to approach the object of his affections. The suspicions of the fathers would impede her from even coming to the door or the balcony. If the young man pleased the family, he would have to spend months on end giving proof of his good intentions, until, after many demands, they would consent to the indispensable engagement, an act attended by the father or mother of the suitor to guarantee the seriousness of the case and the good intentions of the boyfriend.

Usually a date for the wedding would be set.

On the other hand, if the suitor was not well regarded by the family of the young woman, then there would erupt a kind of civil war within the home; and woe if the young man's affections were returned by the girl! Punishments, deprivations, severe orders and at times even blows were received by the wretched young woman. These misunderstandings sometimes led to fatal results.

Since in those days it was the custom to bring serenades to the object of one's affections at midnight, there were cases when the father, irate, would get out of bed and with less than courteous words, pack the musicians off.

So even the natural right that every woman has of choosing the person who will be her companion for life was haggled over for the female of yesteryear.

But the step to marriage, when they managed to take it, was a sort of change of master. From the government of the father she would pass to the authority of the husband, supreme chief of the home. The wife continued being the humble serf, humble and virtuous mother of the family.

The Acción Feminista Dominicana was founded on the 14 of May of the year 1931

This dynamic association was born in the bosom of the prestigious Club Nosotras.

Before proceeding with the topic already introduced, we allow ourselves to remember that the Club Nosotras, a women's institution formed especially for intellectual ladies and artists, had existed for some years, and in its salons were scheduled lyrical presentations, scientific conferences, painting expositions, introductions of personalities visiting the country. The Club Nosotras met in the house located in El Conde at the corner of Isabel la Católica, in front of El Parque Colón.

Its founding was the result of concerns by some educated women, among them, Abigaíl Mejía de Fernández, who was its first president.

For a long time Club Nosotras was the home of poets, reciters, artists of the keyboard and public speakers.

In the warmth of its cultural activities, the idea to organize a society for the purpose of working for the rights of women in the Dominican Republic was born. There, plans unfolded and rules were postulated. Finally we were able to announce the surprising news, unexpected by all.

There in the salons of Club Nosotras the idea came to life, and the birth of Acción Feminista Dominicana was proudly proclaimed, giving an account at the same time of its goals and the faith that guided the spirit of its founders.

We regret not writing down the names of all of the ladies who with patriotic ardor and humanitarian sentiments proclaimed these ideals.

The first board of directors was constituted in the following manner:

General Director:	Lic. Consuelo González Suero
Sub-Director:	Prof. Abigaíl Mejía
Secretary General:	Dr. Gladys de los Santos
Treasurer:	Prof. Celeste Woss y Gil

Principles of the Acción Feminista Dominicana

This group will be made up of women of good conduct, who have reached their eighteenth birthday and who know how to read and write. Its main goal is to tend to the betterment of the intellectual, social, moral and legal condition of women, as well as to campaign for social defense against alcoholism, prostitution and narcotic drugs, etc., to fight so that laws will be passed for the protection of mothers, children, adolescents, the aged and the blue-collar workers, etc. To advocate for the establishment of tribunals for children, to work to instill in women the understanding of the necessity to be frugal and to dissuade them from spending on unnecessary luxuries; to persuade Dominicans not to sell their land to foreigners; to fight so that our traditions are preserved and to sponsor every idea that would mean the advancement and welfare of the Republic.

The establishment of the Junta Superior Directiva with a headquarter in Ciudad Trujillo, with provincial juntas in each head of province and communal sub-juntas in each of the communities, will ensure the rapid spread of feminist ideas, so poorly understood and unjustly criticized.

The spread of feminist ideas can reach the corners of the cities and in the most remote sections, neighborhood delegations have been created, which are in charge of conducting registration, explaining the principal mission of women facing difficult problems and looking for a place appropriate to their aspirations, as has taken place in other countries in Europe and America.

The Acción Feminista aspires to enroll in its rank all their compatriots, so that a true feminist union would result, formed by ladies and young ladies who live, some by their rents and incomes, others by teaching, by industry, blue-collar work, students, etc. One of its principal goals will be to accustom Dominican women to the agreement of thought and of mutual tolerance and protection at work. The Acción Feminista wishes to form mothers truly conscious of their mission; it wishes that mothers prepare themselves to earn in a dignified manner their sustenance and that of their families, should the need arise; it wishes that although women might possess a great fortune, that they receive such a preparation as to prepare themselves to administer their fortune and make them fit to sustain the moral and material equilibrium of the home, because lest we forget, whosoever says balance at home, says balance in the fatherland.

Feminism will tend to bring about the happiness of women by preparing them so that they always marry for love, and not for necessity and in a hurry with the first to come for fear of facing the demands of life; it will work so that laws are passed that would support marriage and the stability of the family.

Translation by Daisy Cocco De Filippis

CAMILA HENRIQUEZ UREÑA
Santo Domingo, 1894-1973

Camila Henríquez Ureña is one of the finest intellectuals of the Spanish speaking Caribbean this century. Born in the Dominican Republic, the only daughter and fourth child of the distinguished writer and educator Salomé Ureña and the political figure Francisco Henríquez y Carvajal, Camila Henríquez Ureña's figure has often been overshadowed by her two better known siblings, the literary luminaries, Pedro and Max Henríquez Ureña.

Henríquez Ureña spent most of her life in Cuba where she moved with her father in 1904. Her mother had died in 1897. In 1926, she became a Cuban citizen. She received her doctorate in philosophy, letters and pedagogy from the University of Havana. Moving to the U.S., she also studied at the University of Minnesota and at Columbia University. For years she was in the teaching faculty of Vassar College. She also directed summer programs at Middlebury College. Camila Henríquez Ureña gave up her pension from Vassar College to return to Cuba and teach at the University of Havana after the Revolution. She died while visiting her native Dominican Republic in 1973.

Few women in the Spanish speaking world, let alone the Spanish speaking Caribbean have been able to transcend the boundaries of their own immediate cultural borders. Camila Henríquez Ureña's essays on feminism and literature, however, have reached countless women of our generation in the Caribbean and elsewhere, and have had a profound impact on the intellectual development of more than a generation of women writers. "Feminism", included in this publication, is one of the better known and more anthologized essays written by Camila Henríquez Ureña. Going back to ancient times and basing her analysis on a Marxist understanding of history, she traces the role of women in society through the centuries. She clarifies the need for women to take charge of their lives, on their own terms, without reproducing the failed models created by men.

Selected Bibliography

ed. with Dolores Nieves Rivera. *Teatro y narrativa medieval.* (essay) La Habana: Editorial Pueblo y Educación, 1974. 2nd. ed. 1990, 126 pp.

Estudios y conferencias. (essay) La Habana: Editorial Letras Cubanas, 1982, 644 pp. Prologue by Mirta Aguirre.

Invitación a la lectura, notas sobre apreciación literaria. (essay) Santo Domingo: Taller, 1985, 211 pp. Introductory note by the editors.

Feminismo y otros temas sobre la mujer en la sociedad. (essay) Santo Domingo: Taller, 1985, 157 pp. Introductory note by the editors.

Las ideas pedagógicas de Hostos y otros escritos. (essay) Santo Domingo: Secretaría de Educación, Bellas Artes y Cultos, 1994, 382 pp. Presentation by Jacqueline Malagón.

FEMINISM *

Ladies and Gentlemen:

WOMEN DECIDED ONE DAY TO TAKE OVER the reins of government of the States from men, in light of their complete failure in that matter. "It is necessary for us to take over the government for the welfare of the Republic," they said, "because things cannot continue such as they are: neither by sail nor by paddle does the ship of State move. This is going no where!" A trustworthy account of such a happening is given by Aristophanes in his comedy *The Assembly of Women* produced about four hundred years before Christ. And if we do not have eyewitness accounts that in earlier days women posed that question, it is because comedy had not been born yet, joyful mirror of present customs and jocular vaticination of things to come. Because the problem is as old as the human couple. It was set forth from the day it was constituted, emerging from the primitive horde. But, since in the life of the universe the days that man measures are infinitely small fractions of unlimited time, the problem is still throbbing without a solution. The struggle between the two halves of humanity is due to motives of such complexity, it comprehends such multiple and various aspects, that there is no vital manifestation in which it is not felt, and to try to interpret it and to expound its development in brief words, is to attempt at once analysis and synthesis of the entire existence of humanity.

The history of feminism is but the feminine side of that eternal question, and therefore, it is the history of a struggle between two very uneven parts, because however we consider the problem, we have to take as a point of departure the inconvertible fact that the feminine half of the world has found herself always in a condition of inferiority with respect to the masculine half. The vital problem for woman is double. The whole history of humanity is a history of struggles: man has always battled to improve the conditions of his existence and woman, fatefully although not always consciously, has taken part in that general struggle against illness, war, famine, slavery, misery and death, common lot among all human beings. But at the same time, she has confronted her male counterpart with problems specific to her sex: biological problems and problems that have been created by the social condition which has been imposed upon her.

If we glance at history to examine the situation of woman throughout the ages, we find it, in the forms of social life more primitive that we can observe directly, considered by the male as a being that occupies (perhaps) the first rank among domestic animals, and that is also a necessary instrument for the satisfaction of sexual instinct. In that form of savage life the union of the sexes is purely bestial, and the concept of love in whatever meaning it has among the more civilized is totally unknown. There usually is not even in their vocabulary a word that would denote affection. The males regard their women like their dogs, by the services they provide. As soon as they age or become incapacitated, they are put to death. Frequently they are devoured, so that they even serve the purpose of satisfying the hunger of the tribe in times of penury. In other words, they are not even buried. Oldfield the traveler declares not having found the grave of a woman in untamed Australia. Monogamous or polygamous union is not the rule. Promiscuity is practiced and woman obeys might. Children become new arms for the tribe. Their number is reduced by infanticide, which is practiced as natural, in particular with young girls, because they could become burdens. According to the needs of the tribe, women are beasts charged with more or less hard labor, even at times when their masters are resting

---

*   Lecture given at La Institución Hispano-Cubana de Cultura, July 25, 1939, included in *Estudios y conferencias*. (La Habana: Editorial Letras Cubanas), pp 543-571.

from fatigue brought about by war or hunting. Fitsroy the explorer observed that among the inhabitants of Tierra del fuego when the winter was rough and food was scarce, they would roast and devour first the oldest women. He asked one of the savages why they did not eat the dogs first. "Because dogs help us hunt for otter," he replied. The women were considered, therefore, as animals with relative usefulness. Of course, in that social state family is non-existent. Man has no woman; the tribe has female slaves. The idea of paternity is in its inception still. In many tribes the role of the male in the generation of children is unknown, and they are believed to be the product of mysterious outside forces that act upon woman. The condition of woman does not admit more than one description: beast of burden.

Among people in a more advanced stage of civilization, the idea of progeny, the base of a family, predominates. Without doubt it appeared first as a feeling in woman, since the love of children is instinctive. In the male the feeling of paternity is the product of civilization. It points to a material and moral progress, and to judge from the extreme ease with which the male of the most civilized nations are accustomed to abandoning and ignoring their children even in our day, we are justified in believing that such a sentiment has not reached its most developed degree. The idea of progeny developed in primitive man with the notion of individual property. The male removed woman from the state of promiscuity and made her his personal slave. The male at that stage of civilization possesses one or more women, who work for him and serve to provide his pleasure exclusively. If children are born from those unions, they are new servants for the father. Only he can dispose of them and exercise the right of life and death over them. This male considers his woman and his children as his ax, his harpoon, or the strength of his muscles, or the domestic animals that plow the land that nourishes him: they are the signs and the basis of his might. Man's egoism prevails absolutely. There is no love in him. He unburdens himself of his relatives without hesitation or remorse the moment they are in his way. The basis of the original family is, therefore, the nascent concept of individual property. The condition of woman within this social state is that of slavery: the slave of an individual master. That rudimentary family represents, however, a progress in the situation of woman, who moves from belonging to the tribe to belonging to one individual defender who, in order to keep his property, will protect her from all others. In turn, the male begins to impose on woman a new duty: sexual fidelity. She is exclusively his. She is to belong to no other, except when he makes a gift of her, sells her or lends her, as he is also able to do with his weapons. But from the moment that a man possesses exclusively one or a few women and their children, habits of mutual services begin to take shape, since the male, by defending them, begins to give something to them in exchange for what they give to him. There begins to develop, I say, a new moral force. What belongs to him appears preferable to each man than what the rest of the tribe possesses. Familial affection is born. The man who already possesses something, searches for a place to establish himself with his family. Patriarchal society is organized.

In rare cases, in some races where women were exceptionally vigorous and scarce in number, the family organized itself around a woman. Genealogy was established by her and children belonged to her, the father remaining unknown and without authority. This social organization is called matriarchy.

The existence of that state of affairs, indicates to us that in woman the desire for freedom and predominance has never ceased to exist, and that where she has been able to obtain it, she has put it into effect. Therefore, her submission has not been the product of her natural will, as some pretend, but of force. Woman is subjugated because she is physically weaker. In the people in this period of civilization, if women are strong and are scarce, polyandry is established at times: Woman may have a few husbands at the same time. This may happen in people with an advanced degree of civilization. So we see, in the great epic poem of ancient India, the *Mahabarata,* the beautiful Drapandi, with eyes the color of the blue lotus, is the wife of the five Pandava brothers, warriors favored by the gods.

With the establishment of the primitive family, the union between man and woman remains tied to limitations. Marriage begins. This is done by means of abduction or sale of the woman by the male. What is purchased is, principally, her fecundity, the children that she is to produce to the point that if the husband does not meet the stipulated price, in some tribes he is not the owner of the children that are born of the union. The wife becomes the progenitor: she who gives many children, gives wealth, power. Religion intervenes to make of marriage a ceremony of the cult, something sacred. The purchase of the wife is transformed into a sacrament.

The State and religion rule the family, which is no longer a personal business of the father and mother nor of the human group. Polygamy is restricted. In many places, they begin to deny man more than one legitimate wife, who has authority over the children of all others in the rank of concubines. This is due to the promotion of the question of inheritance of property. It would have created complications to give equal rights to all of the women and children of a man. That is why one woman was designated among all, sometimes two. Thus monogamous marriage makes an appearance, which later is established on new material and moral bases. But monogamous marriage has never meant perfect monogamy. Considering it in its general constitution, human society always has been polygamous, for various and complex causes: among them, the number of women exceeds, by far, that of males.

Woman, then, continuing her historical evolution, is already the slave whose highest function, maternity, usually frees her of other onerous burdens and confers upon her a certain rank. Her mission is to give children to man. And "for a child," Manu says, "man gains the kingdom of the heavens." But woman, in what we may call her third social state, the progenitor, continues to be subordinated. All men are superior to her. Her son is her master and lord, after her father and husband. Telemachus, in the presence of the suitors, orders the noble queen Penelope, his mother, to withdraw and she obeys him with humility. Already the harshest labors in the field have been left for the slaves. The free woman dedicates herself, nevertheless, to many labors in the home: she spins, knits, sews, prepares medicines, takes care of the ill and the children, maintains cleanliness and order...Her work, which can be symbolized by Penelope's cloth, never ends; but this is worth only the right to be supported by man only as he so wishes to do. Thus, from the most remote of times, woman has worked harshly, has rested little; but no one ever thought that that work was worth other compensation. Slaves, among whom she occupied the highest place, were not compensated for their labor.

Morally, the situation of woman has improved; materially, it has exceeded the beast of burden; but legally her state remains the same: she is the property of the male.

That is how we find her in ancient Rome. Morally, the matron occupies a high place. The Free Roman woman is not denied the benefits of a good education; but the family persists, primitively patriarchal in its constitution.

In Athens, on the other hand, woman has some legal protection. She is allowed to own property; her husband is punished if he does not meet his obligations to support her, as well as the children. But this does not occur because Athenian democracy is preoccupied with the personhood of woman, but because she is at its service: she must give it citizens, which represent strength and wealth. She is not given any other consideration. She is denied any instruction outside domestic work. She is relegated to the gynaeceum, and she can barely leave the house. Her children are separated from her while still young to be educated by the State. The male leads a public life and does not usually converse with his wife. But the Greek male was too subtle when it came to the spirit to deprive himself of the exchange with the female mind. He cultivated and appreciated it in the hetaera, who was able to instruct herself, to philosophize and to enjoy the pleasures of the world. The Greek male kept his admiration for the courtesan; sometimes, his love; but not his respect. The price of her relative freedom was the moral contempt of man.

Thus, in republican Rome, where the law made a slave of woman, she enjoyed moral esteem; in Athens, where the law gave her protection for the welfare of the State, she saw herself morally reduced.

We can say that the esteem of woman as a human being begins in Rome. The matron was honored and venerated by her relatives and clients. Her voice was heard in family councils. She influenced the government of the State through her husband and her children. She was not relegated to the home; she could go out and be seen in public. In public festivities she was given the first place. Men bowed before her. She had importance in the life of the nation, and if the laws forgot her, custom did for her more than the law did for women in other places. It is Cornelia who advises her children the Gracos, not to give up the struggle for the welfare of the people, even if they endanger their lives. It is Veturia who disarms Coriolannus to save Rome. This is a fact that moves us to reflection: because it makes us see how different are the various aspects that woman has to consider with regard to the problem of her betterment. That moral predominance is, perhaps, the only one in which woman has managed in the past to surpass the male. It constitutes her unarguable strength and it would be desirable for her not to lose it, not even at the cost of obtaining other gains. That strength of the Roman matron was conferred to her in part by maternity; but it was more than that; it was the moral quality, the excellence in the advice, the nobility of spirit, the dignity in action, the serenity, what the male found in her that would give him inspiration and fortitude. It was virtue, virtus, that signifies energy in the ancient language of Rome.

But that greatness lasted only as long as the Roman Republic. It could only be produced where there were men capable of respecting her. It disappeared with the corruption of the Caesars. A thing that seems strange: in that period of decadence, laws were created to protect the Roman woman without taking the liberty that customs gave her. She was made owner of her property, the right to life or death was abolished, she was protected from abuse by her father or her husband. But such advantages in a period of corruption only had as a result that women would give themselves over, just like the men, to the most unrestrained licentiousness. The law could prohibit that woman give her money to her husband; but nothing could impede that she give her fortune to her lovers. Those women achieved immense power: they destroyed thrones, made and unmade emperors, they took their sexual passions to politics, they made their coarsest, most miserable and imbecile lovers senators and ministers. Actors, clowns, libertines, rogues of the worst sort were raised to the highest positions in the State by feminine influence. Woman almost reaches equality with man; but equality in vice, in crime, in a rotten society, on its way to extinction. Nevertheless, that society bequeaths to the future, after the cataclysms in which it is shipwrecked, the legal foundations for progress in the condition of woman.

In the Orient, everything takes on a mystic form. The preachings of Jesus Christ and the tentative social revolution that accompanied them arrived in Europe only as religious reform. Paul of Tarsus, the first to preach Christianity in Europe, advocated a moral reform and a spiritualistic religion, imbued as he was with the theories of Greek metaphysics. A noble and fertile idea he had taken from the preachings of Christ: the idea of equality. Paul asserted, the first one to do so, the equality between man and woman; although he compared it only before God. Both sexes had the same mystic duties and rights. "There is no longer," the apostle says, "neither Jew, nor Greek, nor slave nor free man, nor man or woman; we are all one in Jesus Christ." The initial struggles of Christianity confirmed such a comparison: woman was equaled to man in faith, in heroism and in martyrdom. She was admired, exemplified, sanctified. And since that equality was only in Jesus Christ, the early Christians did not reject it. But the egalitarian wave invaded matrimony, where both spouses remained subjected to the same moral law: "What divine law prescribes for one of the spouses, it imposes on both", Saint Jerome would write. And when the State adopted the Christian religion, that moral equality was passed to the legal and economic terrain: the contribution of the husband must match the wife's dowry; gains during marriage should be followed by equal distribution...Naturally, when it came to that, the comparison was not honored. It was necessary to pass some laws to protect the fortune of a woman from her husband. Pauline Christianity was contaminated by old beliefs and traditions. The equality of the sexes survived only before God. The Fathers of the Church, which began then to be a powerful organization, had very particular opinions about woman. In the first place it felt for her such a profound contempt that it was argued whether woman had a soul, a discussion which was inherited from paganism; but which was incongruous with the teachings of Christianity. Not only was woman impure, but contact with her created impurity; therefore, marriage was a state of impurity, and was discredited. Priests imposed restrictions on marital relations. The pater familias himself remained subject to tyrannical laws. Only the son, as heir, was granted legal protection. While marriage was discredited and ambitious men speculated with divine things, the more libertine or sensual ones engaged licentiously in concubinage. Constantine, in order to combat that situation and to regulate wealth for the benefit of the State, granted all rights to legitimate children and deprived all rights to bastard children, establishing the tragic system of inequality which still survives. The Church, straying further from nature, denied the body all rights. It could not proscribe the union of the sexes; but it restricted it. It glorified celibacy; it made widowhood eternal, considering a second marriage an act of adultery; it substituted divorce, which Ancient Times accepted, with the separation of bodies, another sterilizing arrangement; it prohibited the marriage of the clergy. All relations between man and woman, with their economic and social consequences, remained under the control of the Church. Canonical laws were especially humiliating for woman, and pushed her further back in her traditional condition of inferiority. The clergy with one hand caressed her, remembering the mother of Jesus, and with the other flagellated her, in the name of the temptation in Paradise. She was the great culprit. She was cursed, declared diabolical and obscene. Saint John Chrisostomus accused her of staining man by means of sexual unions. Were it not because of her fault in Paradise and original sin, God would have found a less shameful manner to perpetuate the species. "Woman," Tertulian says, "you should go dressed in mourning and tatters, in order to redeem yourself of the sin of having corrupted the human race. You are the gate of Hell! Because of you Jesus Christ died!"

And after Saint Paul said that celibacy was a more perfect state than matrimony, all based themselves on this assertion, forgetting all others. For canonical law, only the male has been created in the image of God; not woman. In consequence, she must be subjugated by the male. She is not allowed to serve as witness before the law, because her testimony is not trustworthy. All the laws to protect woman dictated by the emperors, all those inspired by primitive Christianity, disappear in canonical laws. Organized Christianity, powerful in all Europe, considers woman an impure being, that only seclusion in a monastery can bring about forgetfulness of her sin through prayer, humiliation and abstinence. If she remains in the century, her life must be almost equally restricted, and, adhering to those practices, she might rise, in spite of everything, until she reaches sainthood, because the ultimate equality, before God, subsists.

We have seen how man has established monogamous marriage, while the tolerance of concubinage has permitted de facto polygamy outside the law. The Church, although it imposes monogamy, cannot get anything else either. In the last days of the Roman Empire there came to historic life a people of simple and severe customs: the German people. They practiced monogamy, and Tacitus affirms that adultery in man was punished equally as that of adultery in woman. Tacitus probably exaggerates; but the German woman seems to have enjoyed many rights. She could rule her family in the absence of the male, she could own property and she had not only a dowry but gifts from her husband. She was protected physically by man because she was less strong, but she attended assemblies with him, her voice was heard during deliberations and her intelligence was greatly esteemed. Germanic laws soon changed in contact with canonical laws. In the north of Europe they were preserved for a longer period of time; in the south they were lost sooner. With Charlemagne, an era of new slavery began for woman. This emperor placed her under the tutelage of the government, and on his death that tutelage was passed to the hands of innumerable lesser lords of gallows and knives. A particularly repugnant time in the history of woman begins. The noble woman who had no brother could not be the heir of the feud unless under a male tutor, who was who really enjoyed its benefits, and that tutelage was sold to the highest bidder. To facilitate the transaction, the lady was also sold in marriage, in equal manner. Woman of the working class belonged in work and body to the lord under whose tutelage she was, and even if she were to marry with a male of her social class, her body belonged in the first term to the lord. The popular revolutions that resulted from the abuses of lords momentarily bettered woman's lot, reestablishing old Roman and German laws, but when new codes of law were drafted in the sixteenth century, woman remained in the same situation of inferiority as before, declared impure, pernicious, incapable of spiritual things and, therefore, in perpetual minority of age and relegated to the distaff or the needle in the inside of the home.

Nevertheless, the period of the middle ages we have referred to is that of the troubadours of courtly love. Noble women were able to study, consoling themselves in their oppression and making fashionable the most spiritual sentimentality, without doubt as a reaction to a crass reality. There were knights and pages who would court and serve them. The Renaissance later produced wise women, humanists and poetesses; but these are exceptions, deceptive foam. The bottom of the sparkling goblet was black and bitter.

Absolute monarchy did not help the emancipation of woman. Excluded from public life, her strength in the family annihilated, separated from the domains of the intelligence, she had two main roads: to go populate the convents or to take advantage of male sensuality. Victory belongs to flirtatious women. The favorite sits next to the king, she strolls with the knight, she sits at the table of the ecclesiastical dignitary. The favorite could come from the heart of nobility like mademoiselle De la Valliere, or could climb from the common folk, like the Pompadour woman or Nell Gwynne.

In the seventeenth and eighteenth centuries woman is allowed some attempts to obtain intellectual importance, as proven by the existence of the Hotel de Rambouillet and the salons of madame Necker. But the laws do not change fundamentally. The criterion to judge women does not change. One continues to think as Moliere indicates, that she is sufficiently prepared

Quand la capacité de son esprit se hausse

A connaitre un pourpoint d'avec un haut-de-chausses

Only when absolute monarchy is shipwrecked in the furious ocean of the 1789 Revolution, are new rights for women established. The laws of the 15th and the 18th of April of 1791 establish the civil equality of man and woman in the family and in society. That equality was falsified immediately by the codification of matrimony; but it represents the point of departure of a new legislature.

Well, now. What is the general situation of woman at this time when she enters the contemporary age as a part of bourgeois society in the making? In what condition has she been left by the abuses of the middle ages persisting into modern times? She finds herself separated by group according to her sexual life, a division which is not identified with the division by class. That is something else. It depends on the fact that woman in the middle ages and in modern times only had sexual importance, and her only virtue, at least her fundamental virtue, was chastity. The middle ages had proclaimed celibacy and sexual abstinence as an advantage and a merit, converting women from slaves into victims. We can consider them as forming four groups: a) nuns or religious women; b) spinsters; c) prostitutes; d) matrons or widows. I will continue to talk in the past tense, but this situation endures to our days, modifying itself slowly. The religious ones represented celibacy sanctified. Women gathered in a religious order acquired—by means of the union, under the protection of the Church, by means of its distance from the world, because of the sacred mission and the mystical environment that surrounded them—an importance that alone and in the century they would not have achieved. They entered the convent for diverse reasons, in the first, true place, because of sentimental and visionary temperaments. The cases of vocation are less frequent, predominating, perhaps, in the middle ages, where daily life was impregnated with mysticism; but day by day they became more rare. They would enter, in the second place, in search of protection, because they felt alone, without strength or preparation to struggle against life. Or because of disillusionments, especially disappointments in love. Or because of vanity, since not having resigned themselves to enter a disadvantageous matrimony or to remain single in the century, they preferred to enter the convent. Or by force, for many were forced, morally and even materially, by those persons under whose tutelage they were. Although the number of nuns has diminished today, it is still quite high. The convents of the Good Shepherd alone hold, if we are to believe what we read, many thousands of nuns. Formerly, the majority of recluses achieved no more beneficial labor to humanity than prayer. Nowadays almost all of them are in contact with the outside world, because they practice pedagogy and nursing. This group or class of women, isolated by society, suffered a physical and spiritual deprivation of human contact, a limitation in life, that has given rise among them, through the centuries, to great mental disorders and numerous illnesses, individual and collective in nature.

The old maids constituted a type created by the laws and the customs of the Middle Ages. We have no news that it existed in pagan antiquity. It was formed by the obligation imposed on woman to live in chastity until she entered legal matrimony, added to economic dependence. The number of women then exceeded that of men even more than nowadays; further, not all men would marry, since chastity did not have to be the virtue of single men; many entered religious orders and could not be married. The more attractive women and especially those women who had a good dowry, would get married; but there remained a large number of single women; in the lower classes, prostitution and concubinage did not allow for the problem to be postulated; but in the comfortable classes, particularly in the bourgeoisie, they remained obliged to live parasitically. Also, forcibly limited in her physical and spiritual life, the old maid used to become ill of mind and body if it were not possible to dedicate her energies to an interesting activity, which was no mean task. That type, because of the multiple activities in which a woman can participate today, has begun to disappear with great speed; but she still can be found with relative frequency in small communities where all progress is slow.

The prostitute is the type of feminine social victim which is the reverse of the former. In addition to the polygamy that is achieved through concubinage, man has generally practiced sexual promiscuity, with certain limitations. Establishing on the one hand a forced sexual restriction on women considered virtuous, but not obliging men to practice the same virtue, has necessarily led the other portion of feminine humanity to live in promiscuity, resulting in misery, scarce salary, difficulty in finding a paying job, which for a long time was an impossibility for woman, and also causing the moral and physical weakness of exploitation, these women made a commerce of their promiscuity. Prostitution has existed from the time civilization merited its name. It has been regulated and exploited by religions, the states and individuals; but in no period of time has that regulation and that exploitation been more repugnant, more injurious to human dignity than in the middle ages and modern times, under the influence of hypocrisy and cupidity. It is still one of the more frightful problems, that will be resolved only with the complete economic and social reorganization of the world. Meanwhile, the only thing prostitutes do for humanity is to propagate the most horrifying, because of its consequences, of all illnesses. It is another sterile and antisocial feminine group, the same as the two former ones. That is to say, three important divisions of the feminine humanity, from centuries ago, have been absolutely annulled, incapacitated to carry on a useful life either for humanity or for themselves, in the name of custom and with the complicity of the laws. The strange and surprising thing is that the same individuals who have lived in a social state that imposed sterility to a numerous portion of the feminine sex are frightened by the specter of birth control according to present concepts. It seems that it would be more rational to evolve toward an organization where the economic conditions and the customs would allow every healthy and capable woman to have a limited number of children and to raise them with the most efficacy possible. It would be more rational than what has been done until now: to discharge the obligation of maternity upon only one group of women: the married ones, also victims of the social organization. Marriage, just as it is understood by bourgeois society, is another legacy of the middle ages that has undergone slow modifications. It is, ideally considered, a union founded on mutual spiritual and physical love, which is followed later by the responsibility of paternity. Such a perfect love is, without doubt, a novelty introduced in marriage. The same middle ages, despite praising it, did not believe in it. Pas d'amour dans le mariage, was one of the beliefs of "Courtly Love". But bourgeois society did not admit discussions about the matter. Perfect love had to be constant and faithful, which logically would make the union permanent and indissoluble. Divorce is, as we know, an institution which we have revived recently from pagan times.

For woman, marriage was the only way to achieve a secure existence, coupled with a protected and respected maternity. No one can say that the ideal of love lacks beauty or that those securities are not extremely desirable. But let us examine reality. Marriage constituted legally the absolute annulment of the personality of the woman: she owed obedience to her husband, she could not dispose of the wealth she had or earned (if such thing came into being) without her husband's permission. She could not defend herself legally against him or against others without his authorization. Her personal rights remained absorbed by those of her husband. Her children were not under her authority, but under paternal authority.

The single woman—despite the authority of the parents, despite the shame and the persecutions that made her life almost impossible if she risked illegal maternity—had more rights than the married one, who remained permanently under tutelage. But, what did the marry woman need rights for? Tied to a husband by a love that could not have any imperfection or fault, it would suffice her to have the good will of that man in order to achieve a happiness without gloom. Thus it would have been; but perfect love is a blue bird impossible to find. Not even an approximation was easy to find, and it is not easy now. Marriage opened the door to a series of injustices and tyrannical abuses from which woman could not free herself except when she could achieve it by the separation of bodies, another injustice which placed her in the same situation as her sisters from the groups already mentioned, depriving her in life of the right to live. Marriage used to be a speculation or an exploitation. The wealthy, the men of the world, would marry a dowry, a social position; poor men, a maid. Women often would turn marriage into a form of prostitution, marrying for money, for position, to have someone to support them. They often had many children, because that was their unavoidable duty.

Widows had, as single women, some rights; but lest they inherited a fortune, they were persecuted by the ghost of misery and death, the same as her children, and were at times without any alternative but prostitution, although they might have practiced it in a shamed manner. The single mother did not usually have another alternative. Illegitimate children represented the largest proportion of infant mortality, which took place shortly after birth or in early infancy for lack of care, or they would go to increase the numbers in the foundling hospitals. The single mother had the right to her child but not to seek the father, who would unburden himself of all responsibility with the complicity of the law. And even today, as this situation persists, in the majority of cases the doors to honest work are closed to single mothers, and if she has a relatively high social position, she loses not only the possibility of work, but of continuing to move about in her usual circles.

Woman entered that situation as a part of the new bourgeois society. Her education, save exceptions of the comfortable class, was rudimentary. Men had just begun to extend to all classes the benefits of education, and in the slow process of improvement, woman has always marched at the rear. Her political rights were non-existent and she still did not think of claiming them. Her possibilities for work, except in the domestic area, were scarce. Therefore, she did not think of obtaining economic independence.

That is to say that at the dawning of the nineteenth century a situation that would allow woman free development of her human personality had not been produced. I would remind you that this has barely happened for the male either. But there were free men who lived the Greek miracle. There were men in the Renaissance who gave themselves to creation without limits. The male has achieved many accomplishments. Woman has not known anything other than restrictions. Individually, she sometimes escaped the annihilation of her personality and became philosopher, poetess, governor, saint; but those exceptions did not influence collective progress. The fact is that woman, because she is weak, has always been economically a subject; she has never been the producer, the promoter of wealth, its owner or distributor. And she did not consciously rebel against this, despite Aristophanes' predictions, which were nothing but mockings of Plato's utopias, as long as she could not glimpse the possibility of being economically independent. Up to that moment, she was always dragged by circumstances in which she had no direct influence. From centuries earlier we heard the cause of maternity celebrated; the praises to motherhood from the mouths of men have never ceased throughout time. But even that fundamental mission woman has achieved by chance. The idea of maternity as a fulfillment of her personality is a new one. Woman accepted maternity as an instinctive impulse, as a duty, as a biblical curse, unsurmountable, as a relief for her many humiliations; or she had it as a sin and a shame. Because maternity has never been respected and protected for its own sake: it has been so under matrimonial contract. It is not true that the child has always been protected: a legitimate son, for economic reasons, has been protected. Woman has never had the right to be free and conscious. That is one of the victories her efforts seek.

Woman consciously began this movement to improve her integral condition, and today finds herself on the road to development. This is what has been called feminism. It began in the nineteenth century after the French Revolution had declared, pompously, women's equal civil rights with men. But it would be the greatest error to believe that the movement was the work of a handful of superior women who, imbued by revolutionary ideas, kindled their sisters' fire and propelled them to the conquest of a determined goal. That period came later. The feminist movement has been the consequence of social processes that have unfolded implacably and fatally. What woman has done is to acquire consciousness about the processes and to cooperate with them. Feminism is itself a natural process. It could not have been avoided without destroying or paralyzing social evolution. It cannot be asked to turn back nor to stop definitively. It will continue to run its course as all historical processes. As we have seen, it is tied to all evolution of humanity; but now a set number of circumstances have propelled woman to take a more active part in the realization of her historic destiny. That is why discussions about whether there should or should not exist feminism are so useless. We might as well discuss whether the industrial revolution should or should not have occurred in our civilization.

Woman, who is not usually aggressive by nature, did not seek out the struggle: she saw herself hurled into it by circumstances, at times against her own wishes and looking back with nostalgia because

> to our understanding
> any time past
> was better

The determining fact was the transformation of feminine work. Not the fact that woman works. Woman, we have seen, has been one of those beings who has worked the most in this world. What were called "labors appropriate for her sex" have included all sorts of obligations, from plowing the earth to the education of children. Prior to the existence of machines the housewife with her own hands would make the cloth her family wore, the soap they washed with and the bread they ate. The development of industry took the manufacture of articles of first necessity outside of the domestic center. Public school removed a good deal of the work of educating the children from the mother. And as that transformation took place, the privilege was extended to the wealthy bourgeois woman that before had belonged only to some of the women of the idle nobility: living as a parasitic being, without working or spinning, like the lily of the fields.

Surely the woman of the wealthy bourgeoisie found herself rather comfortable with such an arrangement, while she had someone to support her; her psychology as a surrendered being would not have taken her to rebel against forced idleness. According to her inclinations, she could channel it to the reading of novels, to the practice of some religion or to play bridge. But it is the case that, in the less privileged classes, woman's work still continues to be necessary. When domestic industry in great scale, which constituted feminine work, was destroyed by manufacturing, the cost of living went up and the salary of man did not, so that it was no longer sufficient for the support of the working class family and even that of the lower middle class.

At the same time, the invention of the machine eliminated what could have made impossible the employment of woman outside the home: the necessity to have muscular strength. In that manner woman could have made herself equal to man in her capacity to do certain jobs. The working class woman went to work in the factory and increased the family's income. The manufacturers did not refuse to hire her because they saw the possibility to contract the work to woman for less money. Thus, scientific and industrial progress, which has lavished the world with marvelous inventions, from the motor to the radio, has caused economic upheavals which have propelled the workers' movement and the women's movement. They are convergent: their causes are complex; their origins, remote; but both have been hurled into action by the laws of economic determinism.

Woman, upon beginning to work in the factory and in the workshop, realized that she neither had the preparation nor counted with the protection of the law for such an undertaking. She could be exploited by her boss in conditions worse than the male and she could be dispossessed by her father or her husband of whatever she earned.

On the other hand, the woman of the lower middle class, in order to address her family's needs, had to go out to work in the offices, and she became aware of not only her legal inferiority, but her cultural inferiority. She needed to find her way in commerce, in industry, in bureaucracies, in careers in liberal arts, and she had no knowledge.

The polemic about the intellectual and practical preparation of woman that then raised a dust storm has not subsided yet. Books, speeches and treatises were written to prove that woman was incapable of cultivating herself, because she was mentally inferior to man. Governments and governing councils of educational centers intervened in the issue to grant or deny the possibilities of study. This has all led to prove sufficiently the mental and moral inferiority of some men, as well as the open mindedness of some others because it was not a matter of finding out whether woman was capable or not of creative genius, a question that had no bearing, because genius is also exceptional among males, but of allowing her to struggle to earn a living outside of the home, putting an end to a very real but changeable inferiority: scarce instruction and legal incapacity. The movement continued, against the wind and the tide, propelled by necessity. The harshest has been the legal issue. When man stopped being the sole provider of the family, it would not have been possible to continue having all-embracing legal authority. Then there began a bitter aspect of the struggle, because it was directly about power. Passions and feelings mingled. Men and women militated indistinctively in one or the other camp, because some of the most violent opposition to the progress of women was recruited from the feminine ranks themselves. That fact appears to be a contradiction, but it is not. Many women of the types classified by men as honest have been educated in the belief that women who are different do not deserve protection or regard. Any law or custom that could favor the others interpreted by these women as a measure against the rights acquired by them at the price of maintaining their virtue. Laws that would make marriage less rigid, that would protect the illegitimate child, that would grant women of no virtue the right to live, appear to them as an attempt against their own security. Many other women, because of the education they have received, are not worried and look with absolute indifference on feminine problems of a social nature. When the National Feminine Conference met recently in Havana, it fostered discussion about problems of concern to humanity, among them, the special problems of women. A woman of comfortable means and of uncommon education, told me: "I did not attend that conference because I am not interested in it. None of those problems have anything to do with women of my class. We don't have those problems. If some have attended, they may have done so out of altruism." When that lady left my company, I remained thinking about a play by that great defender of women, the Norwegian writer Bjornstjerne Bjornson. In a very intense tragedy, as a consequence of an economic conflict, of the sort so common in our social organization, the ruin of a family is imminent. It would bring with it dishonor and death. Through its scenes we live moments of anguish in an ominous environment. Over the head of the father, the children, the woman, therefore, catastrophe looms. And she, the wife of the protagonist, the mother of the family, comes and goes muttering with the air of a person who has to solve the most arduous of problems: "What will I do, what menu will I order for dinner tonight?" It will not change, it cannot change in a few years, the mind-set that has reached such a state of nullity.

But those women who had to face other aspects of life and to intervene in the sour struggle soon acquired the understanding that in order to modify codes it was important to have a stake in legislative power. And feminism attained a political projection. At the end of the nineteenth century and the beginning of the twentieth it took the shape of a struggle for feminine suffrage. The war of 1914, which gave women the opportunity to prove their capabilities in labor of every kind, placed them at its conclusion in 1918, in the position to obtain the recognition of their right to elect and be elected. England, the United States, the German Republic prior to nazism, Czechoslovakia and Austria, before being absorbed, Poland and republican Spain, Mexico, Cuba, have recognized it. Finland and the Scandinavian countries had done so before 1914. It is not necessary to mention the Soviet Socialist Republics, that have not only granted that right to woman, but have made her equal to man in rights and obligations more so than any other country in the history of the world. Other countries have granted her limited rights to suffrage. The pinnacle of the feminist movement was reached in manufacturing countries or those that are under this control. In regions where the social state does not require great use of machinery, the movement is slow or finds itself in its inception. That is the case of some of the countries in Spanish America. That victory has been achieved after a long struggle, in which woman has had to face up to man in terms that have reached heights of misunderstandings and violence, a struggle that has had moments worthy of Aristophanes' satire, in the fury of some suffragists and the ridiculous imitation of masculine behavior and dress. Gradually we have arrived at a certain degree of mutual understanding, in the degree that the feminine problem identifies with vital problems of humanity at present day.

At present, what began as a struggle for the rights of a social group, has developed into the participation of that group in the solution of general problems afflicting society at present. The struggle is very far from siting an end. But what is important is that woman can work, and she does it, to achieve modifications in law and custom that allow the advance along the road she proposes to take, whose fundamental points follow: a) economic emancipation, that implies the reform of social conditions that limit the development of her capacity to work and to produce; b) complete legal ability, by reforming all laws that maintain her in the condition of inferiority in relation to man and the establishments of laws favorable to maternity; c) obtaining all political rights; d) the right and the possibility to obtain a complete education; e) the revision of the foundations on which sexual morality rests. And it is equally important that woman realize that those gains cannot be obtained alone nor do they benefit her alone, that she is aware of being a part of the social union.

In all of the areas we have just pointed out, woman has gained ground; but as she finds herself in a moment of transition; such gains until now have granted her relative advantages. She has acquired the burden of life outside of the home without freeing herself altogether from domestic ones, so that, in the poor classes, her life is an exhausting double labor. Often she cannot tend to her children or she cannot have them, because she is obliged to go out to work. The salary of the home, if it exists, would not be enough to support the family even temporarily. The access of woman to blue collar work and in bureaucracy has given way to a new and shameful exploitation that degrades her morally and materially. The laws that are passed on her behalf and that of her children are ineffective. In addition many of the more necessary ones are still to be passed in the majority of countries. Woman has a right to be educated; but economic conditions allow only some women to do so. She has the right to work; but the scarcity of employment opportunities oblige her to prostitute herself. Many of the problems find themselves, thus, linked to the working class and their solution must come the same way. In some countries, today, the condition of woman is experiencing a retrogression toward traditional inferiority. We are not lacking men nor women who applaud this. Despite all of that, it is a transitory phenomenon, because social evolution considered in its total sense, cannot stop or regress.

The point referring to the revision of sexual morality faces a more resilient obstacle than the law, which is custom. The evolution achieved in this aspect can be observed rather well in the educated middle class. Woman presents herself to man with her own personality, which she lacked in the past, since she does not see herself requiring his support. She has ceased to belong to him as property. Marriage loses its character of obligatory perpetuity. It is a legal contract that can be undone. It loses its character of ceremony of a sacred cult, its religious celebration remaining as a matter of personal beliefs in all of the countries where the State has freed itself from the dominance of the Church. Families have had to reduce their numbers because of social and economic conditions, which sees woman unburdened from her biological mission. Woman can have a life separate from man, outside the home; in study, work, politics. She does not dedicate herself as before entirely to the home, whose labors do not demand that. She cannot dedicate herself every minute to her children, who from an early age spend a great deal of their day in school. She cannot dedicate herself every minute to her husband either, and in that manner her moral dependency on the male begins to cease, her interior slavery, that "love is all in the life of a woman and only an episode in the life of a man," that was one more expression of her inferiority. It is not to say that love cannot be the greatest thing in a life, but that the concept of love inculcated upon women was one of servitude. Love is the only thing; marriage is the only thing. Result: a very long list of failed, aborted lives, because woman had only one reason to live and that was situated outside herself, absolutely alien to the dominion of her will. The cure of woman from that hypertrophy of feeling will be one of her great advances; but the revision of all sexual morality, that she aspires to, is not a problem that can have a short term solution.

Woman demands freedom to organize her sexual life with regard to human personality. That is to say, she asks a reform of the laws, a transformation in customs; and something else: a change in mental attitude. Here comes to my mind the protestant minister that, to the stupefaction of his parishioners, used to pray to God to grant women courage and men modesty. Yes: let man get rid of the psychological attitude of the master, each time more anachronistic, of the dishonest attitude of the seducer, of the cynical attitude of the defamer. And woman must give up the wages of her fragility, her inside-out virtues: shrewdness, hypocrisy, wantonness, the exploitation of male sensuality. Both sexes then would be in a position to establish relations on the basis of mutual understanding.

When woman has achieved her true economic emancipation; when she changes the situation that obliges her to prostitute herself in a pragmatic marriage or in the public sale of her favors; when the prejudices that weigh on her sexual conduct have been destroyed by the decision of every woman to manage her own life; when women have become acustomed to exercise their freedom and men have improved their detestable sexual training; when we live days of freedom and peace, and, through many attempts, we find a new basis for the union between man and woman, then decisive words would be said on this complex issue. But we will not hear those words. The time we have been given to live is that of knocking down barriers, clearing obstacles, demolishing, so that building can take place later, in all aspects of the relationship between human beings.

There is a ground, however, where we women have to build now: our interior. Our traditional virtues have been negative: submission, obedience, silence, separation, fragility. The functions of the new life we glimpse demand of us positive qualities: independence of mind, serenity, a spirit of cooperation, a feeling of human community. That is very difficult.

It was much easier to remain with limitations and to obey, even if in doing so we ignored dignity. That stage has ended, and although the fearful regret it, we must move forward. Now it seems easy to follow the route of the morally lax male and, like him, lose ourselves in vice and libertinism, as woman did in Rome with untimely-gained liberty. There are women today who complain that man does not respect woman. Neither with the lapsed virtues of yesterday nor with the vices of today we will achieve men's respect, nor deserve our own. In the last instance, I don't know what is to become of woman's greatest contribution to the new life of humanity, but in the long term her public participation has to have an impact on the spiritual roots of social organization. Perhaps she will contribute to moderate the worst male characteristics of the present organization, the predominance of violence and brute force, the selfishness and sensuality, with a mixture of the better feminine characteristics of serenity, peace, spirituality, maternal altruism. Perhaps the memory of a secular inferiority will compel her to assist in the construction of a social order where inferiority would not exist. But if we are to create anything, let us grow now in science and conscience; let us become what the Roman matrons could have if, having obtained the enjoyment of their rights in the severe times of the Republic, they would have carried the struggle outside the home and displayed the motto: "constientia propugnat pro virtute," consciences that fight for goodness.

Translation by Daisy Cocco De Filippis

ABIGAIL MEJIA SOLIERE
Santo Domingo 1895-1941

Born in Santo Domingo to a family of intellectuals, Abigail Mejía Soliere went to Spain at the age of thirteen when she began attending classes at the Colegio de la Compañía de Santa Teresa de Jesús in Barcelona. She received her high school degree in teaching at seventeen, traveled to Italy and France, and returned periodically to the Dominican Republic where she participated in a number of cultural and political activities. The North American invasion of 1916 fueled some of the passion in her earlier writings. She was part of the group that organized la Semana Patriótica.

Mejía Soliere returned to settle down in Santo Domingo in 1925. In 1927 she founded the Club Nosotras and in 1931 she became the founding president of the Acción Feminista Dominicana. An indefatigable worker, she lobbied, organized and presented a proposal for the foundation of a National Museum. When this dream became a reality in 1933, she was asked to serve as Director, in addition to her obligations as a teacher of literature in La Escuela Normal and as organizer of the women's movement. She held these posts until her last days, dedicating herself completely to her work and to the raising of her only son by herself. She died in 1941, one year before women were granted the right to vote.

One of the more combative voices on behalf of women's suffrage in the Dominican Republic, Abigail Mejía's introductory essay to *Ideario Feminista*, reproduced in these pages, gives evidence of her passion, militancy and determination. Mejía's prose, infused with quotes, dates, statistics, logic, cajolery, flattery, anger, and excitement, presents a veritable tour de force of the art of persuasion. In the process, however, and in the examples she draws upon, a reader today might find the limitations of her class, including a certain insensitivity for the lot of the lower classes and an overly optimistic and naive embrace of modern technology. The reader should keep in mind, however, Mejía's commitment to the education of women of the working classes, which includes the opening up of night classes in several cities and public high school instruction for women.

A mistress of the exclamation point, dots and dashes, puns and colorful phrases, she gave as good as she got, and did not shy away from responding swiftly and openly to newspaper articles, by men who believed ridicule to be the appropriate weapon to fight the women's movement in the Dominican Republic. Unfortunately, lured by Trujillo's promise of the vote in his fateful 1932 speech (alluded to in a couple of instances in this essay), the women of Acción Feminista Dominicana opted for a conciliatory stance, ignoring the facts of the bloody dictatorship and silencing some of the more polemic and powerful voices in the movement, among them Abigaíl Mejía's, as the bitterness expressed in the Preliminary note underlines.

Selected Bibliography:

Obras escogidas. Santo Domingo: Secretaría de Educación, Bellas Artes y Cultos, 1995. Vol I & II, 498 p & 514 p.(selections of fiction and non-fiction publications)

Ideario feminista y algún aporte para la historia del feminismo dominicano. Santo Domingo: Imprenta P.A. Gómez, 1939. "Nueva Edición," Vol I. 53 p. (essay)

Historia de la literatura dominicana. Santo Domingo: Imprenta Caribes, 1936. 446 p. (essay)

Vida de Máximo Gómez en Santo Domingo. Santo Domingo: Imprenta Caribes, 1936. 71 p. (essay)

Biografía de Meriño. Barcelona: Imprenta Editorial Altés, (Primer Premio), 1933. 107 p. (essay)

Historia de la literatura castellana. Barcelona: Imprenta Editorial Altés, 1929. 318 p. (essay)

Brotes de la raza. Barcelona: Editorial Araluce, 1926. 168 p. (essay)

Sueña Pilarín. Barcelona: Imprenta Altés, 1925. 246 p. (novel)

Por entre frivolidades. Barcelona: Imprenta de Hermenegildo Miralles, 1922. 232 p. (essay)

FEMINIST IDEOLOGY*
and Some Notes Toward a History of Dominican Feminism
Dedication

to Dr. Gregorio Marañón, illustrious Spanish feminist who established the principle of the just science and the pleasing truth...;

to my friend, the great CONCHA ESPINA, glory of Spanish letters...;

to CLARA CAMPOAMOR, Republican fighter and feminist...

to my dearest MOTHER, a great feminist, who raised, virtuously, six children of her own and six mothered by others...

Preliminary Note

When we hear individuals preach and act now — as if they had forgotten our work - those same women we taught to dare to do precisely that—we are reminded of what Lamartine de Rouget de L'Isle, creator of La Marsellaise, once said. One day, pursued by the very Revolution he had lent his voice to, tired, hungry, upset, almost out of his mind, he asked: "What hymn are those hordes of people singing?" "It's the Marsellaise," they told him. "How could you not know that?"... So it is today that we are horrified by the assurance of those who displace and censure us. We ask: "Who are those women, the ones speaking in such a manner?" ..."Feminists"...they tell us. "Don't you recognize them?"...

It is then that we bow our head...

---

* First publication: *Ideario feminista y algún apunte para la historia del feminismo dominicano.* Santo Domingo: Imprenta P. A. Gómez, "Nueva Edición," Vol. I, 1939, 53 pp. (1) Paragraphs from an article about "Feminism and femininity," published in "Cosmopolita," in the year of 1919, by the author. That complete "Ideology" first appeared in the Sunday pages of the "Listín Diario," January to July of 1932, in the midst of a campaign by the Acción Feminista Dominicana, and later as a pamphlet (1933). DCDF

FEMINIST IDEOLOGY

The only flirtation some men do not forgive is that of having talent.

Nature, according to the recalcitrant, has given females their mission: maternity. That is to say, a role similar to that of the hens...

...But there are times that neither the Beloved nor the Awaited-for or his true effigy appear. There are times when for that woman, the one who was taught only the Road to Weddings,...the years pass by and the doors to Love remain closed!... "Why- if she is endowed with a head and a heart-can't she dedicate herself to an activity more useful than the useless task of waiting?"...(1)

And that is what many "crazed" idealists do...

(Son of mine, nestled in my arms, and that to give you life I almost lost mine; who drinks from my breast the vital juice of my blood; that taking care of you is continuous labor of all of my days and the insomnia of my nights; will you be like those other VALIANT sons of other mothers who are bothered by the fact that the MOTHERS of SONS ask for their RIGHTS?...)

Woman has been and has done everything man has allowed her to be and do: and she was QUEEN AND SAINT, HEROINE, ARTIST, WISE WOMAN, MOTHER, WOMAN, DOLL...How can she not be PREPARED to vote and even TO DO NOTHING, as it IS DONE many times in Congress?...

We ask for woman ALL THE RIGHTS and also ALL THE DUTIES, except that of going to war. She must not take away life. She gives it...

What is FEMINISM? A vindicating doctrine that wants that it be granted to the female or woman, that is to say the weakest sex but not the LESS INTELLIGENT, the same HUMAN rights her companion MAN abrogated to himself alone; the ability to carry on in all positions and functions, provided she demonstrates the talent to do so...(Although we may agree on the fact that many men arrive at this position only by virtue of wearing pants...)

FEMINISM is VINDICATION, liberation for woman: a somewhat late DEMAND. It asks for no concession, because this would imply a grace or gift. And one demands what belongs to one...Nothing more.

"It is convenient that the husband be allowed to express without punishment a solecism" said the cunning Latin writer...There is the QUID, the why of the dread and war being waged against us by mediocre beings!...Petty jealousies, fear of cutting a poor figure when those who are stooped over raise themselves...And surprise everyone perhaps by their stature!

To plant a tree, to write a book, to have a child, to found something or to preach an ideal, these are all difficult things. It is easier and more doable to become a celebrity and to reach the heights of fame by insulting those who are doing that. (The bad part about this is that there are others who believe that such a profession is not MANHOOD but COWARDICE AND PERVERSITY.)

FEMININITY is the scent of Woman; but do not believe that by changing the vase, the flower, which is a flower, would no longer perfume the environment. If such is its mission, it is the same in an extremely delicate flower vase as in a miserly clay pot, near the smoke of the cigars in the office as in the sewing basket, and it will spread its perfume. One has to be near it, quite close, to inhale it...

It happens, yes, on occasions, that by a miracle of universal germination, the flower is nothing but a case, seedling for a wide tree, that will take shape and grow, and I don't wonder why it would later admire itself and forget in its greatness that it came from a flower...

In England FEMINISM is conservative or labor; in Spain republican or moderate; in Mexico, catholic or atheist; in Russia red or ultra radical; in Finland, it is already ancient and reasonable, like the people of that climate; in Venezuela, it is pro labor and Christian...And only in this miserable barren isle of Quisqueya will it fail to adapt itself to its ways and idiosyncracy?...Or is it that, according to what that gentleman said: "This will never be a NATION, only a country...?"

When one says MAN one speaks many times GENERICALLY and one understands, IN GENERAL, MEN AND WOMEN OF THE WORLD. Nevertheless, when the time came to proclaim the RIGHTS OF MAN it was understood in practice in a manner SPECIFIC and selfish (despite the fact that the head of Madame Roland fell off the guillotine in the same manner as that of Danton's)...In our century, this is clarified and what remains in the inkwell is proclaimed: THE RIGHTS OF WOMAN.

To pretend to oppose the planting and cultivation here, as we see fit, of the grain that is already mature sprig, harvested in nothing less than FIFTY FOUR COUNTRIES, is a scandalous pretension, much like the useless stone placed in the middle of the stream to impede the flowing of the water...and A TRIUMPHANT FEMINISM will get here some day, like all facets of progress, a bit late, like the airplanes, the automobiles and the radio have arrived. "Woman is not fit for anything other than being a woman," decreed Mr. Platitude in a vapid ditty currently circulating. Monsieur de la Palisse would correct this by saying: "Male is not fit for anything other than being a male." With which MALE AND FEMALE would be reduced to a pure zoological and reproductive mission...(Although one or the other might aspire to something more).

Between MAN and WOMAN there is no difference than that imposed by Nature: man begets and woman conceives. But the great number of idle hours could be employed in other activities, fecund not only for the species but also for the sake of UNIVERSAL Society.

If a MODERATE form of FEMINISM has raised such a ruckus here, how is the so-called INTEGRAL FEMINISM or BOLSHEVIK to take hold? ..."The gallows, the bonfire, the gibbet, would not be sufficient punishment for such daring design!

"Who will mend our socks?" "Who will cook our snacks?"— cry out with feign alarm those who never worried about such things while their frivolous wives ran after the movies, while Maritornes did her thing between the cooking stoves...Sweet "poetry of the home" that vile feminism might come to spoil!

Saying that we are not PREPARED has become a worn beyond words cliche...when so well prepared, without a doubt, are those ignorant peasants, illiterate cane-cutters, innocent ignorant men who come to the polls without knowing what it means, nor how to sign their names!...And instead, women already successful in schools, universities and life -that one who founded a home, that one a doctor in Medicine, the one further down, an illustrious educator who supports her family with her profession...do not participate in the election of heads of government and legislators, even when they are teachers and hold degrees in Letters and the Law; but this right is granted to the unaware, to poor little illiterate men...THIS IS THE JUSTICE OF MEN...

Maternity is "the highest and only mission of WOMAN". But there is not any law among us that would protect this "noble" mission...Instead, such "noble" mission is used as the PRETEXT to prevent woman from participating in the making of her LAW...What are we saying then? Does this deserve reward or punishment?...

Nature was such a good mother to MAN that he began to believe himself KING OF CREATION; but, as a bad stepmother, it left only pain and physical miseries from puberty in the female breast. And it completed that fatal gift of impious inequality before SOCIETY and before the LAW, fabricated by the strongest.

Intelligence lacks gender and it is puerile to consider it a masculine monopoly. Mythology tells us that Minerva, who was a female, came about complete and PREPARED from the head of Jove. (Although this might be only a feminist joke by Mythology, since I know some who are incomplete and empty...)

FEMINISM is not an exclusively socialist, nationalist or bolshevik problem. It is a SOCIAL problem, and in each country it can be channeled according to national and sociological currents.

We do not pretend to be either superior or inferior to our companion. Neither above his head nor under his feet, but at the height of his heart or his brain, CORDIALLY AND REASONABLY EQUAL before the law.

Just as it was said that "man does not live by bread alone" neither does woman live by rags alone. Women have already conquered their RIGHT TO BOOKS! Rags have turned into paper! Let new problems shaking the NEW WOMAN in the world vibrate on the open pages for those women as well!

We are placed in an altar at times, and we are thrown incense, a lot of smoke, as if to make us dizzy for a while and have it go inside our nostrils, so that we don't notice that further up there is a brain, and it occurs to us to say, parodying Andrea Chernier: "What a shame! We had something here.."

Carnival!...The joy of a farce and living, when, jocund, youth dresses up as old age! But how sad and ridiculous is poverty wearing the mask of opulence, old age behind the mask of youth; and FRIV-OLITY with the appearance and the mask of FEMININITY, futile pretext to walk away from any serious thought that might wrinkle the nards of a forehead!...

For many to say WOMAN is to say a SUBLIME BEING, ethereal, incomparable...A FAIRY...Better yet: an ANGEL, a virgin, an immaculate mother...(But let her not ask for any rights. Then, by strange metamorphosis, she no longer is even a HUMAN CREATURE...)

Although mothers bear on their flesh the greatest of pains, they enjoy - more than the shedding of blood- to wipe away the hurts and the blood of Humanity. And, Horatius has already said it, the beautiful one: "Bella matribus detestata..." Mothers do not love war.

"That we are not PREPARED"..."That we should prepare ourselves"...And all that for a miserly electoral ballot? Without doubt, we will find in the coal seller and the farmer and in the miserable illiterate man who votes, nervous claimer of employment or the one who goes as "counsel to Madrid" an able leader of Public International Right...

The weak sex? The one that goes around the world and launches herself trying out a parachute or swims across the English Channel, and the Atlantic on the wings of a plane, like Ruth Elder or Amelia Earhart...Where is the WEAKNESS? Oh, yes: before the UNEQUAL LAW that does not protect her!

We women have not invented GUNPOWDER...nor dynamite...But a lady began the RED CROSS; another, the first HOSPITAL; and to the abolition of slavery another one contributed a book; and the Nobel Prize for Peace was won by yet another. She planted only LOVE and now she wants to collect JUSTICE, poor merciful female!...

According to the biblical myth from the Genesis, Jehova got woman from the rib of a MALE, and he called her MANLY, that is to say, his EQUAL. Thus he would be able to exclaim: "This is the bone of my bones and she will be blood of my blood"...

A PUBLIC WOMAN is reprehensible because she sells her person. A PUBLIC MAN (although he too might sell himself...) is something respectable and envied...

Of all animals, an INTELLIGENT woman is most like an intelligent man. Between any old illiterate royal groom and Shakespeare there is a greater distance, in the human zoological scale, than between Napoleon and Madame Stael, for instance...

Why is that THEY do what they have not been prepared to perform and WOMEN on the other hand, no matter how PREPARED they are, cannot do these very same things? It means to condemn MOTHERS to be citizens, but not to have the power TO DO WHAT THEY, THE MALES, DO.

JUSTICE AND LOVE is our motto. But in the name of LOVE an injustice should not take place, not with the most noble of our traditions, our FOREFATHERS, nor with the weakest, woman.

"Do not beat woman even with a flower"...goes an oriental proverb. And Dominican feminists were at times whipped with these FLOWERS: "unprepared, impertinent, insufficient, whiny, tricky," and other weeds. The horn of plenty of GENTLEMANLINESS runneth over...

"But if they earn their living LIKE MEN!"- "Well they are not PREPARED."

"But they are Dominican women and SISTERS of yours!"-"Well, they are not PREPARED."

Who is the monomaniac with the refrain? I looked: I saw a tiny house sparrow that was beginning to fly...

To the misogynous Euripides, himself, it is owed, from his Medea, the first CRY OF REBELLION BY WOMEN— a chant taken up by English suffragettes. Today-as a writer says-"the sweet Ofelia, like the sarcastic Medea, would answer with a laugh to an authoritarian Hamlet who would send her to the nunnery" or order her to confine herself to the kitchen...

Ancient men even believed that we had no soul; but they also had the mistaken belief that the slave was a THING. Aesop and Epictetus, from their ergastulum, prove false that theory. As the other was proven false by ZENOBIA in the desert, or CORINA defeating Pyndarus, or Helen Keller, miracle of our sex and of our century.

To love those who love us is NATURAL LAW. And to argue CAPACITY AND PREPARATION with those who have argued with US, is pure LOGIC. Who gave it to THEM?...

How curious! Spaniards judged "in illo tempore"- that the Englishwomen who voted were PREPARED but their compatriots were not. Nevertheless, Spanish woman got the vote at last. Some CUBANS were of the opinion, not long ago, from their pulpit in Congress, that CUBAN WOMEN were not yet PREPARED for SUFFRAGE. And from here, for a change, some WISE MONKEYS discovered that yes, the CUBAN WOMEN were PREPARED for FEMINISM; but that DOMINICAN WOMEN were not...The moral of the story: "Neither Anne nor anyone is a prophetess in her Land..."

How much admiration would be bestowed on an honorable President of a Republic called DEMOCRATIC if he were to name a FEMALE JUDGE for Macorís, La Vega or Santiago of the gallant Caballeros (knights)! And nevertheless, many centuries ago, the stale Bible (so retrograde, so little democratic, eh!) tells us how Deborah administered justice, under a palm tree, in Israel...

Even in grammar masculine strength prevailed, but with the condition that, in agreement, or when we say GENERICALLY: MEN or BOYS (CHILDREN)-to mean boy and girl- we understood it included EQUALLY the two halves of humanity: man and woman.

And that is why, when it was said THE RIGHTS OF MAN, it should have applied to both.

France, Italy, Paraguay...Latin, ardent countries: much admiration and much ecstasis. England, Ireland, cold and serene countries: less ecstasis. And they were the first to give practical rights to women.

The beloved no longer needs Werther to commit suicide because of her, but that he make her life soft, within the parameters of JUSTICE AND EQUITY...

What is a good understanding of the word feminism? Let us consult Calleja's dictionary: "FEMINISM. A SET OF DOCTRINES THAT HAVE AS THEIR GOAL TO RETURN WOMAN TO HER RIGHTFUL PLACE IN SOCIETY" TABLEAU! According to this, those who do not understand well are the sophists, anti-feminists...

A French Revolution was necessary so that the world would notice THE RIGHTS OF MAN...Would we need as much to proclaim those of woman?...Never! We women only ask that, as a consequence of today's civilization, HUMAN DUTIES AND RIGHTS be proclaimed.

Femininity, frivolity...Just as it was said "man does not live by bread alone," neither ought woman to live by rags alone.

Feminism destroyer of femininity!...Here it is, the eternal war horse of those who would have us with the foot on the distaff, forgetting that the middle ages have become the dark ages forgotten...

Those pseudo-gallants who would want only dolls for their salon are shocked and surprised to find that instead of sawdust we have in our heads a brain not unaware of the evolution of ideas. Miserly gallants, before our femininity you regale us...much smoke, and before our feminism...you dedicate insults to us! (If the first is femininity, the latter must be VIRILITY in their eyes...)

"The nineteenth century saw the triumph of the RIGHTS OF MAN; the twentieth century will see the glory of those of WOMAN." (This was not announced by me, but by the great Victor Hugo.)

"Everything said against FEMININE SUFFRAGE is said against reason and EQUITY." (And this was written by HOSTOS.)

"The uselessness and indelicacy of the fact that laws should not be equal for both sexes makes, from whatever point of view, such an enormous injustice, that only the greatest excitement in the most zealous of suffragettes is justified. How could MAN have been so unjust with the sex that gave him his being and to whom he refers as WEAK?"...(And this was not invented by me or any other woman, but by Dr. MARAÑON...)

"We do not want woman to enjoy only the same rights as man, for that would be an injustice to her. We vindicate for the femenine sex SPECIAL RIGHTS, inaccessible to men." (And such thing GURLITT dares to declare, who is a male.)

And when great men write such things, we small women must reflect and accept.

"In illo tempore"...Yes, at that time, when we began the planting of the new seed...what loneliness!...In space they were lost, without an echo, words, handfuls of germs...Later the number of believers grew. Today, already a resolute company prepares for the struggle. How many stragglers will not come later, at the time of the "harvest" as they are saying in some quarters?...

The humble little teachers that disseminate science in their classroom to gather ingratitude and forgetfulness, in the opinion of modern Gedeons, less PREPARED than any charcoal vendor who ever passed by a school, but who had the right to vote since he was a young man.

FEMINISM is an educational system and a SOCIAL THEORY. As EDUCATIONAL SYSTEM it demanded for young women the study and the exercise of the liberal professions: Medicine, Pharmacy, Law, Accounting, etc. Later, as a SOCIAL THEORY, it comes to ask participation in the administration of nations (of which man had reserved the lion's share among lambs...)

"The great ones-said Hugo-appear to us even greater because we see them on our knees: Let us get up!" And so men appear even greater when we see them from afar: Let us approach them! And then, many times, we discover...a big boy that needs to be told what justice and LOVE are...

Himeneo causes suffering...and all trust to be married; being a mother is painful...and all yearn for the CHILD, because life must be lived and the law of progress of the species must be submission. And FEMINISM and SUFFRAGE are signs of progress and evolution, whose time to toll, like all...

After planting many benefits, it would be a good "affaire politique" to concede, with other rights in the magnanimous hand, access to the voting booths to the favored ones. Women would only vote for those who would favor them with the RIGHT TO VOTE.

Some have been born to be queens and others busy bees,-although all are needed in a good REPUBLIC and in a good beehive... Even the good for nothing drones who are only good to aid reproduction!...

If because we defend tenaciously THE RIGHT OF ALL our sisters we call ourselves FEMINISTS, those who settle for the "status quo" of the rights of the male we should call MASCULINISTS... Isn't that so?...

Each Holy Week has its Easter Saturday...And (after a period that now seems to us to be short; but long in the struggle, organizations, mockings and truths), we saw the dawn of Saturday, the fourteenth of May of 1932, when our leader of State made this solemn and FEMINIST declaration: "We can begin to consider the NEED to grant CITIZENSHIP to WOMAN."

"I sympathize with that movement of SOCIAL JUSTICE in favor of woman," he said.

And the women- the FEMINISTS, at least-we sympathize with that declaration of PRESIDENTIAL JUSTICE.

It will be funny, when elections get nearer, at the time of the vote and triumph, to see how the up to now stragglers and lukewarm women will hook on the wings made by us and fly...

Equalizer progress drags all with you and will show as equals those who love you and fight for your advancement and those who are routinely reluctant to see the new light!...

All of us women fit in this world! For a woman to shine she does not need to darken another; for a man to stand out he need not dim the light of women...

Great and noble MOTHER'S DAY CELEBRATION! And how much cheap literature, one day a year, in honor of whom, in the daily reality of her home, is not THE ONLY AND UNIQUE TUTOR of her children, when the father is absent, not even a CITIZEN still before substantive law, nor privileged by any objective law, made all by those she put in this world, with the pain of her flesh!...

It is common to see a MACAQUE being supported BY WOMEN who later dedicates himself to the sweet chore of ranting and raving AGAINST WOMEN...His GREAT VIRILITY is proven there...

Why, when the ill named POPULAR OR UNIVERSAL SUFFRAGE was promulgated (as if we daughters of Eve were not the daughters of the PEOPLE or of the UNIVERSE...) THE RIGHT TO VOTE was not contested as restricted to the educated, and now the not so galant notion comes up of whether THE VOTE ought to be RESTRICTED and only for those who can read and write? Adam THE CITIZEN is a man of letters and illiterate; Eve THE CITIZEN, must she forcibly have a university education?...

Men who are truly GOOD AND NOBLE have been pained by the RELEGATION that the majority of others-because of different secular customs-imposed on women. WITH THEM (WOMEN) there was no need to consult; but it was legislated on HER BEHALF! And that without taking into consideration THE RIGHT nor THE OPINION of those who were their wives, daughters and sisters!...

Many women are still hanging on to the old theory of Nietzsche: "Cats" there you have what women are, cats and cats and birds. Or, when things go well, cows...(What bull!-we would have to tell old Nietzsche...)

Why should there be DOUBLE STANDARDS, one for MAN, the other for the poor woman, one with a WIDE SLEEVE, another with a NARROW ONE? Why should there be TWO STANDARDS, TWO LAWS and UNEQUAL? "Half of one thing-as it was pointed out in geometrical terms by a feminist at the Assembly-must be exactly equal to the other half-as the axiom says, "Are we not half of HUMANITY?" Where were we?...

Some presumed (and presumptuous) GREAT MEN of the intellect are like the cathedrals only in this: they are majestic and EMPTY. And still we search in those temples for the Virgin and we cannot find her. There the only thing virgin is their talent...

The early English suffragettes were the martyrs of ridicule in the annals of ANTI-FEMINISM and insulted and censured FEMININITY. We first Dominican feminists were also tortured in various ways by injustice and incomprehension, in this our apostolate without a crown...

To study the LAWS! To improve PENAL CODES! To preach incessantly about FEMINISM...Whatever for? It is better to dedicate oneself to plant IDEAS that would be for the good of ALL WOMEN on the day of triumph than to submerge oneself in the sharp NARCISISM of contemplating oneself in the mirror, selfishly and sweetly, like SO MANY OTHERS...It is sad to confess it!...

The greatest mystery of PLEASURE is...a CHILD in the arms of a MOTHER. A presumed WEAKNESS sheltering another small one! And where can we find a good LAW that would protect both like a shield?...

The apostles of all IDEAS are almost always tormented, because of their preaching and talking too much. But perhaps there is more beauty in Saint Peter, nailed to the cross, than in the Pope himself, resplendent in that Rome that crucified his predecessor. One died head down, so that the other might wear a tiara years later...(I was given the cross...)

When in the tall Dominican zenith a HEAD OF THE GOVERNMENT declared himself prepared to begin CONSIDERING THE NECESSITY TO GRANT CITIZENSHIP TO WOMEN, the scarce TROGLODYTES still remaining either kept their council surreptitiously or whispered in Napoleonic fashion:

From the bottom of the caves, forty centuries of INEQUALITY regard you with amazement!...

The miserable mother of the small colt WORKS as hard as the stud or more, by pulling the cart. The weak ivy CLIMBS as tall as the corpulent oak. And from the delicate flower comes the strong and juicy fruit, that remembers the flower. Only among HUMANS has the theory prospered that woman-flower, ivy, mother-, COULD not or OUGHT not to reach as high as the MALE, her complement!

We want to do THINGS like MEN; we want TO BE LIKE MEN...But, Mother of God! We must ask with the ingenuity of a Franciscan: Is it possible that our LITTLE BROTHER MAN does

SUCH BAD THINGS that WE cannot do them the way that HE does?...

The truth is this: man PROPOSES and woman DISPOSES and the Devil INDISPOSES, when it comes to LOVE. So an EQUITABLE AND JUST Divorce Law must be passed, in the bilateral sense, for both.

A donkey may be a PROFESSOR OR AN ACADEMIC (there are instances...) and teach, like the monkey in the fable, with his lantern's light out...But, when it comes to woman (let her be Pardo Bazán or Concha Espina), there are all sorts of impediments and obstacles for their unheard of pretension...And that, without a doubt, is done out of gallantry and CONSIDERATION for the WEAK sex...

Even the spirits who engaged in conversation (as he says) with Allan Kardec were FEMINISTS! They did not refer to beautiful cases or moving stories-as Dante asked those in hell or Faustus was told, but like well-educated spirits and before this century they declared EQUAL RIGHTS before HUMAN law, the same as equality in the tomb...

It is good to note that the great WOMANIZERS are not generally great FEMINISTS. One thing is to love WOMEN and another is to love and to give consideration to A WOMAN. Between Don Juan who spurned them and the Son of Mary who dignified them, there is an abyss.

How many wretched women BECAUSE THEY DID NOT KNOW found themselves, almost without any awareness of it, divorced, despite being innocent and believing, in their ignorance of laws and Codes, that evil would never choke them in its merciless clutches.

THE MORAL:-woman MUST KNOW and be interested in the laws that pertain to her existence.

In the France that passes for the brain of the world, with its divine Paris of triumphant gallantry and free love, woman still does not have the right to vote...Nor is she in a hurry, there, in the "Ville Lumiere", to demand her RIGHTS, because when it suits her—and that is quite frequently—she takes them all...

If we did not fear being beaten, we would say that FEMINISM, far from aspiring to MAKE US MASCULINE, aspires to the contrary, to MAKE men a little bit FEMININE, to soften them, to make them sweeter...Let no one laugh, because we have discovered that throughout history the more noble examples of HUMANITY—Christ, Budha, Socrates, Leonardo da Vinci, Pestalozzi—all had a touch of FEMININE delicacy and sentiment.

On Monday, bridge at the Perez's; on Tuesday at Mrs. Terry's; on Wednesday at Nanú's place; on Thursday...How are beauties made drowsy by the sweet henbane of frivolity and uselessness to think about feminism or about any other RIGHT than the right to PLAY and to waste...time?...

If we know nothing, that would serve as fertilizer to the theory of our supposed INFERIORITY; if we know something, we would be called Misses Know-it-all; if we do nothing, silly and wild; if we attempt to do a lot, tomboys...We will have to exclaim with the divine Sor Juana Inés de la Cruz: "Love them as you make them...or make them as you would want them"...

"When women ruled the world,"I hear some say, "gossip would have its day." If that were true, it can be argued that while ONLY MEN have ruled there have been too many WARS and too much BLOOD has been shed. Our gossiping has always hurt HUMANS less than THEIR wars...

ANTIFEMINIST criterium: "Man, undoubtedly, is superior to woman, because he is a sort of very BIG ANIMAL (and more dough, in general...) He MUST WORK for us like a donkey...Woman MUST BE queen and lady of the home, because her mission is having children...if she has them. If not, she can dedicate herself to dancing, going to the movies, or spending on luxuries; that is why her husband earns a living. Let us not be silly or look for any more RIGHTS or reforms than those already in place."

FEMININE AND FEMINIST criterium: Man is our mate and brother; we must help him with our vision and knowledge. The only superiority of the male is his strength: woman has hers, MATERNITY. And, because she achieves this mission, she must be supported by the law. In everything else we are equal to our FELLOW CREATURE AND COMPLEMENT. The donkey works; but the female also works. And the wise man works, and his wife helps him sometimes, as witnessed by Madame Curie.

"That we are attacking a lot, that we are FINISHING OFF men" a timid antifeminist tells us as he feigns alarm. But, by God, how is that going to be possible! What would we women do without men?...Get bored...And that would be the end of the world....

An accomplice to the INEQUALITY OF RIGHTS has been FRIVOLITY, nourished by certain elements. One is permitted luxury, the movies, automobiles, constant dances and beauty contests, the home turned into a gambling den from morning to night; let them smoke, let them play cards, let them neglect their children...Anything except THINKING!...

BEAUTY has its scepter, like TALENT, like VIRTUE...But there is the difference that only beauty shines, dazzles...and vanishes; virtue is sometimes lost and intelligence nurtures and fortifies itself with the passing of the years. Why not cultivate it, Oh, Woman!

To preserve the veils, the gate, silly traditions, the charm of the harem and of the aged, against FEMINISM invading the Universe, there can only be weak reasons to prevent that in Bagdad and in Istanbul, in Tokyo and in Jerusalem, old poetry is destroyed by the marvelous RADIO, the portentous ELECTRICITY, the modern TALKIES and the BLIMPS AND AIRPLANES...No one can oppose PROGRESS even if they wish it!...

And...let us repeat it, like at the beginning, at the end: For woman ALL THE RIGHTS but also ALL THE OBLIGATIONS, except going to war. She cannot cut life down...She gives it...

Translation by Daisy Cocco De Filippis

DELIA WEBER
Santo Domingo 1900-1982

Poet, playwright, painter, narrator, cultural worker, feminist, Delia Weber is one of the most outstanding Dominican women of this century. In her eighty-two years of life, Delia Weber participated actively in many aspects of Dominican life. A feminist by her own definition, for many years she was a member of the board of directors of the Acción Feminista Dominicana where she had the opportunity to study the condition of women and to take a stand on behalf of women's rights.

Delia Weber understood, however, that her voice gained authority when she spoke from the position of mother or future mother and many of her writings present "the compromise" between her wishes for freedom and her total acceptance of the position and responsibility of women as mothers. After reading Weber's theories and studying her life as an activist we would hope to find the same optimism and vitality in her poems and short stories. A reading of her collection of short stories, *Dora y otros cuentos*, for example, presents a series of feminine characters who show their inconformity with the lot of women by running away from home.

It is understood then that despite her public conciliatory statements, as the essay included in this selection shows, her stories betray her dismay at the situation of women. A dismay, we can only imagine, which also represents the great anguish that as leader of the Acción Feminista Dominican she must have felt, as a woman with a great sense of justice and artistic sensibility who had to work with Trujillo's regime in order to gain for women the right to vote. In the last instance, the women of Acción Feminista Dominicana lived through the sacrifice of the integrity of the group, coopted by a promise they had to wait a decade to see it come to fruition.

Selected Bibliography

Ascuas vivas. Ciudad Trujillo: Editora Montalvo, 1939. 83 p. (Poetry)

Encuentro. Ciudad Trujillo: Editora Montalvo, 1939. 80 p. (Poetry)

Los viajeros. Ciudad Trujillo: Imprenta La Opinión, 1944. 2nd. ed. Colección Antología de Nuestra Voz, No. 43, 1991. 30 p. (Drama)

Apuntes. Ciudad Trujillo: Editorial La Palabra de Santo Domingo, Colección Antología de Nuestra Voz, No. 47, 1949. 67 p. (Poetry)

Los bellos designios/Lo eterno. Ciudad Trujillo: Editorial Stella, 1949. 43 p. (Drama)

Los bellos designios. 2nd. ed. Santo Domingo: Colección Antología de Nuestra Voz No. 41, 1991. 21 p. (Drama)

Lo eterno. 2nd. ed. Santo Domingo: Colección Antología de Nuestra Voz, 1992. 20 p. (Drama)

Dora y otros cuentos. Ciudad Trujillo: Imprenta de la Librería Dominicana, 1952. 69 p. (Short Story)

Espigas al sol. Ciudad Trujillo: Editora del Caribe, 1959. 69 p. (Poetry)

Estancia. Santo Domingo: Editora del Caribe, 1972. 52 p. (Poetry)

Poemas a mi madre. Santo Domingo: Editora Frahegio, Colección Antología de Nuestra Voz, No. 2, 1982. s.p. (Poetry)

La india: renacimiento en Bengala/Personalidad de Rabindranath Tagore. Santo Domingo: Colección Antología de Nuestra Voz, No. 13, 1987. s.p. (Essay)

Pensamiento inédito. Santo Domingo: Colección Antología de Nuestra Voz No. 32, 1987. 72 p. (Essay)

The Meaning of Civilization and the New Woman*
In memory of the luminous shadows Gastón Deligne and Domínguez Charro

The sensible space of a conference is not sufficient to satisfy my desire for spiritual exchange with a dedicated and viril people, such as the one in San Pedro de Macorís.

Thanks to my companions in ideals, the enthusiastic collaborators of the Union Femenina Ibero Americana of this city, I enjoy the privilege and honor of this moment.

I hesitated quite a bit in the selection of the topic for so precious a time. I wanted to speak of feminism, of my intense work with the Acción Feminista Dominicana (AFD), of my favorite topics about art and poetry: "The Renaissance in India". The personality of Rabindranath Tagore or of Maurice Maeterlinck or Romain Roland. I wanted to speak of Buddha, the precursor of Christ, of the aspirations of the United Nations, of peace, etc. etc. At last, I have chosen: "The Meaning of Civilization and the New Woman" because it seemed to be an adequate choice.

We observe through history that the values of civilization at a particular moment—Morals, Rights, the State, Religion, the Arts, the Fatherland, Humanity—are problems very relative to the human capacity acquired up to that moment. That is to say, depending almost always on the times and circumstances. In synthesis: everything is instability, movement, change, apparently. In truth, everything is relation, dependency, fusion, unity, harmony.

Life acquires meaning in relation to those unstable values that civilization achieves. But the sources of nature and of the human spirit are inexhaustible virgin quarries. The idealists or utopians conceive their most daring ideas in the secret of their spirit or of nature, according to the degree of sensibility of their understanding.

Today civilization is the development of innumerable needs. The absolute technical dominion over nature. Man believes he succeeds when he defeats the obstacles nature places before him. But this is the sense of civilization in the West, drunk with industrialization, mechanism, vortex. Western man, the North American in the highest degree, with the astounding development of industrialization, demonstrates that he defends himself and defeats nature as if it were a hostile enemy.

It is as if we were looking to protect ourselves from the harm that would come to us from our own mother.

---

* Selection from *Pensamiento inédito.* Santo Domingo: Colección Antología de Nuestra Voz, No. 32, 1987.

We forget that we are children of the earth, of the beneficent earth that knows not about rich and poor when it swells the seed that would germinate the tree, the cool shade for the travelers and the delicious fruit for man.

We forget that we are children of the purifying earth, in its heart, the water that springs up to quench all thirst and clean all filth.

We forget that we are children of the earth that gives us the caress and benefit of the air that sustains life, and the symbolic ardor of the fire that purifies by destruction.

We are the children of the earth that will embrace us one day forever, free from the anguish of being.

The Eastern interpretation of civilization leans man toward nature. He loves it. He respects it. He looks for it. In its secrets the solution for all man's problems is to be found.

It is based on this that man in the east, profoundly spiritual, links as a whole social sentiments—responsibility, facts, individuals, economic, moral, aesthetic—to the unlimited plan of the spirit narrowly fused with nature, with the wise mother, who solves elementary necessities, of the tender small bird as well as the transcendent situation of man.

The goal in life for men in the west is, generally, to acquire. First the job that would allow us to save, in order to own the beautiful little house. Beautiful furniture. Immediately more expensive needs. The refrigerator. The electric stove. The car. The house in the country. Or the apartment house to rent out and be able to live increasingly more comfortably. And the time that remains we use to cultivate reading, poetry or the fine arts. All material goods. Objective. Concrete. Acquired. Acquired for the benefit of our material person. And of our spirit as an appendage. For luxury. To meet our aspirations, only.

The goal in life for men in the east, generally, is dispossession. True goods are derived from meditation and the understanding of the secrets of nature. And the meaning of life is the search for truth. The answers to the big questions:

Where is the eternal rush of human struggle and continued battle leading us? What is the truth about human existence?

Hope and certainty are fixed stars in the firmament in the Orient: They almost possess the secret of the meaning of life.

In the West, pessimism and the reason for this unquenchable thirst for machines, pulls away from us the deep rhythm and the sweet sound of meditation which awakens hope in the human heart.

From both senses of life, as much in the east as in the west, work is the ideal unifier. It appears to be the most powerful motivator in life. It is a natural law, inherent to existence. Some beings: the ants, the bee, the spider, etc., carry, awake, within themselves the stimuli for this activity. The rest of the beings animal or vegetable and the earth itself, carry with them the motor energies sufficient to meet the requirements of this law of life.

The present panorama shows us man in his struggle for subsistence during a time of peace. It is a true daily battle which man calls peace. Nevertheless, we do not know which of the battles is the fiercest, the one at war or the one during peace?

Man in the west goes to war to kill. Most of the times without knowing why. The foundation or motive of wars is always to defend the interests or conveniences of one minority of individuals or states.

Man in the east opposes war with his tame Christian gesture of non violence, in the fashion of

Christ, or Gandhi. A political strategy at the moment not understood but a beginning of a future superior stage.

Civilizing humanity rises to the level of its men of highest consciences. But the civilization of a people is measured by the level of the majority. Not by its chosen ones, although these might be the guides that shake the inner workings of the soul and its vibrations are extended throughout the earth.

The politics of Non violence, advised by Mahatma Ghandi in India, and observed by the majority, almost the totality, of hindu citizens, is the same politics that was practiced by Jesus "who sacrificed himself for the redemption or vindication of humanity".

When the practice of this religion of Non violence dominates the human race then the force of the spirit would have imposed itself. And we will leave for the brute the brute force of his fists and for the beast the brutality of bloody combat.

I have seen in my reveries a humanity bathed by this light of love and piety. Of confidence and peace.

I have seen joy retained on earth. And death to be the rest, from happiness not grief.

At the present stage of civilization woman appears as a new and different kind of woman. The emancipated woman. The new woman.

This new woman who makes present society uneasy and puts at risk the tranquility of her male companion is the same woman of 1948 and all other previous eras. But time and circumstances have changed. The creation of living beings opposes the action of time and circumstances. Then, today not only woman is new but man is new and the truth is new.

Life with its claims and needs is the great moderator. It shapes the soul of living beings as needed by its present ideal.

Modern woman is the product of the economic system of the great capitalism. And it is, clearly, a natural and inevitable consequence of her participation in the flow of economic and social life.

She is transformed with the rhythm of the new truth circulating about. She has the need to earn her bread. To defend her freedom. That freedom that she counts on to struggle in life. That freedom that authorizes her with certain arrogance to maintain her dignity without undermining her beautiful gifts of femininity.

The characteristic of woman in the past was the predominance of sentimentalism. Contemporary reality demands of woman the double goal of knowing how to control her feelings and strengthen her will. It demands, also, that it be she alone who solve the economic difficulties, the moral crises and other assaults that destiny has in store for her as an independent being, yearning to present with integrity her personality. It is she, principally she, who has seen the great responsibility contracted by human beings to achieve the peace and felicity of man on earth. If she gives life, she ought to preserve it. And look for the necessary means to achieve this end.

It is she who turns her back to the obsolete civilization of yesteryear to receive with open arms the new light that is approaching. That is gaining on us little by little. Wanting it or not. Only because of the overwhelming force of what is to be. As Jesus said, "What is written, has been written. And it is useless to oppose the wish of my father who is in heaven."

The new woman is nothing more than the product of circumstances and the new truth.

In synthesis: I say that there is no such new woman. Nor such feminism. Nor masculinism that would place at risk our tranquility. All concepts derive from a common source whose roots carry with them the needs that create the deeds.

Time and circumstances change life minute by minute. They are the powerful agents of erosion that modify the strata of social life as the wind and waters erode the layers of the earth. And from this erosive struggle emerges the truth we all know. And it is taken from the environment. From the level of our ideas. From the secret aspirations that compel the facts to the surface. And of all that exists around us.

In the intimate consortium the mutual influence of beings is felt. Lyric poetry is the archive for these studies.

As a corollary to my thesis I will read an intimate poem which I entitle: You made me strong

I was like the flower in the opium poppy: I closed the bloom trembling with strange emotion...

You rocked violently the calyx to the wind. And you made me strong...

I was like the drop of dew waiting for hot lips to come to drink of it.

You drank the freshness, and quenched your burning thirst. And you made me strong...

I was like the new leaf moving at the end of the branches and fearing the harsh wind that comes to cut it down.

You burnt the tender bud. And you made me strong.

The individual achieves the social, moral and aesthetic level of his family in particular, and of the people to whom he belongs in general. The cosmopolitan man is he who knows (here is a reason for the importance of traveling) the social, moral and aesthetic level of many families and of many people, an appreciation which allows him to have a critical understanding and knowledge of its flaws and conveniences. Against the antifeminists I will say that women are not predestined by nature to be inferior and even less the serfs of men. It is only that, defeated by the dear implacable winner, she has been his prisoner for many long centuries.

The inheritance of customs and of ideas is a biological-social fact.

Spencer has forecasted "a new era for humanity where morality would constitute an instinct that would be exercised automatically." Despite his respectable adversaries, like Guyau, for example, I believe it is possible to achieve such perfection—when the moral of society would guarantee the greater number of collective satisfactions and injustices would disappear, when morality would teach that the only admissible and just differences among men are those of character or psychological mental abstracts underlined by the environment, by nature which is superior to men, and when subsistence of material life assured, the work would be the development of the power to assimilate spiritual goods.

Why are we not to believe, a stage that is not too distant, in a beautiful humanity that struggles only for the acquisition of better ideas, better feelings, and more perfect yearnings?

When the spiritual bread and the advances of an altruistic science become more delicious than the acquisition of a beautiful cadillac or a summer home.

When the emotion of art and its success, or union with the beloved, makes our being vibrate with a higher feeling than the emotion of possessing a beautiful emerald or a diamond from the Urals.

When human interest and stimuli are placed in the field of worldly goods, then the light singled out by Jesus and however many wise men our humanity has seen will be reached.

Having broken the barriers of an exclusivist home by extending its activities in all senses, woman has began her period of training.

She has been self-teaching in contact with reality. She is trying out her strength in the limits of her domain and knowledge of all tasks.

This conscientious woman will comfort, consolidate the new home, know how to love her child and her husband better, and how better to educate her child.

Dramatic poets will not be able to create "Doll Houses" like the genial Ibsen where the home crumbles down because of a lack of mutual understanding.

But humanity always advances. Even in its falls and leaps there is future progress. We must make haste to work for the beautiful days of the reality we dream of today.

Inherent ability and the theory of evolution guarantee us that beautiful future.

Once hurled, the wave of whatever human aspiration is never detained, forever and ever, until the end of time, because the wave is circular and in constant motion in space and in the time of eternal things.

Now then: It remains for me to insist on the great responsibility of woman in all periods of time in the lot of men and the destiny of humanity. And as her conscience wakens each time the demands grow more deeply in the subconscious of her destiny in the future reality of the new civilization, and therefore of education.

Education ought to aspire to assure the spiritual growth of men. And woman is the only one capable of doing this because of her animic condition and because of the law marked on the curve of her breast.

She must give life with her body and spirit.

Thank you, Lord, for having created me a woman...

The happiness and peace of the world depend greatly on the new education that woman imparts and gives out.

On her weak shoulders weighs all the responsibility and the meaning of future civilization.

The bloody period of transition that we have lived through claims from grief the right to happiness.

Intelligences frustrated by wars, energies consumed by frivolous living are shouting: sense and wiser justice.

Be alert, woman, go on to fight and to win!

Paper read at the Club 2 de julio in San Pedro de Macorís, 1948.

Translation by Daisy Cocco De Filippis

HILMA CONTRERAS
San Francisco de Macorís 1913

Fiction writer and essayist, Hilma Contreras has distinguished herself during several decades for her dedication to her craft. In his *Narrativa yugulada*, Pedro Peix singles out Contreras as "the first Dominican woman short story writer." This assertion is arguable, as we remember the writings of Virginia Elena Ortea and Delia Weber, among the most distinguished forerunners of short fiction in the Dominican Republic.

What is unquestionable, however, is the existential angst, very much of our century and times, we find in Contreras' stories. Her collections point out, as I have indicated elsewhere, that Contreras has struggled with the problem of finding a voice, to give witness that she has lived not only in the existential space between two absolute silences, but also in the context of a Dominican society and a contemporary world whose prevalent condition is alienation.

I am including in this publication *Doña Endrina de Catalayud*, the only essay Contreras has published in book form. As an essayist, we find in Contreras a comfortable use of language which moves from a conversation with this character in the Archipreste de Hita's masterpiece, *El libro de buen amor*, to reflections on customs, lexicon and the definitions of the concept of honor in hispanic culture at the end of the middle ages and in the Dominican Republic of the day (1957). Hidden among perceptive interpretations of this episode in one of the classic works of Spanish literature, we find reflections on the situation of women in light of public opinion, and the role of the procuress, "trotaconventos". We need not extend the metaphor too far to remember that this essay was published in the "Ciudad Trujillo" of 1957 where women bore the weight of the harassment and the consequence of the abuses of the patriarchs and henchmen of the regime.

Selected Bibliography

Cuatro cuentos. Ciudad Trujillo: Editorial Stella, La Isla Necesaria, No. 3, 1953. 39 p.

Doña Endrina de Calatayud. Ciudad Trujillo: Impresora "Arte y Cine", 1955. 42 p.

El ojo de Dios: Cuentos de la clandestinidad. Santo Domingo: Colecciones Baluarte, Ediciones de Brigadas Dominicanas, 1962. 26 p.

La tierra está bramando. Santo Domingo: Biblioteca Nacional, Colección Orfeo, 1986. 134 p.

Entre dos silencios. Santo Domingo: Biblioteca Taller, No. 241, 1987. 129 p.

Facetas de la vida. Santo Domingo: Taller, 1993. 118 p.

Doña Endrina de Calatayud

Castile in the year thirteen hundred something. The reign of Alfonso XI and of the long fur robe with skirts, whose elegant width had not yet led to a prohibition by the Courts of Alcala de Henares regarding their use by women of humble lineage. A bloody era, that, of cruel revenge and of love. But a sensual love, lived as another escape valve, or better, lived where the ecstacy of life begins to flow from life itself. It is then that the transition from a primitive feudal society to a bourgeois society begins, when the king predominates as a consequence of the Crusades. The knight, no longer a hero or a soldier, finds himself facing a townsman, wealthy, sarcastic, and a parody of his chivalrous ideals. In order to defend himself from these, his rivals in terms of the ostentatiousness of his clothing, the noble embroidered his clothes with his coat of arms, alternating colors in the quarters of his shield. These suits became more popular later so that even the common people wore bi-colored breeches and doublet.

From the early middle ages, the ascetic branch of Christianity emanated, contrasting and at times mixing with an epicurean delight in life, a precursor of the Renaissance. From this stems the profound contrast or paradox of those times, and it is that amalgam of the profane and the sacred, of lewdness and devotion, which scandalizes us today. Medieval Christianity — in a rapture of mysticism— had taken in its anointed hands the massive form of the romanesque church, to raise it to the firmament like a prayer. But, if the gothic church signified the symbolic ascension of the religious spirit by its fine, airy needles of towers, it seems that the winds of the Renaissance determined an opposite movement. Having lost the gentling spirituality which had permitted them their flight to the heavens, men tugged at the mantle of the Virgin and God, pulling them toward earth. But we will learn what happened in that year of thirteen hundred and something if we enter the City.

When the traveller advances along a narrow, somewhat torturous and dark street toward the plaza of a town, his surroundings come alive in a multi-colored hustle and bustle around the shops and warehouses. A narrow stripe of blue sky unfolds itself at the top of the houses, while below creak the iron chains of lions and horses in a colorful display of inns and hostelries.

The knight comes from afar. There is mud on his breeches and on his roving mule. To the picturesque tumult of the shelters of the market they add another note of color with his short crimson gown, his blue toque with its pink stripe. Voices, shouts, and laughter blend with the bells of Saint Mary's in a froth of people. Someone recognizes the traveller and says:

"A long walk, Don Love"

Don Love crosses the plaza at the whim of the impatient mule, not without first taking a long look at the people leaving the church. Next to the escutcheoned portal of a house our traveller boldly pauses. It is cool outside. He dismounts and waits. At noon, the man he was awaiting arrives.

"—May God keep us in his peace— he says in a hoarse greeting.

The knight smiles, and since the new arrival is ready to continue on his way, he holds out his arm:

—I know you, Juan Ruiz.

Angrily, Juan Ruiz asks him:

—And you, who are you?

—Love, your neighbor. Doña Venus, my wife, sent me to watch the door of your rival don Melon while she "punishes" him.

—If you are Love, you cannot be here. You are a liar, you are false, you can save no one, but you can kill a hundred thousand. —Leave me alone. Go away."

The traveler with the crimson gown does not move for a bit:

"—Archpriest - he says— don't be so enraged, I beg you. It is better to hear my advice and you will succeed in finding another lady. Understand it well, my irate friend, your love does not work on every woman. Listen to me. Doña Endrina secretly loves Don Melon.

—Love, you liar, keep quiet. Go on your way!

—Don't insult me, because from a little fight great rancor is born. Come tomorrow to the plaza and you will see with your own eyes.

Oh God, how beautiful doña Endrina is as she comes through the plaza!

What a figure, what grace, what a long, swan-like neck!

What hair, what a mouth, what a complexion, what a gait!

With arrows of love she wounds you when she lifts her eyes!

In the glittering plaza the bells ring. And how well do her black widow's weeds suit doña Endrina. Woman of great ancestry, a young girl, this widow surpasses all the women of the city with her grace, beauty and lineage. She is the neighbor of don Melon de la Huerta, a clean living man, well mannered, as gentle as a lamb, the most handsome young man from the most noble home in the neighborhood.

According to the repeated descriptions found in the *Libro de Buen Amor* (*Book of Good Love*), beauty, youth and good lineage seem to be the most propitious conditions for love. This belief is confirmed in two lines from Don Love's response to the Archpriest.

"If you can, you don't want to love a peasant woman,

Because of love she knows nothing, she's like a simpleton."

This piece of advice corresponds to the aristocratic concept of beauty and love found in Provencal literature, where only ladies can be beautiful and only gentlemen can fall in love.

When, years later, the poet relates this event, he tells us that doña Endrina was from Calatayud. But he does not clarify whether she lived in that city or was merely born there. This biographical detail laconically authorizes all kinds of conjecture. If for many, the event took place in the Aragonese city, we are inclined to locate it in Castile. Castilian is the atmosphere of the city. Castilian is the profound silence of the houses, the simple robe and not the Italianate "coat" from Aragon, and above all, that tyrannical concept of honor, whose rule no one whose veins ran with that normal Spanish blood which history was distilling in its vials, could escape.

Doña Endrina came to Castile like doña Beatrice of Suabia, the queen who imported the wimple: through marriage. Doña Endrina of Calatayud, Aragonese by birth but Castilian at heart, united Castile and Aragon in her soul more than a century before the crown of the Catholic Monarchs covered both kingdoms.

And so, having been widowed by that most noble gentleman, Castilianized to the extent of reacting exactly like a woman from Guadalajara, life continued on slowly.

"—Ay! —complained don Melon to his neighbor— if such a disdainful beauty were not my close neighbor it would not be so difficult; because the further a man gets from the fire, the less he feels its heat. Ay! Woe is me!"

He said this while restlessly pacing through the wide chamber, inflamed in his heart and in his clothing. The youth had a very gentle bearing in his red tunic beribboned with white, and his bright red stockings. Back and forth he paced, moaning his afflictions, because he had been sighing over

Doña Endrina for two years. Many times he dared to try to woo her and he remained badly insulted by the scorn of the young widow.

Doña Venus came to help him move beyond such an impasse. She advised him to approach the young woman again, and the seed he planted began to germinate. Later, he would use one of those old crones, wise in the ways of the procuress. Love without a third party is never attained; it is like sown land without dew. Sooner or later one must rely on such intermediaries.

Having fastened his wide, gentlemanly cape on his right shoulder, don Melón is encouraged by the sound of his own voice as he puts on his purple hat, which goes so well with the happy knight's clothes.

"—I am going to speak with the lady,...
I hope to God that she answers me favorably!"

He goes out, walks down the road, observing everything, not knowing if he is seeing with his eyes or with his heart, and in the middle of it all, doña Endrina appears in the shimmering sunshine of the plaza.

Don Melon, don't get cold feet. Speak to her, do not be afraid to tell her of your desires. Don't you see that this haughty Aragonese woman dreams of loving you? Or is it that in your tribulations you have forgotten the wisdom of your advisor: that of a thousand pleasant women scarcely one will deny you their heart? In our times, women's teeth are unset precious stones and in their eyes there are happy little stars. But you are a knight of the Middle Ages, and she is one of its women. Go on, talk to her.

The daughter of Endrino is courteous, prudent, very exuberant and pretty; she was proud of her honor. She rarely left the house, as was the Castilian custom which is still maintained in small Spanish villages. But the black of her skirts and the frequent praying of the Psalter do not completely drown that little spark of desire, that unconscious little hunger for a new husband that she had deep within her. The desire grew little wings in the vague territory between the subconscious and the conscious. There he awaited his opportunity in the form of a neighbor. Like Marcel Proust we believe that just as microbes are on the lookout for an organism prepared to accept them, one does not fall in love with a given being unless one feels the necessity of loving. This conception of love, if we can make Eros prosaic, has the advantage —for women— of diminishing male arrogance since —according to such theories— it isn't men who defeat women but women who allow themselves to be defeated. No one defeats anyone. Everyone is defeated by him/herself. The struggle within these conditions comes from actions taken to fight prejudice and fear of a bad reputation:

"From a little thing fame is born in the neighborhood.
Once it's born, it's slow to die, even when it isn't true." and the fear of suffering and of ridicule:
"The woman who believed the lies you were telling
And believes the lies the men have sworn,
Her hands are twisted around her shackled heart
How badly her tears wash her face."

These last two verses are —in our judgement— some of the most beautiful in the whole Book. They are beautiful as much for their psychological content as for the visual nature of their imagery:
"Her hands are twisted around her shackled heart
How badly her tears wash her face."

A picture of the scorned woman, twisting her hands in pain and bathing her face in sobs. Black tears which do not clean, but rather, soil. Hands that squeeze the heart as if they wanted to wring its feelings out of it, and make its silence the unending scream.

The Archpriest's profound understanding of feminine sensibility, of a woman's feelings and reactions is amazing. It is a knowledge born of the confessional as well as the love he has for them. At each step, throughout the narration, we come across a rich vein of psychological experience. Some of these are relevant only to the Middle Ages, others are as relevant now as they were then, because the human heart persists through time, unchanged in the shifting surf of social customs.

Don Melon de la Huerta, an apprentice to those flirtatious knaves who in that licentious environment pursue widows and single women through the streets, "trying to speak with them, entering churches they went to and even sending them jewels and little gifts in order to corrupt them", has truly fallen in love.

"Oh God, how beautiful is doña Endrina as she comes across the plaza!"

His color changes, his hands and feet tremble, and he feels as though he will lose consciousness. He has prepared a few words but the radiant presence of his beloved and the crowds around him confuse his thoughts. He hardly knows her nor does he know where she is going. How could he talk of love in such a place?

"—My Lady..."

Doña Endrina had become serious.

"—My Lady, my niece who lives in Toledo, sends you her regards..."

The curious watch and one woman friend after another wags her gossiping lips. But little by little the plaza drains itself of people who slide out into the streets. Don Melon recovers his nerve. Next to the elegant lady he begins to open his heart in a whisper. His declarations of love can no longer be contained. He narrates, explains, swears to God, and suddenly, her apparently inattentive silence disconcerts him.

"I fear you have not heard anything which I have just told you."

Doña Endrina was thinking and mulling it over. Her heart had been listening, and her brain said no. Therefore she launched her wounding reply:

"—I do not give two figs for your words.

They deceive many others, many Endrinas."

But her reply does not stop her from accepting Don Melon's invitation to walk under the arcade of the plaza. It is certain that the invitation is motivated by the desire not to be seen by everyone walking down the street, and certainly, the modest, simple woman of the middle ages, might pray the psalter but still wouldn't refuse a love note slipped to her at a soiree. But, would she hide herself from the eyes of the public with a man whom she disdained? For the first time doña Endrina betrays her still unconscious attraction toward her handsome neighbor.

"Step by step doña Endrina enters the arcade"

As soon as the possibility of rumors is eliminated, doña Endrina softens and calms down. There in the shelter her exuberance shines forth. Despite her great pride, the closeness of the young man makes her look at the ground. While he begins anew to tell of his love and affirm his good faith with oaths, she listens, seated on the stone bench. With the sparkle of her eyes hidden behind her eyelids, doña Endrina listens meekly and because no one is watching them, don Melon loses his timidity and his tremors.

"—Grant me this, my lady, in good faith

That you will come another day, just to talk;

Because in talking, hearts come to know each other.

—This I grant you— replies doña Endrina. But, to

put his complacency in its place, she adds: —You, or anyone else.”

She is not afraid of being alone with her lover, except when the public might discover them, because people then would gossip and tarnish her good name. But in front of witnesses there is no problem in meeting to converse.

In doña Endrina we observe the constant preoccupation with honor, the theme of so many of the best dramatic works of Spanish literature. The preoccupation with public opinion is the source of honor. There is a horror of scandal. Don Miguel de Unamuno, in an essay on the Castilian spirit, studies with his customary keenness his obsession with "what people will say", which he synthesizes as follows:

"One shouldn't weaken, and if one does, nobody must know it, above all: nobody must know it, for God's sake, nobody must know it!"

Castilian honor is an extroverted sentiment, that is, above all it tries to conserve one's good name. It does not reside so much in the intimate satisfaction of having an impeccably clean conscience, as much as in retaining public respect. Therefore, nibbles at honor are bathed in blood and one dramatist carried the idea of honor to such extremes that a man punishes his wife with death for a supposed conjugal infidelity, although he is convinced of her innocence.

Even the Archpriest of Hita's wicked fourteenth century feels the chill of public dishonor. Even in those years of fondness for concubines, ladies and gentlemen of good manners held the Castilian concept of honor in high esteem and they were united in holy matrimony.

Doña Endrina, then, accepts the company of her lover in future meetings. But don Melon is inflamed by this first success and acting like someone who will take a yard when he's given an inch, asks to embrace her as if it were the time and place. It isn't the innocence of the young girl who answers him but the experience of the widow. She knows well that a lady will lose herself if she gives the valuable jewel of her kiss, and just how great the flame becomes when she is embraced.

"—This I do not grant you— she says—, only my hand."

You give him your hand, and in your hand, your heart, Endrina. Although the Archpriest does not recount it, you were surely sleepless within the curtains of your high bed, singing to yourself of the declarations of love of your genteel neighbor, his oaths, and the kiss you are afraid to give him. If not, why did you promise him your hand, you who are so proud, modest, and disdainful toward lying suitors? You are going around with an empty head, Endrina, if you even think of anything else. And that visit in the arcade is enough to make your mother doubt your good sense. Because you recognize him, you left for home early, before the dismissal of the Mass:

"My mother will be coming from Mass, I want to leave here early,

I don't want her to suspect that I have lost my senses."

Who do you hope to fool? Not don Melon, because he shares our thinking:

"—I love a lady—he says to doña Urraca— above all the others I have seen. She, if I'm not fooling myself, seems to love me."

A pretty woman who walks under the arcade and offers her hand to a man who asks for a kiss, is a bell that will chime if someone knows how to play her.

For the job of bell-ringer, no one is better than the busy procuress. Pious church-goer, mid-wife, and a peddler in a black cape, she weaves her tapestry of intrigue and enchantments between two hearts. The old woman cries out her wares to the sound of jingle bells: jewels, rings, pins. She cunningly sells her knickknacks for money and honor.

"—Buy these tablecloths for next to nothing!"

From across the patio doña Endrina says:

"—Come in, don't be afraid."

Doña Urraca loosens her smooth tongue. She mentions don Melon's name once, but doña Endrina doesn't notice. Only when the old woman questions her directly does the young woman come out of her distracted silence.

"—Who is this whom you praise and who has so much wealth?

—Who else can it be but don Melon de la Huerta!

With so much pride and dignity she replies:

—...Stop this preaching, because this smooth talker tried to trick me;

Many other things he came to try.

But neither he nor you can praise me."

Yes, much pride and even more dignity. But, how does this explain, if she feels so much anger towards her aristocratic neighbor— that she doesn't notice the first time his name is mentioned? Perhaps, its a ruse to hear more of the elegies about her suitor that doña Urraca has prepared. But her attention is interrupted when the stimulus or her interest flag; at least she shows a good dose of courtesy. We must remember then that along with being pleasant and beautiful, Endrino's daughter is polite. Courtesy causes her to pay attention to doña Urraca's exuberant conversation. On the other hand, the attention inhibits; that is, it denies all stimuli for the sake of one: in this case, thought. Doña Endrina is distracted because she thinks. About whom? About what? Only about the many boors who seek her hand for her estate? The reactions of doña Endrina contradict themselves throughout this dialogue with the bawd. These contradictions are born naturally out of the struggle between pride and fear on one hand, and on the other, the desire for love.

Don Marcelino MenÇndez y Pelayo, in his detailed and intelligent analysis of the *Book of Good Love*, underscores the careful progression of the seduction scenes of the episode we are discussing. Avoiding as far as possible repetitions, our preferences lean toward the unconscious manifestations of doña Endrina's amorous feelings. How weakly she responds to the subtle logic of the procuress who only sees happiness, pleasure and blessings in the house where the good man flourishes.

"—It would not be good for me to marry before the year is out.

Why not..."

It is not fitting for the young widow to marry before finishing her year of mourning. And this weighs on her, since she calls it a burden. Once again the tyranny of honor torments her. She would be defamed if she married before time, and even in the eyes of her second husband she would become less worthy. She wouldn't be so honorable.

Note that all these gradations of her intimate feelings are revealed in the first session with the seducer which ends or seems to end with the negative reply -weak but nevertheless negative— by doña Endrina, who declares that she cannot go against customs and she wishes to maintain her good reputation by not marrying don Melon or any of the hundreds who seek her hand in matrimony. It is the triumph of prejudice over the heart.

The plot quickly thickens. In the face of the imminent marriage forced on doña Endrina, perhaps by her mother, doña Rama, ("—Ah, the old hag! May the cross carry her to the devil, with holy water!") or astutely invented by doña Urraca for the purpose of collecting more money, don Melon's pain explodes.

It is an exuberant, profuse explosion, as vivid as an open vein. It is an important incident because of how much flows from the delicate description of the effects of love on the completely defeated doña Endrina. How far away is her pride!

"—The great love kills me...,
You see my will, advise me what to do..."
And the old woman advises her:
"—Well, if you want love, why don't you go to him?"

With the great burning passion there has been a change in the character of doña Endrina'a moral struggle. If the constant note of honor still reverberates —that fear and shame to which doña Venus attributes the chastity of women and the obstacle to the satisfaction of the female heart—, its persistence is losing ground. The profound complaint of the young woman which begins "Oh God...the loving heart —How many guises does it adopt in fear and trembling?" and ends "Now I want to die his death than live in suffering", reminds us in its tone of the sad words of Dorotea in the Sierra Morena when she washed her lovely feet in the clear water, but not her wounded heart. Two discordant pains which tire her night and day; there where love and honor are in conflict the happiness of one is the sadness of the other. Nevertheless, the custody of the mother represents an element of great weight in the new situation. Who knows if thanks to doña Rama, doña Endrina has not kept the promise made days earlier in the arcade.

"—I would do much for my love — she confesses to doña Urraca—, but keep my mother for me, never take her away from me."

In addition, where will she find a suitable place for the desired meeting?

A woman with doubts is easy to convince. Therefore, you, Endrina, blind in sight and understanding, do not see nor understand the rope held out to you. Above all else, you worry about your honor. The horror of a scandal, Endrina, the what will people say. "Your reputation will not be touched" — the old woman told you— "I will guard it well."

And you, did you believe her? Did you really believe that she was inviting you to play ball and eat ripe fruit in secret from don Melon?

For the Archpriest, yes. But we seem to feel your hidden anguish when a day after the feast of Santiago, as quietly as you please, in your robe, at noon, while the town was eating lunch, you went with the old woman to her house If doña Rama stayed to pray the psalter, much would weigh heavily on her.

Now doña Endrina is in the shop. Now don Melon arrives, forewarned, and he pounds on the closed doors and shakes them like cowbells...

"—Lady Endrina, my beloved!"

Why recount the rest, if your good fortune wanted to mislead the indiscrete stanzas. Oh, Endrina! How were you afterwards? These are your own words:

"The woman who believed the lies you were telling
And believes the lies the men have sworn,
Her hands are twisted around her shackled heart
How badly her tears wash her face."

Doña Urraca tells you to hide your problems when you are hurt to the quick. What do you expect, this is the Castilian concept of honor. The same one that Spain brought to our American lands: "Be quiet, watch your reputation; do not go out of your house" For God's sake, nobody must know! But the deceived woman in love does not understand these things. Complain and you defame yourself with your complaint. You will do worse, you are going to lose yourself because of the world.

How can this weakening be explained? The preoccupation with her good name operates on doña Endrina's decisions until the moment when the ardor of her passion makes her vacillate. Even then, she had in mind the fear of defamation: "that she would be found out." She agrees to go home with doña Urraca, even after she has heard the frequent warnings about taking precautions and guarding her reputation. And now, keeping the offense silent, she can keep her good name, but ignoring this, she only pays attention to her wound. From this it becomes clear that for doña Endrina honor means more than her good name. It is this and also the feeling of possessing it. A good public reputation and a mortified conscience is only partial honor. And if the great haste of their love is added, doña Endrina's defeat is understandable. No, she could not accept marriage after what happened, except to the man who caused her problem. Doña Urraca, not completely bad in those days, thinks of this and brings about the marriage. We do not believe however, that her influence over the will of men was so great that she could force them to restore honor. If don Melon returns to the beautiful Aragonese woman, he is strictly moved by his love for her. Not in vain do we note that this time when he proposes, the flirtatious aristocrat has truly fallen in love:

"Doña Endrina and don Melon, are now joined as one;
The bells ring happily for this wedding, and rightly so."

Translation by Margaret A. Ballantyne

AIDA CARTAGENA PORTALATIN
Moca, 1918-Santo Domingo, 1994

One of the most important Dominican women poets of the twentieth century, Aida Cartagena Portalatín began her literary career as a member of the group of poets in *La poesía sorprendida* (1943-1947). Her poetry from this period is defined by its lyricism and by its search for language. After the closing of the journal, Cartagena Portalatín traveled and studied in Europe, Africa and Asia.

She returned to her country in the mid-fifties and it is then when she publishes her best known poem *Una mujer está sola* (*A Woman Is Alone*) which, in the opinion of a new generation of critics, among them Chiqui Vicioso and the author of this introduction, is the defining moment of feminism in Dominican poetry.

Her literary career is defined by formal experimentation and her engagement with political causes. Her last collections of poems, *La tierra escrita*, *Yania tierra* and *En la casa del tiempo*, are the result of this personal quest which is also her cry of solidarity with oppressed humanity.

She also distinguishes herself as editor with her collection of "Brigadas Dominicanas" (ten issues between December of 1961 and March of 1963) and "Colección Baluarte" (12 issues). These publications gather the work of "engaged" artists in the immediate post-Trujillo era.

The defining characteristic of her contribution, however, is her identification with the African heritage in Dominican culture. In the essay included in this publication, a chapter in her book about African cultures, Portalatín expresses in a very personal way the dilema of the mulatto intelligentsia in different parts of the world.

Selected Bibliography

Víspera del sueño. Ciudad Trujillo: La Poesía Sorprendida, 1944. 10 p.

Del sueño al mundo. Ciudad Trujillo: La Poesía Sorprendida, 1945. s.p.

Mi mundo el mar: poema. Ciudad Trujillo: Editorial Stella, "La Isla Necesaria No. 2", 1953. 28 p.

Una mujer está sola. Ciudad Trujillo: La Española, "La Isla Necesaria", No. 5, 1955. 47 p.

La voz desatada: poemas. Santo Domingo: Ediciones Brigadas Dominicanas, 1962. 38 p.

La tierra escrita: elegías. Santo Domingo: Ediciones Brigadas Dominicanas, 1967. 99 p. comp.
    Narradores dominicanos. Caracas: Monte Avila Editores, 1969. 153 p.

Escalera para Electra. Santo Domingo: UASD, 1970. 153 p.

Tablero: doce cuentos de lo popular o lo culto. Santo Domingo: Editora Taller, 1978. 105 p.

La tarde en que murió Estefanía. Santo Domingo: Editora Taller, 1983. 212 p.

En la casa del tiempo. Santo Domingo: Editora Taller, Colección Montesinos, 1984. 75 p.

Culturas africanas, rebeldes con causa. Santo Domingo: Editora Taller, Colección Montesinos, 1986. 156 p.

Sedat Senghor - Dakar: African Experiences*

I have already said that a living being is made up of celebrations and memories. Also of experiences. I have in my hands the poem *Prayer of the Death Masks*, by Leopoldo Sedat Senghor, which brings me to recall how I fell like a skydiver in a gathering of not more than six poets who used to meet in a small informal salon. Some were from African Presence in Paris. I came because I learned that Senghor would be there that night and I had not seen him since he had stopped frequenting the house of Andre Breton and his wife. Also at the meeting was Aime Cesaire, the poet whom Breton, passing through Martinique, discovered. He was shocked by the depth of his work, finding that his poetry, like that of Senghor, resonated with the same surrealist technique of discovering a deeper and more mysterious state of exploration, "A mysterious and mystical life which develops just beneath the conscious".

I came to see Senghor, and also to catch up on the latest news. The founders of Negritude, including the Guyanese Leon Dumas, were discriminated against by other members of their race. Those who had denounced them had published a most scathing attack, for reaching out to the white intellectual elite, especially for the "adoption" by French-speaking blacks of the associative forms with which the surrealists experimented. In fact, the very structure of the African mentality had moved Breton to incorporate in his new movement the three major poets and founders of Negritude. For many African intellectuals Negritude merely had literary value since it separated itself from the political, social and economic evil which the colonial powers in Africa represented. This attitude was to become even clearer after the reform and broadening of its cultural horizons by Frobenius and Delafose two decades later.

In the war against them, these poets were condemned for thinking that Negritude had lost the appreciation of its own people and tried to introduce itself to the white civilization which it could only enter stooped over. In spite of these recriminations, Senghor continued to consider himself an African; he was considered by many to be the voice of his roots, the re-discoverer of the poetic potential of his nation and of his race.

That night Senghor came and sat with the others, like a bard in the retinue of a lord who sanctions deeds by singing of them. His poems always anticipate a theme of invocations, fitting for the ritual formulas and ceremonies of black Africa, fitting for a descendant of a noble of the Serere tribe. He continued on in Paris, surrounded by the fire of the poet-philosopher- politician Alexis Kagame and the writer-politician Ezekiel Mphalele, who proclaimed the need to revive the spirit of combat so that Africa could fulfill its destiny as the bearer of the torch of liberty.

The Negritude movement had split into several bands. Senghor remained in his own. Without a doubt he owed his formation to the missions, to his French education, to his academic status. He found himself caught between lines of fire. The long years spent in the metropolis had made him a citizen of two worlds. But he never bestowed his poetry on France because he felt a sacred obligation to the land of his birth, continually calling the members of his own race back to their ancestral roots.

* Selection from *Culturas africanas: rebeldes con causa.* Santo Domingo: Taller, Colección Montesinos, 1986.

That night of my free-fall a friend begged him to read, yet again, his poem Prayer of the Death Mask that Armand Quibert had included in his book, L. Sedat Senghor, the Poet and his Work. As I look at that poem now, beside me on my desk, I still hear the poet's voice.

> We may call out present at the rebirth of the world,
>
> like the leavening which is needed for white flour
>
> because, otherwise, who would teach rhythm to the dead world of machines and canons?
>
> Who would send up the shout of joy that will awaken the orphans and the dead at dawn?
>
> Tell us, who will give back the memory of life
>
> to the man whose hopes have died?
>
> They call us men of cotton, of coffee, of oil,
>
> They call us men of death.
>
> We are the men of the dance whose feet
>
> gain strength with each step on hard ground.

In the midst of the fire the prestige of Senghor as a poet, a scholar and a politician continued to grow. He was considered to be a glorious representative of his country. The French, without questions, meddled again in the affairs of the prosperous colony and made Senghor the first President of Senegal. For several years I did not see him again until the Pan- African Cultural Congress held in Algiers, where leaders of the continental liberation launched a violent attack against him for having abandoned the Marxist line.

The poet invited me to visit Dakar for the celebration of a festival of the area's native cultures in 1975. Poets of the western coast and the regions bordering the mighty Niger were also invited. There, in the middle of that enclave, Senghor, the Senegalese, begged with his own voice for the conservation of the yet unspoiled natural environment; for a re-evaluation of rhythmic cultural elements vis a vis western intellectualism and for the supremacy of cultural dynamism over western technique and formalism. His worries of old.

After re-uniting with old friends in the poetry and intellectual circles of Upper Volta which the Commission of the area formed, and of which I was made a member during the Annual Assembly of UNESCO which took place in Paris in 1965, the poet-president offered me the opportunity and support to travel to other lands. Of all the unforgettable impressions made during that trip, the most outstanding are those of the cultural and artistic programs of Dakar, a modern, European-styled city; the folk-songs, dances and drums of the villages; the probing words of the Nigerian poet Moukue, who attended the Festival:

> Here we are
>
> at the hinge of two civilizations.
>
> I am tired, tired of floating at the halfway mark,
>
> but where can I go?

Or the affirmation of the Ghanian poet Dei-Anang:

> Go backwards?
>
> Back to the days of drums
>
> and the festival dances in the shade
>
> of the sun-bathed palms?
>
> Or, go forwards?

Forward! But where to?
To the factory
where time is painfully threshed
in a human mill
in an eternal nightmare?

I am grateful to the poet for the opportunity to have experienced those peoples surrounded by a natural environment that is either a furious desert or an angry jungle, where the natives live together surrounded by misery, protecting themselves because they have learned the taste of spoiled meat.

At last, the formal farewell. The limousine to the airport and the thoughts and memories of my last night in Dakar with the rhythm and the voice of "Maria Kindanga is shameless, a shameless woman who wants her mistress' man..." I return. The water on the shores turns a diffuse grey. I love these memories because we are a mulatto people. I am. And I am happy to have been able to bring objectivity to, as well as correct, what is often asserted about Africa by scholars at home in their libraries.

Translation by Margaret A. Ballantyne

MARIANNE DE TOLENTINO
Santo Domingo, 1930?

For more than two decades, Marianne de Tolentino has distinguished herself as a journalist on culture and as a critic of plastic arts. Her writings have advanced more than one artistic career and are well read and respected at the national and international levels.

Presently, Marianne de Tolentino is the president of the Asociación de Críticos de Arte (AICA) in the Dominican Republic.

Selected Bibliography

Balzac y García Márquez. Santo Domingo: Taller, 1971. 39 p.

Estudio crítico. Santo Domingo: Biblioteca Taller, No. 60, 1975. 22 p.

El árbol de los pájaros. Santo Domingo: Editora Taller, 1983. 32 p.

WOMEN AND YOUNG ART*

Very recently we read, in an analytical article on a worldwide event, that the condition of minorities and women was becoming more difficult. Although realistic in its facts, the analogy is a surprising one. Women, who constitute a little more than half the population, are assimilated in ethnic minorities, small percentages of the population and whose means of oppression and repression have very different causes. Nevertheless, the word minority is striking, in another context, because of the theme of this conference, Women and Dominican Art Today.

We are not discussing past eras of Dominican Art, nor its great masters, themes which other colleagues have dealt with in their presentations. We are limiting ourselves to the importance of women in Young Art. It is an expression that is at once clear and complex, because there are artists from all generations bringing novel, fresh and bold changes to the imagery. They speak a visual or graphic language that can easily be considered Young Art after it is read. Nevertheless, the definition of youth in the arts, and in its primordial meaning, concerns age, artists younger than 35 years of age, a chronological frontier which is sometimes stretched to the 40's, truly a crucial moment in the life of a woman.

In the Young Dominican Art movement, women are a "minority", not in the sense of marginalization, but rather in the quantitative aspect, both in proportion to the total female population and fundamentally in relation to the number of male artists whose ages range between two and four decades of life. With an optimistic vision, we would say, estimating a global number of professional

---

*   Selection from Myrna Guerrero Villalona et al. *Mujer y arte dominicano hoy, homenaje a Celeste Woss y Gil.* Santo Domingo: Amigo del Hogar, 1995.

artists who fall into this age group, that the ratio is one woman to every five men. And we maintain that this "self-discrimination" has been improving, if we compare, for example, the post-65 (to 70) generation with the one which began to work in the 1980's.

We speak of self-discrimination, or at least of the inhibition that does not come from barriers imposed by the artistic community or the market. It comes more from the resistance related to the role of women in society. As Michele Mattelard says:

> *In the social sphere woman is called upon to exert a regulating force in relation to the subtle interplay of ideological and cultural mechanisms. In the economy (...) woman is invited into the workplace when she is needed, and then, frequently, sent back to the home when she is no longer needed. The transmitter of life, security of the family, base cell of society, the material, emotional and moral balance. Tradition makes her the pillar, the guardian, of the home.*

We cannot continue the quote, despite its interest, since it talks about a global and universal context, but it does still speak to female participation in artistic creative endeavors. Practicing her art is made difficult, especially for the young woman artist, because of her multiple roles within the family.

In the Dominican Republic even an unmarried woman artist does not enjoy the same freedom as a male artist. She continues to be a victim of the prejudices of her surroundings, which deny her the wider movement, contacts and meetings, which are not merely convenient but necessary for inspiration, dialogue and relationships in general. We believe that this surrounding pressure, these apprehensions and these ambitions for more substantial work, are, even in the last two generations and decades, elements which explain the quantitative imbalance of men and women in Young art. It is one thing, especially in the upper middle class, to bring your little girl to painting classes — this has always been the practice— and to children's workshops, and later support a vocation based on that. When it comes to a career that will guarantee the support of a family, it is preferable to direct the young woman toward a less uncertain field... and, in such a case, art constitutes an education and activity which are merely accessories. But, when it is a question of devoting oneself even half time to one's art, we observe that in these circumstances, young female talents become discouraged, withdraw and disappear.

We will give one more example of these problems. If a man is born and raised someplace in the interior where there is no opportunity -or if there is, it is deficient— of an artistic training or professional opportunities —museums, galleries, cultural centers, competitive spirit— if the adolescent male shows talent, naturally a solution will be found to enable him to move to the capital—or to the provincial capital if he is from a rural area. However, today the fear still exists that a young girl will lose herself, will be "corrupted" in the big city and her artistic "bohemia", if she cannot rely on the support of nearby relatives.

Now then, once these obstacles have been overcome, the future young female artist usually studies very seriously and completes her education —for the most part at the National School of Fine Arts, in accord with a tradition which dates back to the first class in 1945. She does not rely on self-training or an "informal" apprenticeship as much as men do. Generally in less of a hurry to enter the art marketplace than her male counterparts, a young woman artist looks for opportunities for apprenticeships, to perfect her technique, or for post-graduate work abroad, even if only for a few months. Frequently the young female artist is a graphic and/or advertising artist, art instructor, licensed architect —a profession in which discrimination against women is as strong as in the past —often the holder of a doctorate in aesthetic theory and practice. That academic focus is in accord with her disciplined and persistent temperament as well as with the educational habits developed since childhood.

The young female Dominican artist participates in collective "Mixed" exhibitions, if we can call them that, both multigenerational and for their own generation, as was the case of the Generation of the '80s Collective Exhibition. Nevertheless, there has still not been a group show dedicated solely to Young Female Art. Might it be a question of numbers? In part, yes, since there continues to be a clear minority of visual and graphic artists who are women. But we also believe that, among the young women, there exists a certain skepticism about introducing oneself in a gender segregated show. It is not always good for them from the point of view of their place and intrinsic value within Dominican art.

Also, this is a point which we will reiterate, in their professional development they are objects of a certain marginalization, exploitation or discrimination. We repeat, we are speaking about a particular field, not a general social condition.

It would seem that that sense of family, of a responsibility to the inner heart of the group, leads her naturally, if there have been no objections, to enroll in the Dominican College of Fine Arts. However, like their predecessors and teachers, the young women have not founded an Association of Women Artists as they have done in Puerto Rico. That is a very unique and powerful group since presently there is no comparable integrated College of any real merit. It seems that among us there is not a sufficient solidarity nor spirit of confrontation nor desire for dialogue to call for the creation of a special entity. The other reason is of a quantitative nature, but at the same time, if the young women artists or members of the art-related professions are united, perhaps their numbers will become an active factor in increasing not only the number but also the conviction of women who want to embrace art as a full-time career. Of course, this proposal does not include the hundreds of amateur women painters...

Young Art is a major support of the Competitions and Biennial Art Festivals through the participation of its members. It has been so since the first events, but that generational tendency has been growing. Therefore, the young female artists make a very strong showing in national competitive events in relation to their numbers, while, internationally, their disadvantage is more evident: up until now foreign curators almost never chose them and only one has been given an award in an international competition. In the domestic competitions, once they have crossed the threshold of selection, the female participants between 20-40 years of age —which make up more than 80% of the women present— are the clear minority in relation to their colleagues of the stronger sex, if we rely on a numeric evaluation. Therefore, in the Nineteenth National Biennial, where not a single woman was selected in the categories of ceramics, architecture and video, of the 171 total participants only 25 were women and of them, 21 were young. Of the 27 prizes awarded, women won four: one in drawing, one in engraving, two in the free category, an extraordinary achievement since there were only three entries total in that category! In the Fifteenth E. Leon Jimenes Art Competition, a few months later, 23 of the 162 contestants chosen were women; 20 of these were young. They did not receive any of the eight prizes given and only one woman received one of the three honorary mentions. Although we do not attribute despotic intentions to the decisions of the Juries, there is no doubt that more recognition would be encouraging for our young women artists, who nevertheless have not lost heart and continue to enter competitions.

We must reiterate the fact that recovery must direct itself to the condition of the Dominican woman in the global sense of her social, familial and economic roles. For art is one of the fields in which women are less marginalized, and in terms of the eventual exploitation or rejection of the avante garde, men face the same problems as women. This is particularly true of Young Art. In the various exhibitions, museums, cultural centers and collective or individual galleries, the female artists are on an equal footing. Likewise, in terms of art criticism, they enjoy exactly the same consideration and if a pen spews negative judgements, circumstantially or systematically, it is more a personal problem and in no way a discrimination based on gender. We would even go so far as to say that in terms of the attitude of the public and the critical establishment, there is a favorable disposition toward Young Art: curiosity and interest increase when the artist is a woman. We must point out too that male artists recognize and back their professional sisters.

It is true that paintings and painters dominate, and continue dominating in our visual arts and that at this time, sculpture, speaking candidly, plays the role of a poor relation. This tendency is confirmed in young women artists and is aggravated by market forces, by the price of tools, materials, and work spaces. Young, competitive female sculptors are needed, as innovators in materials and forms or as followers of a carving tradition. In the mixed media and in ceramics, the disproportion according to gender is frightening, but there is vigor, personality and concept. We could also give similar criteria for drawing and engraving, where new female artists are making their mark on new graphic worlds. If they distinguish themselves and excel in two-dimensional forms, psychological factors, such as delicacy, patience, discipline and introspection certainly are brought to bear, as is a rush for the commercialization of the work. Of course, female painters abound, in an equal proportion to male painters, and we will outline their respective characteristics. And, we would like to also point out that in the two latest generations, a multifaceted creativity is manifest, which if still not practiced, is attractive for its multiple values and perhaps as a way of continuing, even partially, to work with sculpture. On the other hand, there is cause for great happiness in the appearance of young women photographers, technically demanding, sharp and powerful in their images. Lamentably, no weaver has come forward, an artistic specialty -not just a craft- which has gained many practitioners in several Latin American countries.

Having examined the condition of the young woman artist on various planes, and having mentioned their modes of expression, we ask ourselves if a young female art with its own properties exists, and if, globally, it forms part of the context of our fin de siecle age. We believe that women's art is integrated within the panorama of contemporary young art. If an individual study of these transformers and reinventors of reality is necessary and permitted, because of her situation in her society and her family, and without denying visions and individual feelings based on her physical constitution and psychological development, we will one day soon speak of genetic predispositions. In our country, there is not, due to the factors already discussed, a separate culture or prohibitions of any type. The young woman artist of yesterday or today, fits the parameters of the national personality, including the "New Image." Her tendency is toward audacity, craft and imagination. We will see that her singular side has something fascinating about it, which concerns the complexity of her status, the sincerity of her language, the frequency of her emotional, personal, and collective message and a tenacious if not profound investigation.

We shall recall, in a very brief synthesis, the traits which we consider distinctive of the so-called Young Art in terms of the artists' ages in order to later try to delineate the modalities proper to female creativity. We observe, each time more purely, over the course of the past ten or fifteen years, not only an inclination to refute the division between representation and abstraction, passing naturally from one to the other - frequently within the same work or in the same series— but also in the resurgence of abstract art, with a lyrical discourse and a predilection for large formats. The image is constructed and interpreted with liberty; versatility rules. The pictorial and graphic signs integrate, without vacillation, biological, anthropological, zoomorphic and environmental and landscape elements with spots, lines and graffiti.

Almost always conscious of their origins and regional identity, the young also long to make their re-creation of the Caribbean world more urban and less bucolic, more pre-Columbian and less exclusively Afro- Antillean, more referential and less visceral. When they "represent" they elaborate their own super-realization in the same figures and in the combination of the signs. And their strange atmospheres are not simple to decipher, inspired by myths, syncretism and the subconscious. Certainly the commitment of Young Art has distanced itself from the traditional political and social iconography; their preoccupations revolve more around immigration and ecology.

Expressionism —a true tradition in Dominican art, and principally among women artists— continues to be in vogue, with its figurative or abstract vehemence, its magical-fantastic components, with its ingredient of rebellious humor. Its corresponding elegance rests in a virtuosity of drawing that permits everything, contrary to the disdain of the academy, tilted toward color and the baroque. Nevertheless, in their writings, no matter the stand, they mix styles and tendencies, the multiple references including the absorption of other national, regional or universal artists, materials and techniques. This is not about eclecticism and confusion, but rather a conscious goal, although the results do not always match the level of the intentions. Personal experiences, ideas, optical illusions constitute an authentic language for such tangible and intellectual processing; the installations are compound spaces which frequently contain an ideological charge.

Young Art has adopted a post-Modernism "a la Dominican", at once solid in its cultural identity and well-informed about movements and works abroad. This is not to confuse it with those silent plagues that any knowledgeable person will soon diagnose. A Colombian observer, Felix Angel, in 1986, on the occasion of a group exhibition by young Dominicans in the OAS, "Signs and Symbols of the Dominican Republic", has written the following in his analysis of the exhibition:

> *Romantic, without rules at times, the representational is combined with the abstract in a spontaneous and informal manner. The majority of the images make allusions to the regional realities and to attitudes which range from the rational to the magical. Above all there is an independence of artistic expressions, free from the constraints of the local market which unfortunately has often led established Dominican artists to make concessions of a decorative nature, diminishing their plastic authenticity.*

We do not think that there exists a different attitude on the part of women in the Young Art movement, and with existential and sociological shades inherent to their condition, we observe common denominators in their artistic formulations and aesthetic solutions. If, at times, we find an intimacy, a subtlety, a reserve, in short, an atmosphere which spontaneously we attribute to feminine inspiration and style, in other personalities and works, the provocation, aggression, and lack of restraint habitually attributed to the masculine mind and hand also bursts forth.

We also want to point out that despite the fact that they constitute a minority in the Dominican Young Art generation, just as in the case of male artists, new names continue to surface, some too new to be mentioned, others already showing undeniable promise or talent. Here, at the impressive exhibition organized by the artists and art historians Myrna Guerrero and Danilo Santos, an admirable and memorable event, are the majority of the young visual artists. As often happens, some have not had works available, or were not able to be contacted —such as Rosario Marrero and Charo Oquet, temporarily residing abroad. We must also name -and this additional list is probably also incomplete— Rosa Daisy Lantigua, winner of the María Ugarte Prize in 1994, Anabelle Batlle, Zenobia Galar, Milagros Arias, Yolanda Naranjo, Marisol Cabrera. Not all of them belong to the Generation of the 90s, but the female presence is growing, and we hope that it will be strengthened, in number and in artistic merit, thereby demanding consideration in a broader context.

In terms of style, in painting as well as in drawing, the young woman frequently continues the lineage of her elders: the neo-expressionist exuberance requires their energetic expression, decisive outlines, its emotional, at times furious, brushstrokes. It is fitting to associate drawing and painting, since in the pictorial, color and line reinforce one another, in the graphic, chromaticity often intervenes technically and expressively. In this respect we will mention Maritza Alvarez, Yolanda Monción, Anabelle Batlle, Scherazade García, Luz Severino, Belkis Ramírez, among others. In the works of Alette Simmons-Jiménez and Inés Tolentino, the stylistic references are multiplied in post-Modern versions; in Amaya Salazar, they are inclined towards Symbolism, and in Grecia Rivera, "sensitive geometry" currently predominates.

We were alluding to a certain intimacy, not to be confused with what amongst ourselves we qualify as "infantilism" or oversentimentality, but rather an intimacy which values the family and the female social condition, the importance of the everyday domestic world and psychological and affective expressions. Amaya Salazar constucts, in different versions, sentimental atmospheres where the creatures resemble one another physically and spiritually, in a luminous stillness. Inés Tolentino rewrites the memory of the past and of childhood, while all the shades of nostalgia and the time that has passed, "of a strange flavor and a particular form of mystery" according to the appreciation of the critic Laura Gil. Alette Simmons also has depicted and demystified the woman at home, (cocoon or cell?) These are examples of strong and accusing works within a feminine, not feminist, poetic.

Humor is sharpened in the drawings and paintings of Maritza Alvarez, with her canine fauna, her schematic and neo-infantile iconography. Other young female artists content themselves with the manipulation of the image based on the sign, the sign based on the image, such as Luz Severino — one of the stars of Dominican engraving— with her chairs, or Yolanda Monción with the umbrella, things that they animate as though they were living beings. In several of those that we have just mentioned, there are allusions, direct, symbolic and metaphorized, to the situation of women. This allusion is most highly charged in the work of Yolanda Naranjo, and is present also in the surprisingly gifted Scherazade García and her extremely masterly pictorial ability.

Inhibitions and taboos do not weaken the expression and the transmuted pulsations of the young female artists such as Grecia Rivera in her erotic series. And certainly, they do not limit themselves to a psychological transcription or reconversion of the present -object, surroundings, subject, "I"— Taino pictographs; the voodoo pantheon and the "vevés"; the journey through past eras of Western art shows through in the ritual paintings and drawings of Gina Rodríguez, the experimental Rosario Marrero and the referential richness of Inés Tolentino.´

We are still waiting for the appearance of an important sculptor in the Young Art generation. We celebrate Belkis Ramírez for her outstanding work —recognized at the Worldwide Biennial in Johannesburg—, using resources from wood engraving in the third dimension, raising a voice of protest against the barbarousness striking at people as often as at the environment. Certainly Belkis Ramírez, committed to her own aesthetic renewal, is affirming her status, with a growing efficacy, in multiple graphic and visual values. Today, it is in ceramics that the young woman artist is making her statement on sculpture, with a "sophisticated" rusticity, with wrinkled and decorated matte textures, a mixture of anatomy and archaeology; here Jacqueline Soto and Grecia Rivera come to mind. Like the male sculptors of their generation, the women must deal with the lack of good materials —traditional or synthetic— and it is very difficult for them to realize their goals, which happened to Milagros Arias, a passionate defeat of material and formal experimentation.

We would like to dedicate a special elegy to the young female photographers ... because finally a voice is raised, or better, a woman's eye has opened in Dominican photography. We are pleased that they have chosen to express themselves in the fundamental idiom in which the "writing of light" is inscribed and best read: black and white. Several women show much promise: Clara Barletta, so effective with her images of childhoods which are abandoned or maturely poetic; Mary Rosa Jiménez, with her very beautiful and conceptually profound Parisian scenes. Marisol Cabrera not only shows a social look through the eyes of her camera, she simultaneously examines it in her painting. Nor can we leave out the young talent, Mariana Balcácer, who has brought an excellent training to a multiple and transcendent vision of the contemporary world, without forgetting her impeccable technique. We also discover Scarlett Victoria.

The young Puerto Rican artist Nora Rodríguez, winner of the Prize of the Second Biennial of Caribbean and Central American Painting, said the following in regard to the meeting on female artistic production:

> *In this room the works of artists from different places in their professional development share space. This gives us then, a rare opportunity in the art world to cooperate instead of compete, to support one another from diverse points of artistic processes. Aided by this spirit of solidarity, the possibility for a constructive dialogue is growing.*

That comment fits this exhibition-seminar perfectly. We sincerely congratulate Myrna Guerrrero and Danilo de los Santos for this reconciliation and fruitful dialogue among male and female artists. In this way we will see male and female professionals in graphics, in fine arts and Young Art: each one, man or woman, contributes to the advance of Dominican art today and tomorrow. They share the same exalted territory, a single challenging responsibility toward his/her country, and international perspectives. We must not forget that it is not infrequently the minorities who stimulate historic evolution and the treasure of a nation!

Translation by Margaret A. Ballantyne

CELSA ALBERT BATISTA
La Romana, 1944?

Celsa Albert Batista is a teacher and historian who graduated Magna cum laude in 1977 from the Universidad Pedro Henríquez Ureña as Licenciada in Education, Minor in Literature. She received her Masters and her Doctorate from the Universidad Nacional Autónoma de México, with honors in Latin American Studies and History.

Dr. Celsa Albert Batista has held a number of positions at the university level including professor of Dominican history, world history, culture. At present she is the Director of Curriculum and Educational Assessment at the State Education Department in the Dominican Republic and Dean of Humanities and Director of the Department of History at the Universidad Católica Madre y Maestra. Dr. Albert Batista has presented numerous papers at national and international conferences, in such diverse places as Venezuela, the United States and Mexico. The central theme of her presentations is the influence and importance of Africa in American cultures and societies.

Selected Bibliography:

Mujer y esclavitud en Santo Domingo. Santo Domingo: Ediciones CEDEE, 1990. 130 p.

Las ideas educativas de José Martí. Santiago de los Caballeros, Rep. Dom.: Universidad Católica Madre y Maestra, 1992. 2da. ed. 1996. Premio UNESCO. 205 p.

CHAPTER 2: INTEGRATION OF THE AFRICAN WOMAN IN THE SYSTEM OF SLAVERY DURING THE COLONIAL PERIOD

Slavery is a means of production which rises from the ashes of the primitive community (the primitive communal regimen) and which offers humankind the creation of the state as an organ which provides, systematically and hierarchically, the hegemony of one class or group over another.

In the beginning, slaves were not originally black Africans, but later, Africa became a major source of slaves through historic necessity. Let us recall that the four centers of ancient civilization were: Egypt, Mesopotamia, India and China, and all of these practiced slavery without linking blacks to it. Likewise, in Greece and Rome, slavery existed without this link to blacks.

African slavery in America, then, should not be seen as a damning of the black, but rather as a result of the class struggles of a concrete, historic period of human social development. For example, Hispaniola, as the center of the colonial enterprise in America, reflects these contradictions since the characteristics of the means of production are not genuinely slave-based, due to the fact that while capital is generated by so called pre-capitalist means, it is done so on the base of social relations built on slavery. The coexistence of these two types of economies not only emphasized the ties and char-

---

* Selection from *Mujer y esclavitud en Santo Domingo*. Santo Domingo: Ediciones CEDEE, 1990.

acteristics of the transition from one type of production to the other, but also the mechanisms utilized by the power elite in the history of the society in order to permanently maintain their power. One must also consider the fact that slavery was a fundamental spur for the development of capitalism.[1]

The subordination of women as a form of slavery dates back to the patriarchal structure of classical societies in which the woman, while not banished from the means of production, principally fulfilled her role as producer of children, as provider of sexual satisfaction for men and as a domestic. This tended to reduce her capacity to develop as a human being, equal to men, a result blessed and encouraged by traditional male chauvinist societies. This ideology or concept of women keeps her, in the majority of cases, in a state of psychological slavery which forces her to assume a dependent, weak role and forces her to avoid or fail to achieve her potential as a woman in all the interactions which are rightfully hers as a member of society. In this regard Margarita Cordero states:

> *Patriarchal ideology is any system of values which maintains the supremacy of the male over the female. It is an ideology which is not merely exclusive to the dominant social sectors, but permeates all the men of the subjugated classes as well.*

The obviousness and truth of these observations in the development of contemporary society points to a situation of social discrimination against women, no matter their racial origin. But the situation becomes much worse if we go back in time three centuries and look at the situation of the black African slave woman, or in contemporary society if we look at this phenomenon as regards the black or mulatto woman.

In addition to the characteristics of the patriarchal society, slavery arose as a result of wars in the framework of ancient times, when vanquished peoples went on to be enslaved. In the case of women, this meant being doubly subjugated by both the system and by her own social condition.

2.1 The African Woman in the Development of Pre-Colonial Society

The role of the African woman within the parameters of pre-colonial society in Africa is tied to the development of production in economic activities. Therefore, her image reflects in African life an important role in economic activities from the colonial era to the present, sharing with men the different tasks which characterize the African economies since before colonization. Among these are: agriculture, gold-mining, hunting, fishing, shepherding, tending animals, pottery making, manufacturing and artisanry. To these must be added the so-called domestic labors, housekeeping, caring for babies, and others; all of which demonstrates the noteworthy responsibility of women within the framework of societal development.

This function of women in the economy has two fundamental meanings whose principal parameter is the mythology which conforms to the African cosmovision as it refers to fertility. The woman is seen in light of these ideas and beliefs as a fundamental element in the economy and in the growth of production. Therefore, in the field of agriculture, the men will prepare the fields and the women will dedicate themselves to sowing and harvesting. In regards to procreation, women will have the responsibility for giving birth to the children that society needs.

Regarding political activity, the customs of pre-colonial Africa are organized in accord with the

---

1 Karl Marx cited by Juan Bosch in his work *Dominican Social Composition*, p. 9.

caste system, and the characteristics of clan and tribal societies, in which wealth is seen as an indication of political power for a woman. Achola O. Pala, in a study of the situation in Kenya states the following:

> *In practice, it must be pointed out that in recognition of a woman's ability as a the provider of basic nutrition and as the producer of children, her rights to the use of land and cattle are strengthened. This security gives women a "voice" — a political position— in the community. A man who is unjustly cruel to his wife, who disregards his family duties or restricts her rights as they have been defined, exposes himself to the sanctions of the men of his family and of the community. Such behavior can cause him to lose his social position and prestige.*[2]

It is also important to point out the advantages which maternity and the production of food brought, since they were very highly regarded by the community. Nevertheless, this position should not lead us to generalize about the treatment of women in Africa, because if we look at infertility or the lack of property, women are made the victims of a double exploitation and of complete dependence on their husbands.

In the opinion of a few authors, this treatment is due, in addition, to the fact that they are women.[3] Likewise, in several societies of Western Africa, such as those of the Soca, the Swazi and the Fula, the men look for a submissive, almost servile attitude from women. Therefore, although women in these societies hold property, they are not guaranteed an equal social or political position with men, not to mention any lack of personal freedom.

In reference to Mandingo society, Madina Ly, in a study of the pre-colonial African economy, places emphasis on the work of women in the region of the Northwest of Africa extending to the south of the Ivory Coast. This study focuses on the cultivation of family fields in which women toil several hours a day from Monday to Friday, and the rest of the time tend the individual fields close to their huts. Until ten in the morning they do their housework which ranges from feeding children to fetching water; later they gather with their co-wives and daughters to tend the fields. They return to the bustle of the home until ten at night when they cook and clean and then take care of the nightly activities which include teaching the children and teenagers the stories and legends which they learned as children from their parents.

As can be seen, the Malinke woman is an exemplary work companion to her husband and an indefatigable worker in all that has to do with the development of society, working in excess of fourteen hours daily. It is important to note that in this regard the Malinke woman is helped by the old women who also take care of the adolescents at night.

Madina Ly, paraphrasing Leopoldo Seda Senghor states: "Woman is the beginning and the end of the Mandé."[4]

In respect to the social role of the Malinke woman, much has to do with the type of matrimony, such as in the case of polygamy, where the first wife has a very important role and is given the same

---

2   Pala, Achola O. *La Mujer Africana en la Sociedad Precolonial,* Serbal/UNESCO, 1982. pp. 79-80.

3   Information given by O. Pala in the study *La Mujer Africana en la Sociedad Precolonial.*

4   Pala op cit. p. 148.

obedience from the other wives as the husband. As a mother she enjoys the great love, admiration and respect from her children, as they reward her maternal self-sacrifice and responsibility.

The sister is loved by the brother, who should help in any way possible. When a woman's hand is asked for in marriage, and after a process of negotiations with the suitor's family - if these have been concluded satisfactorily— she goes to take part in the chores at the fiance's home. In that group virginity is required, adultery is punished and divorce very difficult.

As concerns the religious aspect, the woman is the object of great admiration and believed to have powers to communicate with the ancestors; these powers are considered to be even superior to those of men. The making of fetishes as protection in dangerous situations was one of the religious practices that conformed to the beliefs of that society.

The social and familiar deference which women enjoyed in the Mandingo region were important, yet it cannot be said that she was equal to men. However, this respect enabled her to exercise notable political influence, as in the case of the mothers of kings, the favorite wives, women friends of the chieftain and his sisters. Nevertheless, in respect to political decisions, it is rare to find occasions in which women played a determining role. This brings us to other phenomenon which characterizes northwestern Africa, but which points to the unequal treatment of women, despite their personal achievements and their accepted responsibilities as social beings.

As we have seen, the African women who participate in the forced diaspora to America have a broad and effective experience in the social, economic, cultural development of African society. Their integration in the new colonial environment in America, although forced on them, signifies the presence of the special conditions and qualities of the Mandingo woman because geographically this is the source of so many contingents of men and women who are uprooted from their lands and dragged to Santo Domingo and other places in America. There they will be governed by an inhuman and abusive system, ignorant of individuality and human dignity.

2.2 Interation of the Black Woman in the Work of Slavery and her Role in the Socio-Economic Formation of Santo Domingo

Men and women were equally victimized by the machinery of slavery and the variations which existed can be explained in relation to the different goals of the Crown. They were dispersed through various regions according to the wishes of the authorities, the administrators and the colonists.

The Africans, after being dispersed for their incorporation into the various activities of the colony, were divided into three types or classes, tied to the work assigned to be done. These were: field slaves, for working in the sugar mills, the plantations and farms; day laborers, whose masters rent them out for this purpose. They performed various tasks such as selling crops. What they earned or the profits they made were for their master. In the third class we find the domestic slaves, whose work was done in the bosom of the house, estate or palace.

The female African slave was also incorporated into this system, and her classification depended on her "nature" and the goals of the system. As a field slave she worked primarily for the subsistence of the farms called "conucos": planting, cultivating and harvesting; in the caring for domesticated animals, etc., in which she would have some help from the old men and slave children.

As a day laborer she was hired out and worked for the benefit of the master: she was a vendor of food stuffs, cloth, firewood, flowers, clothing, etc. She was required to hand over a daily sum to her master, and she was under threat of punishment if sales were slow. This custom of punishing slaves if sales were not good led, in the opinion of Larrazábal Blanco, to prostitution for the women, and robbery for the men. The proof of this assertion is found in a Royal Decree made in Madrid on December 2, 1672:

> *It is given to understand that in the Indies, the owners of slave women send them to sell things and if they do not bring back the presupposed earnings they are let out at night in order to earn said amount by dishonesty and lewdness. Therefore I order that the Viceroys etc., of all the Indies, do all in their power to punish such scandalous abuse, that they give orders, imposing appropriate penalties, so that black women, slaves or free, do not leave their master's homes after dark; and the Bishops and Archbishops are charged with quickly finding a solution to this and any similar abuse.[5]*

The Decree also included all the Indies, which shows that this practice was widespread throughout the empire. The alarm of the Monarchs which prompted a decree to stop this activity probably was not sufficient to guarantee that the decree would be successful, since we know of the laxity in enforcing laws, especially when these favored the native peoples, the free blacks, the slaves and mulattos.

To our judgement, the day laborers were the cause of another facet of the wildness of the Spanish colonies. The freedom with which they were able to carry out their assigned tasks over the years removed them from the circle of their masters and male and female slaves united in a phase of great cultural creativity, both material and spiritual. This behavior, on many occasions, took place with the complicity of the owner, as we see it, as an incentive for a particular laborer because it led to greater earnings for the former. Our assertions are supported by some regulations found in the Negro Code. These appear without a date, but we surmise that they correspond to the first half of the Sixteenth Century, because the style and content is similar to those dictated in April of 1544, on page 144 of the Negro Code. It reads:

> *3a. Because, in this city many negro men and women work at diverse occupations, deals and contracts as agreed upon by their owners and likewise both parties have agreed upon the amount to be handed over per month, week or day, and this causes many inconveniences especially when they do not recognize their owners nor enter their homes unless it is for the payment of the daily wages. And little by little more liberty is taken, so that it is hereby ordered that from now on, no person who has slaves can enter into a direct-indirect contract with them so that if they are hired in this city without a license from the city council it will be a crime; that those who work for a daily wage be required to hand over what they have earned, and not a previously agreed upon sum. The owner will gather and keep their blacks in their home at night to sleep, and will guarantee that they not leave until morning as agreed. If he or she is hired out for more than one day, that this master be held to the same regulations and that he or she not be permitted to leave the house, beyond sleeping there nor do they hand over money only to their owner. Any infraction of these regulations will result in a fine of three gold pesos to be divided in thirds as follows: one third to the coffers, one to the judge and one to the plaintiff.*

5 Malagón Barceló, Javier. Op cit p. 254.

> *5a. No one may deal with them, nor sell them anything, nor buy them even a trinket but their own master, and if they do sell things, they must be wild things or things of little quantity and with permission of the master or the mayordomo or estate manager in writing previous to the sale, and they must bring the slave with them, or, if it is in the city, it must be with a legal license because there are some blacks who on feast days and Sundays sell things from these warehouses in the country.*

In addition, the colonial administrators had day laborers of both sexes and the wages or sales they earned were used by the town councils for the development of the capital city, in the construction and repair of streets, public establishments, etc., which means that slaves were taken advantage of as a source of public labor.

As a domestic, the slave woman undertook a broad and important function, principally because of the type of relation she established, not only on an affective level, but also due to the role played in everyday life, in customs, where the process of the fusion of the tasks of master and slave were going to create or establish the Dominican and/or American way of doing or being.

Therefore, this woman worked on domestic chores in general: cooking, cleaning, laundry, manufacturing, etc. In these tasks the African woman would transmit her own customs, learned in Africa, linking them to those of the master.

Another transcendental function which the domestic slave undertook was, in our opinion, that of the wetnurse-nanny and nanny; although it was a job which was forced on her by the irresponsibility of the white mother or the aristocratic customs of the day, the African woman in this role as slave-mother to kings and lords, gave life and love to her surrogate offspring. This created a new type of emotional relationship between these women and the children of Europeans and white creoles. In addition, this became an important way to transmit African culture.

The living arrangements for single slave women consisted of rows of huts separated from the men. When chores began they formed two lines, one facing the other. In between these two rows of huts the women washed clothing and did other chores. These huts were dirty and unhygienic, as Esteban Montejo tells us in his interview with Miguel Barnet for the latter's book *Biography of a Runaway*.[6]

Punishments differed from those of the men, but were not less severe. They depended on the nature and circumstances in which the woman was found, and so, the slave woman was also thrown into the stocks, taken out to a patio and tied to the trunk of a tree or pillory where she was whipped. Slaves were given between 50 to 200 lashes; in 1784, the Carolinian Negro Code legislated a maximum of 25 lashings as a punishment due to the frequent death of slaves at the end of their owner's or overseer's whip. Something else which came about through legislation must also be pointed out. In the case of Hispaniola we found the second agreement from May of 1544 which states:

> *Under said penalty it is ordered that no black woman leave a house in the city to go to the country for any purpose that may be related to the forests or the orchards and that whoever may find her must take her, bring her back and put her in the stocks until she be brought to court so that said punishment can be ordered. The*

6 Barnet, Miguel. *Biografía de un Cimarrón*. Colección Mínimo, Siglo XXI Publishers, Mexico, 1976, p. 37.

Spaniard who brought her in shall receive a reward of three silver reales *from her owner.*[7]

It is important to note that owners who did not mete out the mandatory punishments for their slaves were fined by the authorities. The character of the owner or colonist always influenced the punishments and the general relationship between slave, male or female, and the owner, as did the personality of the overseer, the one person closest to the slave.

In the case of African slave women we find that very often it was their mistress who gave the lashings. The sanctions were generally for escaping, complicity in acts of violence, the death of the mistress, failure to complete work assigned and jealousy on the part of the wife, etc.

In applying the punishment, the foot was the instrument most commonly used on slave women on Hispaniola (Haiti and the Dominican Republic) as well as in Cuba, Brazil and elsewhere. In Cuba and Brazil, when a slave was pregnant, a hole or cavity was dug and the woman put face down so that her stomach fit into the cavity and the stipulated punishment was given to her back. This was done so as to not injure a future slave.[8] There is, at times, evidence of Sadism in certain relationships between owners and slave women. For example, Larrazábal Blanco y Deive in studies on slavery in Santo Domingo tell the story of a pregnant woman whose master killed her with a dagger as she bathed. Several days later a group of other slaves killed him and became runaways. According to Esteban Montejo, there were dungeons which contained whips where the women were sent for punishment. There were also subterranean wells where slaves were thrown, and where they generally drowned.[9]

In the case of Jamaica, Edward Brathwaite[10] relates that a screw would be put in a slave's thumb until it bled and then he would be sent back to work.

The bad treatment, hard labor and lack of care of African slave women was so evident that it came to the Crown's attention and led to the promulgation of Laws 2 and 3 of Chapter 26 of the Negro Code.

LAW 2

The notable rate of infertility among women field slaves as compared to their urban counterparts has been attributed to the illnesses they contract in the dampness and humidity of the fields when they go to work so early, as well as to the disturbances to which they are exposed on the estates where the number of males is so much higher.

Therefore, owners and overseers must take utmost care, first not to permit them to begin their work until the sun has dissipated the noxious vapors of the earth, that they work shorter hours and that single women are given separate rooms cared for by the old women, day and night, and a room for each married couple.

LAW 3

Strenuous or dangerous work shall not be imposed on pregnant slaves in the months prior to

---

7   Malagón Barceló, Javier. Op cit p. 147.
8   Eduardo Galeano gives this information in his book *Las venas abiertas de América Latina.*
9   Miguel Barnet relates this fact in his *Biografía de un Cimarrón.*
10 Brathwaite, Edward, "Cuadernos Latinoamericanos." UNAM 83, Mexico, 1978.

giving birth, during which time they shall receive better food, and later, taking painstaking care of the upbringing and education of their progeny.[11]

These texts reveal and partially confirm our thesis that one of the principal objectives of the presence of African woman in the colonial period was to be a "slave factory"; these texts also show the inhuman treatment which she received, especially in the case of the rural slave, thanks not only to her owner but also to her fellow slaves.[12] Although these imperial laws tried to prevent the continuation of these abuses for their daughters, the same situations are found after three centuries of colonial life and female enslavement.

The variety of areas in which the African woman slave, and later, the creole (that is born in America) black woman worked are evidence of the importance she had in the economic development of her day. Forced to do this work, often for 12 hours a day, her experience and her work ethic from Africa are seen in her attitude throughout the centuries: she is intelligent, nervous, hard-working, worried, sufficient, suspicious, daring, capable, diligent, sacrificing and tenacious, qualities that have accompanied her into the present. This is the work ethic that the African woman transmits as part of the cultural heritage of the Dominican woman, urban or rural. She fulfills various functions, from multiple domestic chores, to agricultural chores to work as a street vendor, even to those chores supposedly reserved for men.

In our present context there are other schema which direct our economy, and these are not entirely racial. However, it is undeniable that all the rich are whites or very light skinned mulattos, and all the poor are blacks or mulattos with dominant negroid features. Analyzing the characteristics of the present economy and the role of women of color in it, we quote Rubén Silié (et. al.), when he states

> *The Dominican economy, in general, is a capitalist economy, that is, world-wide capitalism has penetrated the nation's economy and established its way. The black Dominican woman is part of this economic reality. Despite its capitalist nature, influenced by the United States' economy, the Dominican economy is based, above all, on capitalist agricultural production and an agricultural subsistence economy.*[13]

If by the term "of color", one means black people, one does not fully capture the Dominican reality since nearly 90% of the population is of mixed origin and therefore, "of color". The population in the broad sense is mulatto, and especially so in the case of women. But the general population maintains a hierarchy in its social structure in which racial mixes are evident. Nevertheless, those who occupy the three lowest strata are, in their majority, blacks or mulattos with dominant black features. But it is important to note that in the last 25 years there has been a notable rise in the social and economic status of the persons with the features just described. These clarifications are made in order to better delineate the phenotypical characteristics of the Dominican woman that are found in the Dominican socio-economic context to which the author made reference in the quote presented above.

Translation by Margaret A. Ballantyne

11 Malagón Barceló, Javier. Op cit p. 215.

12 This situation is confirmed by Esteban Montejo in *Biografía de un Cimarrón* (op. cit.) who tells us that the obligatory sexual abstinence of the male slave due to the lack of women led, in many cases, to sexual deviancy among male slaves.

13 Silié, Ruben, et. al. *La Femme de Couleur en Amérique Latine* Anthropos Editions, Paris, 1974, p. 177. (Trans. by the author.)

M A R G A R I T A C O R D E R O
Santo Domingo, 1947?

Journalist, political pundit and researcher, Margarita Cordero has made a name for herself through the seriousness of her writings and her indefatigable work on behalf of her political ideals. Cordero's columns in *El siglo* have earned her a first-rate reputation and the respect and the trust of her readers. Currently Cordero is the general editor of the journal *Rumbo*.

Selected Bibliography:

Mujeres de abril. Santo Domingo: CIPAF, Ediciones Populares Feministas, 1985. 187 p.

Nicaragua: las mujeres frente al proceso electoral. Santo Domingo: Editora Búho, Ediciones Populares Feministas, 1985. 54 p.

Evaluación general de avances y obstáculos para la participación de la mujer en el proceso político del país. Santo Domingo: UNICEF, 1987.

Mujer, participación política y procesos electorales (1986-1990). Santo Domingo: CIPAF, 1991. 121 p.

et al. *Con trabajo de mujer: Condiciones de vida de la mujer rural*. 2nd. ed. Santo Domingo: Centro de Solidaridad para el Desarrollo de la Mujer, 1991. 46 p.

Comunicaciones para la mujer en el desarrollo. Santo Domingo: CIPAF, 1994. 97 p.

The Definitely Forgotten Woman*

There was a common role, as can be seen in reflections and testimonies. There were also exceptions to this role, affirmed in careful and detailed memories of the events. But either one of these represents only a partial picture of the role women played in the early days of the war, when the sporadic nature of the battles had not yet imprinted their burden of habit on the daily tasks of the combatants. The former is a partial reflection because it is true but too general; the latter, because being exceptional meant it was usually forbidden for women.

Nevertheless, April gave birth to a presence that we must not forget: A public, militant female presence that escaped, on certain occasions, all the restrictions of a patriarchal culture which relegates women, permanently, to a secondary status. This presence faced death and all the other risks, in the same way that it faced the minutia of daily life.

How do we evaluate that presence? It has been said, since the start, that today it is impossible to get the testimony of the women who fought in the most crucial times of the war. Nobody knows who they are, no one remembers them. And, if they are remembered, very few people think that identifying this source has any historical value.

* Selection from *Mujeres de abril*. Santo Domingo: CIPAF, Ediciones Populares Feministas, 1985. 187 p.

The occurrences of the war, today more than ever, have been turned into an echo of its reality. The common people are the undifferentiated, faceless masses who, due to political or ideological convenience, have had their true possibilities or their capacity to respond in a way that was more than merely casual, taken away from them.

It bears repeating that this homogenization of the struggle of the masses hides the presence of women more than that of any others. The common woman, those who did not have then nor ever, a name to identify them or pull them out of anonymity, would never be placed in the pantheon of the new, but defeated, makers of History.

Nevertheless, these women performed incredible deeds, deeds that the men who received the laurels, could not take pride in. Why they did what they did requires a more detailed and lengthy analysis than is the purpose here. We could attempt to resolve the debate with a commonplace and trivial truth: that as a social class, these women responded out of their own self-interest; they could do nothing less than fight those whom they identified as the cause of the misery in their lives. And, yes, it is possible that this trivial truth may be the only one, the fundamental explanation for the brusque rupture of the musty routine of domesticity which previously had been broken only for rare emergencies.

It is worth noting too, as a not unrespectable fact, that women of the working classes took on their roles within their own settings: there, where the repression of the anti-nationalist and imperial forces was most virulently concentrated on crushing opposition. They were faced, then, with a choice between survival or extermination: they chose survival over all else. This desire for survival grew beyond individuals and took on a collective nature. Perhaps it was for this reason, that the women of the working classes, without previous ties to politics or political organizations, were able to develop relationships which more closely approximated utopian theories.

They did not have time to build a response brick by brick, in the way a building is constructed. They never even attempted it; instead, almost intuitively, they undid the hierarchy of social functions. They could fulfill the same traditional roles, certainly. But the imminence of danger, not its mere echo or shadow, grew closer to their world by the second, radically transforming every aspect of their lives, including their emotions.

When they buried the unknown dead with their own hands, although there were no emotional ties with them nor did they share political or party allegiances, they were placing themselves on a plane much wider than their former lives. When they reached the trenches to distribute food they had cooked at command stations or in their own home, they often met with bullets and their own deaths. When they took risks to save others whom they had identified with the future, selfish invidualism was shattered as they freely chose pluralism.

Of them, we have, I repeat, only an image, sometimes vivid, sometimes faded by the distance of 20 years. But even faded and fragmentary, the indirect testimonies about them exemplify one way to raise them from their circumstances, and we must rescue them.

Mercedes Ramirez (La Rubia/Blondie) "I will tell you that all those women had incredible valor. Because it wasn't just those of us who had weapons and could defend ourselves who were the brave ones. They had nothing, but they dedicated their lives, you could say, to carrying the wounded, to cooking for the soldiers. I admire those women as much as if I were one of them. When "Operation Clean-Up" was going on, I was on duty on a corner there, where the command was and I had to flee;

I ran into a house with my rifle on my shoulder and hid myself, rifle and all. Well, there was a woman in the house, who had given birth five days earlier who still ... she can't give any testimony because she died, but her son is alive. You can say that the boy saved my life. When I entered she said to me, "Oh Blondie, come in, they'll kill you," and she put the baby in my arms and put me in her bed. When the people from "Operation Clean-Up" arrived from the Transportation and Quartermaster Unit, they were yelling: "This is where the Communists are! The Communists are here." She told them "Keep in mind, my sister is here, and she just gave birth five days ago." With all this, and having my rifle and my revolver, I said to myself, "fine, I am going to risk it all; they will kill me, but I am not going to go like this." The only thing I felt sorry about was the baby and the lady who was helping me; I didn't want anything to happen to her."

Sagrada Bujosa: "I had a group of women in the Academy, and the one I remember in a special way was Tina—I don't know her last name—because she left such a strong impression on me, not just as a professor, not just as a soldier, but also as a teacher. To know her was to know a woman, not of the petty bourgeoisie like I was back then, but as a woman of the lower classes who had fought and who had had totally different experiences from mine. This always impressed me. Tina was the bazooka operator from the POASI command, and when they say to me, "These are the comrades you are going to teach," I think of her, that young but worn-out woman of the people whose face was covered with scars. We very quickly became good friends. I remember that at the beginning she would always call me "Professor", and I used to say to her "I am not your professor, I am just another comrade." I always saw her hitching on the back of a jeep. At first our conversations were very timid and limited, more on my part because she was a very impressive woman. She always dressed in olive drabs. Later, we would settle into conversations and she would speak to me of the battles in the North in such a natural way, telling me about her combat wounds with the same simplicity that other people describe their daily chores at home. She was one of those who grasped instructions easily, someone very clever, and she was different. She was a woman who represented the common people. She was the woman who had seen battle, because few of the women under my command, no—none of us including myself, the instructor—had seen combat. Only Tina."

Brunilda Amaral: "I only remember one, whom they called "Blondie". I can't remember the names of any of the other women at the Academy; I am sorry about this because they did more than the rest of us. Not because they fired shots, no, but because they tried as well to be, to communicate with us, to tell us their experiences, to tell us without bashfulness that they had been prostitutes, or were prostitutes, and they tried to respect themselves. And one said "I am a homosexual but I respect all of my comrades. Don't be afraid of me because I will not disrespect any of you." And I never heard anything more of it; as far as I know that was the beginning and end of it. There, in the Academy, it was accepted; now, on the outside, it wouldn't be. This woman was a bazooka operator, and she never told anyone about blowing up half the world with her bazooka. That was the important thing for me. Not that they did things, but that they placed importance not on what they had done, but on what they were going to do. That is where the valor of all those women stemmed from; they didn't walk around with a rifle just to say they had a rifle oiled and ready, but that they had it to shoot it. "Blondie" for example, used to say "I have a son but I don't know what will become of him, because he lives with my mother and she doesn't know where I am." She was sixteen years old, an old woman of sixteen. She had walked many roads and had come back. She used to say that she couldn't conceive of a world where her son would live with those people (she was talking about the gringos) living in the country. She would say "I cannot allow, if I can help it, my son to live in a world where he will not know if he is Dominican or something else. That is why I am here." She was a prostitute, yes, and it hurt me greatly when I learned that they had killed her on the Duarte bridge, shot her like a little animal. I never knew her name, and that hurts me more. But at least I spoke to her a lot and she told us her story (to those who would listen, because there were some who had no interest whatsoever in what she had to say). To hear her tell how she was sold, how a man bought her for five pesos, how that man sold her, how she was treated like toilet paper, and then, how she was sent from bar to bar. From twelve (she was sold at the age of twelve) to sixteen are four years and in that time she had become an old woman. It was all the same to her now. That is, the only reason she had to live for was the war, because, she thought that her position as a woman, of someone oppressed and marginalized three or four times over, was going to change. She thought that the revolution was going to help her find herself, reform herself; that was her hope. She vindicated herself in the eyes of many. But not now, not after her untimely death. And so it was for others who got the worst of it for being prostitutes - in the jails they were given more beatings than anyone else. After the revolution, Belkis was given many beatings in jail, because she was a revolutionary prostitute. Being both was like having dynamite and gunpowder together. And she always maintained her revolutionary identity and her dignity; she demanded respect, even when it was rarely given to her. But at least, she demanded it; that is what stirred it in me. "The Colonel", whose name I also never knew, entertained herself with the frogmen. This woman was one of the ones who had been up North. When any armed skirmish broke out, she was the first to go running; she went around in a jeep, not to be a show off, but to get there, and she never talked about what she was doing. Those women lived a very enriching experience; they felt good, because knowing that they were excluded by us, and knowing or feeling that they were different from the little middle class ladies we were, didn't bother them. It wasn't about social status, but about social conscience, and they knew that in this regard, they were the betters, in spite of everything else. And they always tried to be the first to arrive, to be the sharpest, to pay better attention. I remember Tina saying "I am a thick woman, I am a woman from the docks. I am so stupid, but I have to learn, so I have to pay double attention."

I don't know, but this type of woman, this unnamed woman, who may never appear in any of the many histories that will be written about women and their role in this or that event, those women were precisely the ones who dignified the role of women in the April War. Those women. Yes, because they, as the little old man with the wart said, taught us by their example. They hadn't read a book, some were illiterate, totally illiterate, and they didn't know what your tendencies were, or whether that leader had a higher position than the other, or if this woman was more militant than another, or what everyone's place in the hierarchy was. This did not interest them in the least, not for anything. They were not interested, because they had not gone there to find out such things. Neither did they know of internal strife, nor of innuendo, nor of the lack of personal relationships between those other women, nor the lack of communication or warmth, or affections.

Picky Lora: There were women who had never heard the sound of a bullet and who lived in the interior of the country who came to Santo Domingo to join the struggle, hoping to go into combat side by side with the men, and they stayed the whole time in the Constitutional zone and never left. There were young girls —sixteen, seventeen, eighteen years old - who escaped from their families and joined the war in the Constitutional zone, and they never left. And there were, at times, scenes that were practically hysterical, of fathers looking for daughters, looking for them from command post to command post, in order to force them to return to their cities, and they wouldn't do it. They never left.

Ivelise Acevedo: The women of the lower classes had no knowledge of the handling or bearing of arms, but they were capable of the most incredibly valiant deeds you could mention. The women from the North took part without arms side by side with armed participants in the resistance. They formed an invaluable communications network and exhibited incredible valor in the face of death. You know that in the North there were deaths in genocidal proportions. In New City they resisted "Operation Clean-Up" as soon as it started and concentrated the constitutionalist movement within the cordon. And they resisted heroically under the leadership of Colonel Caamaño and his order that "any Yankee who enters is a dead Yankee," but attacks were isolated attempts, especially those of June 15 and 16.

But getting back to the women of the popular sectors, I tell you that they behaved valiantly in the face of the amount of deaths that we had up there. There were comrades who were buried right there, as soon as they fell. I remember one case, which happened a little bit away from the house of comrade Aniana Vargas, on Juan de Morfa Street. A woman and her two children died. In the morning we received word that the advancing troops were coming and on one corner near Dominican Radio-Television where there is a triangle, only a few women remained to do the burial because we knew what was coming. The men were in their combat stations, some in the outposts, others in their siege positions. There, in that place where two children are buried, another woman fell, because despite the fact that we insisted that the grave be left open, she said no, she couldn't leave them unprotected. The woman died trying to cover the grave of those two children. It will be said that this was a maternal stance: they weren't her children. It will be said that this is a Christian stance, to be sure that the dead are buried. I say that it was a furious stance, a way of saying "I am going to bury the dead. They cannot be allowed to bury our dead. I myself will bury them." I don't know, perhaps some people are more stubborn than others. I still remember how, from a nearby patio, I watched her, alone, trying to cover the grave of those two children with her bare hands. I don't know when she fell, or where they buried her.

Gladys Borrell (The Colonel): The women of the masses participated a great deal, I keep telling you. Not only did they collaborate. They bore arms in the revolution. There were a great many of them who performed many different functions in the '65 Revolution. Even if they had no gun, they were there curing comrades, administering injections, transporting materials from one place to another, clandestinely. That was a great thing, very brave, you have to risk your life to move arms from one place to another. When we were in the Northern zone, many female comrades came back down to get us ammunition, because we had no shells up there; we needed ammunition. And they came, smuggling them in their underclothes, little packets of shells, which they passed us. The little shoe-shine boys hid ammunition for us in their boxes, sent from down South, and since they were just little shoe-shine boys, the Americans didn't search them. And that was how we were able to survive up there, to last more days to fight. That then, for me, was as courageous as picking up a rifle. There were even many housewives up North, who, as I passed their houses would say "Oh, Miss, come in, come in." And I would say to them "No Ma'am, we can't come in, we have to keep advancing." They would reply, "Take care, take care." Sometimes we would get to a place and ask for water and the women would say "Look, Ma'am, I am going to take a little water first, so that you can be sure." A lady called Niña did this, in the Luperón development. And she gave us a big can of water. When the Americans arrived, they went to her house and detained her."

Translation by Margaret A. Ballantyne

SHEREZADA (CHIQUI) VICIOSO
Santo Domingo, 1948

Born in Santo Domingo, Chiqui Vicioso spent her adolescence and early adult years in the U.S. She lived in New York for eighteen years where she studied in distinguished institutions of higher education. Vicioso received her B.A. in Sociology from Brooklyn College and her M.S. in Education from Teachers College of Columbia University.

Vicioso has worked as a sociologist and coordinator of programs in various organizations, among them the Women's Program at the UNICEF. Since 1980, Vicioso has lived in Santo Domingo where she has been the driving force behind the promotion of the literature and the defense of civil rights of women. She is a founding member of the "Círculo de Mujeres Poetas". Vicioso is a poet, essayist and playwright. Her poem "Desvelo", an imaginary conversation between the nineteenth century Dominican woman poet Salomé Ureña and her North American counterpart Emily Dickinson, was staged as a ballet. In 1997, Vicioso received the Premio Nacional de Teatro for her play *Wish-Ky Sour*.

Selected Bibliography:

Viaje desde el agua. Santo Domingo: Visuarte, 1981. 71 p. .

Un extraño ulular traía el viento. Santo Domingo: Alfa y Omega, 1985. s.p. .

Bolver a vivir, imágenes de Nicaragua. Santo Domingo: Editora Búho, 1985. s. p. .

Julia de Burgos, la nuestra. Santo Domingo: Alfa y Omega, 1987. s.p.

Algo que decir, ensayos sobre literatura femenina 1981-1991. Santo Domingo: Editora Búho, 1991. 143 p.

Internamiento. Santo Domingo: Editora Búho, 1992. 60 p. .

Working with rather than for Women. Haiti/Dominican Republic: UNICEF, 1995. 24 p.

In Search of Equal Opportunity. Haiti/Dominican Republic: UNICEF, 1995. 24 p.

Salomé Ureña de Henríquez, a cien años de un magisterio. Santo Domingo: Publicación de la Comisión Permanente de la Feria del Libro Dominicano, 1997.

The Paths to Solidarity Among Women Writers
In her essay on the "Intellectual She-Male", the poet Carmen Imbert suggests that women are "sisters and enemies" when the "individual search touches on the measure of your worth as a person", and adds

---

* Selection from *Combatidas, combativas y combatientes, antología de cuentos escritos por dominicanas*. Santo Domingo: Taller, 1992.

It is with difficulty that you will extend your hand to those who are still immersed
in the well from which you managed to escape with great effort, and you will take
on the attitude of the "she-male", that is, of the woman with the prejudices and atti-
tudes proper to the "traditional intellectual" man.

The attitude (arrogance, preponderance, discrimination, elitism or stinginess) that Carmen defines as that of a "she-male" in the intellectual field, is the same as for any woman in the fine arts (the negative reputation of some ballerinas, actresses, painters and critics is known to all), or for any other professional woman who has not experienced an ideological-moral transformation which would separate her from the rest, or rather, which would both separate and unite her, in a dialectic relation, just as water momentarily separates the dust from the ground when someone is washing it.

And it is always the same because, no matter the field, competition is twice as strong for women in our society, due to their historical marginalization by the "cultural establishment", as has been shown to the saturation point in essays by Angela Hernández, the aforementioned Carmen, and the woman addressing you now.

Joined to the social reality which marginalizes women is the stereotype or traditional myth about the writer as a solitary Quixote, who in one marvelous image after another, goes about constructing a world; the writer as an isolated, asocial being, who, in a room of her own or in the back part of the house, (in Santo Domingo there are few garrets) takes part in a duel of words in order to reaffirm freedom: freedom to define the world in her own image and likeness. The verses of Neruda come to mind, where he describes in "The Invisible Man" (which could well be the "Invisible Woman") that washed-out, super-individualistic being who idealizes and merges his identity with his role as poet or writer:

> I laugh... I smile
> at the old poets,
> I adore all the poetry written
> all the dew,
> moons, diamonds, drops
> of silver submerged
> which was my brother
> embellishing the rose.
> but
> I smile
> every time he says "I",
> at each step,
> something happens to them,
> it is always "I",
> through the streets
> only they walk
> or the sweet thing they love,
> no one else
> ....he is so great
> he contains himself,

he tangles and untangles himself
he declares himself cursed,
he carries his cross with great difficulty
in the shadows,
he thinks he is different
from the rest of the world,
every day he eats bread
but he has never visited a bakery
nor has he ever attended a union meeting
of bakers
and so my poor brother
broods darkly,
he twists and turns
and finds that he is
interesting,
that's the word...

INDIVIDUALISM AS A REFLECTION OF IDEOLOGY

Mary Castro, the Brazilian intellectual, affirms that the youth of today, writers or not, are victims of the three horsemen of Capitalism: individualism, nihilism and materialism, though not necessarily in that order.

Of the three, I believe that the last two can be summed up by the first: Individualism, that "virtue" which, crowned by divine mandate, propelled the great capitalist revolutions, the class struggles, the domination of smaller countries by those with greater strength and force, and the domination of the "ignorant" by those who had an understanding of a certain type of knowledge —that of the West or Western Civilization— over the rest of humankind.

I insist on the ideological, in broad outlines (there is no reason to repeat what Marx or Marcuse have said here) because it is impossible to speak of solidarity among women, whether they are writers or not, without a reflection on ideology and its impact on social conscience, on attitudes, on day-to-day interactions.

To speak of solidarity, or of the roads to solidarity among women writers, is to speak of a change in the ideology which governs women's relationships to one another. It is a change which does not necessarily precede immediate structural changes, as the difficulties which revolutionary societies have faced in creating the new man, or even the new woman, have shown us.

The testimonies of Che Guevara, without doubt the purest and most beautiful man of our times, has contributed little to the creation of a new type of relationship among women, perhaps precisely because they do not specify gender, lost in that nebulous term "man" which represents two very complex and very different halves of the human race.

What has been missing from the discussion?

Specificity. This is the feminine contribution to the creation of an ideology where fraternity and solidarity will form the keystone. A new world view which will translate itself in a new language, exempt from (as Roland Barthes would say) that "obstinate remnant, left behind by all the writings that have gone before us, even our own earlier writings, which muffles the voice of our present."

FUNDAMENTALS OF A NEW IDEOLOGY

The lack of that ideology which we must construct does not deny the existence of women who were pioneers in pointing out its absence and the ways of creating it, the most honorable of whom (to my way of thinking) in the Dominican Republic is Camila Henríquez Ureña, whose stature continues to grow. (See my essay: "La Mujer en la literatura dominicana: A 47 años de Camila Henríquez" in the book *Sin otro profeta que su canto* by Daisy Cocco DeFilippis.) In a pioneering work which she read at the Congreso Nacional Femenino in Havana in 1930 Camila insisted on what must be the foundations for new feminine creativity, namely

1. Exceptional women of centuries past represent in their isolation progress in the vertical sense. They were precursors whose examples, at times, bore fruit. But an important cultural movement is always a collective movement and must propagate itself horizontally.

2. Women must develop the collective aspect of their nature in order to carry to completion a struggle which is now in its early stages.

3. Women need to work at the propagation of the cultural advances they have made in order to continue to progress.

> These foundations which at the same time spring from the recognition that as women we are
> "—Sisters in suffering.
> —In resolve.
> —In duty.
> —Human beings with analogous problems in life, and not rivals for power or strangers who hate one another."

I dare to suggest that in the Dominican Republic the "important collective cultural movement" of which Camila speaks has been Feminism. This Feminism must be understood, not in the way some have chosen to deform it (in order to discredit it) as a movement seeking the domination of men by women. Rather, Feminism must be understood as the basic solidarity among women as sisters in suffering, in duty, in resolve, as human beings with similar life problems.

The evidence of the correlation between a collective cultural movement, such as Feminism, and the appearance of the means of solidarity among women, is found in the creation of the Women Poets Circle.

Until the early '80's women poets in this country found themselves in dispersed groups or workshops founded for the most part by male counterparts, a few of whom were as well-intentioned as Mateo Morrison, who was justly recognized as an "honorary woman" by our Circle.

In 1983, as an offshoot of a series of meetings and discussions about common problems which affected us—isolation; lack of respect for and recognition of our work; sexual harassment and inadequate means of publishing our work—a group of women poets decided to form a Circle and introduce ourselves to the public with a homage to our national poet, Aída Cartagena Portalatín.

The story of the problems caused by choosing to name ourselves poets and not poetesses (following the example of the "poetas sorprendidos" who in their tribute to Gabriela Mistral's Nobel Prize wrote "a poet from our Spanish America has received the award...", thereby establishing that women could merit the name poet) is only a reflection of the intransigence of a society not accustomed to women claiming their place, not even linguistically, and is a topic for another essay. For our purposes, it is enough to point out that without the solidarity of the Center for Research on Feminine

Activity (CIPAF) we would not have been able to organize the homage, just as we would likewise not have been able to organize the First Ballad and Poetry Contest for Rural Women and the orchestration of the winning ballads for a concert. Both activities were sponsored and financed by Women in Development (MUDE).

The Homage to Gabriela Mistral on her Centenary was another activity sponsored and financed by CIPAF, and all of you know that this conference is made possible thanks to CE-MUJER, and to the initiative of that well-known feminist and poet Angela Hernández, who in fairness, must also be recognized.

This solidarity among women poets, principally from the capital, has spread to the interior, headed by Emelda Ramos in Salcedo, and a budding movement in Puerto Plata which calls itself the Renewal Society.

PROBLEMS

But all is not, nor has it been, a bed of roses. —Still we doubt ourselves before giving a collection of poems to a sister poet. —Still we doubt ourselves before sharing our anxieties or fears. —Still the ghosts of betrayal are awakened when a counterpart doesn't explain her actions or acts thoughtlessly. —Still our mistrust is reinforced when we learn that a writer has defamed another unjustly or caused problems with her partner (because of envy or jealousy or who knows what other motivation or complex). —Still we are products of this century, of this ideology, of the philosophical superstructure which hangs like the sword of Damocles over our consciences, lying in wait for any weakness, for any insecurity, any meagerness or smallness, in order to reaffirm itself.

NEW MORALITY

We cannot therefore, speak of new mechanisms for solidarity among women if we do not speak of a new morality, a new morality for all of humankind, centered on solidarity, on a re-definition of the other as yourself, which will lead us to the essential rule of relationship, not between women, but between all human beings. This will lead us to that FINITE UNITY where, as the poet Carmen Sánchez sings,

> It must be shown many times
> sheltered in time
> nature and the road
> shown that arms are not meant
> only to be tied up
> nor the mouth closed
> in the face of fatigue
> nor do hands have fingernails
> merely to calm rebellious secrets
> It must be shown that feet
> do not walk alone
> that there are other bridges to cross
> and other wines in the cellar
> and another aroma in the café
> and other lips awaiting a new kiss

it is not a question of bets
why bet on faded numbers
and play at being happy singing songs
while we go on cutting legs off
with hatchets made of human bones?

Translation by Margaret A. Ballantyne

EMELDA RAMOS
Salcedo, 1948

Poet, fiction writer, educator, librarian, feminist, Emelda Ramos was born in José de Conuco (Salcedo) on the 16th of September of 1948. She received her Licenciatura in Education, Minor in Philosophy and Literature at the Universidad Nacional Pedro Henríquez Ureña in Santo Domingo. She has been teaching since 1971 and has held for a good number of years the position of Chief Librarian at the Biblioteca Universitaria in San Francisco de Macorís, Dominican Republic.

A strong woman with a generous disposition, her efforts have contributed much to the dissemination of the writings of Dominican women. To that end, Ms. Ramos has participated in a good number of colloquia, conferences and seminars in such far away places from Salcedo as Wichita, Kansas, where she presented one of the articles included in this selection. Publications such as *Combatidas, combativas y combatientes, antología de cuentos escritos por dominicanas* (1992) and this anthology owe much to her generosity and efforts as a librarian who is also a researcher.

Selected Bibliography:

El despojo o por los trillos de la leyenda. Santo Domingo: Taller, 1983. 102 p.

TOWARDS A FEMININE NARRATIVE IN DOMINICAN LITERATURE

In her invaluable work *Women in the mirror: Twentieth Century Female Narrators of Latin America*, Sara Sechojovich compiles an anthology of all the women throughout the continent who are currently writing, and upon arriving at the Dominican Republic, she notes that we know little of what is happening here today since there is no Max Henríquez Ureña to inform us. And from that fertile dialogue between author and reader, the painstaking essayist from the Institute of Social Research at the UNAM managed to convince me of the need for such a project: first of all, for a catalog, and then for a critical examination. This study is the result of that dialogue and I undertake it as renewal of my own writing and as a member of the last generation of Max Henríquez Ureña's students.

Name them, as Carpentier would say, in order to know that they exist. We are facing a virgin universe, and therefore it is imperative to rescue their names and to establish from the outset that although our country was the place where women's writing began in the New World with the composition of five sonnets and poems in blank verse by the Dominican nun Leonor de Ocando in the Regina Convent, writing at the same time as Elvira de Mendoza, nevertheless, the inclusion of women in the field of literature as it developed throughout the continent is precarious due to the vicissitudes of the socio-historic and political-economic situation. And, in spite of the fact that the birth of the Dominican Republic was witnessed by and recounted by a woman, Rosa Duarte, whose writings brought us information about the life of Juan Pablo Duarte, the Father of our Country, and about the "Trinitarians", the clandestine movement which gave birth to our Independence, I repeat, there has not been a prodigious female presence, in neither quantity nor quality, in the field of narrative fiction. Let us look at those who did attempt to create a world narrated by themselves, those who did not succumb to the fatal impulse which seems to have consigned so many of these worlds to the dark emptiness of the family cupboard.

In 1849 Manuela Rodríguez, "La Deana" (The Dean) who conducted her political and literary activity in her own small printing shop, wrote a type of autobiography entitled *Historía de una mujer* (*Story of a Woman*), but it was 1850 (the year in which Salomé Ureña de Henríquez, our stellar poet was born), when Amelia Francisca de Marchena, hiding behind the pseudonym Amelia Francasi, would become our first woman novelist. She would publish *Madre culpable* (*Guilty Mother*) in 1893 and *Francisca Martinoff* in 1901 but she was already successful by 1892 with the serialization of her novels, following the literary paradigm so in vogue in Europe throughout the nineteenth century. Also in 1901 Virginia Elena Ortea (1849-1903) published *Risas y lágrimas* (*Laughter and Tears*), a collection of stories, articles and chronicles by the author of an operetta that was produced in theatres at the end of the century.

Francisca A. Vallejo García (1859-1909) published *La mano de la providencia* (*The Hand of Providence*) and Rosa Smester (1859-1945), educator and outstanding activist during the American occupation, wrote *Juveniles: Cuentos de color de rosa* (*Youthful Dreams: Stories in Pink*). In 1925 one of our most prolific writers, Abigail Mejía (1895-1941) published her novel *Sueña Pilarín* (*Pilar Dreams*) and her contemporary Jesusa Alfau wrote *Los débiles y Teletusa* (*The Weak Ones and Teletusa*). A feminist like her predecessors, Delia Weber, who was born in 1900 and excelled as a painter, published poetry and in 1952, *Dora y otros cuentos* (*Dora and Other Stories*). There is also our first story writer, Hilma Conteras, who was born in 1913. Although her first volume *Cuatro cuentos* (*Four Short Stories*) only came to light in 1953, the proof of her primacy is found in 1937 in a letter by Juan Bosch in which he critiques her story "La desjabada" saying "our country has seen the birth of an accomplished female writer, not a novice, nor even a talented amateur. A mature writer." And he added, referring to the woman still known at that time by the pseudonym "Silvia Hilcom", "with this page Hilma Contreras greets the nation. Let us welcome her as a special friend." Another Dominican writer, Virgina Bordas, published *Toeya* in 1949, but this is more of an indigenous fantasy than a short story, a tale whose central figure is a native princess whose name has been given to the island that we know today as Catalina.

Let us return to 1945 when Beatriz Roldán wrote her novel *A través de los años* (*Through the Years*), and to 1947 when María Antonia Sagredo published her novel *Ercilia* in *La Información*. Back again in 1945, the novel *La Victoria* (*Victory*) by Carmen Natalia Bonilla, our militant poet, was chosen to represent the Dominican Republic in the United States' Hispanic-American Literary Contest. Melba Marrero, who achieved renown as a poet was also known for her novel *Caña dulce* (*Sweet Sugar Cane*), followed by *Postales sin estampillas* (*Postcards without Stamps*) (a travel book) and her novel *El voto* (*The Vow*), her best works were to remain unpublished. In 1953 a biographical essay was published, "Sor Juana Inés de la Cruz", by a short story writer recognized for her works in *Listín Diario*, Milady de L'Official. In 1955 *El destino manda* (Destiny Calls) by Marta Polanco Castro was published. In 1964 Euridice Canaán presented her novel *Los depravados* (*The Corrupt Ones*) and in 1969 she published *Los monstruos sagrados* (*The Sacred Monsters*) and in 1980 *Morir por Última vez* (*Dying*

---

* Study edited by Elías Miguel Muñoz.

** Sara Sechojovich, *Mujeres en espejo: Narradores latinoamericanas siglo XXI.* Folios Ed., 1981.

for the Last Time); she also wrote seventeen manuscripts that were not published.

In 1967 Altagracia Vargas de Toya published her first novel, *Sueño ideal* (*Perfect Dream*) and in 1969 Carmita Henríquez de Castro did likewise with her *Cuentos para niños* (*Stories for Children*), pioneering in this genre in which others would follow: Lucía Amelia Cabral with *Hay cuentos para contar* (*There are Stories to be Told*) [1977], *Gabino*, a selection from the same in 1979, and in 1984 *Sorprendido el plátano* (*The Surprised Plantain*). María Cristina de Farías would follow with *Cuentos en versos para Maricris* (*Stories in Verse for Maricris*) as would Eleanor Grimaldi with *Cuentos infantiles y juveniles* (*Stories for Children and Young People*).

In 1969 Aida Cartagena Portalatín was a finalist for Seix Barral's "Biblioteca Breve" Prize with her novel *Escalera para Electra* (*Stairway for Electra*); in 1978 she published *Tablero* (*Checkerboard*), a collection of short stories, and in 1984 with *La tarde en que murió Estefanía* (*The Afternoon that Stephanie Died*), the woman who was initially the only female presence in the "Poesía Sorprendida" movement made herself famous. In 1972 Jeannette Miller published her *Fórmula para combatir el miedo* (*Formula for Fighting Fear*), a book of poems, and *Suplementos culturales* (*Cultural Supplement*), a collection of modern tales. Miller's concentration primarily on her work as an art critic and essayist, which bore fruit in her *Historia de la pintura dominicana* (*The History of Dominican Painting*), probably meant that the Dominican narrative lost a potential talent. In 1979 Mary Rosa Jiménez won an honorary mention in the Casa de Teatro competition for her story "Tan sólo unos lirios" ("Just a Few Irises"). In 1983 Emelda Ramos won a regional prize for narrative with her *El despojo o por los trillos de la leyenda* (*The Rubble or Through the Legendary Thresher*). In 1984 Aída Bonnelly de Díaz published *Variaciones* (*Variations*), an exquisite surprise for Dominican literary criticism.

It is precisely with the assistance of current criticism that we can approach the following task. Up until now, we have only dealt with history in the sense of naming or defining a catalog. To track down this information we follow the usual channels: the literary market. Now we must try to scrutinize what it is that women write as they labor to bring forth a feminist Dominican narrative. It is imperative to note themes, tendencies, codes, the use of universal feminine archetypes, underlying rebelliousness, in order to place these women writers within the broader Latin American literary context.

Dominican fiction in the last twenty years has rejuvenated itself and the choices of themes has been widened to include urban as well as rural problems, but despite this breath of fresh air, prose, especially short works, continues to be scarce and of limited quality. The Dominican novel is still a work in progress. A look at the works written tells us that since the 1960's novelists have been absorbed by the following concerns: 1) the dictatorship and its effects on the people; 2) the guerrilla war of 1963 with its attempt at restoring a constitutional system; 3) the April 1965 war and the second American occupation; 4) splitting from old narrative forms; 5) the search for forms which are adaptable to social reality. Do our women novelists of today fit this mold? Let us examine what they have written.

The fact that a country's first short story writer is still alive shows how young that country's narrative tradition is. According to Pedro Peix, that pioneer, Hilma Contreras, is "a short story writer of surprising and unexpected poetic resonance."* Contreras published *Cuatro cuentos* (*Four Short*

---

* Peix, Pedro. *La narrativa yugulada* (Santo Domingo: Editorial Alfa y Omega, 1981).

Stories) in 1953, *El Ojo de Dios* (*The Eye of God*) —stories of the underground published in 1962—, as well as an essay, *Doña Endrina de Catalayud*. In addition, she kept in secret hiding places various stories which were unpublishable due to the omnipresent literary persecution. These stories are really miniatures which depict the facts and scenes of Dominican family life under the dictatorship. This woman painted these with the bold prose and strong content of social protest. The power of the military can be seen in "Biografía de una hora" ("Biography of an Hour"):

> *A jeep rode down "Rosa Duarte", a damned military jeep. In a flash I wanted to scream. The whining buzz of one of the jet helicopters sold for a vote in the United Nations passed overhead. We live in a filthy world. Par for the course. The ideal — which is like talking about the anger of dignity— to hell with it!*

Another theme, repressive persecution, is an important part of "The Eye of God":

> *"Hi Abel!... I'm warning you that I really insist that you accept the trusteeship. Who killed that man?" - he asked pointblank. Half closing his sharp eyes, the governor in turn asked "What man?" "The one you ordered to be put on public display." The story ends: On seeing him pass by, the "Eye of God" abandoned Cain, in order to dedicate himself entirely to the persecution of Abel.*

And, last of all, terror and crime are examined in "Los rebeldes" ("The Rebels"):

> *"Does Marcelino Torres live here?", asked the driver as the ambulance stopped short. "Yes", he answered, barely interrupting the sweet task of sucking his pipe. "What is going on?" The driver motioned to the man seated next to him. They had already opened the door of the ambulance when the second man deigned to answer him: "Well then, this dead body is yours" ... Shocked, don Marcelino removed the pipe from his greedy lips. "This is a mistake", he protested. "We don't have anyone sick in the hospital." "But this is yours." They took a bundle from the ambulance, pushed don Marcelino to one side and without any further glances dragged the package to the middle of the portico. Inside the house a woman screamed. The old man looked at her without daring to lower his horrified eyes to look at ...*

Escalera para Electra (*Stairway for Electra*), by Aida Cartagena, is not only one of the first worthwhile narrative experiments proposing the actualization of the Dominican novel, but is also possibly the only one which posseses a high degree of coherence, that is, an adequate formal and thematic relationship which does not render gratuitous or forced its literary techniques," says Alcántara Almánzar. In effect, this work -very abridged in anthologies, schools and universities- becomes a real challenge to metatextual analysis, because in it the author leads us, by means of a stairway of overlaying and alternating planes, to the structure of the text, monologuing in one moment of her narration:

> *Ah Helene's things! Into what labrynth has she fallen? It isn't that she isn't curious about the fickleness of others because there are many women who are like her. After writing: "The Earth," she broke down Swain's book into disconcerting planes. She took a notion that a mechanism had begun that she should continue on that stairway. That mechanism corresponds casually with the so-called "modern styles" which*

make fun of Aristotle, Nebrija and Cervantes and any other son of a bitch that
tried to imprison the profession of writing. (33)

Important and well defined aspects of Cartagena's discourse are revealed to us here, making it possible for us to appreciate at a glance what space does not permit us to express, no matter how succinctly we try to examine the metatext. First, Helene is the biographer of Swain, the Dominican Electra from the hometown of the author, and therefore, Helene is Aída Cartagena, fragmented into a third person. She is the "she" of the "I". Second, the goal of breaking with canonical novelistic forms must be the compass for the journey towards modernity for this archeologist-anthropologist-art student, travelling through the Greece of Euripides. Third, the discovery of the "technique of planes" will make us participants of her own discovery, when she states: "I see that stairway, it grows in height, so that at times I feel dizzy. Will my stairway fall? Who will knock down my stairway?" The novel is constructed on bits of memories, epochal testimonies, cables sent to Dominican friends, illustrative commentaries on the art of ancient Greece, the political situation of the country, existential doubts and contradictions, messages to Paris, while she continues to unroll the parchment scroll of the old story of incestuous love and tragedy. Fourth, the anxiety inherent in the process of producing a book and watching its reception, a new reference point for our women's narrative, will become pathetically clear from one plane to another throughout the text: "What do I have to gain or lose with this book which will never find a publisher because they will say that it is not a novel, it is nothing to talk about. That Helene is not a writer..." Anxiety will turn to doubt and to the almost total denial which then leads to the denouement of the tragedy, beyond the Greek chorus: " Miss Helene, Do you insist on having us believe that this is a novel?" (159). Cartagena embodies the reality of all Dominican writers which caused F. García Godoy to say: "to everything already said must be added the poverty and low state of our literary environment which does not allow an author even a glimmer of hope of earning a decent living." Without falling into the momentary pessimism in which the considerations of Robbe Grillet seem to sink her, she says:

> Now I am sure that I am leaving this and I throw Swain's papers and organize
> *the boxes of Bingo that a Swedish woman left in that room. A game. Bingo! I say to*
> *myself: Girl, you are no Swede, wake up and use your very own judgement, yours*
> *alone and no one else's and finish your novel. I throw the notes and the boxes. I*
> *promise myself to finish the Swain case. (136)*

The promise follows her consciousness raising, product of the search for her identity. A woman who follows a previous retrospective plane observes almost confessionally: "I must fight a little longer, because I was born a woman: I must control my own development, which is necessary to self control: there is no redeeming aspect of it for the opposite sex: the obligation to develop as broadly as possible, human intellectual potential." (26). These few steps of Electra's stairway are enough for us to see that this is a feminist novel par excellence among novels written by women.

While Aida Cartagena's prose has been deemed refined and Hilma Contreras' called virile, Aida Bonnelly's prose allows us to consider the present theme: Is there women's literature? Or, is there only literature? And it is the prose of this pianist and professor of music that harmonizes descriptions which are elegant examples of careful, regular syntax, a marvelous economy of words, a "feminine" exquisiteness, all contained in an artistic work of exceptional richness and taste. To further complicate this burning argument, I must confirm her use of elements of every-day life as the predominant reference points in the text. In structuring her novel the author has made use of a device: the adaptation of the musical pattern of theme and variation to narrative form, resulting in a feminine, maternal composition in which melody, rhythm, harmony, language and most importantly, the quality of its content are presented. In these variations the sonority of the words is important, but I believe that the silences are more so, just as is so with time and its persistence, and its management within the theme of "El Baño" ("The Bath"). In "El Amor" ("Love"), a figure appears in each and every one of its variations: the dog, who as a symbolic character will play a very unique role in each story.

This is precisely what Bonnelly de Díaz writes, not stories, not novels, not tales, but narratives. (Narrations) Doubts remain about their genre, just as in the case of my book *El despejo*, (*The Clearing*) classified now as a novel, now as a long tale, or an updating of a legend from my region where the characters speak in a local dialect, the focus of an investigation by Pedro Henríquez Ureña. Finally *Variaciones* by Aida Bonnelly has, from beginning to end, 1) a didactic intent; 2) the message of love; 3) a call to beauty.

And now, as a sort of conclusion, I include a conversation among the women writers discussed in this essay.

E. Ramos: Has being a woman influenced your work and its development?

H. Contreras: No, I do not believe that being a woman influences you but rather that the barriers are in the individual's temperament.

A. Cartagena: Think about that woman whose works I read since childhood and who is a central figure in world literature: Teresa of Avila: agitator, advocate, combatant...

A. Bonnelly: Yes, being a woman in Latin America influences a writer because we still are not free from cultural alienation, not free from preordained duties, not free from following archaic patterns that limit the vision of the woman in our present day.

E. Ramos: Is there a common feature among Dominican women novelists? You have all visited the continent: will this be a determining factor in the narrative direction of our insular imagination?

H. Contreras: Yes, I went to secondary school in Europe, I returned to my country and I completed my undergraduate studies and then took courses in Anthropology, Civilization and Culture at the Sorbonne. Yes, in Europe one comes in contact with the intellectual and artistic movements of the world; although I have always kept a diary, it was on my return home in 1935 that I felt the need to write stories.

A. Cartagena: On the continent one comes into contact with other cultures, one is broadened and nourished by that. Travelling teaches you so much about everything you read and study. I wrote *Stairway for Electra* while I was travelling through Greece working on a report that the magazine *New World* in Paris had hired me to do.

A. Bonnelly: Distance gives us perspective on the great and the small, the everyday and the transcendent. I was in New York from 1945 to 1950 earning my Master's Degree in piano; I studied in Paris from 1954 to 1955 and I lived in Washington for ten years.

E. Ramos: Finally, to what do you attribute the fact that there are so many women poets, and a good number of women who write journalistic or historical essays but that there are so few women writing prose fiction in our country?

H. Contreras: I believe the phenomenon is world-wide, but I can say that this is related to your first question: the milieu is narrow and does not permit us to narrate with much imagination and we are accused of any actions we describe and so the timid are inhibited from writing, they won't risk the scandal or the public hostility.

A. Cartagena: Poetry is easier even now, although it is a very serious thing, requiring knowledge, because it is no longer only inspirational: looking at a moon that is no longer there and no longer shines. Narrating is something else: you have to research every thing you present. And there are things which need to be told: exploitation, hunger, repression—the artist is obliged to tell of these things, to be on the side of the other man and the other woman, to be with those who suffer.

A. Bonnelly: I believe there is a shortage of women novelists and more women poets because when all is said and done, the world we imagine comes from within our lives and the restrictions on the Latin woman. Now, with the freeing up of traditional roles, the access to the means of production and work, working in the public forum side by side with men, in time there will come a crop of women writers intellectually equal to talented male writers.

With this sketch of the women who write fiction, it can be seen that Dominican women narrators share the same thematic and formal concerns as others. Like their male counterparts, they suffer from the lack of a strong, well-defined narrative tradition, but they also search for those new forms of expression, adaptable to and representative of our social reality, which will bring our narrative to a place of importance within contemporary Latin American fiction.

Translation by Margaret A. Ballantyne

DAISY COCCO DE FILIPPIS
Santo Domingo, 1949

A native of the Dominican Republic, Daisy Cocco De Filippis has lived in New York City for the past thirty-seven years. As many other immigrants, Dr. Cocco De Filippis studied at the City University of New York where she received her B.A. Summa cum laude, in Spanish and English literatures from Queens College and her Ph.D. from the Graduate Center.

Dr. Cocco De Filippis is Professor of Spanish at York College where she has taught Spanish language and Hispanic literatures since 1978. A prolific writer, Dr. Cocco De Filippis has devoted much of her time in the past two decades to disseminate Dominican letters in the U.S.

An active participant in Dominican community activities in New York, Dr. Cocco De Filippis is the founder of "Las tertulias de escritoras dominicanas en los Estados Unidos," and the founding President of the Dominican Studies Association/Asociación de Estudios Dominicanos.

Selected Bibliography:

Estudios semióticos de poesía dominicana. Santo Domingo: Biblioteca Taller No. 178, 1984. 174 p.

ed. *Sin otro profeta que su canto, antología de poesía escrita por dominicanas.* Santo Domingo: Biblioteca Taller, No. 263, 1988. 231 p.

ed. *From Desolation to Compromise: A Bilingual Anthology of the Poetry of Aida Cartagena Portalatín.* Santo Domingo: Colección Montesinos No. 10, 1988. 125 p.

ed. et al. *Poems of Exile and of Other Concerns, bilingual selection of the poetry written by Dominicans in the U.S.* New York: Alcance, 1988. 146 p.

ed. *Combatidas, combativas y combatientes, antología de cuentos escritos por dominicanas.* Santo Domingo: Taller, Publicaciones del Instituto del Libro, 1992. 446 p.

ed. *The Women of Hispaniola: Moving Towards Tomorrow.* New York: York College, Executive Report No. 1, 1993. 152 p.

ed., et al. *Stories from Washington Heights and Other Corners of the World.* New York: Latino Press, a Publication of the CUNY Latin American Writers Institute, 1994. 204 p.

ed. *Asian Culture: Tradition and Diaspora.* New York: York College Executive Report No. 3, 1994. 105 p.

ed. *Tertuliando/Hanging Out.* Santo Domingo: Publicación de la Comisión Permanente de la Feria del Libro Dominicano, 1997. 280 p. U.S. edition. New York: Alcance, publication sponsored by the CUNY Caribbean Exchange Program, 1997. 210 p.

INDIAS Y TRIGUEÑAS NO LONGER:
CONTEMPORARY DOMINICAN WOMEN POETS SPEAK*

Women have had the power of naming stolen from us...
To exist humanly is to name the self, the world and God...

Women's isolation and silence are the subject of many recent feminist studies. Elaine Showalter's collection of essays *New Feminist Criticism* illustrates the need to end the traditional silence of women and the urgency to fill blank pages with the voices of female experience. As Mary Daly states, women need to own language in order to exist and to control their universe. In the past, since "women have had the power of naming stolen from us," women have been forced to accept someone else's definition of their womanhood. Any study of Dominican literature would certainly confirm that this has been the experience of Dominican women. Although this claim is not limited to Dominican poetry, we wish to emphasize that all of its literary canons of traditional Dominican literature reiterated and gave witness to the false image and the artificial identity which Dominican women had been obliged to accept. Unable to express themselves, women became a mere reflection of the fantasies of that "Other," who, like a new Adam, allows himself to recreate the world to suit his needs.

Dominican poetry in general has preserved and protected European canons, standards and values, with the image of Dominican women as mere copies of European womanhood. For the better part of our literary history, the proverbial muse of Dominican poets has been a close relative of that Laura who caused many a heartache to that venerable Florentine bard in the 1500s. Neither the passing of the years nor the geographical changes in the racial composition of her new land have altered her in the least. This identification with the European is translated in many Dominican literary creations, as in the works of other Caribbean and Latin American writers, into an open rejection of the African element in its cultural heritage. In *The Black Image in Latin American Literature*, Richard L. Jackson explains that the aesthetic ideals of a society are determined by the physical characteristics of the dominant group, the somatic factor. The search for that somatic ideal may result in the loss of one's own identity. Solaum and Kronus explain that:

> *The acceptance of these aesthetic standards produces those practices common in Latin America and the United States by which individuals seek to "whiten" themselves.* (Jackson: xii)

The rejection of the African element in Dominican poetry is expressed in the representation of women in a constant antinomy between a virginal and submissive white woman and a sensual and sinful negress or mulatto woman. It should be remembered also that the negress or mulatto woman in better known Dominican poetry, especially that of Manuel del Cabral and Tomás Hernández Franco's *Yelidá*, are of Haitian nationality. (Cocco De Filippis: 1984: 57-58; 79-83) The mulatto woman as icon of Dominican womanhood does not enter the Dominican poetic landscape until well into the twentieth century; and even then she must be hidden under a protective cloak of euphemisms, such as india (indian woman) or trigueña (olive-skinned, dark-complexioned brunette).

* An earlier version of this paper was first published in *Cimarrón*, the journal of the CUNY Caribbean Studies Association. I, No. 3 (Spring 1988) 132-150.

The traditional muse of Dominican poets has three basic characteristics: she is white, virginal and submissive. This angelic and delicate creature has been placed on the highest pedestal since the beginning of Dominican literary history. Her presence is a constant from the poetry of Gastón Deligne in the late nineteenth century to the works of Manuel Llanes halfway through the twentieth century.

In Deligne's poem "De luto" (In Mourning), black, the color of mourning, serves to underline the race of his heroine:

> Una blancura astral de azules venas,
> como la tuya, inmaculada y suave;
> formada adrede con pulmón de ave
> y con pulpa de nardos y azucenas.
>
> (Contín y Aybar: 37)

> (A star-like whiteness adorned with blue veins,
> such as yours, inmaculate and supple;
> expressly created of down
> and of the pulp of nards and white lilies.)

The reiteration of nouns and adjectives which point to European, lady-like attributes, categorically affirms the author's aesthetic. Years later, Víctor Garrido, the Modernist poet, in his "Elegía blanca" (Elegy in White) uses his muse's color as the basis for requesting God's favors:

> Ten piedad de su boca
> que es un lirio
> de sus ojos azules
> de sus manos nevadas como un cirio...
>
> (Contín y Aybar: 74)

> (Look with favor on her mouth
> for it's a madonna lily
> on her blue eyes
> her hands, snowy as candle wax)

Again, the repetition of elements which underline the color of his muse implies that being white is synonymous with being pure and, consequently, worthy of God's special favors. By choosing nouns such as "cirio" and "lirios" whose semantic value is precisely whiteness, the poet not only points to the woman's color but also to her "holiness". A white woman then possesses all the attributes of a madonna lily, the delicate flower which withers easily and only appears to fit into, to be comfortable within the walls of religious enclosures. God must feel compassion for her since a woman so white, the poem implies, does not deserve to suffer but should thrive so that she may adorn the sacrosant places and decorate the interiors of man-made structures. White women in the poetry of this period are always to be found inside their homes, in sedentary positions, awaiting the arrival of that "Other" who will bring them, albeit vicariously, to life.

The mulatto woman or the negress, the antithesis of that virginal muse, appears for the first time in Dominican poetry in Francisco Muñoz del Monte's poem "La mulata" (Mulatto Woman) where she is born eager to dwell in wickedness:

> *No más, por Dios, no más. No es piedra el hombre.*
> *No hay más que un ser de bronce: la mulata.*
> *Plegaria inútil. Ella goza y mata,*
> *abre y cierra la tumba a su querer.*
>
> *Cuando al son de la lúgubre campana*
> *a la fosa su víctima desciende*
> *la cruel mulata su cigarro enciende*
> *y a inmolar va otro hombre a su placer.*
>
> (Morales: 329)

> (Stop, by God, stop. Man is not a stone.
> There is no other being than this bronze creature: the mulatto woman.
> Wasted prayer. She rejoices as she kills,
> opens and closes tombs at her whim.
>
> When at the toll of the sorrowful bell
> her victim descends into the dreaded dwelling,
> the cruel mulatto her cigar lights
> and to inmolate another she moves on.)

This persona contrasts sharply with the proverbial muse of earlier poems: clearly the quality of goodness, innocence and fragility attributed to the white woman are absent. Instead, the mulatto woman is presented as a being who destroys and annihilates man. What was postulated at first as an aesthetic preference, degenerates into an attack on the moral fiber of a female representation of an entire race.

Even when the woman of color is described in "positive" terms, she is not allowed the right to occupy the exclusive place reserved for that luminous being, her opposite pole: the white virgin. Vigil Díaz, one of the creators of Dominican avant garde poetry, illustrates this attitude in the poem "Tímpano de la montaña" (Eardrum of the Mountain) when he states:

> *Mi querida,*
> *que es una negra retinta,*
> *dulce y armoniosa como el cuello de una cítara de ébano,*
> *con pulpa de coco en la sonrisa*
> *y esencia de mandrágora en las dobleces...*
>
> (Contín y Aybar: 59)

> (My paramour,
> a dark negress,
> as sweet and harmonious as the neck of an ebony zither,
> has coconut meat in her smile
> and mandragora's essence in her curves...)

The first verse indicates that however she is described, the poet has no intention of integrating his lover into Dominican society. The dark negress is a rather exotic being who cannot be anything other than man's concubine. The sensuality explicit in the verse "mandragora's essence in her curves" immediately closes the door to what has been presumed to be a better status. The negress, because of her voracious sensual appetite, cannot be the immaculate virgin destined to bring forth man's descendants. This is why she must be relegated to the position of "paramour": to exist without legal and social status.

In the second decade of this century, the mulatto woman begins to be known as the trigueña who inhabits a poetic world which is still a copy of the European. Héctor Incháustegui Cabral, the Dominican poet and critic, explains this presence in his essay "Los negros y las trigueñas en la poesía dominicana":

> *Pienso que a las trigueñas se les hace figurar para no pecar de irrealistas, por un lado y por otro, para no usar una designación como sería mulata que recuerda bastante crudamente al negro de los antepasados y del cual pocos querían acordarse hasta que aparece en las Antillas la poesía negra y la poesía social que describe y condena la situación de los biznietos de los esclavos que son, con mucha frecuencia, también biznietos de los colonizadores.* (Incháustegui Cabral: 329)

> (I believe that the trigueñas are included simply not to be too unrealistic on the one hand, and on the other, in order to avoid calling women "mulattoes," a designation which rather crudely brings to mind the blackness of one's ancestors; a blackness few wanted to be reminded of in the Caribbean until the creation of a black poetry and a poetry of social protest which describes and sanctions the lot of the great grandchildren of black slaves, who on the other hand, are also quite often the great grandchildren of the white colonizers.)

The most elegant trigueñas in Dominican poetry appear in the *Criollas* of Arturo B. Pellerano Castro, also known as the Dominican "Byron." These are women whose gracefulness and exquisite poise remind one of the *Serranillas* written by the Marqués de Santillana six hundred years earlier. Although the setting and their courtly manners are so similar to those of European models, here Castro's trigueñas are dark-skinned women:

> *Desde el día en que en el cierre del monte,*
> *cojida (sic) la falda,*
> *el arroyo al cruzar me dijiste*
> *sonriendo, ¿me pasas?...*
> *y sentí ganas enormes*
> *de que fuera muy ancho el arroyo*
> *de que fueran muy hondas sus aguas...*
> *desde el día en que te cuento, trigueña,*
> *yo quisiera ser burro de carga...*
>
> (Contín y Aybar: 46)

(Since that day at the end of the woods,
by the edge of the stream,
your skirt slightly gathered,
you asked as you smiled, "would you carry me yonder?"...
I felt a yearning
for the stream waters to widen,
for its waters to deepen...
since that day I recall now, trigueña,
I pine to be a hardworking plodder.)

As the poem indicates, the image of woman as an exquisite, delicate being in need of protection has not changed. What has begun to show a transformation is her color, which has become more representative of the racial composition of the Dominican people. Nevertheless, the poet is still not willing to accept the African element in his heritage; to avoid alluding to his race he finds excuses, pretexts, which in some instances are rationalized by an alleged pride in the indigenous past of the island, as in the case of the poem "India" by Domingo Moreno Jimenes:

> *India, desde la cabeza hasta los pies,*
> *in-dia*
> *debí decir mestiza*
> *pero ya ves, escribí india*
> *y no me arrepiento,*
> *a veces la salvación de un porvenir está en el pasado.*
> (Moreno Jimenes: 236)

> (In-dia, from head to toe,
> in-dia
> I should have said mestiza
> but as you see, I wrote india
> and I don't regret it,
> sometimes the future is saved by its past.)

Moreno Jimenes' poem presents a very unconvincing argument. To return to a remote indigenous past totally removed from contemporary Dominican existence does not represent salvation. Indeed, it is an evasion of a writer's responsibility to face up to the real problem: his people's escape into an indigenous past in order to avoid recognizing the African element in its racial composition.

The image of woman as a submissive being completes the false portrayal of Dominican womanhood. Helene M. Anderson in her essay "Rosario Castellanos and the Structures of Power" reaches conclusions about Mexican reality which can be applied to the universal condition of women and, in particular, to the situation of Hispanic women:

> *Neither women nor Indians were given the privilege of choice. As an instrument of repression, the mythification of traditional role models for Mexican women has glorified the negation of choice as one of the most desirable qualities in a "proper" woman.* (Meyer and Fernádez Olmos: 25)

By denying women the right to make choices, to decide on their own, to err, to learn, and to grow, men have kept women in a child-like condition. Unable to decide for themselves, women then become a property in need of care and protection, forever young, forever helpless, forever foolish. Moreno Jimenes' poem "Maestra" (School Teacher) is an example of this paternalistic attitude in Dominican poetry:

> *Trocar los sexos y con qué objeto,*
> *siendo como eres en realidad de un sentir*
> *prolijo y tierno.*
> *Así minuciosa, sensible y sumisa*
> *te soñó mi egoísmo*
> *y te anhelan mis hijos*
> *que están en gestación desde la infancia.*
>
> (Moreno Jimenes: 106)

> (To change your sex, whatever for?
> being as you truly are of a tender
> and generous disposition.
> Thus meticulous, sensitive and submissive
> you were created in my dreams,
> and you are yearned for by the children
> who have been gestating since my childhood)

Thus centuries of seeing their reflection in someone else's mirror has in many instances distorted women's self-image. A glance through the thin pages of the "Paréntesis femenino" (Feminine Parenthesis) in Contín y Aybar's anthology reveals poems which express the ambivalence of women who, though not quite ready to lose masculine support, nevertheless, feel the uneasiness of knowing themselves unfulfilled. Martha Lamarche's poem is a case in point:

> *Aligérame, Amado,*
> *quítame de los hombros esta carga*
> *de locas ambiciones,*
> *que desfallece mi alma...*
> *Aligérame, Amado,*
> *y otra vez en las noches*
> *seré la chiquitina*
> *que en tus brazos se duerme*
> *soñando como niña...*
>
> (Contín y Aybar: 132)

> (Remove this burden, Beloved,
> lighten the load on my shoulders,
> those foolish ambitions,
> for my soul is languishing...
> Remove this burden, Beloved,

and once again
night-time will find me
the little one
who fast asleep in your arms
dreams as little girls are bound to...)

In this ambivalence we find the seeds of a changing attitude in the formerly static representation of the "muse," a change which would produce new configurations.

The last two decades have witnessed what the critic Bruno Rosario Candelier has termed "un boom femenino" (Candelier: 209-224). The word "boom," explosion, generally points to the impact caused in the sixties by the publication of works by a group of Latin American writers. In the Dominican Republic, this "boom femenino" of almost thirty years later represents the breaking of the silence traditionally attributed to women. Young Dominican women poets among them Chiqui Vicioso, Miriam Ventura, Carmen Sánchez, Sabrina Román, Angela Hernández, Marianela Medrano, Yrene Santos, following the footsteps of Aida Cartagena Portalatín refuse to accept the judgement of the old poetic establishment. These women understand that they must not inhabit a literary world created by men and they cease to be sumisas, blancas, virginales, indias o trigueñas when they come to terms with their own voice and identity. This new Dominican woman derives her strength precisely from her mixed heritage. In some instances, this strength is achieved by studying the African component of her culture. In others, her mixed racial heritage is proposed as the key to open doors to a much wider world.

Aida Cartagena Portalatín began to publish her poetry around the time that Contín y Aybar edited his anthology *Poesía dominicana*. Then there were no female role models to emulate; there was no one to mentor her. Known today as the most important woman writer in the twentieth century, Portalatín's career began as one of the collaborators, later editor, of *La poesía sorprendida*, the literary journal closed down in 1947 by Trujillo's regime.

The closing down of the journal forced Portalatín into a decision: She had to travel in order to break down the barriers limiting her life. To a younger generation of Dominican women writers, Portalatín's travels have come to symbolize Dominican women's flight from her imposed surroundings. Portalatín's poems of this period indicate that they have been written down in such diverse places as Athens, New Delhi, London, Paris, New York and Santo Domingo. In an interview, granted shortly before her death in 1994 to the writer of this article, Portalatín confirmed this interpretation of her work and explained how much her travels and associations with such influential figures as André Breton and Pablo Neruda had changed her poetry, giving it strength and audacity.

This newly found energy and self-assurance spilt over into every aspect of her life. Upon her return to Santo Domingo in the fifties, Portalatín undertook the rigorous task of being co-founder and co-editor of a series of publications which appeared under the name "La isla necesaria". This collection published the works of young as well as older, more established poets, who were writing without the benefit of apoyo oficial. This was Portalatín's way of taking a stand against a system she did not approve of but could not openly confront. In "La isla necesaria" she also published her own books of poetry under the titles *Una mujer está sola* and *Mi mundo el mar*. Her collection of poems *Una mujer está sola* speaks frankly of her condition as a woman alienated in a male dominated world:

No creo que esté aquí de más.
Aquí hace falta una mujer y esa mujer soy yo.
No regreso hecha llanto. No quiero conciliarme
con los hechos extraños.
Antiguamente tuve la inútil velada de levantar las tejas para aplaudir los párrafos
de la experiencia ajena.
Antiguamente no había despertado.
No era necesario despertar.
Sin embargo, he despertado de espalda a tus discursos,
definitivamente de frente a la verídica, sencilla y clara
necesidad de ir a tu encuentro.

(Portalatín: 1955; 7)

(I don't believe I am not wanted.
A woman is wanted here, and I am that woman.
I am not weeping. I don't want to reconcile myself
to someone else's deeds.
In the past, it was my useful lot to lift my voice
In praise of some other's experience
In the past, I had not awakened.
I felt no need.
Nevertheless, I have turned my back
on your tired words,
finally facing the truthful, clear and simple need
to find myself)

Portalatín is not weeping since she has no intention of looking back. No longer interested in gaining male approval, she is free to forget those images found in alien mirrors and to move on to create her own world.

Although the poet is determined to knock down the lofty pedestals to which she had been prescribed, she has no illusions about the difficult task she is facing. Portalatín understands that her search for identity will end only after a long, painful and lonely struggle:

Una mujer está sola. Sola con su estatura.
Con los ojos abiertos. Con los brazos abiertos.
Con el corazón abierto como un silencio ancho.
Espera en la desesperada y desesperante noche
sin perder la esperanza.
Piensa que está en el bajel almirante
con la luz más triste de la creación.
Ya izó velas y se dejó llevar por el viento del Norte
en fuga accelerada ante los ojos del amor.

Una mujer está sola. Sujetando con sueños sus sueños,
los sueños que le restan y todo el cielo de Antillas.
Seria y callada frente al mundo que es una piedra humana,
móvil a la deriva, perdido en el sentido
de la palabra propia, de su palabra inútil.

(Portalatín: 1955: 3)

(A woman is alone. Alone with herself.
With open eyes and open arms.
with a heart opened by a wide silence.
She awaits in the desperate and despairing night without
losing hope.
She believes herself to be in the leading vessel
lit by creation's saddest light.
She has sailed away,
fleeing from love,
the North wind guiding her flight.

A woman is alone. Binding her dreams with dreams,
the remaining dreams and the open blue Antillean sky.
Thoughtful and quiet,
she faces a stony, aimless world,
 lost in the meaning of
its own word, its own useless word.)

With Cartagena Portalatín the demythification of the role of women begins. In the fifties Portalatín discards from Dominican literary lexicon sumisa, virginal, blanca as she begins to redefine the boundaries of the female world. Yet even as she assumes her position as citizen of a much wider world, Portalatín realizes there is much work to be done. In her later poetry, having come to terms with her own independence and her right to her own voice, Portalatín's concerns become those of humanity as a whole and, in particular, those of the peoples victimized by bigotry and racism:

Vertical camino derribado
reducido a esencia original
fatalidad: el hombre
 su problema inherente
simplemente la raza.

(Portalatín: 1984; 47)

(Vertical road trampled
reduced to its original being
misfortune: Said simply,
race is the problem man inherits)

In a courageous blow for Dominican racial identity, until recently linked in poetry to the European not to the African ancestor, Portalatín speaks of her own racially mixed background, and for the first time in Dominican poetry a poet faces her own racial identity without having to resort to euphemisms or justifications:

> *MI MADRE FUE UNA DE LAS GRANDES MAMAS DEL MUNDO*
> *De su vientre nacieron siete hijos*
> *que serían en Dallas, Memphis or Birmingham un*
> > *problema racial*
> *(Ni blancos ni negros)*
>
> > > (Portalatín: 1967; 35)

> (MY MOTHER WAS ONE OF THE GREAT MOTHERS OF THE WORLD
> from her womb were born seven children who would be
> in Dallas, Memphis or Birmingham
> a racial question.
> Neither white nor black)

Clearly the "racial question" alluded to is a point of daily discussion in journals all over the world, as in the case of the senseless death of four black girls in Birmingham:

> > *OTOÑO NEGRO*
> > *elegía*
>
> *'Redoblado tambor redoblando...'*
>
> *Sé que era otoño sin alondras ni hojas*
> *yo que lloro al árbol, al pez y a la paloma*
> *me resisto a los blancos del sur*
> *a esos blancos con su odio apuntado a los negros.*
>
> *No les pregunto nunca porque responderían*
> *que en Alabama pueden florecer las dos razas*
> *Mas, después del verano de Medgar W. Evers*
> *hicieron un Otoño de cuatro niñas negras.*
>
> > > (Rueda: 239)

> > (BLACK AUTUMN
> > elegy
>
> 'Echoing drums, echoing on...'
> I know it was already autumn,
> without leaves and a lark's song
> I, who cry for the trees, for fish and for doves,
> reject the white men of the South,
> those whites with their hatred aimed at black men.

I'd never question their motives
because they would answer
that in Alabama both races can blossom.
But, after the summer of Medgar W. Evers,
came the fall of four black girls)

In this poem, the trees, fish and doves, symbols of a graceful, innocent and generous nature are the counterpoint to an act of gratuitous violence. As it can be seen in the fragment cited above, Portalatín has undressed her verse of adjectives and has given it emotions as its only ornament. Yet her poetic line, sustained by a strong and unyielding anger maintains a lyricism and a beauty which poignantly underscore the loss of possibilities: what can exist when both nature and human beings are in harmony.

In *En la casa del tiempo* (1984), her last collection of poetry, Portalatín's experimentation with form and content culminate in an angry verse characterized by the reduction of the poetic line which gains strength and becomes the visceral shriek of an anguished poet who needs to shake down the foundations of injustice:

> *ay ay ay ay*
> *asesinaron*
> *otra vez a africa otra vez en sharpeville*
> *ooooooooooh oooooooooh*
> *OoooooooooooooooH*
> *nadie grita: castigo*
>   (Portalatín: 1984; 48)

> (ah ah ah ah
> they've murdered africa again
> once again in sharpeville
> ooooooooooh oooooooooooh
> OoooooooooooooooH
> no one shouts: curses)

Aida Cartagena Portalatín's contributions have had a powerful influence on the work of young women poets. In 1984 a group of women writers, organized by Sherezada (Chiqui) Vicioso, formed a "Circle of Dominican Women Poets." According to their manifesto, Vicioso, Carmen Imbert, Carmen Sánchez, Dulce Ureña, Miriam Ventura, Sabrina Román and Mayra Alemán believe that:

> *Se nos puede construir con las palabras del sueño que nos impiden, aunque la voz que permite descuartizar estas palabras, gritarlas, unirlas, no se quiere dejar oír. El temor a su timbre la calla....Porque ya es tiempo de que digamos como querramos la poesía, que expresemos en un ensayo lo que nos plazca, que cantemos nuestros propios cantos, hagamos nuestros propios dibujos, creemos nuestras propias danzas y bailemos al SON de nuestra propia música.* (*El Nuevo Diario*: [I, No. 3] 1984)

(We can build with words born of the dream they forbid us, although the voice that allows destruction, screams, unification of those words cannot be heard. Fear of its own resonance paralyzes it...Because the time has come for us to say whatever we like in our poems, to express whatever we please in our essays, to tell our own tales, to draw our own sketches, to create our own dance and to dance to the beat of our own drum.)

Women's writing in the Dominican Republic today reflects a wide range of themes and styles. Chiqui Vicioso's work on behalf of women and her writings reflect their highest aspirations. In 1980, Vicioso returned home to the Dominican Republic after having lived in New York City for eighteen years. Shortly after her arrival, Vicioso published *Viaje desde el agua* (*Journey from the Water*), a work that established her as one of the literary voices to be heard in the Dominican Republic. As Jane Robinett affirms in her unpublished monograph "From a Woman's Perspective: The Poetry of Sherezada (Chiqui) Vicioso", Chiqui "is a poet who observes and records." Indeed, *Journey from the Water* attests to this need to record ("hacer constar"), and the reader finds in its pages a world without artificial frontiers. Everyday survival in New York City, for example, goes hand in hand with the struggles of the African people or of a Dominican youth drifting, seeking to find direction. This journey brings Vicioso to the realization that as an inhabitant of the world she has arrived at a safe port, the comfort to be found in her solidarity with other human beings:

> *Haití,*
> *caminante que afanosa me sonríes*
> *interrumpiendo siestas de veredas*
> *ablandando piedras, asfaltando polvo*
> *con tus pies sudorosos y descalzos*
> *Haití que tejes el arte de mil formas*
> *y que pintas las estrellas en tus manos*
> *descubrí que el dolor y el odio*
> *como tú se llaman.*
>
> (Vicioso: 1980; 42)

> (Haiti,
> traveller who eagerly greets me
> interrrupting the quiet of paths,
> softening stones, paving dust
> with your sweaty, bare feet
> Haiti who can give art a thousand shapes
> and who paints the stars with your hands
> I found out that love and hate
> share your name.)

In Vicioso's poem, Haiti is the personification of a vital human spirit that transcends the limitations imposed by the realities of everyday living. Haiti is also an explosion of color and light, constantly reminding us that in the end the cause of the just will prevail. Neither political nor economic setbacks can crush the spirit of a people thirsting for life and artistic expression. Furthermore, Chiqui understands that the problems facing the Haitian nation are similar to those of the Dominican people struggling to create art and to survive under difficult circumstances.

From the particular to the universal to the personal, Vicioso voices in her poetry an interest and an empathy for all aspects of human experience:

> *A $1.15 por semana*
> *3 panes diarios me indican que*
> *alguien sabe donde vivo*
>
> > (Vicioso: 1985)

(At a dollar fifteen a week
three daily breads corroborate
someone knows where I live)

Her poetry and her activities as sociologist and activist reflect Vicioso's need to understand, to recreate and to rewrite the history of her people:

> *Antes la identidad era palmeras*
> *mar, arquitectura*
> *desempacaba la nostalgia otros detalles*
> *volvía la niña a preguntarle a la maestra*
> *y un extraño ulular traía el viento.*
>
> > (Vicioso: 1985)

(Before there were palm trees,
the sea, the architecture
once again, the girl would question her teacher
betraying a need for further explanation
and a strange howling was heard in the wind)

The poetry of Vicioso often poses questions that go unanswered at the same time that they communicate the urgency to capture the essence or the "truth" about her culture. In June of 1994, the CUNY Dominican Studies Institute sponsored a conference on "Dominican Literature at the Turn of the Century: A Dialogue Between the Native Land and its Diaspora". Vicioso's presentation owed as much to her Dominican childhood as to her North American experience. It focused on the issue of a young woman's apprenticeship in the world of Dominican womanness. Double standards, sexism, and racism were discussed from the point of view of a narrator who is at times a young girl, at others the reflective adult who has has dealt with learning difficult lessons:

> *I discovered the geographical limits of my world when I was still quite young. One,*
> *two, three, four, five vertical streets until you reached the main road, Sun Street,*
> *with its shop windows, sunny and inaccessible...*

I discovered also the limits of my grandmother's home which streched like a
worm, long and lanky, eating up ever so slowly all that was green. Each one of
us, like bees, had her own cubicle... (Unpublished manuscript)

The narrative continues to trace the gradual realization that there were, in fact, two worlds:

The entire universe appeared to be masculine then. Boys could go fishing. Boys could stay playing in the street until eleven (we, girls, only until nine). Boys could go out alone...

These two worlds take additional significance when racial differences are at play:

I always do things wrong. You should have looked like Juan and Antonia should have looked like Luis... But, Mama! But, nothing! Imagine yourself a white woman with Juan's green eyes. And Antonia with Luis' blue eyes and blond curls? Wouldn't that have been something! But, Mama! To have you turn out like your father. It isn't as if I didn't love him but the boys should have looked like him and Antonia and you like me.

The issue of racial identity is put to rest only when the young woman meets the gatekeeper in her new land:

Your passport... Aquí está. What is this business of india clara? ®Dígame? No buts... That is my color. In Santo Domingo we are classified by skin color. I am india clara, that means "light indian"... Indian is not a color... Pero No buts...Look, I don't have time for this nonsense...

For Dominican writers in the U.S., the admission of a shared African heritage as well as the understanding of their position as marginilized members of North American society, has brought about another level of consciousness to be shared with other Dominicans who in the past had accepted anti-Haitian sentiment in the island. As a member of the diaspora as well as the Dominican community of writers, Vicioso offers a more inclusive approach.

Concern for unearthing their history as women, writers, linked to a homeland whose history and women's participation in it have been problematic can also be found at the heart of the writings of a group of Dominican women writers currently struggling to maintain a sense of equilibrium in New York City. Marianela Medrano's poetry, in particular, has elements which are of particular relevance to this essay. For Marianela Medrano, one of the members of the second Circle of Women Writers in the Dominican Republic where she published her first two collections *Oficio de vivir* (*Survival Is My Business*) and *Los alegres ojos de la tristeza* (*Sadness' Lively Eyes*), being a poet in the Dominican Republic is a painful profession:

> *Hay veces en que el dolor*
> *se levanta con nosotros*
> *cosquillea las pestañas*
> *nos crece junto al silencio*
> *desparramando en la tristeza*
> *un intento de poesía*
> *y su golpe de olas*
> *nos maltrata las neuronas*
> *hay días irreverentes*
> *que asesinan versos*

(Medrano: 1986)

> (There are times when pain
> 　　awakens with us
> 　　it tickles our lashes
> it grows beside our silence
> 　　spread out in sadness
> an attempt at poetry
> 　　and its tidal strike
> 　　upsets our neurons
> these are days filled with irreverance
> assassins of our verses)

From the personal, existential anguish to maintain the spirit alive when all around us appears to be plotting against us, when we are what we do not wish to be, emerge Medrano's earlier verses:

> *De pronto*
> *siento ganas de llorar*
> *y sonrío*
> *ganas de pelear*
> *y hablo de paz*
> *ganas de no ser*
> *y soy*
> *quien dijo que vivir*
> *no es un oficio*
> 　　　　　　(Medrano: 1986)

> (Suddenly
> I feel like crying
> but I smile
> I feel like fighting
> but I speak of peace
> I feel like ceasing to exist
> but I am
> who said that surviving
> is not a business)

　　Living in the U.S. since 1989, Medrano presently resides in Connecticut. From an existence that weighs her down, that bothers her, that interferes with her ability to write, exemplified by the use of short verses in her earlier poetry, Medrano awakens in the U.S. to face her situation as a single parent in an alien land. This is a world Medrano is beginning to understand; one in which, nevertheless, she has begun to define herself as one of a specific class: of those on the fringes of society.

　　For those living on the fringes, like Medrano, it is difficult to articulate a better world for the future generations: the many Dominicans being born everyday. In the poem "Generación del Post X" Medrano presents this concern:

Mi hijo nació en el Harlem (nació en el Harlem)
He comenzado a recoger mi talle
        en la estación del tren
donde un ojo pregunta por mi trasero
A más de la envidia del pene súmese la envidia de nalgas
Fantasma ahogado
revendido en el barrio chino por diez dólares

Procédase al siguiente caso

Las muchachas, las elásticas y suaves muchachas
interrumpen la clase para una acción metafísica
En el salón de al lado amamantan a sus infantes
    Progresa la praxis institucionalizada de
    los demócratas o los republicanos

        o es la misma mierda?
          (Unpublished monograph)

(My son was born in Harlem, was born in Harlem
I have begun to gather my waist
      at the train station
where an eye is inquiring after my ass
Let penis envy be joined by that of buttocks
Drowned ghost
resold in Chinatown for ten dollars

Let us move on to the next case

The girls, those yielding and soft girls,
stop the lesson with a metaphysical act
In the room next to mine children are being breastfed
    Progress is being proposed in bills
    by democrats or by republicans

    or is it all the same crap?)

Loneliness, alienation, objectification, marginality is a far cry from the orderly depictions of genteel womanhood painted by a long-line of paternal poets. Medrano's poetry is introspective even as it is invaded by the sound and assaulted by the violence of her encounter with this brave new world: her new North American homeland. Consequently, her writing reflects an understanding of the need to redefine her existence and the impossibility of accepting or taking for granted cultural givens in her present or a past she unmasks in search of self-definition:

La abuela de ojos azules
oreja retinta
narraba cuentos
de cuco de cuco negro
Historias de pañitos bordados
sábanas blancas
> *sexo virgen*
Secretos de olla y habichuelas
> *bastón mágico para cocinar la dicha*
Perdí la zapatilla de cristal en el polvo
y no vino el príncipe a acariciar las magulladuras
Luego fueron los cactus no los tulipanes
> *fue el encierro no la libertad*
En las horas fijas de la guerra abuela
> *sus cuentos resbalaron por la piel*
-negra no trigueña abuela-
-mujer no muñeca abuela-
> (Fragment, "The Black Bellybutton of a Bongo,"from *Tertuliando*)

(The blue-eyed grandmother
ears of a blueish black
used to tell tales about boogey men
about black boogey men
Stories made of embroidered linens
> white sheets
> virginal sex
secrets brewed in pots and found in the flavor of the
beans by the magic wand to condiment happiness
I lost my crystal slipper in the dust

but there was no prince to soothe my blisters
Later on it was all about cactus not tulips
It was about confinement not freedom
During the hours arranged for our struggle
your stories slid down my skin
> black-not trigueña, grandmother
> woman-not doll, abuela)

The work of Marianela Medrano and of the members of the Tertulia de escritoras dominicanas en los Estados Unidos, among them Josefina Báez, Yrene Santos, Virginia Moore, Miriam Ventura, Ynoemia Villar, Nelly Rosario and Annecy Báez and the publications by Dominican women writers in the past two decades justify Candelier's assertion that there has been an explosion of female voices filling with fresh air the closed quarters of male dominance. Art has taken a thousand shapes in publications such as *Demando otro tiempo, Internamientos, Distinguida señora, Hubo una vez y dos son tres, Geometría del vértigo, Música del agua, Arca despejada, Piano lila, Mi silencio roto* and *El libro de Alamí, antología del placer.* These works speak of the experience of women who elude easy definition and who cannot be fitted into ready-made molds. By writing about their racial identity, searching within themselves for answers, and by identifying with those who share a bond, Dominican women have taken the most important step in gaining their own voice. In the words of Miriam Ventura, there is much to celebrate because

> *Hay mujeres que por sus encantos es el mundo quien le adeuda*
> *otras piensan en conflictar auroras*
> *a estas una duda de años acaricia las sienes*
> *para ellas levadura y felicidad pueden ir juntas*
>
> *Hay mujeres hay mujeres*
> Miriam Ventura, *Clave para fantasmas.* New York: Alcance, 1996.

> (There are women whose charm make the world
> their own a gentle probing caressing their temples
> others think about creating new dawns
> for these women yeast and happiness can go hand in hand
>
> There are women there are women)

Bibliography of Works Consulted

Arias, Aurora. *Piano lila.* Santo Domingo: Editora Buho, 1994.

Candelier, Bruno Rosario. *Ensayos literarios.* Santo Domingo: Editorial Santo Domingo, 1986.

Cartagena Portalatín, Aida. Una mujer está sola. Santo Domingo: "La Isla Necesaria," 1955.

_____. *La tierra escrita.* Santo Domingo: Baluarte 15, 1967.

_____. *En la casa del tiempo.* Santo Domingo: Montesinos, 1984.

Cocco De Filippis, Daisy. *Estudios semióticos de poesía dominicana.* Santo Domingo: Taller, 1984.

_____. *From Desolation to Compromise, The Poetry of Aida Cartagena Portalatín.* Santo Domingo: Montesinos, 1987.

_____. *Sin otro poeta que su canto, antología de poesía escrita por dominicanas.* Santo Domingo: Taller, 1987.

_____. *Combatidas, combativas y combatientes, antología de cuentos escritos por dominicanas.* Santo Domingo: Taller, Publicación del Instituto del Libro Dominicano, 1992.

_____. *The Women of Hispaniola: Moving Towards Tomorrow,* Proceedings of the 1993 Conference. New York: Executive Paper, Vol I, No. 1, York College CUNY, 1993.

_____. *Tertuliando/Hanging Out, Dominicanas y amiga[o]s*. Santo Domingo: Comisión Permanente de la Feria del Libro Dominicano, 1997. U.S. edition. New York: Editorial Alcance, Publication Sponsored by the CUNY Caribbean Exchange Program, 1997.

Contín y Aybar, Pedro. *Poesía dominicana*. Santo Domingo: Julio D. Postigo, 1969.

Goede, Johanna. *El libro de Alamín, Antología del placer*, Santo Domingo: Amigo del Hogar, 1994.

Hernández Nuñez, Angela. *Arca despejada*. Santo Domingo: Editora Búho, 1994.

Incháustegui Cabral, Héctor. *Escritores y artistas dominicanos*. Santiago: Universidad Católica Madre y Maestra, 1978.

Jackson, Richard L. *The Black Image in Latin American Literature*. New Mexico: New Mexico University Press, 1976.

Medrano, Marianela. *Oficio de vivir*. Santo Domingo: Colección Separata, 1986.

_____. *Los alegres ojos de la tristeza*. Santo Domingo: Editorial Búho, 1987.

Mejía, Rosalía. *Música del agua*. Santo Domingo: Editora Corripio, 1995.

Meyers, Doris et al. *Contemporary Women Authors of Latin America*. New York: Brooklyn College, Brooklyn College Humanities Series, 1983.

Morales, Jorge Luis. *Poesía afro-antillana y negrista*. Puerto Rico: Universidad de Río Piedras, 1976.

Moreno Jimenes, Domingo. *Obras poéticas, del gémido a la fragua*. Santo Domingo: Taller, 1975.

Pantaleón, Adalgisa. *Mi silencio roto*. Santo Domingo: Editorial Centenario, 1995.

Rivera, Marta. *Geometría del vértigo*. Santo Domingo: Editora El Nuevo Diario, 1995.

Rueda, Manuel et al. *Antología panorámica de la poesía dominicana*. Santiago: Universidad Católica Madre y Maestra, 1972.

Sánchez, Carmen. *Demando otro tiempo*. Santo Domingo: Offset y Encuadernaciones, 1995.

Ventura, Miriam. *Trópico acerca del otoño*. Santo Domingo: Huellas, 1987.

Vicioso, Sherezada (Chiqui). *Viaje desde el agua*. Santo Domingo: Visuarte, 1981.

_____. *Un extraño ulular traía el viento*. Santo Domingo: Alfa y Omega, 1985.

_____. *Internamientos*. Santo Domingo: Sin casa editorial, 1992.

Villar, Ynoemia. *Hubo una vez y dos son tres*. Santo Domingo: Publicación Moira, 1993.

MYRNA GUERRERO
Santo Domingo, 1951

Myrna Guerrero is an artist, cultural activist and critic of art. She is a member of the Asociación Internacional de Críticos de Cine (AICA) and of the Asociación Latinoamericana y del Caribe de Agentes para el Desarrollo Cultural (ALCAGEC).

In 1995 Myrna Guerrero organized the first seminar-exhibit about the contribution of Dominican women to the field of plastic arts. A homage to Celeste Woss y Gil, the seminar-exhibit and the publication of the proceedings, as well as biographies and descriptions of the art in the exhibit, represents a priceless contribution and a pioneering effort to begin to write the history of women in Dominican culture.

At present, Myrna Guerrero is the director of the literary and artistic supplement of the daily newspaper El Caribe in Santo Domingo.

Selected Bibliography

Guerrero Villalona, Myrna and Danilo de los Santos. *Mujer y arte dominicano hoy, homenaje a Celeste Woss y Gil, Exposición-Seminario, Casa de Bastidas, 1995.* Santo Domingo: Amigo del Hogar, 1995. 146 p.

Woman, Art and Marginalization*
1. Some considerations on the woman artist and her creation.

Everyone knows the aberrant situation of dependence, marginalization and oppression in which a large proportion of women throughout the world find themselves, simply because they are WOMEN. This situation can reach unheard-of levels, in such cases as that of mainland China, where the definition of gender can be a death sentence because of the state limit of one child per family and the generalized preference for a male child as transmitter of the family surname.

In our country we might think that the situation for us as women is less extreme. However, the growth in domestic violence, whether psychological or physical; the alarming rate of sexual abuse of girls; the ignorance of the right of women to equal treatment as a HUMAN RIGHT; the legal impediments in our legislation which curtail full socio-economic participation of women and the apparently unsolvable difficulties of revising the legal code to incorporate laws which will guarantee equal rights and opportunities for all Dominican men and women, make us realize that here, too, marginalization is a fact.

When, in addition to being a woman -a condition we do not choose— we decide to follow the call of our vocation as an ARTIST, our destiny will be crisscrossed by marginalities, and from this

---

* Paper presented in the Seminar on Women in Dominican Art Today, held in the Casa de Bastidas, Santo Domingo, Dominican Republic, March 21, 1995.

intersection a strength to overcome the majority of traditional impediments will be born. Yes, because a woman, in her development, has to surmount innumerable obstacles in order to be an artist: disapproval from her immediate family, lack of understanding from her circle of friends, mistrust in her school or academy... until, when she has already been accepted into the nucleus of artists and she seems to have left behind her limitations, then we notice that there is still a struggle and marginalization continues in the most subtle guises.

Very little is understood of the specificity of being a woman; of the uniqueness of her language; of her singular eye for detail; of her prodigious perception of her reality; of her intuition; of her concept of time and of space; of her metacommunication....And although for many the work of art is ASEXUAL I believe, and I wish to share this with you, that just as a man and a woman are two expressions of one reality -that of the human being biologically differentiated—the product of our creativity in one way or another should translate our specific gender without in any way signifying a qualitative deterioration. And since today we understand and accept the quality of diversity, this concept should be validated in the work of art by a man or a woman.

I present various examples to clarify the above. The first is a text by André Bretón, the father of Surrealism, quoted by Lourdes Andrade in her article "Tres Mujeres del Surrealismo" ["Three Women of Surrealism"] (*Revista México en el Arte* No. 11, 1985-86).

Bretón presents us with the following image of woman:

> *...Love is a transformational force, it is a magnetic process which draws the lovers toward a wider union with the universe, toward a fusion with the diverse forms of the earth ...The agent of love is the woman: the woman is part of the unfathomable, the magnetic, she is the spark that illuminates the world around her and invigorates the senses... Magician, depository of mystery, within her move telluric forces which are incomprehensible to man; initiated in the secrets and purposes of the earth, she manages hidden energies and finds herself near dreams and instincts....* (André Bretón, quoted by L. Andrade, 1985).

The author of the article adds:

> *...and thereby the surrealists bestow on women the roles of magician, enchantress, intuitive, vital beings initiated in the secrets of the world. This determines the character of their creation..."* (L. Andrade, 1985).

In the second text I quote Michele Mattelart in *Mujeres e Industrias Culturales* [*Women and Cultural Activities*] where the following is posited:

> *... This measure specifies that feminine subjectivity attributes and defines time simultaneously as repetition and eternity: the return of the same; the eternal return, return of a cycle which unites her to a cosmic time, a motive of incredible pleasures in union with a natural rhythm, and on the other hand, this infinite matrix, this myth of permanence, of monumental duration....It can be said that feminine time appears, along with the perception of the body itself, at the center of the research being done by women at present in order to come to a consensus on cultural expressions manifesting the uniqueness of a feminine contribution, showing what she feels as a woman....This diffuse investigation leads them to explore their archaic memo-*

ry linked to the space and time of reproduction, in which one part of her sensibility continues to be constructed and defined as part of her uniqueness. It is an irreducible difference, since it depends on the psychological, biological and sexual difference that tradition has used to alienate and dominate, a difference that is currently expressed in the form of alternative meaning and symbolism...

By 1968, René Passeron, in *Historia de la Pintura Surrealista* [*History of Surrealist Painting*] had pointed out, in regard to the works of Leonore Carrington, Dorothea Tannin, Toyen, Leonor Fini, Frida Khalo and Valentine Hugo, the following:

...We find then that the majority of female surrealist painters are grouped by analysis. Is this a coincidence? In addition to their fondness for careful depiction, they have in common a certain psychoanalytic symbolism. They do not experience the influence of Dalí, nor have they let loose the fantastic. But yes, the unfathomable, the repugnant, delicious... concerning, above all, the worries, fears, mysteries and marvelous hopes or anxieties of feminine eroticism. The theme of maternity does not appear, generally, in their work. The theme of conquering beauty is absent, as is Dionysian pleasure. In retaliation, the woman as victim, the mistreated ingenue, the woman-child lost in her dreams... constitute the response to the cruelty with which the male surrealist painters imbued the essence of their homage to woman...

It remains to be stated then that it is necessary for us to revise our interpretive codes for the analysis of the work of female artists with the goal of beginning to eliminate the conditions which arbitrarily hold that work in low esteem at the present time.

2. Regarding Marginalization: Its Characteristics and Their Effects on Women Artists.

This phenomenon should be analyzed on both axes of marginalization: the internal and the external. By the first we understand self-alienation, with which we often feed ourselves, that alienation which is not imposed upon us by anyone or anything, but rather which we promote when we assume comfortable postures of laziness at work, when we accept the lack of research, when we do not accept the challenge of participation; when we feed FEAR, yes, the fear of confrontation, taking refuge in the shadow of the reigning injustice or inequality, lacking the courage to overturn the established paradigms. It is lamentable but may times we lack the claws with which to defend our rights and our work, shielding ourselves in the peace of anonymity and satisfying ourselves in the familiar market.

But marginalization also includes another reality: that external world dominated by male patterns, where the law of the strongest rules, he who speaks loudest and shows off more, the improvisation and the attitude that all that matters is getting what's mine. That world many times makes us assume the roles of "intellectual she-males", as Carmen Imbert Brutal has pointed out, disdaining solidarity in favor of opportunism and the non-recognition of the values of others.

Further, external marginalization establishes itself on other slopes, dissimilar in appearances but which, when all is said and done, are no more than different aspects of the same problem: ALIENATION.

2.1 Disclosure-Promotion. It is undoubtable that the lack of familiarity of the work of women in art is a world-wide phenomenon and the inequality in the promotion of their work in terms of the publicity which a male artist receives is enormous. For example, how many are familiar with the sculptures of Barbara Hepworth or Alicia Peñalba? With the photographs of Julia Margaret Cameron and Dorothea Lange? With the paintings of Maruja Mallo and Maria Blanchard? The works of Georgia O'Keefe, Maria Helena Vieira Da Silva, and Sophie Taeuber-Arp? Who recognizes that Toyen is the artistic name of a Czech surrealist named Maria Germinova? Perhaps we have not heard of some of these names before, but it is certainly true that they sound familiar: Henry Moore, Ansel Adams, Joan Miro, Juan Gris, and Robert Delaunay. Why? Simply because their names appear more frequently in publications while one must go out and search for the names of the female artists.

In the Latin American milieu the situation is similar. We are unaware of the social painting of the Peruvian Teresa Carvallo and the Bolivian Magda Arguedas. We are ignorant of voluminous aggressiveness of the sculpture of the Ecuadoran Germania de Breihl and that the Cuban Lolo Soldevilla made luminous mobile reliefs before the apparition of film. The lyric abstraction of the Haitian Marie-José Nadal, the native primitivism of the Paraguayan Olga Blinder and the Brazilian Djanira and the syncretistic magic of both Judith Gutierrez from Ecuador and Costa Rica, and Louisanne Saint-Fleurant from Haiti seem strange to us. We do not recognize the geometric painting of the Venezuelan Elsa Gramcko or the kinesthetic murals of the Argentinean Marta Boto. According to the majority of publications, it would seem that the woman is a stranger to the visual arts in Latin America, since the only artists who appear regularly are Orozco, Rivera, Soto, Guayasamín, Lam, LeParc, Obin, Obregón, De Szyslo, Botero, Tamayo, Zuñiga, Cruz Diez, Kingman and many other men.

Happily, the work of the Brazilians Anita Malfatti and Tarsila Do Amaral, the Puerto Ricans Noemi Ruiz and Myrna Baéz. the Cuban Amelia Peláez, the Venezuelans Marisol and Gego, the Mexicans Remedios Varo and Frida Khalo are beginning to be evaluated on their own merit.

But, how many noteworthy women artists succumb to oblivion because their socialization promotes, in the first place, men, and the competition, ruled by sexist patterns and discourses, slights women?

The national situation is not any more gratifying. How many of us are familiar with Adriana Billini or Genevieve Báez, Noemi Mella or Aida Ibarra?

Our top institution for the visual arts, the Museum of Modern Art (MAM) has organized three homages to Dominican artists: Yoryi Morel, Gilberto Hernández Ortega and Eligio Pichardo. Not one was a woman, making this event the first homage dedicated to Celeste Woss y Gil, as much an artist and master, and with as solid a production as the three previously mentioned.

The same institution has published three monographs dedicated to Paul Giudicelli, Gilberto Hernández Ortega and Fernando Peña Defilló. Also missing from these honors are the women. The Volunteers of the Royal Houses, run by women, is the only institution which has published a monograph about the work of a woman artist: the volume on Elsa Núñez. The only other book in existence is on Amaya Salazar, and is the product of her own initiative.

Likewise, in the coloring book "Dominican Fine Arts" by Leon David and Maria Aybar, 39 male artists and only 6 women artists appear. These are: Celeste Woss y Gil, Clara Ledesma, Ada Balcacer, Elsa Núñez, Soucy de Pellerano, and Maria Aybar. Likewise, in the *Anthology of Dominican Painting* by Cándido Gerón, only 6 of the 47 artists presented are women; five of the women appear in the previous list and Adriana Billini replaces Maria Aybar. These are only two examples of a cruel reality. Nevertheless, we must point out that women artists have received better treatment in the books by

Danilo de los Santos , *La Pintura en la Sociedad Dominicana* [*Painting in Dominican Society*] (1978) and Jeanette Miller, *Historia de la Pintura Dominicana* [*History of Dominican Painting*] (1979).

Nevertheless, there is still much to be done in the field of the promotion of the woman artist. Research is needed to rescue the artists buried in oblivion; there is a need for monographs to study our principal artists; exhibitions and television programs which reevaluate the role of women in visual arts are necessary; we need, in short, places for discussion where the work of women artists, work that is at times anonymous or very timid, underappreciated, can be continuously evaluated and their larger contributions to national art be appreciated.

2.2 Selection of participants in national and international events. The disproportion of men to women in the selection process is our daily habit. Let it suffice to recall the national participation in the most recent international events:

Cagnes-sur-Mer Festival (1994)

Sao Paulo Biennial (1994)

Cuenca Biennial (1994)

Havana Biennial (1994)

Inter-American Arts/DOMECQ-Mexico Biennial (1994)

Caribbean Biennial (1994)

Johannesburg Biennial (1995)

For a total of seven international events 26 artists were selected. Of these only three (12%) were women: Belkis Ramírez, Inés Tolentino and Amaya Salazar. We consider this ratio to be disproportionate when we consider the present quality and quantity of women visual artists. We must call upon our institutions and those responsible for the selection of participants in international shows to establish mechanisms which will guarantee equal treatment for all our artists, male and female alike.

This is reaffirmed when we consider that when an open invitation is given, the participation of women increases considerably. Let us take as an example the Nineteenth National Visual Arts Biennial (1994) and the Fifteenth Leon Jimenes Art Competition (1994) in which, of a total of 167 artists selected for the first and 158 for the second, women comprised 16% and 18% of the participants respectively. This number approaches the ratio of men to women in the visual arts nationally (20% are women).

2.3 Art Criticism. We continue to do critical analysis with sexist parameters. Mea Culpa. We critics have been trained using texts and references written by men, with their vision and their language. For centuries, the aesthetic parameters have been drawn by men without, until now, the consideration of the possibility of the validity of a different vision. We are repetitive in our analyses and our critical judgements, ignoring the particular vision of women and the unique properties of a feminine aesthetic. Vigor, aggressiveness, robustness are values traditionally identified with masculinity and many times we translate this as a quality of art. It is now time to begin a different kind of criticism which will make possible the consideration of other values as qualitative aspects of a work of art. If in contemporary film women's vision is more and more valid; in music, having a good voice does not mean being a tenor or a baritone, and in dance there are specific postures and expressions for men and women, it is then possible that in the visual arts we can also utilize different codes to evaluate the expression of each gender. This is the challenge.

3. Recommendations.

As a sort of conclusion we submit the following recommendations:

3.1. Encourage research about women artists in schools of art and universities for the purpose of broadening our knowledge of these artists and their media.

3.2. Support the creation of forums of this type where the analysis of women artists, their problems and their talents can be studied without interruption.

3.3. Create a center for women artists or a section of the Dominican College of Fine Arts (CODAP) dedicated to matters of gender which will establish contacts with women's museums and the ONGs which support the work of women artists, with the goal of obtaining scholarships and exchanges for our female artists.

3.4 Create incentives for solidarity among all of us as a resource for our improvement and strengthening as people and as artists.

Speaking of other things:

Aida called herself a writer. She loved writers and
artists.

She endured privations and failures
For these she declared herself against the enemies of
culture;

against those who corrupt art.
Against those who solicit the rewards of the Prizes.
Against those who compromise
the Juries in their favor.

Aida Cartagena
"Ninth Elegy"
La tierra escrita

Bibliography

Andrade, Lourdes. "Tres Mujeres del Surrealismo" in *México en el Arte*, Journal of the Instituto Nacional de Bellas Artes, No. 11. Mexico, 1985-86.

Calzadilla, Juan and Montero Castro, Roberto. *Visión de la Pintura en Venezuela*. Cuadernos de Difusión No. 3, Publications of the Dirección de Cultura Gobernación del Distrito Federal, Caracas, 1975.

Catalogues. *Catalog of Works, XV Concurso de Arte E. León Jimenes*. Dominican Republic, 1994.

General Catalogue, Colección Pintura y Escultura Latinoamericana. Museum of Fine Arts of Caracas, Venezuela, 1980.

Catalogue II: Exposición de Arte Boliviano Contemporáneo. Santa Cruz, Bolivia, 1978.

Catalogue XIX: Bienal Nacional de Artes Visuales. Santo Domingo, Dominican Republic, 1994.

David, León and Aybar, Maria. *Artes Plásticas Dominicanas*. García Areválo Foundation, Santo Domingo, Dominican Republic, 1990.

De Los Santos, Danilo. *La Pintura en la Sociedad Dominicana*. Madre y Maestra Catholic University, Santiago, Dominican Republic, 1978.

Falcón, Jorge. Teresa Caravallo. Sabogal Institute of Art. Peruvian Art. Bolsilibros Collection, Vol. 4, Lima, Peru. 1988.

Gerón, Cándido. *Antología de la Pintura Dominicana*. Tele 3 Publishers, Santo Domingo, Dominican Republic, 1990.

Mattelart, Michele. *Mujeres e Industrias Culturales*. Anagrama Ed., Barcelona, Spain, 1982.

Miller, Jeanette. *Historia de la Pintura Dominicana*. Banco de Reservas de la República Dominicana Editions. Santo Domingo, Dominican Republic, 1979.

Nadal, Marie-José and Blancourt, *Gérard. La Peinture Haitienne*. Natham Editions, Paris, 1989.

Translation by Margaret A. Ballantyne

CARMEN IMBERT BRUGAL
Puerto Plata, 1954

Lawyer, judge, professor, writer, poet, novelist and communications expert she has won much praise for the perspicacy and intelligence of her writings and for her work on behalf of women. She has contributed much to the organization of a number of NGOs and to the structuring of agendas on behalf of Dominican women. She has participated in panels, seminars, talks, conferences in the Dominican Republic as well as in other countries.

With her novel *Distinguida señora* Imbert Brugal carves a place of honor for herself as one of the pioneers of the post-modern Dominican novel, and she continues her trajectory as a frank and daring innovator. These elements also define her essays, including this provocative and pathbreaking selection.

Selected Bibliography:

Palabras de otro tiempo y de siempre. Santo Domingo: Editora Imprenta Héctor Blanco Weber, Colección Antología de Nuestra Voz, No. 4, 1983. 44 p. (Poetry)

Infidencias. Santo Domingo: Alfa y Omega, 1986. 73 p. (Short Story)

Tráfico de Mujeres: una visión de una nación exportada. Santo Domingo: Centro de Solidaridad para el Desarrollo de la Mujer, 1991. 24 p. (Essay)

Distinguida Señora. Santo Domingo: Editora Amigo del Hogar, 1995. 230 p. (Novel)

THE MANLY INTELLECTUAL WOMAN*

If we read the traditional anthologies we perceive that literary work has been to great extent alien to women. Could it be true that only two or three women have dedicated themselves to the hard occupation of creating literature in our country? Or could it be truer that traditional editors of anthologies have purposely left out those works?

The names of women that timidly appear makes us think less of a writer than of a languid madonna who for one instant abandons knitting needles, diapers and kitchen, and borrows the pen from her husband as she scratches in a neat piece of paper. The interpretation offered by those males are sufficiently explicit: "Intimate and soft voice of a woman", "poetess of manly intonation".

One critic of our days, in one of his books, recognizes that feminine creation has been and is minimal, and only two names of women appear in his study of Dominican poetry.

From the sixties the number grows, then among the students and readers of compilations the names of Carmen Natalia, Jeannette and Soledad frolick. Even then, if we limit ourselves to orthodox sources, only six women have been able to perpetuate their names in print.

---

* From "Cantidahechizada," *El Nuevo Diario*, February 11, 1985. Also in *Sin otro profeta que su canto, antología de poetas dominicanas*. Santo Domingo: Biblioteca Taller No. 263, 1988.

This number frightens, not only for its meaning in the cabala, but because it could never be in proportion to the quantity of women who dedicate themselves to activities "suitable for their sex". This means that for each poet, who, after sustained production of literature "deserves to be included in a text" that has the quality to endure, there would be six chroniclers of social activities, forty candidates for the Miss República Dominicana title, and one hundred and ninety-eight saleswomen of Mary Kay products. Could it possibly be that women walk away from creative activities and unfortunately, because it is easier, take on roles that have been taught and disseminated?

"Look for the Male"

Something does not add up. If by the mere chance of carrying out independent creation as our first obligation, we forget the patriarchal surroundings that marginalize us, silence comes. It is against those surroundings, defeating the same, that we ought to inscribe the dissemination or aceptance of the literature created by women.

When we manage to have a permanent presence in publications, there is an implicit premise. There was masculine assistance. When one counts on an asfixiating and humilliating sponsorship, that can be disdained after received, it will mark the subsequent attitude of the recipient.

Those who speak are men, those who write are also men. When women decide to speak out, men will have to control the manner, which, in a certain measure, will give trascendence to the creation. Women will have to risk all, counting on the favor of a Mecenas who functions in a certain manner as a pimp.

"Now it is your turn."

And it is because women are "sisters and enemies" when it comes to validation as persons. It is difficult for you to give a hand to those who are in the well, like you were before being able to escape with a great deal of trouble, and thus you will assume an attitude of varona (manly woman).

The vices and prejudices of the male stick to your skin. You will become powerful, and the machista attitude that had kept you down will be your weapon against other women. Indirectly you will have influence over the "other's" decision to rely on that rusty brain which created the first heated beautiful pages but always forgot to include you; you will make the other resort to the dens, within an organization, modern parodies of the "sacred hill", from where dogmas, diatribes and insults are read. Intellectual gatherings celebrate the varona who is willing to sing the praises of her lord. But were the same woman to dare to sing the praises of her own vagina she would be marginalized and plunged into the chaos caused by ugly rumor. Were she to dare to sing in celebration of her body, she would be assailed by the participants, and rumors about her frigidity, lesbianism or possible nymphomania would have their day. That is the risk that the attitude of the winner cannot prevent.

Then, is there nothing to be done?

If the compilers of anthologies do not gather our names, if it gets more difficult each day to be included in the pages of traditional literary supplements, if one has to count on the male for validation of one's work, we are apparently lost; but it is only apparently, because we have the necessary insight to avoid being left out by working constantly, by conscious self-validation, by having the required solidarity.

We can write our own history, to make the product of our creation lasting, which on occasion comes out of a dramatic process, with frustrating consequences.

Translation by Daisy Cocco De Filippis

RAMONA HERNANDEZ
Santo Domingo, 1954

Born in Santo Domingo, Ramona Hernández has lived in New York City for more than two decades. Dr. Hernández has a B.A. in Latin American History from Lehman College of The City University of New York and an M.A. in Caribbean and Latin American Studies from New York University. In May 1997, Dr. Hernández received her Ph.D. in Sociology from The Graduate Center of The City University of New York. Currently, Professor Hernández teaches Latino Studies at the University of Massachusetts, Boston.

An active participant in community organizations in New York City, Dr. Hernández is a founding member of the CUNY Dominican Professors Association, a researcher at the CUNY Dominican Studies Institute and First Vice President of the Dominican Studies Association/Asociación de Estudios Dominicanos.

Selected Bibliography:

Dominican New Yorkers: A Socioeconomic Profile, 1990. New York: CUNY Dominican Studies Institute, 1995. (With Francisco Rivera-Batiz and Roberto Agudini.)

Dominican New Yorkers: A Socioeconomic Profile, 1997. New York: CUNY Dominican Studies Institute, 1997. (With Francisco Rivera-Batiz.)

The Dominican Americans. Westport, Conn.: Greenwood Press, 1998. (With Silvio Torres-Saillant.)

NANCY LOPEZ

A native of the Dominican Republic and a New York resident for decades, Nancy López is an ABD candidate in sociology at The Graduate Center of The City University of New York. An active participant in community affairs, Ms. López is a member of the board of directors of the Dominican Studies Association/Asociación de Estudios Dominicanos.

YOLA AND GENDER: DOMINICAN WOMEN'S UNREGULATED MIGRATION*

No one really knows how many Dominicans flee their homeland illegally in the small, homemade fishing boats known as yolas. But everyone seems to agree that they are simply too many; too many women, men, and children. Dating back to the Tainos hundreds of years ago, traveling in yola is not a new phenomenon. Yet, only recently has it become a frequent means used by those who, seeking to leave, desperately violate the rules that regulate national boundaries.

These frail wooden boats are constructed clandestinely in two to three days and can carry a human cargo ranging from seventy to a hundred people. The space on yolas is small, and all that hap-

---

* First published in *Dominican Studies: Resources and Research Question*, Luis Alvarez-López, et.al. Dominican Research Monographs. New York: CUNY Dominican Studies Institute, 1997.

pens on board—eating and defecating, crying and laughing, getting ill and trying to sleep—must occur in the same diminutive space. Sometimes, from fear of going overboard, women may menstruate and men may soil their pants. There are no individual choices or privacy. The travelers are all one, trying to survive their perilous escape.

Lacking any overhead protection from the unrelenting sun rays, passengers endure unbearable conditions for their two- to three-day ordeal. Once in Puerto Rico, if apprehended by the Coast Guard, they are repatriated to the Dominican Republic, only to attempt the endeavor again. Why are so many Dominican people, and particularly women, leaving their island in fragile boats? And what are some of the socio-economic implications of this phenomenon for the sending society? These are some of the questions we intend to address in this preliminary report.

Purpose of the Study

The aim of this study is two-fold. First, we wanted to examine the socio-economic background of Dominican women who resort to migration in yola. We began asking ourselves whether these migrants fit a homogeneous social class description and whether their socio-economic status resembled that of other women who have been previously studied by scholars of Dominican migration. Second, we wished to explore the nature of social interaction between men and women during the actual sea crossing. Specifically, we were curious to see whether traditional male/female relationships would be modified by the pressure of shared calamity, a harsh and uncertain environment temporarily outside the supervision of the State with its configurations of men and women as dissimilar subjects of law and nation.

Methodology

As researchers, we combined three methodological approaches: (1) one-to-one, in-depth interviewing in migrants' homes; (2) focus groups; and (3) participant observation. Research was conducted in 1993 during the months of June and July for a period of two consecutive weeks in five Dominican towns selected on the basis of two criteria: they were frequently used by migrants as a port of departure, or they were commonly known for their high incidence of out-migration. While in the Dominican Republic, we were assisted by two Dominican anthropologists who had conducted the only existing research on the issue of yola migration.

During the two-week period, we interviewed twenty-five women using a snowballing sampling method. Women were identified for interviewing by "word-of-mouth" or through friends and the two local anthropologists. A detailed questionnaire containing eighty-seven questions was used to collect demographic and socio-economic data. Interviews were typically over three hours long and usually took place in the informants' homes. In some cases, informants arranged for us to talk with them at a friend's home, which, we conjectured, they deemed to be more presentable than their own.

The Towns, The Women

All the towns visited were located on the North-East and the Eastern coast of the Dominican Republic. These, unlike other towns, provided ideal sites for yola departures not only for their proximity to the Caribbean Sea, but also their wilderness, their inaccessibility, and their remote location. The most popular of these towns was approximately four and a half hours from Santo Domingo by bus over bumpy roads.

The principal economic activities of these towns were agro-cattle raising, sugar, and light manufacturing. One of the regions depended mainly on the production of rice and coconut. In addition, in all the towns we found a vast informal economy dominated by chiriperos, people who did not hold steady employment for long periods of time. Though in some of these towns, light industrial production via the free trade zones had proliferated during the last three decades, unemployment was still rampant. Sugar production was seasonal and depended mainly on the use of Haitian laborers. Manufacturing was increasingly based on capital intensive production, resulting in the underuse of labor and generating chronic structural unemployment. Extensive cattle raising production exacerbated the unemployment problem by monopolizing land, since cattle, which occupied more than half of all agrarian land, used an estimated 12.8 tareas per animal for pasturing on the average.

The women interviewed belonged to three different migrant categories. One group had lived in Puerto Rico for some time or had voluntarily returned home after establishing their legal residence abroad. Specifically, nine had been deported and two had managed to become permanent residents in Puerto Rico. Another group was represented by seven women who had been caught in the Mona Passage while trying to enter Puerto Rico. The third group, made up of seven women, had never left the Dominican Republic, having been apprehended in the process of trying to leave the country. After the migrants were recruited for the trip, the yola migration included three stages: first, the hideout in the dense, insect-infested bushes along the Dominican coastlines; second, the actual sea voyage, which may last three days; and finally, the disembarkation process which may include hiding out again in Puerto Rico.

Asked whether they had tried to leave the country through legal means, all the women in our sample responded that they had not because they knew they did not qualify for a visa. Beside their urgent material need and the lack of an alternative means of emigration, the decision to embark in a yola was influenced by the regularity, cost, and rate of success of this mode of transportation.

Informants explained that as many as four yolas may leave the country in any given week during the active months of migration. They also said that usually trip organizers, the captains, are well known, for they have been on the job for some time. The more successful trips an organizer makes, the more clients he or she will have. Some passengers may travel on credit with the understanding that they will pay the captain after a time of living abroad. For those who pay beforehand, prices ranged from $1,500 to $5,000 Dominican pesos per person. Trips organized entirely by family members and friends were becoming increasingly important. They were extremely cheap and, as found by Taveras, Puello, and Selman's 1988 study, occasionally included two or three non-relatives. Family members were not normally charged a fixed amount, but they contributed depending on their own sense of fairness. Among non-paying passengers on a non-family trip, we were able to identify three categories. First, there were friends of the captain. Second, there were those who had earned a seat on the boat by recruiting a number of paying passengers, usually five. And finally, there were the relatives of the organizer.

Preliminary Findings

Socio-Economic Background Early studies in Dominican migration concluded that most Dominican migrants in the United States were predominantly rural, poor proletarians or unskilled workers (González 1970, 1973, 1976; Hendricks 1974; Vicioso 1976). However, Ugalde, Bean and Cárdenas (1979) challenged this notion by arguing, instead, that Dominican migrants were mostly urban and educated, coming from the middle and working class strata of the population. Most recent research on migration to the United States has adopted the finding of Ugalde, Bean and Cárdenas (see for instance, Kritz & Gurak 1983; Bray 1984, 1987; Baez Evertsz & D'Oleo Ramírez 1986; Georges 1991; Grasmuck and Pessar 1991; Portes & Guarnizo 1991).

Contrary to the prevailing socioeconomic model, we found that Dominican yola migration is an all-encompassing phenomenon which includes people from both rural and urban settings. When asked about their birthplace, equal numbers of the women reported having been born in small rural villages and in urban settings. The significant number of women in our sample who came from a rural background suggests that a three-fold migratory process, rural-urban-international, is characteristic of unregulated migration. Our study did not reveal, however, whether migration in yola has reinforced rural-urban mobilization in the Dominican Republic.

Our study found that all the women interviewed were poor, belonged to the working class, and only half of them were employed prior to migration. Most of the women worked as domestics or in a factory in the free trade zones, or in retail sales in the informal economy. None of the women interviewed had a profession or generated a salary that could place her in the rank of the middle class. Salaries ranged from $350.00 to $1000.00 pesos per month. With the exception of two, all women were the heads of their households, and most of them resided in overcrowded homes. In some instances, as many as fifteen people lived a two-room shack, without running water or sewage, which is a typical feature of ghettoes in the Dominican Republic.

Seven of the women interviewed had not finished elementary school and some who had started high school were not able to complete their studies because they needed to work full time to contribute to the household income. Three of the women were high school graduates, but none of them had any college or technical education.

Factors Influencing Migrants Many of the women interviewed were primarily concerned about generating income to maintain their children and families, regardless of whether it was in Puerto Rico or in any other country, including Saint Thomas, Saint Croix, or Antigua. Those who identified Puerto Rico as their destination were asked whether they intended to stay there or migrate eventually to the United States. Those who had managed to live in Puerto Rico for a while, or who had seen it before being apprehended by the coastguards there, invariably said that they always wanted to return home. When asked specifically about using Puerto Rico as a stepping stone to go to the continental United States, with the exception of two who said they had family there, the rest indicated they were not interested in moving further if they could earn a decent living in Puerto Rico. Three of the women who had been apprehended in the Mona Passage said they would have returned home after living abroad for some time. The others were not clear and felt that it all depended on what they found in the host country.

Interestingly, the seven women who had not yet succeeded in leaving the Dominican Republic all wished to leave for good and bring their children and as many members of their family as possible whenever they had the chance to do so. Whether their answer stemmed from resentment towards their home country for repeatedly frustrating their aspirations, or from some other feelings or thoughts, we do not really know. What we do know, however, is that among those who somehow manage to leave, even for a little while, the intention to return is clear.

When asked about why they wanted to leave the Dominican Republic, all women categorically said that they were forced by the economic situation. Specifically, they talked about their inability to find a job and provide a decent life for their children. It is important to note that all our interviewees had children and their children's well-being was identified as the main reason behind migration. They were all the primary caretakers of their children. The number of children among our informants ranged from two to six. Responsible fatherhood was perceived more as a voluntary or optional behavior on the part of the men.

During the interview women were asked to figure out a monthly income which would have allowed them to remain in their country. Their answers indicated incomes which ranged from $1,500 to $8,000 Dominican pesos. The differences in the ideal monthly income reported by informants may be based on the specific class sector each informant represented. For example, while some informants lived in quarters which would hardly fit the description of a house (made from rice bags, wood, thatch and mud), others had homes that were made of wood or cement. Their differing types of jobs and employment status may have also shaped their responses.

Although the majority of the women in our sample were heads of their households, the amount of money they made was not enough for the social reproduction of their families. What prompted them to endure such a perilous trip was not a concern about their own well-being. Instead, they were urged by the desire to enhance the life chances of their family. The survival of her kin, particularly her children, seems to be foremost on the mind of each Dominican woman who decides to migrate in yola.

Impact of Women's Yola Migration

The Economy Informants stated that a good portion of the earnings remitted by those who actually managed to live abroad went towards basic food items. Similarly, the economic impact of yola migration was evidenced in the construction of houses. Some houses were built in cement, while others originally made out of wood were converted into cement houses. Migrant homes, unlike the surrounding homes, possessed electrical appliances and other modern goods, such as video cassette recorders, stereo systems, and cassette players. Also, the migrants' contact with a foreign country was notable in their way of dressing: designer labels as well as gold rings, bracelets, earrings, and chains. These goods are not only for the sake of pure vanity. Informants told us that these items served as barter in moments of economic need. Some migrants who had a good collection of the latest merengues and other Latin rhythms intentionally played loud music in their houses for the enjoyment of neighbors who did not have radios.

A married informant whose husband also migrated in yola and worked in Puerto Rico, managed to save enough money to build an inhabitable wooden house in her town. Though the house, composed of two bedrooms, a living room, and a kitchen, was too small for the five-member family, the informant told us that it took her five years to build it. She explained that every year she traveled to Puerto Rico by yola and worked there for 9 months as a domestic servant. She normally decided to go back to the Dominican Republic when missing her children became unbearable. To return to the Dominican Republic, she bought a route permit (carta de ruta). She usually stayed with her children for about three months, repaired whatever had to be fixed in the house, and again embarked on a yola to Puerto Rico. At the time of the interview, the informant told us that on her next trip to Puerto Rico, she was going to save enough money to build a bathroom and to pay a number of bills amounting to $1,300 pesos. The informant stated that the money she received from her husband, who remained in Puerto Rico while she was in the Dominican Republic, was simply not enough to cover all the necessary expenses to continue to build the house.

Visitors to many of the sending towns would be struck by the number of houses that were boarded up by people who had left, as well as by the mushrooming of cement houses in progress that were surrounded by weeds. For many migrants, however, the construction of livable homes stagnates for years and many empty lots bought by emigrants slated for the construction of homes were literally vegetating in the sending towns. Since migrants who owned these potential houses were no longer in the town, we never had the opportunity to ask why they were not finished or in some cases even started. We hypothesized that migrants either lost interest in returning to their home town or were simply not making enough money abroad to be able to build or finish these homes.

In addition to changing the household finances, yola migration impacts the local economy. The consumption of potential migrants and trip organizers who come to the departing towns stimulates economic activity. Previous research has found that the number of buses for public transportation and the number of trips to these towns has increased considerably since the yola movement began around the 1970s. After reaching the towns, potential migrants need to wait some time before boarding the yola and in the meantime need services such as lodging and food. Informal entrepreneur practices, such as room rentals and the selling of food and beverages in some homes have proliferated spontaneously in these towns. Similarly, the number of formal food and clothing shops have increased as a direct response to local demand for these items.

Migrants also buy a number of goods for consumption during the sea voyage. These items include: Malta Morena (a type of sweet cola), crackers, beef jerky, bread, canned food, painkillers for headaches and Dramamine for sea sickness. When we asked our informants why they did not bring these items from their home towns, we were told that they were trying to avoid appearing conspicuous to police and other government agents who are constantly persecuting potential yola migrants. Also, some of the migrants believed that their presence was well-received by local residents, particularly business people, because, with them there, local demand for their goods and services increases.

The Family   In one home we visited, we found a father left in charge of taking care of his three children because the mother had emigrated. In most cases, however, child-care arrangements followed a more traditional pattern in which children were left in the care of women relatives, especially sisters or grandmothers, or female neighbors. Georges has argued that children left behind in the care of relatives, particularly grandmothers, add an extra burden to the family in question. She noted that taking care of these children involved not only an increase in the care-taker's work-load, but also a high degree of psychological responsibility. A grandmother whose daughter had migrated to the U.S. and had left her with her six children, lamented that she was a "prisoner" since her responsibility towards her grandchildren restricted her from visiting her other daughters in the country (Georges 1990: 201).

In our study we were unable to document any complaint or resentments on the part of the grandmothers and other relatives who were left in charge of the migrants' children. What we found was that in general their increased responsibilities were perceived as an inevitable duty. This was not surprising to us since for most Dominicans it is only normal that relatives perceive themselves as directly responsible for the well-being of other members of the family, whether they are children or adults. There, the prevalent kinship model is the extended family, which may include members who are not directly related by blood or marriage. Often, a family includes a compadre or comadre (co-parents) and even neighbors who have seen the family's children grow up and have developed a close relationship with the family in the process.

Only one informant, a father who was left with the children, was angry and complained strongly about his duty. What is interesting to note is that we do not know whether this man was angry due to the responsibility he had of taking care of his children, or due to the fact that his partner had left him without his approval. As he said "Yo no sé por qué esa mujer tuvo que arriesgar su vida. Como pobres que somos, yo creo que a ella no le faltaba nada aquí. Lo que pasa es que ella es una mujer ambiciosa." (I don't understand why that woman had to risk her life. Though we are poor, I don't think she needed anything more than what we have. The problem is that she is an ambitious woman). As he spoke, the man proudly showed us his home, which obviously was far from meeting the basic needs of a poor working-class family. The so-called house had two-rooms which were divided not by a wall but by a long curtain made of 100-pound rice bags. The kitchen consisted of a couple of tables placed in the backyard of the two rooms. One had two anafes (rudimentary stove made of iron and fueled with coal) and the other had eating and cooking utensils. Yet, he felt that his wife had no reason to leave.

Regular remittances sent to relatives in charge of taking care of migrant women's children constitute a secure income which could play an important role in the socio-economic life of certain households. This is evidenced in the case of María, a woman who had migrated to Puerto Rico three years before, leaving her four children with her older sister, her sister's husband, and their three children in an Eastern town highly recognized for its high incidence of clandestine emigration. María's monthly remittance to support her children was the only regular and secure income of her sister's home. The sister's husband was a chiripero and he was often unable to find jobs. María's sister was a home-based seamstress who produced women's clothing. Many times during the month she was unable to contribute to the household income because there were no orders. As she told us, the money from Puerto Rico always came. Even when it was known that María was sick and could not work for a few days, the money came and at least the food for the household was secured. María's sister had tried to leave the country five months before, using the same captain María had used. Unfortunately, we were told, she was apprehended while still in Dominican waters and could not leave.

While María's remittances to her children came on many occasions to save her sister's household from not being able to meet basic demands, remittances from abroad have been perceived by some scholars as having a negative impact in the recipient family as well as in the national economy. Franc Báez Evertsz and Frank D'Oleo Ramírez (1985) argue, for instance, that remittances received in homes whose members are within economically active ages but where no one is engaged in the labor force, contribute to the development of parasitism and sustained idleness in the country (45).

The prevailing notion among scholars of women and migration from the Dominican Republic is that paid labor in the receiving society has yielded psychological and material rewards for women. It is argued that Dominican couples residing in the United States, for instance, have fostered a new social interaction in their homes, a "movement away from the hegemony of one sex over decision-making and control of domestic resources to a more egalitarian division of labor and distribution of authority" (Pessar 1987: 120). Furthermore, it is contended that before migration to the United States, Dominican women are guided by a "housewife ideology," a set of values and norms that prevents them from complete or full physical movement and limits their sexual behavior and employment opportunities (Georges 1990: 130-35). In this view, male domination in the Dominican Republic is reflected in women's subordination and their oppressed position in their homes. Once in the U.S., whether they articulate it or not, women exhibit a roughly feminist outlook in so far as they seem to act in ways that favor themselves as women. Leaving aside the fact that when compared to men, women in U.S. society still remain in a socially disadvantaged position, whether in politics, the economy, or the home, we wanted to explore the sources of the feminist attitude expressed by Dominican women. Did it derive from their contact with a supposedly more egalitarian society or, in fact, from their own cultural endowment and their social and historical development in the sending society?

Female Yola Migrants and the Feminist Mentality

When women were asked about the ways in which they interacted with their spouses prior to migration, they categorically stated that most Dominican men were "machistas" who believed they had the right to control women just because they were men. They agreed that there were some "hombres buenos" (good men) out there, but these men were too few. The majority of Dominican men were selfish and "mujeriegos" (womanizers). Five women believed that men had the right to control women and saw being womanizers as stemming naturally from this entitlement. The overwhelming majority (15), however, categorically denied men any such right.

One woman, the oldest one, whose mate was much younger and lighter skinned than her, strongly remarked that no man, no matter how he felt about being a man, "podía inventar con ella" (could mess with her). In other words, Dominican men could be as macho as they wanted, but they could not dominate her. This woman had attempted to migrate but was left behind by the organizer who had promised to bring her to Puerto Rico. She told us that she was just waiting to get the money to try again. Three other female neighbors who were very close to our informant and who we assumed wanted to observe the interviewing process, corroborated what our informant had told us by adding as they nodded "eso sí es verdad" (that is very true). Although none of these women had tried to migrate illegally, one who had a daughter in the U.S. had already begun the migration process and was waiting for a permanent visa. These non-migrant women, though, echoed the same sentiment of insubordination to patriarchal imperatives as our yola migrant.

This leads one into some of the complexities of women's behavior in Dominican society. While there were Dominican women who passively accepted their subordination inside the home and who thought that that was how things were meant to be between women and men, a good many held a completely opposite belief. Similarly important was the fact that non-migrant women, women who had not demonstrated the kind of aggressivity assumed necessary to undertake such an intimidating trip, seemed to share the understanding held by the yola migrants that a man should have no control over a woman's life. An interesting piece that problematizes the picture even further is the fact that, even while consciously accepting their subordination inside their homes and openly granting their mates certain privileges they deny to themselves (i.e. the right to have multiple mates), some women reject the subordination imposed by society when they, consciously, may at the same time decide to violate laws concerning the international mobility of people. By moving without formal consent from the sending or receiving societies, these women are acting as subversive agents, showing a type of resistance against rules and regulations of male centered notions.

Upon examining some of our respondents' answers, one gets the impression that in Dominican society a man could understand himself as a macho and not have full control of his partner's life. How could this be possible? How could a man be a macho and not dominate "his woman"? How can a woman live under patriarchal domination and at the same time feel that she is in control of her private life? We believe that the answers to these questions are found in Dominican culture, in which the female/male relationship is not commonly characterized by negotiations expressed verbally, or by women assuming an overtly defiant attitude in society. Through their control of the social mechanisms of communication, Dominican men have the socially sanctioned command of public verbal expression on patriarchal norms. But Dominican women have managed to circumvent this power by simply exercising their agency at will. While men talk of their norms, representing what in sociology is called the ideal culture, women act, representing practices of the real culture. This asserting of their sovereignty in the real culture has been a common form of women's resistance. Thus, social impositions of men's dominance in the public sphere may not necessarily permeate the male/female conjugal relationship.

A good example of this phenomenon is reflected in women's sexual behavior. Dominican men can openly exercise their sexual freedom (i.e., by having multiple and simultaneous sexual relationships). Dominican women, however, forbidden from the same sexual freedom, opt to re-define their sexuality quietly. Publicly, most women are "decent" women, women of respect, who refrain from extramarital sex. Typically, "good and decent" women do not discuss their sexual experiences and many would even deny having any if they are not living with a man. Thus, it is uncommon to hear a woman talking publicly about her sexuality. Yet, in the private sphere, women subversively create spaces to cope with society's sexual mores. News concerning a man who, in a rage, has killed his wife after finding her in another man's arms, suggests that many "decent" women do disobey the patriarchal norms that legislate bedroom activity. That is to say that, despite their awareness that infidelity is socially and legally precluded, Dominican women do exercise sexual agency by deviating from the prescribed morality when they deem it necessary.

An interesting twist to this matter is that although extramarital romance on the part of women is highly condemned, people are fully aware that women may not conform to their mates' or society's impositions in that matter. This is clearly evidenced in a highly popular merengue of 1995 which broke sales records in the Dominican Republic, Puerto Rico, and New York. The song tells the story of a "vena'o" (Dominican pronunciation for venado, deer), a Dominican man who is mocked by his neighbors for his complicity in his wife's extramarital affairs. Apparently, the man's wife had these involvements in her native country as well as in Puerto Rico, where she eventually migrated in search of work. In Puerto Rico the song was banned from public radio stations and other places. Puerto Rican authorities, including the church, alleged that the song portrayed Puerto Rico as a society where women have extramarital involvements, which they believed denigrated all Puerto Rican women.

The existence of such suggestive documents as the aforementioned merengue that highlights the occurrence of female infidelity would seem to accord with the answers given to us by some of our informants who also suggested that women only pretend they are obedient and conform to society's regulations. Yet, when the right moment comes, they act, and, with their actions, challenge prevailing moral conceptions about how they ought to be. Rather than articulating frank violations of social norms, they tell other women "No importa que tan macho sea; pero a mí no me domina" (So what if he is a macho. He does not dominate me). Women act when actions are necessary without involving themselves in face-to-face confrontations with men. Their humoring of machismo, on the other hand, represents another form of women's resistance by trivializing patriarchal standards.

Studies on Dominican women migrants have disregarded the subject of women's resistance to male domination in Dominican society. Yet, most Dominican feminist scholars recognize that women, although uninvited, have been active agents in social change. During the last three decades their activism has become ever more salient, as evidenced, for instance, by the proliferation of diverse women's organizations. Documenting women's activism and changing roles in Dominican society, Carmen Julia Gómez (1990) has explained that Dominican women have historically resisted men's dominance through a process she calls "insubordination."

> *Insubordination is defined by the author as the process in which women resist the limitations imposed on the development of their potential and their full integration to society as subjects who possess the same rights as men. Women's insubordination has expanded social spaces and has either broken or weakened social barriers based on gender division.* (16) [Authors' translation]

Women's resistance to male domination is concretely reflected in their increasing participation in institutions traditionally dominated by men as well as in their participation in redefining some of these institutions. In Gómez's view, the increasing number of homes headed by single mothers represents a direct form of female insubordination to men's concept of the family. Through the process of insubordination, the author explains, "women have weakened patriarchal power structure and conceptualization." (17) [Authors' translation]

Dominican Ideal Culture during the Yola Crossing

Based on the premise that the female/male relationship in Dominican society extends beyond a simple dichotomy of male domination/female subordination, we then became interested in learning the nature of the male/female relationship as it evolves during yola migration. Since yola migration is an illegal activity where people function outside the parameters and boundaries of everyday society, we specifically wanted to see whether or not Dominican social norms remained intact, were altered or perhaps transformed during the migration process.

Women's accounts of their experience identify a non-traditional sexual division of labor during the yola crossing. All the women in our sample said that women were as brave as men, and that in many instances, women assumed positions of leadership in moments of crisis. Informants told of women who persevered through storms encountered during the two-or-three-day crossing, repaired the yola when it was ruptured by the rough sea, and did not tire of emptying water from leaky boats.

Perhaps a wider sense of solidarity may be experienced during the sea migration, a type of solidarity that seems to cut across gender differences. Informants explained that, during the entire yola migration, men and women, acted as if they were family, and important decisions related to the trip were made collectively. We were told that migrants equally distributed any food brought along with them for the sea voyage. In the words of one of our informants: "En la yola, todos éramos como hermanos. Ahí no había distinción entre hembra y varón. Todo el mundo quería lo mismo." (On the yola, we were all like family. There was no distinction between men and women. Everyone wanted the same thing). Only two of the 25 women reported instances of sexual harassment by men during the emigration process. In both cases, the solidarity created during the trip, particularly during the hideout stage, led migrants collectively to come to the aid of the female victims.

Conclusions

International pressure, particularly from Puerto Rico, compels the Dominican government to discourage yola migration. The trips are described as highly unorganized and risky endeavors undertaken by individuals who are abandoning their country, a portrayal contradicted by our informants, who affirmed that all the suffering encountered in the migration process would not discourage them from trying the voyage again. Both the Dominican and Puerto Rican governments are actively engaged in apprehending potential and actual yola migrants. However, in most cases, their efforts prove to be ineffective. In one of the towns visited we found a newly appointed navy official who boasted that no mojados (wetbacks) could circumvent the intensive surveillance operations currently undertaken on the coastline. Similarly in Puerto Rico in 1991, "legislation was introduced...to fine the government of the Dominican Republic $1,000 for each illegal Dominican apprehended" (*The New York Times* 1992a). Also, xenophobic civilian organizations whose aim is to stop undocumented Dominicans from entering or gaining residence have proliferated in Puerto Rico and the United States.

In the meantime, the number of illegal trips has increased considerably during the last years. While in 1988 only 1,958 Dominicans were deported from Puerto Rico, by 1991 this number had more than doubled to 4,093. Immigration officials explain that these statistics do not include an additional 3,000 Dominicans apprehended by the coastguard at sea in the Mona Passage during that time.

The lack of jobs and their low earnings were identified by our informants as the main reasons behind the decision to emigrate, and our study revealed that just as many employed as unemployed Dominican women embarked on yola. But developmental strategies in the country have failed to generate enough jobs and an effective wage policy to address the needs of a growing labor force. The proliferation of free trade zones in the country within the last three decades, particularly during the late 1980s, has not undermined the need to emigrate. The simple creation of an employment policy that does not take into account the elasticity of the labor supply would not prevent people from emigrating. Nor would the implementation of a wage policy which does not consider the inflationary tendency in the Dominican economy. What is required is a an effective employment and wage policy which takes into account the absolute expansion of the labor force and the cost of its social reproduction. Government institutions and xenophobic groups need to realize that any efforts aimed at stopping or controlling the emigration of people without addressing their needs will fail. Dominican women, or men for that matter, will continue to cross the ocean as long as their needs remain unmet in their country.

In relation to the formation of Dominican women's feminist mentality, it seems that women's consciousness has a complex historical formation originating in Dominican society and culture, which goes beyond a given historical event such as migration. Dominican women, as Gómez has stated, have resisted men's domination through insubordination, an insubordination which, we venture to argue, has created the basis for a feminist epistemology, which may manifest itself in patterns unrecognizable to those whose vision is informed by other cultural paradigms. We would propose, then, that it is not only a gender issue which is at stake here, but also a more critical and nuanced cultural understanding.

Works Cited

Báez Evertsz, Franc and Frank D'Oleo Ramírez. 1985 *La emigración de dominicanos a Estados Unidos: determinantes socio-económicos y consecuencias.* Santo Domingo: Fundación Friedrich Ebert.

Bray, David. 1984 "Economic Development: The Middle-class, and International Migration in the Dominican Republic," *International Migration Review* 18.2.

Georges, Eugenia. 1990 *The Making of a Transnational Community: Migration, Development, and Cultural Change in the Dominican Republic.* New York: Columbia University Press.

González, Nancie L. 1970 "Peasants' Progress: Dominicans in New York," *Caribbean Studies* 10.3. 1976 "Multiple Migratory Experiences of Dominican Women," Anthropological Quarterly 49.1.

Gómez, Carmen Julia. 1990 *La problemática de las jefas de hogar: evidencia de la insubordinación social de la mujer.* Santo Domingo, CIPAF.

Grasmuck, Sherri. 1984 "Immigrant, Ethnic Stratification, and Native Working Class Discipline: Comparisons of Documented and Undocumented Dominicans," *International Migration Review* 18.3.

Grasmuck, Sherri and Patricia Pessar. 1991 *Between Two Islands: Dominican International Migration.* Berkeley: University of California Press.

Hendricks, Glenn. 1974 *The Dominican Diaspora: From the Dominican Republic to New York City-Villagers in Transition.* New York: Teachers College Press.

Kritz, Mary, ed. 1983 U.S. *Immigration and Refugee Policy: Global and Domestic Issues.* Lexington, Massachusetts: Lexington Books.

The New York Times. 1992 "Puerto Rico's Coastline: New York's Back Door" by Larry Rohter. Sunday, December 13, p.30

Pérez, Glauco. 1981 "The Legal and Illegal Dominicans in New York City," paper presented at the Conference on Hispanic Migration to New York City, at New York University. Department of Latin American and Caribbean Studies.

Pessar, Patricia. 1982 "The Role of Households in International Migration: The Case of the U.S.-Bound Migration from the Dominican Republic," *International Migration Review* 16.2.

_____. 1984 "The Linkage between the Household and Workplace of Dominican Immigrant Women in the United States," *International Migration Review* 18.4.

_____. 1987 "The Dominicans: Women in the Household and the Garment Industry," in *New Immigrants in New York*, ed. Nancy Foner. New York: Columbia University Press.

_____. 1988 "The Constraints Upon and Release of Female Labor Power: The Case of Dominican Migration to the United States," in *A Home Divided: Women and Income in the Third World*, eds. D. Dwyer and J. Bruce. Stanford: Stanford University Press.

Portes, Alejandro and Luis Guarnizo. 1990 *Tropical Capitalists: U.S.-Bound Immigration and Small Enterprise Development in the Dominican Republic*. Washington, D.C.: Working Papers, Commission for the Study of International Migration and Cooperative Economic Development.

Puello, Rafael and Glenis Taveras. 1996 "Impact of yola migration in the local economy of sending towns" (on-going ethnographic research, 1996)

Riessman, Catherine Kohler. 1987 "When Gender Is Not Enough: Women Interviewing Women," *Gender and Society* 1.2.

Taveras, Glenis A., Rafael B. Puello, and Ana Selman. 1988 Aspectos culturales en la migración ilegal de los dominicanos hacia Puerto Rico, 1982-1987: La travesía en yola. Bachelor's Thesis, Universidad Autónoma de Santo Domingo, Dept. Historia y Antropología.

Ugalde, Antonio, Frank Bean, and Gilbert Cárdenas. 1979 "International Migration from the Dominican Republic: Findings from a National Survey." *International Migration Review* 13.2.

Vargas-Lundius, Rosemary. 1991 *Peasants in Distress: Poverty and Unemployment in the Dominican Republic*. Boulder: Westview Press.

Vicioso, Luisa (Chiqui). 1976 "Dominican Migration to the U.S.A." *Migration Today* 20.

ANGELA HERNANDEZ
Jarabacoa, 1956

Angela Hernández is one of the most respected intellectual figures in the Dominican Republic today. Although she is still quite young, Hernández has published a considerable number of books. Community organizer, activist, fiction writer, lyric poet, her words of love to a soulmate remind her readers of a lost innocence as her poetry envisions a paradise regained. A tireless worker on behalf of the rights of women, Hernández has co-authored a series of handbooks designed to explain women's legal and moral rights. At present, Hernández finds herself at the forefront, earning the respect of the critical establishment in the Dominican Republic who consider her a formidable force on behalf of women and one of the best writers of the moment.

Selected Bibliography

Desafío. Santo Domingo: Editora Gente, 1985.

Las mariposas no le temen a los cactus. Santo Domingo:UASD, 1985.

Emergencia del silencio. La mujer dominicana en la educación formal. Santo Domingo: UASD, 1986.

Tizne y cristal. Santo Domingo: Editorial Alas, 1987.

De críticos y creadoras. Santo Domingo: Editora Búho, 1988.

Alótropos. Santo Domingo: Editora Alas, 1989.

Edades de asombro. Santo Domingo: Editora Alas, 1990.

Libertad, creación e identidad. Santo Domingo: UASD, 1991.

Masticar una rosa. Santo Domingo: Editora Alas, 1993.

Arca espejada. Santo Domingo: Editora Alas, 1994.

ON CRITICS AND CREATIVE WOMEN*

Stereotypes and discriminatory judgements based on sex have incisive effects, as much in their most brutal traits as in the multitude of falsely glittering strands that tint their paternalistic components. These disarm the spirit, vanquish anger, and lead to pretense, generating an adaptive predisposition in the face of deeds and situations inhibiting to the rise and the manifestation of primordial areas of human cultural development.

That men and women produce literature of good or bad quality is a fact.

Well then, in Latin America, and in the world, who judges literary works? Who has the respon-

---

* Translated in its entirety. *De críticos y creadoras*. Santo Domingo: Editora Búho, 1988.

sibility to judge the quality and importance of the same? How many infinite possibilities and combinations do the imagination and the aesthetic possess? Is the critic's judgement exempt from his personal perception of the "correct" order of social and interpersonal relationships? Does the author's specific social context condition his or her perception or manifestation? Can only one scale be established to decide the worth of themes, styles and expressions? How do the terrible intimate schisms provoked by a discriminatory world reveal themselves in the creative process?

This is where diversity shows its conflictive mysteries. This is where complexity manifests itself in distinguishing the reach of prejudicial conditioning. This is where being a man or a woman can bring to bear differences of meanings.

In order to begin to create, to dare to attend a public forum, to be judged, to continue to propose to do better, to resist indispositions and hostilities, to ignore indifference, and learn tenacity on the way, the creative woman requires a mettle and a strength which, generally, is diminished by her gender socialization. Vitality, discipline, enthusiasm and humility will be infused only in the gratification of communication, in the transcendence of the act of authentic expression and the perception of a hint of a promising plentitude. The spirit multiplies itself and flowers on contact with internal and external intensities.

There is only one Literature; however, there exist multiple expectations, degrees of certitude and forces of interpretation and reception of historical and everyday happenings. The perception of time, of place within the sphere of activity, thematic and expressive priorities, intimacy or the displeasure with codes are variables undoubtedly faced in the situation of the artist in his or her relation to the centers of social power. These will become the intratextual parameters.

The great luminaries in the creative sky are, almost unfailingly, men.

In the *Antología Poética Domincana* by Rafael Emilio Sanabia published in 1944, 145 male poets are reviewed. The second part of the book, entitled "Our Poetesses" deals with the names of only twenty-three women.

Joaquín Balaguer, in *Historia de la Literatura Dominicana*, studies 119 men, divided according to whether they wrote novels, stories or poetry. In this book, nine women are reviewed. Carmen Natalia Martínez and Aida Cartagena are included for the period between 1930-1958. The largest number of feminine names is found in a marginal section entitled "Other Outstanding Figures in the Field of Letters". Here are included nine women writers, along with a list of masculine names.

A more recent publication, the *Antología Literaria* prepared by Margarita Vallejo de Paredes, sponsored by the Institute of Technology of Santo Domingo, contains 117 male poets vis a vis fifteen women. In other literary genres the number of writers is considerably lower.

In the section on Essay there are ten masculine names and no female names. Under Biographical Sketches there are no women, neither as writers nor as subjects: 17 male writers study men. In Discourses, there are reviews of 19 men and one woman. She is Salomé Ureña, in her speech upon the graduation of a group students from the Instituto de Señoritas. Of the 63 authors presented under Short Stories, seven are women.

Poetry is the genre most explored by women. This fact is possibly due to the very conditions under which they write. Narrative requires perseverance, free time, concentration, and perhaps, greater audacity. These are necessary elements for the development of productive poetic labors as well.

If there are few short story writers and essayists, there are even fewer novelists. This genre, as José Donoso has noted, requires a singular effort over time, "prolonged, sustained, a continuous effort of sweat and tears, whose interruption can result in paralysis and the loss of months of work."[1] On the other hand, the short story, which is in no way artistically inferior, "can be written sporadically, when the impulse strikes, when the soul awakens and there are interruptions and spaces between one story and another, and changes in direction and time to catch one's breath."[2] Something analogous happens with poetry.

The explanations of the limitations and singularities of exceptional women have to be searched for in the lives of the majority of women, as Virginia Woolf reflected on one occasion. This affirmation possesses a validity difficult to contradict, when women, whether exceptional or ordinary, are placed in their historical context.

One could risk, in advance, the judgement that women in the Dominican Republic have produced more poetry than any other genre due to the fact that poetry can better channel their emotions and sentimental impulses.

At the same time, however, men have also written more poetry than novels or stories; at least that is what the anthologies show us. In terms of women writers, the disproportion continues to be much more noticeable.

Writing is an intimate activity, in which one makes contact with the most delicate and acute perceptions of one's surroundings. It demands concentration and persistence. These are strange elements in an unruly everyday reality filled with children and housekeeping tasks, where other people are always present -especially the husband- demanding and taking what is theirs, and thereby altering the unique and central role of the individual woman.

The fragmentation, the discontinuity and preferences for particular genres among the works of numerous women writers have to be found within this reality. Many others, perhaps the best, have altered important facets of their personal lives in order to ensure themselves their own creative space. Is it a coincidence that among a striking number of women writers there is an absence of children, or that divorce, separation or the choice of a single life are so common?

From 1944 to the present (1987) many names of women writers have vanished. Recent anthologies list only three or four women poets before 1960.

Were they eliminated because the quality of their poetry did not withstand the test of time or because of disdain for their content or style? One explanation which needs to be tested is that offered by the critic José Alcántara: "The majority of our poetesses do not move beyond the little explosions of jubilation or disenchantment which stir their hearts as young girls."[3]

It is not possible to ignore, however, the patriarchal ideological connotations which color the criteria, masculine criteria for the most part, with which women writers are evaluated. Likewise, in order to understand the context of these writers, it is necessary to return to the conditions of their respective eras.

The few women writers of the end of the nineteenth century and those who distinguished themselves in the first four decades of this century were pioneers in literature, in education and in femi-

---

1   Donoso, José. "Temperatura Ambiente." Cultural Supplement "Isla Abierta of the newspaper *Hoy* April 1987. Santo Domingo, R.D.

2   Idem.

3   Alcántara Almánzar, José. *Estudios de Poesía Dominicana*. Editorial Alfa y Omega. Santo Domingo, D.R., 1979. p. 269

nism. The educational and civil rights they fought for are criticized for being as inconsistent as their literary works are. But they began to forge a road, clearing a path for other women.

Until 1940 the law prohibited any woman from practicing any profession or vocation without the authorization of her father, her husband or her guardian. Politically she was nonexistent. She possessed no civil identity of her own. She could not even decide the course of her own life. She lived bound by her reproductive nature and her domestic "duties."

Still into the second half of the last century only a handful of women received even a minimal academic education. Those who did generally had the protection and the intellectual support of some close relative. Such are the cases of the women poets Josefa Perdomo and Salomé Ureña.

Manuela Aybar, La Deana, recounts that in her time, women were only taught to read so that they could study the Bible. Writing was not taught in order to avoid the exchange of "little notes" with the boys.

Economic dependence, lack of mobility, the restriction of personal liberty as well as the non-existence of noteworthy role models who could confirm for girls and teenagers the creative possibilities of women, combined with the limited access to formal education were serious obstacles to the appearance of women writers before the nineteenth century.

Women writers find individual impediments to the unfolding of their creativity and interpretations of their works, when they are judged by sexist criteria.

The negative influence on both sexes by the narrow intellectual framework so characteristic of our Latin societies cannot be denied. Our roots are short and sparse, particularly in those countries where with one bloody blow the indigenous past was erased and nations were born according to the unstable formulas of religious orthodoxies, echoes of liberalism and mixtures of European and African cultural elements along with native products derived from such combinations.

Nor can one question the common boundaries which limit the creativity of both men and women, as equals, in a country where literature itself is marginal—marginal because of the economic hardship which regularly accompanies its practice. Marginal because of illiteracy. Marginal because of the survival imperative of the majority of the population. Marginal, too, it must be said, because in alternative political models, it is common for creativity and literature to be ignored, subordinated or pigeon-holed in imprecise and frozen schema.

The primordial themes of the majority of female poets prior to the decade of the 1960s reveal the narrow limits of their life experiences. Home, children, love (stripped, of course, of any eroticism), religion, Homeland (in the abstract, with traces of romantic nationalism) are the regular sources of their inspiration. Many long centuries defined family and home as the natural boundaries of women. Men became their necessary reference point. Women were subjected to restrictions and scales of importance they did not define for themselves. The themes of the women poets manifest the coordinates of their lives, of the moral constraints on their passions and the unidirectional orientation of the same. Their literary production likewise shows the evolution of their self-perception and the modes by which they capture exterior circumstances.

The women poets prior to 1960—except Aida Cartagena and Carmen Natalia, (I do not dare to include Salomé Ureña)—were discouraged by the "domestic angel", that stranger who inhabits us from within and without, he whom it would be necessary to defeat in order to develop oneself as a writer. Virginia Woolf depicted the noxious influence of this celestial seducer. Entrancing and castrating, he rests on the shoulders and murmurs in the ears of the writer:

Dear, you are a girl, write about a book written by your man. Be understanding, be tender; flatter; trick; use all the shrewdness of your sex. But never allow anyone to suspect that you have your own ideas. And, above all, be pure.[4]

The "Domestic angel" summarizes the qualities designated as feminine, useless, in great part, for creative potential. Wrapped in the "angel's" wings, woman is deprived of a part of her expression, closing off paths of creative exploration.

The "domestic angel" for Virginia Woolf is the spirit of the home, and therefore, woman. She is intensely understanding. Intensely charming. She totally lacks selfishness. She distinguishes herself in the difficult arts of family life. She is self-sacrificing on a daily basis. In short, she was made in such a way as to never have an opinion, a desire of her own, but rather to prefer to adhere to the opinion and desire of others. Needless to say, above all, she was pure. It was thought that her purity constituted her principal beauty.

Among our women poets, Salomé Ureña never succeeded at vanquishing the "domestic angel," but on occasions was able to ridicule it.

The chaste and very sad Josefa Perdomo could not even recognize it, sitting on her shoulders, directing her relationships. She fought in a small place, pursued by insufferable yearnings to rise. And she rose, like a spiral of smoke whose expansion is blocked:

A weak woman, Oh sublime God! is she whom fate with chastity does oppress until its splendid throne and sublime escape are given to her.[5]

The tragic and intense Altagracia Saviñón, employing a style much freer than that of her predecessors, shows the terrible pulsation of her existence. From where do these lethal convulsions of her spirit spring? Would she perish, boldly and furiously fighting the "domestic angel" in the deepest core of her being? Was it a conflict of intelligence, of logic against closed windows, with a sharp perception of what was happening, groping for the unattainable on the other side of the walls? Who can ever know?

My life seemed to me to be a vast desert and my soul a solitary tomb, a barren moor without light where Illusion with his noisy battle broke my wings, a very cold and dark sepulcher where Ideal laid dead.

Brief. With a biting intensity. That is the seventeen - year old Altagracia Saviñón writing on the eve of her madness.

Aida Cartagena and Carmen Natalia, in their most daring works, defeat the "domestic angel"; they kill him and bury him.

Aida is marvelously, impeccably perplexed, cloaked in incandescent intimacy, free from the assigned ghost. She observes her hands, surprised by how few straws there were to grasp at, when the sea gale blew. Fascinated and fascinating.

Already the sails were hoisted and she was driven by the north wind, tacking quickly before the eyes of love.

4 Woolf, Virginia. *Las mujeres y la escritura*. Editoral Lumen. Spain, 1981. p. 69.

5 Iden.

A woman is alone. Fastening dreams in place with other dreams, the dreams
that were left to her, and the wide heavens of the Antilles.
Serious and quiet in the face of a world which is made of human stone.
No one comes forth to offer her a dress to cover her naked voice which is sob-
bing out her truth.

She has touched on the nucleus of her own self-definition. She trembles and she glows. She has reached, through the immense possibilities of her poetic touch, that which she is: a woman. First a woman. Then, a woman extrapolated into her creation.

Carmen Natalia eliminated her "domestic angel" in a double victory. She annihilated him and then ridiculed his ghost. She does not permit any trace of him to cause her tensions, nor does she consent to have him leave behind any trace of his definition of "being a woman" which might color her perceptions.

The crystalline poetry of Carmen Natalia manifests a subjective unity, a balance between personal sentiment and socio-political ones:

> Here I am, newly born and free,
> with no other cord to bind me than the
> moon's golden braid
> and the sash of the wind.
> A new soul, with no traces of remote fossils.
> A heart without memory, open to probable oracles.
> A baby recovered in time.
> Here I stand before you.
> Ransomed from the abyss. With my newly created voice
> and my newly discovered accent.

The contours and ideas of the "domestic angel" are imprecise. And in the desire to rid oneself of him it could come to pass that he were merely replaced by another angel, with folded and hardened wings. If the first is made of fragile glass, the second is pure plaster and silicone. The latter, if one is not vigilant, takes the place of the creative one, gradually mutilating the most vital and tender roots. How to discern the useless from the substantial? That which is innate from that which alienates? The woman writer must tread a difficult and delicate line. Who is she? What must her work be like in order for it to be recognized and appreciated? How must she write in order to express herself authentically?

The feminist struggles, the social evolution, the demonstrations of the equality of intellectual potential revealed by science, the places earned, the challenges accepted, the tenacity shown by women when they are given access to formal education, are factors which continue to crystalize a more solid and realistic feminine image. The writer who is committed to herself, faithful to her own self, contributes to the new concept of what it means to be a woman. She builds and is built. Her labor takes place deep within her core, generating a product which is transitory in its visibility.

These realities turn out to be unrealistic for the majority of the critics of women's writings. Consequently themes referring to home, family, children, and housework become childish and their treatment is confined to second class status.

To penetrate feminine subjectivity, to decipher its expressions and assign value to it, is arduous for a man, especially if he accepts as natural the power relationship between the sexes. It becomes somewhat complicated to evaluate feelings and creations which are different from those that men frequently express, and those which the world at large designates as normal for women. At first contact these feel strange, distant, deforming. It is difficult to comprehend that at times the deformations are the means towards the creation of more complete and well-defined forms. The voice that rises from a throat that has long been mute sounds discordant and even absurd. Little by little it will find its smoothness and its cadence, its unique tonality, its own characteristic timbre. The woman author needs to write genuinely, in intimate accord with her perceptions, moving within her imaginative repertoire. She must adapt linguistic styles and make them more suitable for her own needs, and she must develop an openness which will enable her to enrich her knowledge of the world and sharpen both her sensitivity and her ability to perceive. In this process she will polish her creative individuality and the personal universe which nourishes it.

Criticism has been nothing more than an echo of restrictive, at times almost cartoon-like, stereotypical references when it comes to judging female works of literature.

Speaking about the late nineteenth century poet Manuela Aybar, Gustavo Adolfo Mejía Ricart tells us that she was hideous. Another author points out that along with being ugly she was an old maid. Contín Aybar considers the poetry of the widowed Concha Benítez Valeria to be written "without ostentation, discreetly, femininely."[6]

Joaquín Balaguer affirms that Altagracia Saviñón was a poetess of "a truly feminine style." And of Josefa Perdomo he points out that "there is not even one of her verses that doesn't breathe the most absolute purity" and further he states "Her poetry has a profound domestic flavor."[7]

Salomé Ureña, on the other hand, is a poetess with a "masculine accent" and Virginia Elena Ortea is "an intimate and gentle voice" according to the judgement of the same Joaquín Balaguer in his *Historia de la Literatura Dominicana*.

Mariano Lebrón Saviñón affirms that the poetry of Carmen Natalia is "essentially feminine." According to his vision, Livia Veloz is the voice of "domestic discretion."[8] Amada Nivar de Pitaluga "writes domestic poetry saturated with purity." Likewise, Concha Benítez Valera also produced what is called "domestic poetry."[9] Some poets, according to this poet were able to "play patriotic notes on their lyre."

José Alcántara, a critic who performs his work with rigor and precision, points out that in the past century "only Salomé Ureña escaped to a more intimate schema."[10]

Referring to Aida Cartagena he underscores that her poetry "overflows the plane of intimate confessions, the plaintive lament, the sublimation of amorous frustrations."[11]

---

6   Mejía Ricart, Gustavo Adolfo. *Antología de Poetas Dominicanos*, Editorial La Palabra de Santo Dominigo. Ciudad Trujillo, D.R., 1955. Vol I, p. 64.

7   Balaguer, Joaquín. *Hisotria de la Literatura Dominicana*. 5th ed. Editorial Julio D. Postigo & Hijos. Santo Domingo, D.R., 1970. p. 133.

8   Lebrón Savinón, Mariano. *Hisotria de la Cultura Dominicana*. Editroail Universidad Pedro Henríquez Ureña, Santo Dominigo, D.R., 1982. Vol 4 p. 107.

9   Lebrón Saviñón. Op. Cit. p. 269.

10 Alcántara Almánzar. Op. Cit. 269.

11 Alcántara Almánzar. Op. Cit. 270.

Ambiguity and confusion are common in the criticism of poetry written by women. What are they asking of women? That they write from the home in which they have been confined physically, psychically and culturally? That they write in a manly style? That they do not remain submerged in feminine perspectives? That they take an androgynous posture? How is this multi-faceted woman writer to come forth, subjected to such mutilating restrictions? Where should criticism be placed? In which dimension should it be located in order for it to define itself and give clear, faithful constructive criticism?

Language does not let us forget degree. To be a poetess is not the same as being a poet. A poetess can go very far, but she will always be seen in a lesser light. Her literary rise will be marked on the scale of an inferior hierarchy. The terms do not cross over nor do they transgress. The poetess will never appear in the category of poet. She is part of the "women's league." Her efforts do not matter.

Poetry, as the point where life is met and joined, as the deep conscience of peoples and eras, has to have as its protagonists, human beings: women and men, translating the imperceptible in what we all perceive, examining the intangible, giving new dimensions and expanding sensitivity and mental frontiers, bestowing upon the world words to express the soul of a reality with multiple relationships.

Writing by women in different time periods tells us more about their worlds and their realities than anything we can find in the history or literature produced by men. Octavio Paz is correct when he asserts that "Poetry is the presentation of a moment in time. That moment, for all its intimacy and personal nature, is likewise both historic and social."[12]

More significant than the limits of theme or the lack of real examination of passions which are characteristic of women's literary productions for a time, are the perceptions and interpretations that are made on the frontiers of life, the moral constraints and the more or less inflexible framework in which the writer's experiences take place.

It is no accident that during the last decades in the Dominican Republic a wide spectrum of poetic expressions have appeared in the writings of women: intimacy and eroticism, rebellion and accusation, protest and threat, freedom and invention: a rumor of integrity yet to be revealed.

Of course, the value scale which fragments women's writings, is still in effect. The division between private life and public life; society and family; politics, history and everyday life; production and reproduction: All of this is incorporated into the paradigms preferred by the critical establishment.

It would seem then, that a writer should situate herself on one of two very disparate blocks: intimacy or a masculine, objective expression; social content or private subjectivity.

Today we begin to show, nevertheless, how the spheres are interconnected and how separations are frequently artificial justifications of distorting ideological divisions. In every day life, history is also woven. The family reproduces the society. In tenderness can be found strength, and in strength, weakness. Emotions can explain entirely objective deeds. It is not only the public which defines and influences the private. From the innermost personal experiences that which is public is sanctioned, accepted, tolerated or criticized. And from there spring transforming tensions.

For the woman artist, even after defeating the trap of the "domestic angel," being true to herself continues to be a challenge. It is problematic to dare to freely express her view of the world and configure her own accessible image, distant from that which others have defined for her, and distant too from that insipid, asexual, undefiled and impossible "angel" who encloses her vital experiences in

12 Paz, Octavio. *El Ogro Filantrópico*. Spain, Seix Barral, Biblioteca Breve, 1983. Vol 4 p. 301.

a few square feet of restrictions. It is difficult to break barriers and reinvent oneself while living, thinking, creating and growing in communion with society's impetus for entertainment and change.

Alienated by inequalities and hierarchies, fearful of conflicts and the destructive potential which the super powers have amassed as kinds of treasuries of their strength, the contemporary world cultivates fatality and fatalism: one lives as best as one can in an impoverished and irredeemable environment.

Even in our own Latin American nations, where the immediacy of so many basic needs absorb us, we hear the echoes that dash the hopes of being in control of life, of having a more intense, deeper and enjoyable lifestyle.

Women live, we live, at the right time.

Our forces are growing and the utopias shine forth.

Women are creators in the market or in the field, in the kitchen or in the school, in the factory or the cathedral, in the laboratory or in the farm, they begin to believe that they can change the reality that the world has made for them. The time has come when they will be able to re-make the world.

Women writers and artists bear witness to this project of human regeneration, although they never explicitly say so in their works. The most verifiable witnesses utilize a language of transcendent signs or of apparent silence.

Illusion, a distant Utopia, perhaps. The transcendence, the intensity of the present and the lively impulses of the future originate for humankind in surreal utopias.

We live on consolation prizes.

The woman writer, perhaps more than the male writer, the woman poet more that her male counterpart, need the fabulous patience and perseverance Neruda spoke of in one of his most lucid reflections. It is the attitude of withdrawing without ever isolating oneself, of protecting oneself without being on the defensive, of hearing voices without listening to them. Always alert for the imperceptible beat of something genuine, constantly honing the invaluable ability to bring into harmony the subtlest, the clearest, the most tenuous, light and vivid frequencies found within and without. Always with the calling to subvert and bear fruit.

"The work of writers, I think, has much in common with those arctic fisherman. The writer must search out the river, and if he finds it frozen, must pierce the ice. He must exude patience, withstand the temperature and adverse criticism, defy ridicule, find the deep current, cast the exact fishhook, and after so much work, catch a tiny little fish. But he must fish again, despite the cold, the ice, the water, the critics, until each time out he catches a bigger and bigger fish." (Pablo Neruda, *Memorias*)

Translation by Margaret A. Ballantyne

---

* For a more in depth comparison between the critics Joaquín Balaguer and José Alcántara Almánzar, see the presentation "El Evangelio Según San..." ("The Gospel According to Saint...") by Chiqui Vicioso, the first critical study on these themes presented at the "Conference on Women Writers and Their Works" (1982) sponsored by the Women's colleges of Smith, Amherst and Mount Holyhoke (N.J.E. in the U.S.)

DENISE PAIEWONSKY
Puerto Plata, 1959

Denise Paiewonsky was born in Puerto Plata on July 8th, 1959. She studied in prestigious institutions in the U.S. where she received a Bachelor of Arts in Sociology from Tulane University and a Masters of Science in Sociology of Underdevelopment from Brown University.

She has worked primarily as a researcher, in particular in matters related to the reproductive health of women, and as private consultant. For years now, she has been an active participant in the feminist movement in the Dominican Republic. At present she coordinates the Center for the Study of Gender at the INTEC in Santo Domingo.

The essay included in this selection, although not a current representation of her work on this subject, is valuable because it represents one of the first publications, certainly the first in book form, on abortion in the Dominican Republic.

Selected Bibliography:

El aborto en la República Dominicana. Santo Domingo: CIPAF, 1988. 118 p. (Essay)

LEGAL ASPECTS OF ABORTION IN THE DOMINICAN REPUBLIC*

Article 317 of the Penal Code in the Dominican Republic establishes the following:

"The act of providing food, drinks, medications, explorations, treatment or any other mean whatsoever which would cause or contribute directly to cause abortion in a pregnant woman even when she consents to it, would be punished by imprisonment. This same punishment would be imposed on the woman who would induce her own abortion, or who would consent to the use of a substance indicated or administered to her for that purpose or who would submit herself to abortive measures, whenever abortion would take place. There would be a punishment of a term of six months to two years in prison for those individuals who would put a pregnant woman in contact with another person who would induce an abortion. Doctors, surgeons, midwives, nurses, pharmacists and other medical professionals who, abusing their profession, would cause or cooperate with it, would be subject to punishment for a term of five to twenty years in public service, if the abortion were to take place."

As you can see, Dominican legislation does not permit induced abortion under any circumstance. Unlike the majority of countries in the world, our legislation does not even contemplate the case of therapeutic abortion to save the life of a pregnant woman, much less other frequently accepted instances, such as fetal indicators and pregnancies resulting from incest or rape. The reality is, of course, that an astounding number of induced abortions take place each year in the country with

---

* Selected from *El aborto en la República Dominicana*. Santo Domingo: CIPAF, 1988.

absolute impunity from prosecution by the police or the judicial system. For the purposes of our analysis, we will divide induced abortions in two categories:

1) Legitimate abortions: refers to those that take place under the advise of medical professionals of "good" reputation (that is to say, not "abortionists") in private health centers or in state hospitals. In general they are therapeutic abortions for the purpose of saving the life of a woman or preserving her physical health, although they also take place because of fetal indicators, eugenic factors or at times psychiatric profiles. According to the results of our probing and additional in-depth interviews with some medical doctors, the majority of them reserves the right to decide when they ought to prescribe (or practice) abortion for medical reasons, although the criteria used varies. For example, while all of those interviewed affirmed that they would prescribe abortion to save the life of a woman, their answers as far as eugenic abortions, or psychiatric ones, or because of fetal indicators, etc. were much more diverse.

These medical abortions constitute a practice that is so widespread and so widely accepted, in professional as well as in social and judicial circles, that their execution is formally regulated. In fact, some medical doctors asked about it indicated, erroneously, their belief that these abortions were legal. The formal procedure in these cases consists of obtaining the written approval of a colleague and/or convoking a council of doctors, and later on notifying the appropriate judicial authority about the abortion about to take place. In general, this procedure is followed strictly only in public hospitals; in private clinics, doctors usually consult with some colleague, and in many cases they simply perform the abortion without any other formality than obtaining the verbal consent of the woman's husband.

The presumed impunity for "legitimate" abortions is sheltered by the general principle of penal legislation known as "State of Necessity," in virtue of which jurisprudence recognizes the position of those who cannot save their own legal good without injuring the legal good of the other—that is to say—it is presumed that when abortion is practiced to avoid a greater ill it has judicial validity. What constitutes "a greater ill" has never been defined in specific terms, so that the execution of these abortions could eventually cause judicial problems for those practicing them. It is important to highlight, however, that in the country there is no precedent of doctors who have been publicly denounced or prosecuted for having performed a legitimate abortion.

2) "Illegitimate" abortions: this category refers to those abortions that have been considered in the present work, that is, those self-induced by women and those achieved by clandestine means at the request of the pregnant woman by "abortionists", midwives, herbalists, etc. Although we do not have any indication of how many "legitimate" abortions are performed in the country, we can suppose with sufficient assurance that these constitute a small fraction of the total, the illegitimate ones being the overwhelming majority. Despite the fact that clandestinely performed abortions are precisely those that, by nature, frequently cause lesions, severe illnesses, and even death for many women, in the recent history of the country there is not a case of a woman being taken to court for having solicited or obtained an abortion, and only an insignificant number of those illegal practitioners has suffered penal punishment for his activities. It is good to point out that the scarce judicial prosecutions for this reason are not initiated by police authorities or officials in public health agencies but by the relatives of women who have died because of badly performed abortions—and even in those cases it is practically impossible to obtain a prison term for the guilty party.

In light of the fact that the authorities do not enforce the sanctions stipulated in Article 317, the continued life of this legal rubbish serves only to penalize women, who find themselves obliged to resort to clandestine abortions incurring grave risks for their health and their lives—and enriching in the process the "aborters," who obtain very high profits in light of the illegality of the procedure. If the criminalization of abortion penalizes all women, it is evident that the degree of penalization varies according to their socio-economic status, as we have seen: women of the middle and upper classes who can afford to pay the high cost of an abortion performed by a competent professional, in acceptably asepsic and secure conditions, are exposed to a lesser degree of risk than peasant and poor women who must resort to homemade methods or empirical "aborters." This factor in itself constitutes a powerful reason to reconsider the present legal status of abortion.

Attempts at Legal Reform

As evidenced by its anachronistic references to abortive methods prevalent in the last century, Article 317 is an almost verbatim copy of Article 292 of the French Legal Code of 1832, which was adopted without first translating it by the Dominican legislature in the middle of the nineteenth century. The first national code of law, put into force in 1884, reproduced the dispositions in the French code of law without any substantial variation in its new Article 317. Since then that article has been the object of only one reform, made in 1948 for the purpose of adding the paragraph that penalizes "those persons who have put a pregnant woman in contact with another person who would induce an abortion..."

Despite the obviously obsolete character of the legal dispositions in place, there has been only one attempt to reform it since 1948. This project of law, introduced to the National Congress on the 20th of April of 1976, added one new paragraph to Article 317 which eliminates sanctions in the following cases:

a) Therapeutic abortions, applicable only in situations where the woman ran the risk of death, as diagnosed by three medical specialists;

b) Eugenic abortion, applicable in cases when one or both progenitors were mentally unfit, when the pregnant woman would suffer a teratological illness (rubella, toxoplasmosis) during the first trimester, or when by means of fetal examination it would be determined that the product suffered a grave abnormality (Down Syndrome, idiocy, and others);

c) Medical-legal abortion, when the pregnancy would be the result of rape or incest (presumably only in those cases when the fact could be verified by the authorities).

The proposal of reform which, if it had been approved, would have put Dominican legislation in a position similar to that of the majority of Latin American countries, was propitiated by two events of almost simultaneous occurrence: in September of 1974 the Dominican Academy of Medicine celebrated a symposium on abortion from which the legislative reform proposal arose, written later on to the Congress. Some months later, in January of 1975, the National Council on Population and Family, the Autonomous University of Santo Domingo, and the Dominican Association for the Welfare of the Family co-sponsored a seminar on population problems in the Dominican Republic from which arose a similar legislative recommendation. This last fact has particular relevance because the CONAPOFA is the official organism of the State in charge of the programs for family planning and for maternity-infancy health.

Given the nature of the entities which promoted the reform, it is certain that the proposal of 1976 was submitted to Congress at the most favorable political opportunity up to the moment. The reason why it did not prosper can be found in a declaration made by the Archbishop of Santo Domingo, issued three days after the legislative piece arrived in Congress. We quote briefly from its last paragraph:

"Let God touch the heart of our society and of its legislators so that it [society] is not stained by the legalization of an abominable crime. It would mean to legalize a depravation..."

In subsequent years occasional and weak protests arose, coming in their majority from the medical sector, as public exhortation rather than as direct pressure on the legislative bodies. In April of 1983, for example, the Dominican Medical Association conducted a round table about legal and medical aspects of abortion, which in its public declaration concluded that "it is urgent to revise present legislation on abortion," without later taking on effective measures with respect to this issue. Likewise, in July of 1986, the Dominican Association of Obstetrics and Gynecology issued a public communique in which, after qualifying its members as "the most authorized to issue a judgement," the entity demanded the modification of Article 317 in the same terms already referred to. It goes without saying that this request did not receive positive results either.

Up to the present, the complete elimination of penalty for abortion has never been articulated publicly in the country. Not even we feminists have claimed our unrestricted right to abortion as an indispensable condition to the achievement of true self-determination. Lamentably, the social and ideological climate of the country appears to exclude the possibility of achieving the total removal of penalization in the near future. All the proposals to modify Article 317 arising in public fora, professional events, studies and researches, have had the same objective: the simple modification of the law for the purpose of removing the penalization for therapeutic, eugenic and medical-legal abortions. In other words, what has been sought is to "medicalize" abortion even more, legally granting the doctor the exclusive right to decide when a woman may obtain an abortion and when she may not.* The scarce references to the so-called "social abortion" that have been made to the public are based on demographic considerations or, in the better cases, on socio-economic considerations (i.e. in the case of women who have a large number of children and scarce economic resources).

As we have said, the restricted lifting of penalties proposed by the medical profession would only "legalize" the current status quo insofar as medical abortions, without bringing any benefit to the thousands of women who annually risk their health and lives undergoing clandestine procedures. We must also note that once this reform takes place it would be much more difficult to mobilize public opinion in favor of a second and more just revision of the law. It turns out more than evident, then, that the interests of the medical profession insofar as the reform of Article 317 is concerned do not coincide in the least with the interests of women, in addition to the fact that, if this reform takes place, it would not change in the least the true nature of the problem created by illegal abortions.

---

*   Insofar as abortions as a consequence of rape/incest is concerned, we should note that the legally appointed doctor plays a leading role in the determination of both causes, and that often the final decision as far as whether it was a case of incest or not is placed in the hands of a psychiatrist. The issue of medical-legal abortions is laughable in a country where the majority of cases of rape or incest are not reported to the authorities, and where the reduced number of cases to reach the tribunals have not managed to prove their case to the satisfaction of the magistrates. Council proposers have declared on diverse occasions that one of the principal benefits of the Council would be to impede those doctors who disrespect ethics and the norms of the profession by continuing to practice, pointing invariably to the illegal practices of "abortionists," were a Council to be established, whatever action in this sense would lead to a situation favorable at the level of public opinion to achieve the lifting of penalties for medical abortions.

Even in such cases, the proponents have specified emphatically that the final decision as far as abortions would be taken by a State professional in the area of public health. The possibility that the decision rests with a woman is not even considered.

Recently a proposed law was submitted to the National Congress that would establish a medical Council. Were it to be approved, this project would have considerable impact on the situation of legal abortions, because of two reasons: 1) The doctors, as a professional sector of much social prestige and considerable political leverage, have indicated repeatedly their interest in having the status quo legalized as far as "legitimate" abortions is concerned. The Council undoubtedly would strengthen the levels of the community organization of the profession, providing them a solid base from which to fight for their beliefs. 2) The collegiate organization would grant doctors the right to exercise their profession, by granting the proposed Council the authority to give and withdraw licenses to practice the procedure.

The Current Debate

If we have argued thus far that the definition of attitudes toward abortions have been conditioned historically by factors of a socio-cultural nature, it is no less true that the debate has been, and continues to be, conceptualized in terms of ethics and morality. When we compare the arguments that are most frequently waged we ought to, therefore, begin with those relative to the definition of the moral status of the embryo—or, said in another way, the determination of when human life begins, or from what moment are we to consider the product of pregnancy as a human person with rights of its own.

Once findings in science denied the traditional belief that would place the beginning of life at the point of movement in the fetus, the terms of the debate moved strictly to a consideration of values, where biology contributes little. As Luker wisely points out, at this level contrary ideas about biological facts are not opposed, but ideas about how to interpret and value these facts play a determining role.

Biology tells us that life does not begin, it just continues, pregnancy being a constant progression of stages through which it is impossible to distinguish one that would suddenly confer the dignity of a human being to a fetus. In biological terms, an ovule or a sperm isolated are as "alive" as a fertilized ovule or as the fetus that could result from that fertilization process. The determination as to when life begins or as to when we are to treat the product of that pregnancy as a human being does not belong, then, to science, but implies value judgements in terms of the nature of the human person and the rights pertaining to the woman and to the fetus.

The anti-abortion position states that from the very moment of conception we are in the presence of a fully human life, with all its rights and attributions, so that to terminate pregnancy voluntarily, whatever the motives, is a synonym for murder. The fertilized egg, in as far as a human person, has absolute right to life. Those who support this position in one or another form, base themselves on two important suppositions: first, that potential life is as sacred as actual life, and that it is not valid to establish moral difference between one and the other; and, second, that once an ovule is fertilized, the woman loses ipso facto all right to her body in so far as the continuation or not of the pregnancy, since the rights of the fetus are absolute and not related to hers. The extreme version of this position, supported at present by the Catholic church, states that abortion is not justifiable even when the life of the woman is endangered as a result of the pregnancy. Two deaths, from this point of view, are preferable to one "murder."

Those who, on the contrary, defend the right of women to decide freely on abortion (the so-called pro-choice stance) base their assertions on different propositions. It is not the case, in the majority of instances, to reduce the embryo to a mere inanimate appendix that should be removed at will, as a simple wart. The product of conception, as potential human life, has an intrinsic value, which undoubtedly grants it some rights. But from this point of view, to grant the status of a human person to a fertilized egg or an embryo is as absurd as to equate the seed with the tree. For that very same reason it is absurd to grant prenatal life equal or superior rights to those of the woman in whose body they are sheltered, and who as a real person (and not a potential person) has inalienable and fundamental rights to decide about her own body. The right of the fetus to life is, therefore, relative and not absolute, and it can only be eliminated by the superior right of women.

Another argument frequently made in this debate by supporters of the pro-choice stance relates to the religious nature of the objections to abortion. If the definition of the moral status of the embryo is not based on objective criteria universally accepted but, on the contrary, on religious criteria (and by consequence, subjective), the legal prohibition of abortion constitutes a violation of the constitutional rights to freedom of creed. The State would be, then, imposing on an entire population the religious beliefs of only one segment of that population, so violating the right each person has to choose the religious creed of his/her preference.

The debate on abortion is not limited to abstract considerations of ethics and jurisprudence. There are a series of worldly facts to be taken into consideration, among them the quality of life. When the pregnancy represents a threat to the physical, emotional, social or economic stability of a woman or a couple, it will provoke rejection and hostility. An unwanted pregnancy, far from posing philosophical questions about the possible humanity of the fetus, is the source of earthly problems of various types and magnitudes. When the time comes to decide about the convenience of the arrival of a child, priority falls on tangible life and not on potential life. Catholics and non-catholics make a choice based on the material condition of their existence, among them they include emotional and socio-economic conditions, suitable for the feeding and educating of their offsprings to allow for their healthy growth.

It is required also to take into account that, independent of ethical considerations, religious admonitions and legal prohibitions, there have always been and there will be a considerable number of women who for one reason or another will make the decision to resort to an abortion. In light of this reality we need to think about concrete and objective considerations such as the great risks involved in clandestine abortions, the high personal and social costs of their illegality, and the injustice represented in the disparate economic conditions and access to safe abortions. A notable example in this sense is the promotion of IUD by the State, knowing that the device creates abortion-like conditions. Further injury in the matter is realized when we note that this practice has counted on the tacit approval of the local ecclesiastical hierarchies that have never made an effort to stop it, equal to those waged against clandestine abortions.

(Fragment)   Translation by Daisy Cocco De Filippis

MARGARITA PAIEWONSKY
Puerto Plata, 1960

Historian and researcher of gender issues, Paiewonsky works in the Centro de Estudio del Género of the Instituto Tecnológico of Santo Domingo. She is co-editor of *Género y sociedad*, a tri-yearly publication of the Centro.

In the article included in this anthology, Paiewonsky shows the limited inclusion (a de facto exclusion) of information about the contribution of Dominican women to national history in the history texts published in the Dominican Republic.

THE IMAGE OF WOMEN IN DOMINICAN HISTORY TEXTS

Based on an analysis of the content of Dominican history texts used at the university level, an analysis of gender has been made that proposes to give an account of the absence of women in Dominican historiography.

> *Since all suppers have been cooked, all dishes washed; the children have been sent to school and have found their way in the world. Nothing remains of all that. It has all vanished. Neither biographies nor history books mention anything about it. And novels without meaning to, lie.*
>
> Virginia Woolf, *A Room of One's Own*

The educational system is a fundamental institution in any social organization. Formal education meets two basic functions of socialization. It transmits, on the one hand, the knowledge and technical information of a society, and on the other, its values and norms. (Duarte et al, 1989) In this way, schools not only train individuals for future participation in the job market, but also contribute to the strengthening and perpetuation of ideological structures in society. The Organic Law of Education 2909 of 1951 postulates "free education, universal and democratic" for all Dominicans. However, as can be observed in the statistics, education in the Dominican Republic (particularly at the university level) has shown evidence in the course of history of a marked fragmentation by sex. Thus, by 1960, men constituted 76.6% while women only 23.4% of the university student population, and by 1970 men constituted 62.6% while women represented 37.4%. It is not until recently that the gap has begun to close. According to Duarte et al, these last years have registered a marked increment in quantitative terms in the participation of women in education at all levels. So that by 1981 "there is no significant difference according to gender in school levels." (Duarte et al., 1989: 62)**

---

* The author indicates that the article resulted from research conducted at the Centro de Estudio del Género, supported by a grant from the Ford Foundation. Published in Género y sociedad. Vol. I, No. 1, May-August 1993, pp 30-59.

** Statistics on women's participation in the educational system have been taken from Duarte et al: 1989. university level: by 1981 women represented 46.12% of the university student body in the country.

In 1981, from the total educated male population, 81.67% reached the elementary level, 13.39% secondary level, and 4.93% university level, compared to a 80.74% elementary level, a 15.07% secondary level and a 4.18% university level for the educated female population. In the last decades the most important increase in the participation of women in education was registered at the university level.

Despite this quantitative increase in the participation of women at the university level, in qualitative terms women still maintain to a great measure a tendency to participate in greater proportion in careers traditionally considered "feminine." These careers in turn hold a lesser status and, consequently, provide lower salaries.

Another factor to keep in mind when analyzing the participation of women in education is the concept of co-education (Rich, 1983). In spite of its etymological meaning ("education which is given jointly to children or young people of both sexes") the application of this term to classify the Dominican educational system is highly deceiving. To the merely biological sexual division, culture superimposes a socially constructed separation by gender. This sexual dichotomy is instrumental in the maintenance of attitudes and behaviors that support the sexist ideology of society, due to the fact, in part, that it determines a political distribution of human characteristics which values women less. Sexism, as other cultural characteristics, is transmitted by social institutions, among them the school, which contributes to perpetuating the subordination of women.

It is a fallacy to assume that by the mere fact that they both receive an education together, men and women receive really the same education. The reality is that the ideological content of that education validates men at the same time that it invalidates women; it transmits openly or surreptitiously the message that man is, by natural right, the main protagonist (rather the only) of the events that define the world. (Rich, 1983: 282-283)

The content of the ill-termed co-education denies all that is specifically feminine and presents as the only model the masculine element. As M. Subirats points out:

> *Equality does not emerge from the integration of the characteristics of both genders, but by the denial of one of them...There is no co-education, but the assimilation of women to the education considered exemplary, that of men. It does not happen this way because of ignorance of the existence of forms of behavior typical of women, but because they are considered inferior, have been devalued and therefore, an attempt is made to correct and erase their expression.* (Quoted by Moreno, 1986: 58)

The purpose of this article is to point out how, despite the fact that in this country we supposedly offer equal education to women and men, there weigh factors in the teaching of Dominican history that determine this activity to be intrinsically unequal. In the first place, there is the fact that history is reduced mainly to a chronological narration of political and economic events; and in the second place, and closely related to the former, there is the fact that even within the androcentric narrative of history, the participation ascribed to women is truly insignificant.

In patriarchal society men hold power while women are assigned subordinate positions in relation to men. One of the manifestations of this subordination is the fact that, by means of diverse mechanisms, women are kept from defining themselves: women are, instead, defined by masculine culture, in keeping with male interests and needs. In this way women are placed within determined roles that oblige them to participate in restricted spheres, which in turn have been devalued by society.

Traditional historiography gives a chronological retelling of political and economic events that correspond to the activity in spheres predominantly male. The spheres where women act are determined by their gender; this has been the most significant element of definition in the experience of women through history. This is why, traditional historical categories, such as historical period, class or nationality, have not had for women the same relevance as for men. (Anderson and Zinsser, 1989: XIV-XV)

Traditional historiography "is structured in a way that results in the virtual impossibility to include [women]" (J. Kelly and G. Lerner, quoted by Anderson and Zinsser, p. xiv) This is due to the fact that this structurization corresponds to periods that reflect exclusively men's experience through time or, rather, what they have considered the most salient aspect of their history: discoveries, political struggles, wars, conquests, bloody epics of all type. The experience of women, because it is different, does not fit into traditional historical periods; it has another sequence, another chronology and another content. Women have, nevertheless, been considered insignificant and have been totally forgotten in the chronicles of masculine historians. (Kelly and Lerner in Anderson and Zinsser, p. xiv)

Contrary to the contribution of men, the contribution of women to humanity has been ignored by history. Their participation, since it is circumscribed in spheres different from those of men, have been devalued. It suffices to analyze what has been the economic contribution of women through history to convince us of that fact. Based on gender divisions, women have been traditionally assigned the main role in the care of the family and the home. To this work without recognition or remuneration we must add the ill paid work she has done outside the home through the years. The work of women, whether within or outside the home, has been considered of lesser value or importance than that of men. Consequently, history relates the economic participation of men. Women are not only ignored by history but on scarce occasions when they are noted, in the majority of instances this is defined in terms of their relationship to men. (Anderson and Zinsser, xiv-xv)

Within this framework and considerations—and understanding that the analysis of content is the ideal method to study any form of communication, particularly written ones—we will proceed to analyze the three texts of Dominican history most frequently used at the university level: *Historia social y económica de la República Dominicana*, Vols. I & II by Roberto Cassá, *Manual de historia dominicana* by Frank Moya Pons and *Visión general de la historia dominicana* by Valentina Peguero and Danilo de los Santos. These texts were selected because they are included in the bibliographies of syllabi for courses of introduction to Dominican history (called in most instances Dominican Social History) and/or are used as basic texts for this subject in all the main universities in the country (UASD, INTEC, UNIBE, UNPHU, APEC, PUCMM).

The three texts are structured according to a rigid division in periods established in traditional historiography as far as the internal processes in the country as well as the international framework where these processes are inserted. After a brief description of taino society, they move on to an analysis of Spanish society in the XV century as antecedent to the discovery of America. They narrate economic development of the colony, from the conquest and colonization of the island, within the framework of the political institutions which define them. After narrating countless peripeteia surrounding the demarcation of the frontier that divides the colony in two countries, they continue with a detailed retelling of internal struggles for power which determine the political instability in which the precarious economic evolution of the country is framed.

Within this structure diverse highlights are presented. Thus, Cassá places emphasis on economic aspects, analyzing them from the perspective of historical materialism, while Peguero and de los Santos include in a parallel fashion some chapters about cultural aspects of Dominican society. This, however, in some way implies a deviation from the organizational scheme that by definition excludes women.

Programs at the UASD, as well as at the INTEC, UNIBE, UNPHU, APEC, and PUCMM describe "Dominican Social History" (or its equivalent) as a "global vision of social processes in Dominican history" and they quote as one of their main objectives the development in students of skills to critically evaluate contemporary Dominican history, basing themselves on an understanding of the past. Those programs are designed in terms of the structure of the books used as texts; so that the course on an introduction to Dominican history taught at the universities reproduces the vices that afflict history texts.

Traditional historiography selects for its investigation and study historical aspects deemed more important by androcentric beliefs. According to Moreno, those bases for selection:

> point to a set interpretation of the world, society and the relationship among its components that is founded on the empowerment of force, competition and a desire to control, this explains why this history is centered principally on those who dominate and have power and narrates to us, to the point of exhaustion, the manner in which these forces take one from the other in a manner not excessively original. (1986: 39)

This androcentric vision of history totally ignores women as a whole; in this vision there is only room for those women whose actions resemble those valued in their male counterparts, or for those who because of circumstances more or less exceptional become important actors in masculine epics. A notable example in this sense is the case of Queen Isabella of Castile, who ascended to the throne because her brother Henry IV died without leaving a clear heir. Thus she became a protagonist, we could almost say accidentally, of the discovery and conquest of America.

In those segments of history texts in which a woman by circumstance comes to occupy a place next to a man, the feminine perspective is not recorded. The inclusion of this material is irrelevant "when it is simply integrated to the traditional historical periods which reflect exclusively what has been the experience of men." (Anderson and Zinsser, p. XVIII). For example, traditional cultural spheres have been less close to women than other spheres (political, military, religious), so that the historical accounting that relates happenings in this area allocate more space for the contribution of women. This is what we find in Peguero and de los Santos' text, which, without changing its androcentric vision nor its organizational scheme of history, by the mere fact of including in its text some segments or chapters relative to cultural manifestations in the colony (and later on, in the country) is, of the three texts analyzed here, the one to allocate more space to the contributions of women.

Even as this is the case, it is significant to note that the universities (including those who use Peguero and de los Santos' book as a basic text for the introduction course on Dominican history) exclude from their syllabi for history classes material pertaining to cultural aspects.

Methodology

The texts we analyze basically narrate the social history of power: factional struggles to gain or exercise power, economic factors that have bearing on its practice, military conflict of rival factions in search of territorial control, etc. Given that women have historically been excluded from the sphere of power, it is not surprising to find that they do not appear as protagonists of this narrative.

Their scarce presence made it possible for us to take all references to women when we tabulated the three texts. This includes, on the one hand, those that designate gender; that is to say, mentioning "woman" or "women," as well as feminine nouns pertaining to condition ("goddess," "female slave") or relationship ("wife," "mother," "daughter," "sister"). On the other hand, it includes all references to historical characters such as Anacaona, Queen Isabella of Spain, etc. In the case of men, however, we only tabulated those mentioned by proper nouns; the volume of references to gender made it impossible to do a more detailed tabulation.

As we will see in the analysis, our purpose was not limited to quantifying the total space dedicated to women or specific feminine character, but above all to examine how these women interact with all the other elements in the context of the narrative. That is to say, what factors determined their inclusion in the narrative, or what aspects or condition of life is made reference to, what actions or characteristics are considered of "historical" value and therefore worthy of being mentioned.

The method used in the tabulation was to read the texts carefully, registering each mention of gender or of a female character, and each mention of a male character that appeared. In the case of women, in preparing the tables, we took as a unit each mention of gender, even when in the same sentence several mentions occurred with only one point of reference. Thus, for example, in the following case four mentions were tabulated although all of them referred to taíno women.

> The "marriage" to important women in the villages (daughters or sisters of the chieftains or female chieftains in some cases)...[Cassá, Vol. I, p. 35, emphasis ours)

This same criterium was used with relation to the mention of feminine historical characters. Thus, in the following phrase two mentions by gender were tabulated and one by character:

> Diego de Colón arrived in Santo Domingo by mid 1509 accompanied by his wife and cousin to the king, Maria de Toledo...(Peguero and de los Santos, p. 57, emphasis ours)

Likewise all mentions relative to the same feminine character were tabulated, even when they appeared in the context of one event. Thus, in the following case we tabulated four mentions of character:

> At last by the first months of the year 1504 Queen Isabella's authorization to restitute the apportionment arrived...The Queen ruled against this course of action, ordering that the Indians be considered as free persons... Because according to the Queen's instructions [the Indian] had to receive a "fair" wage for the work he was forced to do...Initially the Indian village granted to Spaniards required, as stipulated in the Queen's instructions...(Cassá, Vol. I, p. 43, underlined by us)

In this context it is necessary to point out that Peguero and de los Santos include a summary of a chronology and three additional documents which appear at the end of the text in addition to the main text. Taking into consideration the criterium of tabulation formerly described, the inclusion of these sections in the analysis would have had as a result a padded accounting which would have overrepresented the real participation of women in these history texts. It is also important to highlight that the actions of the characters which appear in the attachments do not have the same historical relevance as those who appear in the text itself.

Besides the tabulation by mentions (charts 1 and 2), in the analysis of the texts we proceeded to make an enumeration of all feminine characters who appear in the narrative (charts 3.1, 3.2 and 3.3). This was possible because the total number of feminine characters is reduced. This enumeration sheds light on the criteria utilized by different authors to determine which women to select for inclusion in the narrative. Thus, feminine characters included in Moya Pons' text are figures of political relevance (Anacaona, Queen Isabella) or more typically, women whose role is determined by their relationship to masculine figures (Rosa Duarte, María Martínez). In Cassá's text, with the exception of a taina goddess, there are only feminine characters whose relevance is political (Queen Isabella, the Mirabal sisters).

In the case of Peguero and de los Santos we find two categories of feminine characters. On the one hand, there are those women who appear in the main heroic narrative, in their majority figures of political relevance (Queen Isabella, María Trinidad Sánchez, the Mirabal sisters). On the other hand, there are those women who are prominent as artists, educators or of diverse professions who appear in the segment and chapters on culture already cited (Salomé Ureña, Celeste Woss y Gil, Ercilia Pepín, Abigaíl Mejía, Andrea Evangelina Rodríguez). In response to this situation, in chart 3.2 corresponding to the enumeration of feminine characters in the text by Peguero and de los Santos, subdivisions were set up according to the place in the text where women are quoted, which allows for a clear differentiation of those who appear as historical characters themselves, and the more than two third segments which appear outside of the context of the political relation to power, that is to say, outside of the main narrative of the text. The following is an example of the segments on cultural aspects:

> *During the 1940s the first generation of plastic artists was formed in Bellas Artes. Among them sculptors...and painters...Clara Ledesma, Elsa Divanna, Marianela Jiménez, Nidia Serra and Noemí Mella.* (Peguero and de los Santos, 392)

It is as a consequence of the segments and chapters about cultural aspects which appear in a parallel manner to the central narrative, that the tabulation of this text indicates such a high total of mentions of feminine characters. As we compare the figures corresponding to each text, it is important, therefore, to take into consideration the place of precedence of the mentions by Peguero and de los Santos.

The following step was to tabulate feminine characters mentioned in the texts according to their level of involvement (chart 4). For this task, we took the mentions of characters and classified them according to the level of interaction with other elements in the context in which they appear cited. The criterium used to determine the level of involvement was the type of relation (direct or indirect) that the character cited would have with the actual decision making and/or execution of the deed or action narrated. So that we defined as primarily taking the lead those situations in which women act as main character of a deed; and as secondarily taking the lead, those in which women do not appear as figures relevant to the action; and as jointly taking the lead those actions in which women and men appear as equally relevant, either as primary or secondary protagonists. With very few exceptions, when they jointly take the lead, they did so in concert only with other men, never with other women.

This phase of the analysis undoubtedly entailed a certain element of subjectivity, given that the criterium for tabulation was of a qualitative and not a quantitative nature. Nevertheless, the clear definition of this criterium and the consistent form in which it was applied throughout the process confer upon these results a relatively high ratio of credibility.

This tabulation at the level of primary participation of feminine characters allows us to establish the importance of the roles played by these characters, the historical relevance attributed to them by the authors vis a vis their male counterparts. The level of primary participation was determined according to a reduced context; we took as a unit to be analyzed the paragraph in which the character appears and not the global context in which it is inserted. Thus, the following citations, are examples of primary, secondary and joint participation, respectively.

> *This conspiracy was led by María Trinidad Sánchez, an aunt of Francisco del Rosario, who upon being found out in early 1845, was judged and sentenced to death...*(Moya Pons, p. 297)

> *The confrontation of the rights of the Almiral before the authority delegated on the Comendador made the former return to Spain in 1504, the year which would witness the death of Queen Isabella (Peguero and de los Santos, p. 54)...On other occasions [Santana] gave up power voluntarily, first to Báez, and later on to the Queen of Spain.* (Cassá, Vol. II, p. 56)

Charts 5.1, 5.2 and 5.3 show the tabulation of feminine characters according to their occupation, role or condition. This classification allows us to deepen the analysis of these characters, since taking it as a point of departure one can determine the criterium the authors used to base their inclusion in the narrative.

After taking all references to women, we proceeded to tabulate all masculine characters mentioned in the texts. As we said previously, in the case of men the extremely high number of mentions by gender made it impossible to account for. Chart 6 shows the total number of masculine characters and the total number of mentions of the same in the texts, while charts 7 and 8 show the percentage distribution of characters and the mention of characters and mentions by sex.

As a last step, we proceeded to codify and tabulate the illustrations that appear in the books, since these serve to illustrate or widen the content of the narration. As one may observe in charts 10.1, 10.2 and 10.3, first we counted the number of illustrations of human figures in relation to the total number of illustrations; then we established the proportion of human figures, masculine, feminine and mixed within this total; and finally we gave an account of the total number of historical figures, masculine, feminine and mixed which appear in the total number of human figures. A human figure is understood as the representation of a person not known or identified, while historical figures or characters pertain to those persons recognized or identified in the text. Mixed illustrations are those in which persons of both sexes appear, or those in which a crowd of people appears. (From these last references we excluded those where the sex of the characters could not be determined, usually because of the distance.) The numbers in these charts show in a categorical manner that in the illustration of books women are even less represented than in the narrative. Analysis of results:

If we add the total number of pages of the three texts analyzed we obtain a number of 1,480 pages. At first sight it might be surprising to find that in this large number of pages there only appear 253 mentions relative to women. Our surprise might grow if we take into consideration the fact that this number is padded because it includes repeated references to one and the same character. If we were to put aside considerations of gender and we accounted only for the total number of characters, and from these only those who are part of the main narrative, our surprise would be even greater: we would obtain the scandalous sum of 14 feminine historical figures of any relevance within the contents of 1,480 pages.

The number of masculine historical figures in the texts is as high as the feminine one is low. Next to 113 mentions of feminine characters that appear in the texts, we find 7,245 mentions of masculine characters. This marked contrast is by itself sufficiently eloquent to convince us of the insignificance of the space occupied by women in Dominican history text. (See charts 1 and 2)

Cultural androcentrism is a phenomenon that permeates all social institutions, even in our language which reduces the universal to the masculine form and reaffirms and transmits this sexist vision of the world. A careful reading of the texts shows clearly that women, as a social group, are excluded from historical accounting. This fact often remains invisible thanks to the expediency of defining in the masculine the grammatical terms that historiography resorts to insistently. We understand that it functions as a linguistic mechanism of omission of women, if we take into consideration that it routinely gives way, in the same context, to "generic" terms, which without a doubt exclude women totally. (Moreno, 1986). According to García Meseguer:

> This semantic leap constitutes one of the more subtle mechanisms of sexual discrimination, by reinforcing in our subconscious the unjust and traditional identification between the concepts of maleness and personhood. (Quoted by Moreno, 1986:44)

Specialists in "semantic leaps," history texts reinforce the process of internalizing the criterium that the events narrated represent the entire Dominican population, when in fact they only gather the history of a very particular segment of Dominican society; that is to say, that masculine elite tied through the centuries to the political and economic power of the nation.

A clear example of this false use of generic grammatical masculine terms appears in the description made by Moya Pons of taino customs:

> Tainos became farmers without refraining from fishing and hunting at the same time to make a living...Besides farming, hunting and fishing, the tainos used to work in the construction of housing, commonly known as buhíos...In their homes the women dedicated themselves to the making of clay objects, such as pots, bowls, flat griddles, large earthen jars, and other utensils to prepare food. (pp 3-5)

Please note that the references to "tainos," although generic, and thus, supposedly universal, refer exclusively to men. When women are spoken about it is necessary to make specific references to them, which, inadvertently makes evident that the prior use of gender is used to exclude them. In this particular case, the bad use of the generic form has a deforming effect on reality, since in taino society, as in the majority of indigenous societies, women probably played an important role in agriculture—something which is left out in the semantic construction in the description cited. (See charts 3.1, 3.2 and 3.3)

As we can observe in charts 3.1, 3.2 and 3.3 in the historical narrative only exceptional women appear, women who have broken away from the role society has assigned to them. These charts reveal that the few feminine characters considered by the authors as genuinely relevant (that is to say, those who take part in the historical accounting) are those who participate directly or indirectly in the masculine sphere of power, that is in the historical process prioritized by the androcentric vision of history (for example, queens and political activists).

History does not take into account women who lived within assigned roles. It is interesting to point out in this sense that the ten mentions of primary participation in Cassá's text refer in their totality to Queen Isabella. The appearance of other feminine characters in the texts, when it is not given by family ties with some masculine protagonist, occurs in spheres which are far from being considered really important (for example, in cultural life, as in the case of Peguero and de los Santos). [See chart 4]

Symptomatic of the androcentric vision of history the authors of these texts allied themselves with is the manner in which female importance is minimized, even in the case of feminine characters who inhabit spheres considered traditionally masculine, and whose actions are therefore valued by a patriarchal society and its historical chroniclers. This occurs in the measure in which not even those achievements considered prominent make these women entirely deserving on their own merit but, often times, these merits are presented as a representation of family ties to a masculine character to whom they are related. Thus we find Anacaona characterized as the "sister" and "wife" of chieftains and Patria, Minerva and María Teresa Mirabal characterized as "the wives of political conspirators" or simply as "symbols of the trujillista struggle". (See charts 5.1, 5.2 and 5.3)

Considerations as to how history could be written from a perspective that would include women are beyond the scope of this work. Nevertheless, it is this vision of what would constitute a history which would truly include women that gives us a point of reference of what ought to be and allows us, therefore, to evaluate critically what is. A history that would include women, would necessarily have to be conceived outside of an androcentric framework. This would entail not only the abandonment of sexist criteria but would also imply radical changes in so far as the structure itself of the historical account. A history with a feminine perspective and including women would not be organized according to rigid historical periods; the chronology that guides traditional historiography only results in an appropriate framework for events that have taken place in spheres of masculine power, but not for what has been the experience of women. In other words, this chronology has been adjusted to meet the narrative needs of the history of power, and since women have been excluded from this sphere, a history structured according to that chronology by definition excludes women.

Gender has been traditionally the principal element in the definition of women. Their alternative experiences and options have been circumscribed by the constraints imposed on their role by society. This is why a history that makes room for women would have to be conceived and organized according to the function played by women through the ages, and not based on events of a predominantly political nature, which has little to do with what has been the daily experience of women.

The development of ideological and organizational models in the historical narrative capable of incorporating the genuine experience of the totality of the population is the principal challenge facing modern historiography. This task certainly implies overcoming numerous obstacles. Integrating a history truly representative of humanity requires taking account of a multiplicity of elements outside of the establishment of a structure of the narrative. Despite the difficulties, an integral history can be written. A possible alternative to the traditional model would be the development of history with an anthropological focus, a history that would account for the everyday experience of women as well as of men. This history would explain to us:

...the evolution of customs, habits, norms and values of individuals and collectivities according to changes in the economy, science and demography, etc.(Garreta and Careaga, 1987: 153)

The numbers in charts 6 to 10.3 serve as a corollary to those numbers presented in previous charts. The results they give out affirm in an unarguable manner the total exclusion of women from historical narrative. This omission has ominous consequences for women's self-image. The female student of history does not find in the text women who assume roles that serve as model nor that reaffirm their importance as historical subjects with value and merit of their own. In this manner, the texts support a negative image of women and contribute in this way to perpetuate an androcentric ideology on which the subordination of women rests.

By arguing that contemporary women are no longer restricted to the domestic sphere, the theory is put forward that women are now participants in history, in a manner their ancestors were not. This postulate rests on an underlining fallacy: that for the mere fact that they are achieving higher levels of social participation, women are achieving a genuine equality. To the latter we could argue that what really happens is that women lead a double life: at the same time that women are allowed to participate in some aspects of the sphere traditionally considered masculine (public life, salaried occupation), women continue to be entirely responsible for domestic life, and this continues to be the role by which they are defined as women.

Nevertheless, from the perspective of what has been our analysis, we hold the belief that only those activities that insert themselves in spheres traditionally considered masculine are valued, and history only accounts for these. So that in the case of contemporary women only their insertion in these spheres is valued, and only in relation to this aspect of their lives it is considered that women's present participation in society is more visible and their status consequently greater.

True equality, on the contrary, would have to be based on the valorization in equal proportion of all spheres of life and in the eradication of spheres according to sex. While these conditions are not present in society, history still to be written would continue to have the same perspective as traditional historiography, with a focus reduced to the masculine sphere of power. It would simply contain a greater representation in number of the insertions (still really exceptional) that are made by women in this sphere. Conclusion:

Dominican historiography shows a myopic vision of history that excludes half of the population. As the texts analyzed demonstrate, this is the case even in the new generation of Dominican historians, those who, contrary to traditional chroniclers, integrate in their work the perspectives and methods of contemporary social sciences. That portion of the population who by gender definition does not participate in events that belong to the socially relevant sphere is not represented. In order to include women in their own right, Dominican history would have to be rewritten.

The analysis of content which we undertook has had as its objective the analysis of the levels of participation/exclusion of women in history, as well as some of the factors that determine it. Although this analysis of sexism in education has limited its focus on the written word, this (the word) has been used as an index of factors which in our opinion permeate the entire conception of history, its development as an academic discipline and its teaching processes. It is unlikely, for example, that the perspective of those who teach history as a subject differs significantly from the pattern we have analyzed since it is evident that these professionals shared the androcentric vision predominant in all institutions in Dominican society. We can, therefore, suppose with sufficient certainty that the results of the analysis of the content of the texts are a rather faithful indicator of the contents of education in general; that is to say, the total sum of those who can participate in the learning process: professors, students, additional readings, etc.

Traditional approaches to history have to change to include women. Until this is achieved, we will not have a true history of humanity. (Anderson and Zinsser, 1988: XXIII) Deprived from knowing their history because of an education that does not reflect their past, women live without a context, without present reference of their past existence. (Rich, 1983) There cannot be equality when more than half of humanity has no history. Only when the history of women has been written, when their participation and achievements are salvaged, it will be truly possible to begin to put an end to the oldest tradition in our culture: the devaluing of women. (Anderson and Zinsser, p. XXIII)

CHART I
Total Number of Times Women Are Mentioned in the Three Texts*

Text	No. of Mentions
Moya	63
Peguero y de los Santos	152
Cassá	_38
Total	253

*It includes mentions by gender and of characters, multiple references to the same character, etc.

CHART 2
Type of Mentions of Women, according to Reference to Gender or Character

Text	Mention by Gender	Mention by Character*
Moya	42	21
Peguero y de los Santos	75	77
Cassá	_23	_15
Total	140	113

*The difference in the total amounts and those that appear in charts 3.1, 3.2 and 3.3 is due to the fact that for each mention of "The Mirabal Sisters" one mention and three characters were computed.

CHART 3.1
Enumeration of Feminine Characters in Moya's Text

Character	No. of Times Mentioned
Inés the Catholic	1
Anacaona	1
Queen Isabella	3
Elizabeth the First of England	2
María de Arana	1
Rosa Duarte	1
María Trinidad Sánchez	1

Isabel II (of Spain)	6
María Martínez	1
Mirabal Sisters	2
TOTAL	19

CHART 3.2

Enumeration of Feminine Characters in Peguero and de los Santos' Text

Character	No. of Times Mentioned (In the Main Narrative)
Taína Goddess*	1
Queen Isabella	5
Anacaona	2
Iguanamá	1
María de Toledo	3
Elizabeth I (of England)	1
María Trinidad Sánchez	1
Isabel II (of Spain)	4
MirabalSisters	2
SUBTOTAL	20

	(In Sections on Cultural Aspects-Peguero y de los Santos' Text)
Leonor de Ovando	1
Elvira deMendoza	1
María Nicolasa Billini	1
Socorro Sánchez	1
Salomé Ureña	9
Josefa A.Perdomo	1
Adriana Billini	1
Ercilia Pepín	5
Virginia Elena Ortea	1
Aida Ibarra	1
Celeste Woss y Gil	3
Mercedes Cocco	1
María Teresa Ariza	1
Enriqueta Zafra	1
Julieta Otero	1
Catalinan Jáquez	1
Divina Gómez	1
Abigaíl Mejía	3
Luisa Ozema Pellerano	1
Antera Mota	1
Encarnación Piñeyro	1
Andrea Evangelina Rodríguez	2

Armida García	1
Mercedes Heureaux	1
Argentina Montás	1
Urania Montás	1
Clara E. Brache	1
Victoria Sofía Oliva	1
AidaCartagena Portalatín	1
Clara Ledesma	1
Elsa Divanna	1
Marianela Jiménez	1
Nidia Serra	1
Noemí Mella	1
Ada Balcácer	1
Elsa Núñez	1
SUBTOTAL	53
GENERAL TOTAL	73

CHART 3.3
Enumeration of Feminine Characters in Cassá's Text

Character	No. of Times Mentioned
Queen Isabella	10
Guabancex	1
Queen Isabel II(of Spain)	1
MirabalSisters	1
TOTAL	13

CHART 4
Level of Leadership of Feminine Characters in Three Texts

Text	Primary	Secondary	Group
Moya	6	5	7
Peguero y de los Santos	29	16	28
Cassá	10	—	3
TOTALS	45	21	38

CHART 5.1
Occupation or Condition of Feminine Characters in Moya's Text

Occupation or condition	No. of characters
Chieftain	1
Wife and sister of chieftains	1
Queen	3
Landowner	1
Sister/writer	1
Political conspirator	1

Wife/banker	1
Wives of political conspirators	3
TOTAL	12

* We use the characterization given in the book.

CHART 5.2

Occupation or Condition of Feminine Characters in Peguero and de los Santos's Text

Occupation or condition	No. of Characters
Taína goddess	1
Queen	3
Chieftain	1
Taína elder	1
Wife of viceroy	1
Poet	3
Political conspirator	1
Educator	4
Poet-educator	1
Writer	1
Plastic Artist	10
Nationalist/educator/feminist	1
Literary Author	1
Musical artist	6
Educator/writer/feminist	1
Masters in Pharmacy	1
Degree in Medicine	7
Wives of political conspirators/ political activists	3
TOTAL	47

CHART 5.3

Occupation or condition of Feminine Characters in Cassá's Text

Occupation or condition	No. of Characters
Queen	2
Taína Goddess	1
Symbols of anti-Trujillo struggle	3
TOTAL	6

CHART 6
Total number of Masculine Characters and Total Number of Mentions of the Same in the Three Texts*

Text	No. of Characters	No. of Times Mentioned
Moya	439	3,121
Peguero y de los Santos	615	2,320
Cassá	362	1,804

* As opposed to what was done in the case of women, this tabulation encompasses only characters mentioned by proper noun (Colombus, King Ferdinand, Santana). Mentions in other forms such as the Almiral, Discoverer, King, Despot, Dictator, etc. were not tabulated given the large volume.

CHART 7
Percentage Distribution of Characters, by Gender

Text	Masculine Characters No.	Masculine Characters %	Feminine Characters No.	Feminine Characters %
Moya	439	95.4	21	4.6
Peguero y de los Santos	615	88.9	77 1	1.1
Cassá	362	96.0	15	4.0

CHART 8
Percentage Distribution of Mention of Characters, by Gender

Text	Masculine Mentions No.	Masculine Mentions %	Feminine Mentions No.	Feminine Mentions %
	3,121	99.4	19	0.6
Peguero y de los Santos	2,320	97.0	73	3.0
Cassá	1,804	99.3	13	0.7

CHART 9
Total Number of Characters and Mentions in the Three Texts, by Gender

Text	Men Characters	Men Mentioned	Women Characters	Women Mentioned
Moya	439	3,121	19	21
Peguero y de los Santos	615	2,320	73	77
Cassá	362	1,804	13	15

CHART 10.1
Tabulation of Illustrations of Human Figures

Text	Total No. of Illustrations	Total No. of Human Figures
Moya	77	54
Peguero y de los Santos	57	28
Cassá	274	144

CHART 10.2

Distribution by Gender of Illustrations of Human Figures

Text	Masculine Figures	Feminine Figures	Mixed Figures
Moya	54 (100%)	-	-
Peguero y de los Santos	18 (64.3%)	5 (17.9%)	5 (17.9%)
Cassá	117 (81.2%)	4 (2.8%)	23 (16%)

CHART 10.3

Distribution by Gender of Historical Characters

Text	Masculine Figures	Feminine Figures	Mixed Figures
Moya	54 (100%)	-	-
Peguero y de los Santos	9 (100%)	-	-
Cassá	73 (94.8%)	3 (3.9%)	1 (1.3%)

Works Cited

Anderson, Bonnie S. and Judith P. Zinsser. *A History of Their Own, Women in Europe from Prehistory to the Present.* Vol. I New York: Harper and Row Publishers, 1989.

Cassá, Roberto. *Historia social y económica de la República Dominicana.* Vols I & II. Santo Domingo: Punto y Aparte Editores, 1983.

Duarte Isis et al. *Población y condición de la mujer en la República Dominicana.* Santo Domingo: Instituto de Población y Desarrollo, Estudio No. 6, 1989.

Garreta, Nuria and Pilar Careaga. *Modelos masculino y femenino en los textos de EGB.* Madrid: Ministerio de Cultura, Instituto de la Mujer, Serie Estudios No. 14, 1987.

Moreno, Monserrat. *Cómo se enseña a ser niña: el sexismo en la escuela.* Barcelona: Icaria Editorial, S.A., 1986.

Moya Pons, Frank. *Manual de historia dominicana.* 8th ed. Santo Domingo: Editora Corripio, UCMM, Colección Textos, 1984.

Oviedo-Las Casas. *Crónicas escogidas.* Santo Domingo: Fundación Corripio, Biblioteca Clásicos Castellanos, Vol. IV, 1988.

Peguero, Valentina and Danilo de los Santos. 10th ed. *Visión general de la historia dominicana.* Santo Domingo: Editora Corripio, 1987.

Rich, Adrienne. *Sobre mentiras, secretos y silencios.* Barcelona: Icaria Editorial, 1983.

Translation by Daisy Cocco De Filippis

PART II
A SELECTED BIBLIOGRAPHY

DOMINICAN WOMEN WRITERS:
SELECTED BIBLIOGRAPHY

The publication of this selected bibliography of the works written by Dominican women is a continuation of the effort began with the proposal "Toward a Bibliography of Works Written by Dominican Women" included in my publication of 1992, *Combatidas, combativas y combatientes: Antología de cuentos escritos por dominicanas.*

The adjective "selected" assists me in underlining the inconclusive character of projects such as this one. In the present version, designed as a document to support a publication which features the thought of Dominican women, I add to the information on literature, the titles of works by women in other areas in the humanities and in other fields such as social and natural sciences, with the intent to illustrate the valuable contribution women have made to all aspects of the Dominican experience.

As always, I am grateful for the generosity of so many without whose contribution I would not be able to complete this publication. Among them: Chiqui Vicioso, Neicy Zeller, Ylonka Nacidit-Perdomo, Emelda Ramos, Ida Hernández-Caamaño, Myrna Guerrero, Ramonina Brea, Valentina Peguero, Lusitania Martínez, Jean Weissman, Kelva Pérez-Kamber and Franklin Gutiérrez. D.C.D.F.

Bibliographies consulted:

Alfau Durán, Vetilio. "Apuntes para la bibliografía poética dominicana". *Clío,* 33.122 (January-April 1965) pp 34-60; 36.123 (January-August 1968) pp 107-109; 37.124 (January-August 1969) pp 53-68; 30.125 (January-June 1970) pp 50-77.

Biblioteca Nacional. *Anuario bibliográfico dominicano.* Santo Domingo: Biblioteca Nacional, 1984. 263 p. Presentation by Norberto L. Soto.

Coll, Edna. *Indice informativo de la novela hispanoamericana.* V. I. Puerto Rico: Editorial Universitaria de la Universidad de Puerto Rico, 1974. Dominican novelists: pp 171-221.

Collado, Miguel. *Apuntes bibliográficos sobre la literatura dominicana.* Santo Domingo: Biblioteca Nacional, 1993. 535 p.

Moya Pons, Frank. *Bibliografía de la literatura dominicana 1820-1990.* 2 Vols. Santo Domingo: Imprenta Amigo del Hogar, Publicación de la Comisión Permanente de la Feria del Libro, 1997. 404 p. 391 p.

Waxman, Samuel Montefiore. *A Bibliography of the Belles Lettres of Santo Domingo.* Cambridge, Massachusetts: Harvard University Press, 1931. 31 p.

Toward a Bibliography of Works Written by Dominican Women

An Invitation to a Much Needed Project-1997

Abreu de Sturla, Argentina. *Músicos francomacorisanos desde 1884 hasta 1985.* Santo Domingo: Editora Taller, 1985. 72 p. (Essay)

Abreu L., Luz María. *Con las campesinas: Reflexiones sobre mujer rural y desarrollo.* Santo Domingo: Editora Búho, 1988. 140 p. Compilation of papers. (Essay)

Acosta de Pérez, Luz Dalia. *Los derechos de la mujer.* Santo Domingo: Editora Universitaria, 1993. 177 p. + il. (Essay)

Acosta, Ruth. *El Arte de barrer.* Santo Domingo: Colección Pegasos de Poesía, 1992. (Poetry)

Adrover de Cibrán, Belkis. *Renacer.* Santo Domingo: Editora Corripio, 1987. 145 p. (Poetry)

Aguiar, Mercedes Laura. *Discursos y páginas literarias 1872-1958.* Prologue by Argentina Montás. Santo Domingo: Editora del Caribe, 1972. 131 p. Recuerdo amoroso de sus discípulas en el día de su centenario, 16 de febrero de 1972. (Essay)

Alardo de Morillo, Ascensión. *Una mujer vanidosa: Novela corta.* San Pedro de Macorís, Rep. Dom.: Imprenta Femina, 1935. 36 p. (Novel)

Albert Batista, Celsa. *Mujer y esclavitud en Santo Domingo.* Santo Domingo: Ediciones Cedee, 1990. 130 p. Presentation by Yris Rossi. (Essay)

_____. *Las ideas educativas de José Martí.* Santiago de los Caballeros, Rep. Dom.: Universidad Católica Madre y Maestra, 1992. 2nd. ed. 1996. Premio UNESCO. (Essay)

Alejandra, Mayda. *Botones de mi huerto.* Santo Domingo: Editorial Cultural Dominicana, 1974. 202 p. (Poetry)

Alfau Galván, Jesusa. *Los débiles.* Madrid: Imprenta Artística de José Blass y Cía, 1912. 125 p. (Novel)

Alfau, Reyna. *La pieza del mes, 1982-1984.* Santo Domingo: Museo Nacional de Historia y Geografía, n.d. (Prose)

Alvarez Saviñón, Dora. *Voces eternas: 18 poemas en prosa.* Caracas: Imprenta Alvarez, 1945. n.p. (Poetry)

Alvarez, Julia. *Homecoming.* New York: Grove Press, 1986. 2nd Ed. (Revised) New York: Plume Book, 1996. (Poetry)

_____. *The Other Side/El otro lado*. New York: Plume, 1994. (Poetry)

_____. *In the Time of the Butterflies*. New York: Plume, 1994. (Novel)

_____. *How the García Girls Lost Their Accents*. New York: Algonquin Books of Chapel Hill, 1991. (Novel)

Alvarez, Soledad. *La magna patria de Pedro Henríquez Ureña*. Santiago: Ediciones Universidad Católica Madre y Maestra, Colección Ensayos, No. 3, 1981. 132 p. (Essay)

_____. *Vuelo posible*. Santo Domingo: Editora Amigo del Hogar, 1994. 75 p. (Poetry)

Alvarez, Virginia. *Latitud del amor*. Santo Domingo: Agencia Gráfica, 1990. 111 p. (Poetry)

Andino C., Rosa M. *Humilde ramillete de flores místicas en honor de Jesús y María: [Poemas]*. Santiago: Imprenta L.H. Cruz, 1929. 56 p. (Poetry)

Anónimo. *Algunas notas biográficas de la insigne patricia y educadora Señora Ercilia Pepín*. Santiago de los Caballeros: Imprenta de L.H. Cruz, 1932. 14 p. (Essay)

Aretz, Isabel. *¿Qué es el folklore?* Santo Domingo: Ballet Folklórico Dominicano, 1981. 66 p. (Essay)

Arias, Aurora. *Vivienda de pájaro*. Santo Domingo: Editorial Gente, 1986. 58 p. (Poetry)

_____. *Piano Lila*. Santo Domingo: Editorial Búho, 1994. 33 p. (Poetry)

Arvelo, Josefina. *¿Qué pasa, qué queremos, qué podemos hacer? El diagnóstico comunitario*. Santo Domingo: Centro de Solidaridad para el Desarrollo de la Mujer, Colección Presente, 1995. 10 p. (Essay)

Aybar o Rodríguez, Manuela (La Deana). *Historia de una mujer*. Santo Domingo: Imprenta Nacional, 1849. 15 p. (Essay)

Báez, Clara. *La subordinación social de la mujer dominicana en cifras*. Santo Domingo: Editorial Montalvo, 1985. (Essay)

_____. et al. *Fecundidad y mortalidad infantil por estratos de localidades y socio-culturales*. Santo Domingo: Instituto de Estudios de la Población, 1987. (Prose)

_____. *Directorio de organismos gubernamentales y no gubernamentales que trabajan con mujeres*. Santo Domingo: Editora Búho, 1989. 164 p. (Prose)

_____. *Mujer y desarrollo en la República Dominicana: 1981-1991*. Santo Domingo: Banco Interamericano de Desarrollo, 1991. (Essay)

_____.et al. *Mercado laboral para mujeres formadas en ocupaciones no tradicionales: El caso de Los Minas*. Santo Domingo: Editora Palma, 1994. 99 p. (Essay)

_____.et al. *Estado de situación de la democracia dominicana (1978-1992)*. Santo Domingo: IEDP y la Editora de la PUCMM, 1995. (Essay)

_____. et al. *La cultura política de los dominicanos. Entre el autoritarismo y la democracia*. Santo Domingo: Editora de la PUCMM, 1995. (Essay)

_____. et al. *Cultura política y democracia en la República Dominicana*. Santo Domingo: Editora de la PUCMM, 1996. (Essay)

Báez, Clara and Arregui, Marivi. et al. *Mujer, población y desarrollo en el Caribe: El caso de la República Dominicana*. Santo Domingo: INSTRAW, 1988. (Essay)

_____. et al. *Las zonas francas y la mano de obra femenina en el Caribe. El caso de la República Dominicana*. Santo Domingo: Oxfam Caribe, 1989. (Essay)

Báez, Juana. *El hijo de tres amantes*. Santo Domingo: Gráficas William, 1991, 274 p. (Novel)

Báez de Erazo, Melba. *Matemática básica II*. Santo Domingo: Editora de la UASD Vol. 267, Colección Ciencia y Tecnología No. 9, 1979. 195 p. (Prose)

_____. *Matemática básica I*. Santo Domingo: Editora de la UASD Vol. 281, Colección Ciencia y Tecnología No. 2, 1980. 290 p. (Prose)

Barón de Sánchez, Angela. *Poemas del amor sin nombre*. Santo Domingo: Arte y Cine, 1967. 82 p. (Poetry)

_____. *Poemas del amor sin nombre: Segunda parte*. Santo Domingo: Impresora Arte y Cine, 1973. 52 p. (Poetry)

Benería, Lourdes. *Reproducción, producción y división sexual del trabajo*. Santo Domingo: Taller para la CIPAF, 1984. 57 p. (Essay)

Bergés D., Ana Rosa et al. *La prescripción en materia de responsabilidad civil*. Santo Domingo: Ediciones Capeldom, 1966. 58 p. (Essay)

Bernardino, Minerva. *Lucha, agonía y esperanza: Trayectoria triunfal de mi vida*. Santo Domingo: Editora Corripio, 1993. (Essay)

Betances de Pujadas, Estrella. *Unos cuentos para padres con sus niños*. Santo Domingo: Editora Corripio, 1980. 101 p. + il (Short Story)

Bethancourt de Baroni, Daisy. *Auroras en penumbras*. Santo Domingo: Editora Andújar, 1986. 113 p. (Poetry)

Billini Mejía, Lourdes. *El grito esculpido*. Santo Domingo: Biblioteca Nacional, 1985. 158 p. Prologue by Abel Fernández Mejía. (Poetry)

Blanco, Cecilia, Martínez, Vilma, and Román, Solange. *La mujer en "Sólo cenizas hallarás"*. Santo Domingo: Editora de la UASD, Colección Tesis No.3, 1988. 182 p. (Essay)

Bobadilla de D'Esposito, Dolores. *Pilar Constanzo Hernández. Una maestra ejemplar* (Biografía). Santo Domingo: Editora del Caribe, 1964. (Prose)

Bonnelly de Díaz, Aída. *En torno a la música*. Santo Domingo: Premio Nacional de Didáctica, Banreservas, 1978. 2nd. ed.: SEEBAC, 1979. 181 p. (Essay)

_____. *Síntesis de la historia de música dominicana*. Santo Domingo: Banreservas, 1977. 2nd. ed.: Seebac, 1983. (Prose)

_____. *Testimonio del canto y de las palabras*. Santo Domingo: Alfa y Omega, 1981. 338 p. (Essay)

_____. *Variaciones*. Santo Domingo: Taller, 1984. 2nd. ed.: Taller, 1986. (Essay)

_____. *Retablo de costumbres dominicanas*. Santiago de los Caballeros, Rep. Dom.: Editorial PUCMM, 1991. 173 p. (Essay)

_____. *Los niños y las artes*. Santo Domingo: Alfa y Omega, 1992. (Essay)

_____. *Vivencias, semblanzas e inquietudes. Por los trillos del arte*. Santo Domingo: Amigo del Hogar, Serie Arte y Cultura, Banreservas, 1996. 261 p. (Essay)

Bonnelly de Calventi, Idelisa. *Estudios de biología pesquera dominicana*. Santo Domingo: Publicaciones de la UASD, Ciencia y Tecnología No. 159, 1974. 171 p. + il. (Essay)

Bort de González, Fior D'Aliza. *Pequeño...En la montaña hay un niño que espera*. Santo Domingo: Talleres Servicios Gráficos, 1983. 22p. (Short Story)

Brea, Ramonina. *Ensayo sobre la formación del estado capitalista en la República Dominicana y Haití*. Santo Domingo: Taller, 1983. (Essay)

_____. *Propuestas para la reforma constitucional en la República Dominicana*. Santo Domingo: Editora de la PUCMM, 1994. (Essay)

_____. editora. *Temas para la agenda política nacional*. Santo Domingo: Editora de la PUCMM, 1994. (Essay)

_____. editora. *Encuentros de las organizaciones populares: Propuestas de reformas políticas*. Santo Domingo: Editora de la PUCMM, 1994. (Essay)

_____. et al. *Estado de situación de la democracia dominicana 1978-1993*. Santo Domingo: Editora de la PUCMM, 1995. (Essay)

_____. et al. *La cultura política de los dominicanos: Entre el autoritarismo y la democracia*. Santo Domingo: Editora de la PUCMM, 1995. (Essay)

_____. et al. *Cultura política y democracia en República Dominicana*. Santo Domingo: Editora de la PUCMM, 1996. (Essay)

Brenes de Puello, Gladialisa. *En el altar de los sueños*. Santo Domingo: Editora Corripio, 1985. 81 p. (Poetry)

_____. *En alas del ensueño*. Santo Domingo: Editora Elizabeth, 1989. 120 p. (Poetry)

Brito de Domínguez, Elsa. *Al pie de mi escalera*. Santiago, Rep. Dom.: Editora Amigo del Hogar, 1976. 45 p. (Poetry)

Brusiloff, Carmenchu. *Santo Domingo: Key to the West Indies*. Santo Domingo: Dominican Institute, 1970. 113 p. (Prose)

_____. *Santo Domingo: Llave de las indias occidentales*. Santo Domingo: Instituto Cultural Dominicano, 1978. 76 p. (Prose)

Caamaño de Fernández, Vicenta. *La lengua campesina en la narrativa costumbrista dominicana*. Santo Domingo: Centurión, 1976. 207 p. (Essay)

Cabral, Lucía Amelia. *Hay cuentos que contar*. Santo Domingo: Editora Sargazo, 1977. 127 p. + il. (Short Story for children)

_____. *Gabino*. Santo Domingo: Editora Comercial Gráfica, 1979. 12 p. (Short Story for children)

_____. *Sorprendido, el plátano*. Santo Domingo: Intergraphic, 1979. n.p. (Short Story for children)

Cabral, Minerva Urania. *Gotas del alma*. Santo Domingo: Imprenta Arte y Cine, 1947. 124 p. Juicio crítico del Lic. Julio González Herrera. (Poetry)

Cabral de Poladura, Atala. *Casa de los Rodrigo de Bastidas. Apuntes Históricos*. Santo Domingo: Editora del Caribe, 1977. 40 p. [+ 10 fotografías]. (Essay)

Cabral de Valdepares, Edelmira. *Décimas de la leona*. Santo Domingo: Editora Tribuna Hispánica, 1977. 61 p. (Poetry)

_____. *Versos del camino*. San Pedro de Macorís: Universidad Central del Este, 1982. 124 p. Posthumous publication of poety reprinted by her sister Elba Cabral Vda. de la Concha and her husband Julián Valdepares Díaz. Prologue by Virgilio Hoepelman. (Poetry)

Cadilla, Carmen Alicia. *Voz de las islas íntimas: (Poema de viaje)* Ciudad Trujillo: Montalvo, 1939. 34 p. (Poetry)

Caminero Sánchez, María. *Bajo los árboles*. San Pedro de Macorís, Rep. Dom.: Tipografía La Provincia, 1921. 60 p. (Poetry)

Campo de Wittkop, Nora del. *La pequeña Cabonao y su amiguito Matino o El collar de las conchas*. Santo Domingo: Ediciones Infantiles Dominicanas, 1982. (Short Story for children)

Canaán Fernández, Eurídice. *Poesías*. Santo Domingo: Impresora Dominicana, 1959. 62 p. (Poetry)

_____. *Los depravados*. Santo Domingo: Editora del Caribe, 1964. 197 p. (Novel)

_____. *Los monstruos sagrados: 7 libros minitomos 1-2...* Santo Domingo: Librería Dominicana, 1969. 197 p. (Poetry)

_____. *Morir por última vez*. Santo Domingo: Editora del Caribe, 1980, 182 p. (Novel)

Caram, Magaly. *Profamilia: Una institución al servicio de la mujer dominicana*. Washington, D.C.: n.p., 1983. (Essay)

Cartagena Portalatín, Aída. *Víspera del sueño*. Ciudad Trujillo: La Poesía Sorprendida, Colección El Desvelado Solitario, 1944. 10 p. (Poetry)

_____. *Del sueño al mundo*. Ciudad Trujillo: La Poesía Sorprendida, Colección El Desvelado Solitario, 1945. n.p. (Poetry)

_____. *Llámale verde*. Ciudad Trujillo: La Poesía Sorprendida, Colección El Desvelado Solitario, 1945. n.p. (Poetry)

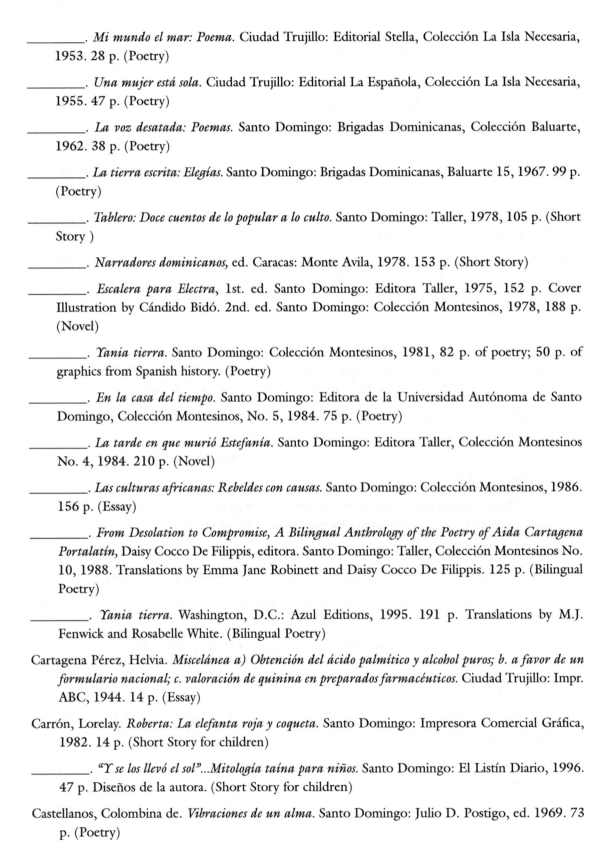

_____. *Mi mundo el mar: Poema*. Ciudad Trujillo: Editorial Stella, Colección La Isla Necesaria, 1953. 28 p. (Poetry)

_____. *Una mujer está sola*. Ciudad Trujillo: Editorial La Española, Colección La Isla Necesaria, 1955. 47 p. (Poetry)

_____. *La voz desatada: Poemas*. Santo Domingo: Brigadas Dominicanas, Colección Baluarte, 1962. 38 p. (Poetry)

_____. *La tierra escrita: Elegías*. Santo Domingo: Brigadas Dominicanas, Baluarte 15, 1967. 99 p. (Poetry)

_____. *Tablero: Doce cuentos de lo popular a lo culto*. Santo Domingo: Taller, 1978, 105 p. (Short Story)

_____. *Narradores dominicanos,* ed. Caracas: Monte Avila, 1978. 153 p. (Short Story)

_____. *Escalera para Electra*, 1st. ed. Santo Domingo: Editora Taller, 1975, 152 p. Cover Illustration by Cándido Bidó. 2nd. ed. Santo Domingo: Colección Montesinos, 1978, 188 p. (Novel)

_____. *Yania tierra*. Santo Domingo: Colección Montesinos, 1981, 82 p. of poetry; 50 p. of graphics from Spanish history. (Poetry)

_____. *En la casa del tiempo*. Santo Domingo: Editora de la Universidad Autónoma de Santo Domingo, Colección Montesinos, No. 5, 1984. 75 p. (Poetry)

_____. *La tarde en que murió Estefanía*. Santo Domingo: Editora Taller, Colección Montesinos No. 4, 1984. 210 p. (Novel)

_____. *Las culturas africanas: Rebeldes con causas*. Santo Domingo: Colección Montesinos, 1986. 156 p. (Essay)

_____. *From Desolation to Compromise, A Bilingual Anthrology of the Poetry of Aida Cartagena Portalatín,* Daisy Cocco De Filippis, editora. Santo Domingo: Taller, Colección Montesinos No. 10, 1988. Translations by Emma Jane Robinett and Daisy Cocco De Filippis. 125 p. (Bilingual Poetry)

_____. *Yania tierra*. Washington, D.C.: Azul Editions, 1995. 191 p. Translations by M.J. Fenwick and Rosabelle White. (Bilingual Poetry)

Cartagena Pérez, Helvia. *Miscelánea a) Obtención del ácido palmítico y alcohol puros; b. a favor de un formulario nacional; c. valoración de quinina en preparados farmacéuticos*. Ciudad Trujillo: Impr. ABC, 1944. 14 p. (Essay)

Carrón, Lorelay. *Roberta: La elefanta roja y coqueta*. Santo Domingo: Impresora Comercial Gráfica, 1982. 14 p. (Short Story for children)

_____. *"Y se los llevó el sol"...Mitología taína para niños*. Santo Domingo: El Listín Diario, 1996. 47 p. Diseños de la autora. (Short Story for children)

Castellanos, Colombina de. *Vibraciones de un alma*. Santo Domingo: Julio D. Postigo, ed. 1969. 73 p. (Poetry)

_____. *Inquietud prenatal: Poemas.* Santo Domingo: Editora Médico Dominicano, Colección La Cámara, 1970. 98 p. (Poetry)

_____. *Dos cantos para una sola América.* Prologue by Raschid E. Zaiter L. n.l.: Fondo de la Cultura, 1971. 58 p. (Poetry)

Castillo, Carmen. *Una conversación interesante.* Santo Domingo: Editora Corripio, 1982. 81 p. (Poetry)

_____. *Todos somos mediums: Dictado medianímicamente por el maestro Joaquín Trincado.* Santo Domingo: Editora Escuela Espiritista Hija de la Verdad, 1979. 170 p. (Poetry)

Castillo, Dinorah. *Lágrimas de pecador rebosante de amor.* Santo Domingo: Editorial Cultural Dominicana, 1976. 102 P. (Poetry)

CIPAF. *Plan de igualdad de oportunidades para las mujeres.* Santo Domingo: CIPAF, 1994. (Prose)

_____. *500 años de patriarcado en el nuevo mundo.* Santo Domingo: CIPAF, Red entre Mujeres, 1993. 151 p. (Prose)

_____. *Programa mínimo feminista.* Santo Domingo: CIPAF, 1990. (Prose)

_____. *Encuesta de hogares y mujeres urbanos.* Santo Domingo: CIPAF, 1988. (Prose)

Cocco De Filippis, Daisy. *Estudios semióticos de poesía dominicana.* Santo Domingo: Biblioteca Taller No. 178, 1984. Includes index for *La Poesía Sorprendida.* 174 p. (Essay)

_____. ed. *Sin otro profeta que su canto, antología de poesía escrita por dominicanas.* Santo Domingo: Biblioteca Taller No. 263, 1988. Includes apendix of feminist essays. 231 p. (Critical literary introductory essay-anthology of poetry)

_____. ed. *From Desolation to Compromise: A Bilingual Anthology of the Poetry of Aida Cartagena Portalatín.* Santo Domingo: Colección Montesinos No. 10, 1988. Translations by Emma Jane Robinett and Daisy Cocco De Filippis. 125 p. (Bilingual Poetry)

_____. ed. et al. *Poemas de exilio y de otras inquietudes/Poems of Exile and of Other Concerns/selección bilingüe de poemas escritos por dominicanos en los Estados Unidos.* New York: Alcance, 1988. Translations by Daisy Cocco De Filippis and Emma Jane Robinett. 146 p. (Bilingual Poetry)

_____.ed. *Combatidas, combativas y combatientes, antología de cuentos escritos por dominicanas.* Santo Domingo: Taller, Publicaciones del Instituto del Libro, 1992. Includes appendix of feminist essays by various authors. 446 p. (Anthology of Short Stories)

_____. ed. *The Women of Hispaniola: Moving Towards Tomorrow.* New York: York College Executive Report. No. 1, 1993. Includes contributions in English, Spanish and French. Proceedings of the May 1993 Conference. 152 p. (Anthology of essays, poetry and short stories in three languages)

_____. ed. et al. *Historia de Washington Heights y otros rincones del mundo/Stories From Washington Heights and Other Corners of the World.* New York: Latino Press, 1994. Translations by Daisy Cocco De Filippis and Margaret Ballantyne. 204 p. (Bilingual Short Stories)

_____. ed. *Asian Culture: Tradition and Diaspora*. New York: York College Executive Report No. 3, 1994. 105 p. English publication en inglés of the November 1993 Conference. (Essays and Poetry in English)

_____. *Tertuliando/Hanging Out*. Santo Domingo: Publicación de la Comisión Permanente de la Feria del Libro Dominicano, 1997. 280 p. Cover designed by Raquel Paiewonsky. (Bilingual essay, poetry, short stories)

Coiscou, Abigaíl. *La ley de policía con sus modificaciones*. Ciudad Trujillo: Montalvo, 1942. (Essay)

_____. *Código penal: Leyes que lo modifican y lo complementan*. 2nd. ed. Santiago, Rep. Dom.: Editorial El Diario, n.d. LXXVI-286 p. (Essay)

Coiscou Guzmán, Grey. *Raíces*. Ciudad Trujillo: Imprenta Arte y Cine, 1959. Prologue by Pedro René Contín y Aybar. 89 p. (Poetry)

Collins de Collado, Mary. *La gatita Mima y sus amiguitas las violetas*. Santo Domingo: Editora Corripio, 1986. 28 p. (Short Story for Children)

Columna de Lockward, Lina. *Legislación y jurisprudencia de seguros en la República Dominicana*. Santo Domingo: Editora Educativa Dominicana, 1977, 425 p. (Essay)

Concepción, Patria. *Quisqueya Ana. Lejanía*. Sao Paulo: n.p., 1990, 55 p. (Poetry)

Contreras, Brunilda. *Ensayos sobre cultura netamente campesina*. Santo Domingo: Alfa y Omega, 1979. 144 p. 2nd. ed. Santo Domingo: Taller, 1985. 94 p. (Essay)

Contreras, Hilma. *Cuatro cuentos*. Ciudad Trujillo: Editorial Stella, Colección La Isla Necesaria, No. 3, 1953. 39 p. (Short Story)

_____. *Doña Endrina de Calatayud*. Ciudad Trujillo: Impresora Arte y Cine, 1955. 42 p. (Essay)

_____. *El ojo de Dios: Cuentos de la clandestinidad*. Santo Domingo: Colecciones Baluarte, Ediciones de Brigadas Dominicanas, 1962. 26 p. (Short Story)

_____. *La tierra está bramando*. Santo Domingo: Biblioteca Nacional, Colección Orfeo, 1986. 134 p. (Novel)

_____. *Entre dos silencios*. Santo Domingo: Biblioteca Taller No. 241, 1987. 129 p. Illustrated by Cover designed by Noemí Mella. (Short Story)

_____. *Facetas de la vida*. Santo Domingo: Taller, 1993. 118 p. (Short Story)

Coordinación de ONGs del Area de la Mujer. *Salud de las mujeres: Calidad de atención y mortalidad materna*. Santo Domingo: Editora Búho, Organización Panamericana de la Salud, 1966, 55 p. Introduction by Sonia Díaz. (Prose)

Cordero, Margarita. *Mujeres de abril*. Santo Domingo: CIPAF, Ediciones Populares Feministas, 1985, 187 p. (Essay and interviews)

_____. *Nicaragua: Las mujeres frente al proceso electoral*. Santo Domingo: Editora Búho, Ediciones Populares Feministas, 1985. 54 p. (Interviews)

_____. *Evaluación general de avances y obstáculos para la participación de la mujer en el proceso político del país.* Santo Domingo: UNICEF, 1987. (Prose)

_____. *Mujer, participación política y procesos electorales (1986-1990).* Santo Domingo: CIPAF, 1991. 121 p. Presentation by Julio Brea Franco. (Essay)

_____. et al. *Con trabajo de mujer: Condiciones de vida de la mujer rural.* 2nd. ed. Santo Domingo: Centro de Solidaridad para el Desarrollo de la Mujer, 1991. 46 p. + ilus. (Essay)

_____. *Comunicaciones para la mujer en el desarrollo.* Santo Domingo: Centro de Investigación para Accción Feminista, 1994. 97 p. (Essay)

Cornielle Mendoza Taylor, Ivelisse. *Saudades.* Santo Domingo: n.p., 1967. 48 p. (Poetry)

Cot, Carmen, *Opus No. 1.* Santo Domingo: Amigo del Hogar, 1983. 16 p. (Poetry)

Cross de Hailu, Elvira Angélica. *Libertad condicional.* Santo Domingo: Amigo del Hogar, 1990. 79 p. (Poetry)

Cruz, Josefina de la. *Agua secreta.* Santo Domingo: Editora Cosmos, 1977. 84 p. Prologue by D. Manuel Alvar. (Poetry) .

_____. *Debajo de la piel y otros poemas anónimos.* Santo Domingo: Editora Cosmos, 1978. 82 p. (Poetry)

_____. *La sociedad dominicana de finales de siglo a través de la novela.* Santo Domingo: Editora Cosmos, 1978. 2nd. edición, Santo Domingo: Editora Universitaria, 1986. 300 p. (Essay)

_____. *Una casa en el espacio.* Santo Domingo: (n.p.). 1986. 160 p. Ilustration by Samech-Aidita Selman y de la autora. (Novel)

_____. *Gineceo.* Santo Domingo: Editora Tele-3, 1988. 50 p. (Poetry)

_____. *Las manos infinitas.* Santo Domingo: Editora Tele-3, 1988. 39 p. (Poetry)

Cruz, María Graciela de la. *Mujer y participación social.* Santo Domingo: Centro de Solidaridad para el Desarrollo de la Mujer, 1991. 27 p. (Essay)

Cucurullo de Engelmann, Gina M. *Sobre museos y servicios educativos.* Santo Domingo: Publicaciones del Museo de las Casas Reales, 1982. 206 p. (Essay)

Chalas, Josefina. *Relaciones entre las mujeres, asociaciones y comunidades.* Santo Domingo: Centro de Solidaridad para el Desarrollo de la Mujer, 1991. 10 p. (Prose)

Delgado de Pantaleón, Mélida, et al. *Diccionario de criollismos.* San Francisco de Macorís, República Dominicana: Imprenta ABC, 1930. xi-67 p. (Prose)

Delgado Pantaleón, Mélida. *La cítara campestre cibaeña: La criolla, poesía, ensayos, cuentos cibaeños.* Hugo E. Polanco Tolentino, editor. Santo Domingo: Amigo del Hogar, 1989. 460 p. (Anthology of popular culture includes poetry, essays, and short stories from the Cibao region)

Díaz, Bertha. *De mis luces interiores: poemas.* Santo Domingo: Editora Taller, 1973. 67 p. (Poetry)

Díaz de Soñé, Inés. *Duarte inmortal: Poemas de una vida.* Santo Domingo: Talleres de Tribuna Hispana, 1977. 18 p. (Essay)

_____. *Francisco del Rosario Sánchez: Prócer de la Independencia Dominicana 1817-1861.* Santo Domingo: Editora Perfil, 1979. 30 p. (Essay)

_____. *Matías Ramón Mella: Prócer de la Independencia Dominicana 1816-1864.* Santo Domingo: Editora Perfil, 1979. 32 p. (Essay)

_____. *Antología biográfica de poetas petromacorisanos.* San Pedro de Macorís, Rep. Dom.: Universidad Central del Este, Serie Centenario de San Pedro de Macorís No. 6, 1982. 320 p. (Essay/poetry)

Díaz de Stern, María. *Mi pucha cibaeña.* Santo Domingo: Amigo del Hogar, 1973. 81 p. (Poetry)

Díez de Planas, Meche. *Este regreso sin fin.* Barcelona: Impresión Grafas, S.A. 1974. 102 p. Cover illustration by Ada Balcárcel. Text ilustrations by Gilberto Hernández Ortega. (Poetry)

_____. *Veintiocho veces.* Santo Domingo: Editora Corripio, 1983. 116 p. Introduction by Manuel Rueda. (Poetry and music)

Dottin, Milagros. *Indicadores sobre mujer y familia rurales en República Dominicana; encuesta nacional de mujeres rurales.* Santo Domingo: Editora Búho, 1987. 97 p. (Essay)

Duarte, Isis. et al. *Azúcar y política en República Dominicana.* Santo Domingo: Taller, 1976. (Essay)

_____. *Capitalismo y superpoblación en Santo Domingo.* Santo Domingo: Editora Amigo del Hogar, Colegio Dominicano de Ingenieros y Agrimensores, 1980. 555 p. + ilus. Premio Nacional de Ensayo "Pedro Henríquez Ureña" (Essay)

_____. *Trabajadores urbanos, ensayos sobre fuerza laboral en República Dominicana.* Santo Domingo: Editora Universitaria, 1986. 314 p. (Essay)

_____.et al. *Población y salud en la República Dominicana.* Santo Domingo: Editora Gente, Estudio No. 5 del IEPD, 1986. 158 p. (Essay)

_____.et al. *Población, crecimiento urbano y barrios marginados en Santo Domingo.* Santo Domingo: Fundación Friedrich Ebert, Colección Estudios Económicos Sociales, 1988. 78 p. (Essay)

_____.et al. *Población y condición de la mujer en República Dominicana.* Santo Domingo: ADPBF, 1989. 170 p. (Essay)

_____.et al. *Menores en circunstancias especialmente difíciles en República Dominicana.* Santo Domingo: IEPD-UNICEF, 1991. 166 p. (Essay)

_____.et al. *Población, migraciones internas y desarrollo en República Dominicana.* Santo Domingo: IEPD, Estudio No. 8, 1991. 148 p. (Essay)

_____.et al. *Encuesta nacional de cultura política y democracia 1994.* Santo Domingo: Editora de la PUCMM, 1995. (Investigative report)

_____.et al. *Estado de situación de la democracia dominicana 1978-1990.* Santo Domingo: Editora de la PUCMM, 1995. (Essay)

_____.et al. *Los hogares dominicanos: El mito de la familia ideal y los tipos de jefaturas de hogar.* Santo Domingo: IEPD, 1995. (Essay)

Duarte, Rosa. *Apuntes.* Santo Domingo: Instituto Duartiano, 1970. 243 p. (Essay and correspondence)

Durán Jourdain, Carmen et al. *Mujer y racismo.* Santo Domingo: CEDEE, 1987. 28 p. (Essay)

Echavarría, Luz. *Voces perdidas.* Ciudad Trujillo: Editorial Stella, 1947. 111 p. (Poetry)

Espaillat de Ventura, Eva M. *El romancero de Trujillo.* Ciudad Trujillo: Impresora Dominicana, 1951. 53 p. (Poetry)

_____. *Primavera en estío.* Ciudad Trujillo: Editora del Caribe, 1952. 96 p. (Poetry)

Espinal, Isabel (Rosi). *Clean Sheets.* New York: La Candelaria, 1996. 8 p. (Poetry/Chapbook)

Espinal, Rosario. et al. *Democracia y proyecto social demócrata en la República Dominicana.* Santo Domingo: Editora Taller, 1986. (Essay) .

_____. *Autoritarismo y democracia en la política dominicana.* San José: Centro Interamericano de Asesoría Electoral, 1987. 217 p. 2nd. ed. Santo Domingo: Editorial Argumentos, 1994. (Essay)

Expósito, Elsa. *Antipoemas.* Santo Domingo: Alfa y Omega, 1986. (Poetry)

Farías, María Cristina de. *Patria mía.* Santo Domingo: Editora Cultural Dominicana, 1975. 184 p. (Poetry)

Félix, Carmela. *Brotes del alma.* Ciudad Trujillo: Editorial Cambier, 1937. 48 p. Introductory words by Juan Bautista Lamarche. (Poetry)

_____ et al. *Unión filial.* Ciudad Trujillo: (n.p.), 1941. 59 p. Prologue by Armando Oscar Pacheco. Includes versos de Rafael Castro Felix. (Poetry)

_____. *Versos del corazón.* Ciudad Trujillo: (n.p.), 1955, 25 p. (Poetry)

Félix de L'Official, Milady. *Sor Juana Inés de la Cruz "La décima musa mexicana".* Ciudad Trujillo: Editora Montalvo, 1953. 24 p. (Essay) F

Fiallo, Ana María. *Brisas: Libro de lectura para segundo grado, primer curso.* Buenos Aires: n.p., 1945. 147 p. + il. (Prose)

Francasci, Amelia (Amelia Francisca Marchena de Leyba). *Madre culpable: Novela original.* Santo Domingo: Imprenta de García Hermanos, 1893. 342 p. (Novel)

_____. *Recuerdos e impresiones.* Santo Domingo: Imprenta de García Hermanos, 1901. 125 p. (Essay and short fiction)

_____. *Historia de una novela.* Santo Domingo: Imprenta de García Hermanos, 1901. 60 p. (Essay)

_____. *Francisca Martinoff: Drama íntimo.* Santo Domingo: Imprenta de García Hermanos, 1901. 235 p. (Novel)

_____. *Cierzo en primavera. Historias cortas.* Santo Domingo: Imprenta La Cuna de América, 1902. 171 p. (Short Story)

_____. *Monseñor Meriño, íntimo.* Santo Domingo: Imprenta La Cuna de América, 1925. 416 p. 2nd. ed. Colección Pensamiento Dominicano No. 53, 1975. Prologue by Monseñor Hugo E. Polanco Brito. Article introduction by Enrique Marchena. (Essay)

Frías de Rodríguez, Thelma. *Diez razones de mi anticomunismo.* Ciudad Trujillo: n.p., 1959. (Essay)

_____. *Inquietudes.* Ciudad Trujillo: Editora Montalvo, 1950. 2nd. ed. aumentada 1962. 62 p.

Gallardo Rivas, Gina. *Buscando la vida. Dominicanas en el servicio en Madrid.* Santo Domingo: CIPAF, 1995. 168 p. (Essay)

Gambaa, Emma. *Nuevo silabario según el método ideo-visual del Dr. Decroly.* Ciudad Trujillo: Librería Dominicana, 1939. 103 p. + il. (Prose)

Garrido de Boggs, Edna. *Versiones dominicanas de romances españoles.* Santo Domingo: Pol Hermanos Editores, 1946. 110 p. (Essay and Poetry)

_____. *Folklore infantil dominicano.* Madrid: Ediciones Cultura Hispánica, 1955. (Essay and Poetry)

_____. *Panorama del folklore dominicano.* Coral Gables, Miami: University of Miami, 1961. 23 p. (Essay)

Garrido de Guzmán, Yolanda. *Al encuentro de la primavera.* Santo Domingo: Editores Asociados, 1983. 186 p. (Novel)

Gimero, Consuelo et al. *Reflexiones en torno a la identidad del maestro dominicano.* Santo Domingo: Centro Poveda, 1988. 96 p. (Essay)

Goede, Johanna. *Aun no sé que nombre ponerle.* Santiago, Rep. Dom: Talleres de Impresora Central, 1991. n.p. Prologue by Oscar Hungría. Cover design by the author. Drawings by Camilo Carrau. (Poetry)

_____. *El Libro de Alimán, Antología del Placer. Libro de cocina, poemas y otras cosas.* Santo Domingo: Amigo del Hogar, 1994. 165 p. Prologue by Bruno Rosario Candelier. (Poetry-prose)

Gómez Mejía, Carmen de. *Altos muros: A la memoria de Juan Carlos, mi hijo.* Ciudad Trujillo: Imp. de la Marina de Guerra, 1961. 136 p. (Poetry)

Gómez, Carmen Julia. *La problemática de las jefas del hogar: Evidencia de la insubordinación social de las mujeres.* Santo Domingo: CIPAF, 1990. 61 p. (Essay)

Gómez de Read, Ernestina. *Poemario de sueños.* Ciudad Trujillo: Editorial Cambier, 1942. 48 p. (Poetry)

_____. *Versos de una vida.* Santo Domingo: Impresora Offset Sardá, 1972. 46 p. (Poetry)

Gómez de Michel, Fiume. *Manual de literatura dominicana y americana, 6to curso de reforma, antología, análisis y comentarios.* Santo Domingo: Alfa y Omega, 1979. 511 p (Anthology of Prose and Poetry)

_____. *Manual de literatura dominicana y americana para el 5to. curso de reforma de la educación media: Antología, guía de análisis y comentarios.* Santo Domingo: Editora de la UASD, Colección Educación y Sociedad No. 13, 1980. 479 p. (Poetry, short story and essay)

Gómez de Peña, Josefina. *Versos y fábulas* (antología). Santo Domingo: Editora Nivar, 1981. 66 p. (Poetry and Prose)

Gómez, María Josefa. *El niño y lo que a él debemos.* La Vega: Imprenta El Progreso, 1928. 21 p. (Speech)

_____. *Sociedad, hogar y escuela.* Salcedo: Imprenta Hacia El Porvenir, 1931. (Speech)

Gómez, Petronila Angélica. *Contribución para la historia del feminismo dominicano.* Ciudad Tujillo: Editorial Librería Dominicana, 1952. (Essay, compilation of historical documents)

_____. *Influencia de la mujer en iberoamérica.* Ciudad Trujillo; Editora del Caribe, 1954. (Essay)

Gónzalez Castillo, Guillermina. *Amistad.* Santo Domingo: Secretaría de Estado de Educación, 1980. 75 p. (Poetry)

Grecia I. Mensaje de S. M. Grecia I: *Juegos Invernales MCMX.* San Pedro de Macorís: Imprenta La Altagracia, 1910. 10 p. (Speech)

Graciano, Berta. *La novela de la caña: Estética e ideología.* Santo Domingo: Alfa y Omega, 1990. 131 p. Prologue by Bruno Rosario Candelier. (Essay)

Grimaldi, Eleanor. *Poesías para ti.* Santo Domingo: Biblioteca Nacional, 1983. 39 p. + ilus. (Poetry)

_____. *Cuentos infantiles y juveniles.* Santo Domingo: Biblioteca Nacional, 1984. 64 p. (Short Story for children)

_____. *Cristal de ilusiones,* 2nd. ed. Santo Domingo: Editora Taller, 1995. 52 p. + ilus. (Short Story for children)

Guerrero, María Angustias. *Tras las huellas de la mujer dominicana en el mundo del trabajo 1900-1950.* Santo Domingo: Centro de Investigación para Acción Feminista, 1991. 98 p. (Essay)

Guerrero Villalona, Myrna et al eds. *Mujer y arte dominicano hoy, homenaje a Celeste Woss y Gil, Exposición-Seminario, Casa de Bastidas, 1995.* Santo Domingo: Amigo del Hogar, 1995. 146 p. Includes essays, biographies, bibliography and photographs. (Essay)

Guzmán de Hernández, Sonia. *Lista de encabezamientos de materia para bibliotecas de Derecho y Ciencias Políticas.* Santo Domingo: Universidad Pedro Henríquez Ureña, ONAP, 1981. n.p. (Prose)

Halal, Farah. *Sol infinito.* Santo Domingo: Editora Paz, 1995, 97 p. (Poetry)

Henríquez de N., Ana Mercedes. *Manual de práctica botánica general.* Santo Domingo: Impresora de la UASD, n.d.. 63 p. (Prose)

Henríquez Ureña, Camila. *Apreciación literaria*. Santo Domingo: Instituto de Superación Educacional, 1964. (Prose)

_____. *Estudios y conferencias*. La Habana: Editorial Letras Cubanas, 1982. 644 p. Prologue by Mirta Aguirre. (Essay)

_____. *Invitación a la lectura, notas sobre apreciación literaria*. Santo Domingo: Taller, 1985. 211 p. Introductory note by the editors. (Essay)

_____. *Feminismo y otros temas sobre la mujer en la sociedad*. Santo Domingo: Editora Taller, 1985. 157 p. Introductory note by the editors. (Essay)

_____. ed. with Dolores Nieves Rivera. *Teatro y narrativa medieval*. La Habana: Editorial Pueblo y Educación, 1974. 2nd. ed. 1990 126 p. (Essay)

_____. *Las ideas pedagógicas de Hostos y otros escritos*. Santo Domingo: Secretaría de Educación, Bellas Artes y Cultos, 1994. 382 p. Foreword by Jaqueline Malagón. (Essay)

Henríquez Almánzar, Carmen Adolfina. *Método ideo-visual alfabetizador dominicano Margarita*. Santiago de los Caballeros, Rep. Dom.: Editora El Caribe, 1942. 72 p. + il. (Prose)

Henríquez de Castro, Carmita. *Cuentos para niños*. Santo Domingo: Ediciones de la Casa de don Fed. y Biblioteca del Maestro, 1969. 63 p. (Short Story for children)

Hernández Nuñez, *Angela. Desafío*. Santo Domingo: Editora Gente, 1985. n.p. Caligraphy by Cristina Cavalcanti and illustrations by Millaray Quiroga. (Poetry)

_____. *Las mariposas no le temen a los cactus*. Santo Domingo: Universidad Autónoma de Santo Domingo. Vol.CCCIXVIII, Colección Arte y Sociedad No. 17, 1985. 82 p. Drawings by José Manuel Sing. (Short Story)

_____. *Los fantasmas prefieren la luz del día*. Santo Domingo: Editorial Gente, 1986. 21 p. (Short Story)

_____. *Machismo y aborto*. Santo Domingo: Editorial Alas, n.d. 20 p. (Essay)

_____. *10 prejuicios sobre el feminismo*. Santo Domingo: Editorial Alas, n.d. 20 p. (Essay)

_____. *¿Por qué luchan las mujeres?* Santo Domingo: Centro de Investigación y Apoyo Cultural, n.d. 100 p. (Essay)

_____. *Emergencia del silencio. La mujer dominicana en la educación formal*. Santo Domingo: Universidad Autónoma de Santo Domingo, Vol. DXXXVIII, 1986. 298 p. Prologue by Víctor Hugo de Láncer. (Essay)

_____. *Tizne y cristal*. Santo Domingo: Editora Alas, 1987. 77 p. Includes a prologue by the author. (Poetry)

_____. *De críticos y creadoras*. Santo Domingo: Editora Búho, 1988. 12 p. (Essay)

_____. *Alótropos*. Santo Domingo: Editora Alas, 1989, 129 p. Includes a prologue by the author. (Short Story)

_____. ed. *Libertad, creación e identidad, selección de ponencias encuentro mujer y escritura.* Santo Domingo: Universidad Autónoma de Santo Domingo, Vol. DCXLI, 1991. 268 p. (Essay)

_____. *Mujer y cultura: Módulo de capacitación.* Santo Domingo: Centro de Solidaridad para el Desarrollo de la Mujer, 1991, 21 p. (Essay)

_____. *Las mujeres en la coyuntura actual.* Santo Domingo: CE-MUJER, Colección Presente No. 1, 1991. 17 p. (Essay)

_____. et al. *Nosotras y en el cambio y la comunidad.* Santo Domingo: Centro de Solidaridad para el Desarrollo de la Mujer, 1991. 36 p. (Educational Folder)

_____. *Masticar una rosa.* Santo Domingo: Editora Alas, 1993. 127 págs. Cover design by the author. (Short Story)

_____. *Arca espejada.* Santo Domingo: Editora Alas, 1994. 64 p. Cover design, watercolor by the author. (Poetry)

Hernández, Carolina. *Brotes íntimos.* Santo Domingo: Impresora La Isabelita, 1980. 84 p. (Poetry)

Hernández de Sepúlveda, Daysi. *Tú puedes ser bella en cualquier edad.* Santo Domingo: n.p., 1982. 142 p. (Essay)

Hernández, Edith. *Manual de estética musical.* Santo Domingo: Editora Taller, 1982. 269 p. (Essay)

Hernández Montalvo, Elbita. *Cuentos dominicanos: La ninfa del lago Enriquillo/Las dos esperanzas.* Santo Domingo: Gewy Artes Gráficas, 1982. 16 p. (Short Story)

Hernández Caamaño, Ida. *Viajera del polvo.* Santo Domingo: Instituto Tecnológico de Santo Domingo, 1993. 64 p. (Poetry)

Hernández, Juana. *Cantos populares.* Santo Domingo: n.p., 1909. n.p. (Poetry)

Hernández, Ramona et al. *Dominican New Yorkers: A Socioeconomic Profile.* New York: CUNY Dominican Studies Institute, Dominican Research Monographs, 1995. 56 p. (Essay)

Heureaux, Casimira. *Esbozos.* San Pedro de Macorís, Rep. Dom.: Imprenta Cervantes, 1930. 12 p. (Essay)

Hidalgo, María. *El niño su gracia y cómo la pierde.* Santo Domingo: Editora del Caribe, 1979. 186 p. (Essay)

Ibarra de Victoria, María. *Alma en penumbra.* Ciudad Trujillo: Editorial Pol Hermanos, 1945. 58 p. (Poetry)

_____. *Ondas de emociones.* Ciudad Trujillo: Editorial la Palabra de Santo Domingo, 1951. 153 p. Prologue by Angel Rafael Lamarche. (Poetry)

Imbert Brugal, Carmen. *Palabras de otro tiempo y de siempre.* Santo Domingo: Editora Imprenta Héctor Blanco Weber, Colección Antología de Nuestra Voz No.4, 1983. 44 p. (Poetry)

_____. *Infidencias.* Santo Domingo: Alfa y Omega, 1986. 73 p. Includes two introductory poems. 79 p. (Short Story)

_____. *Tráfico de Mujeres: Una visión de una nación exportada*. Santo Domingo: Centro de Solidaridad para el Desarrollo de la Mujer, 1991. 24 p. (Essay)

_____. *Distinguida Señora*. Santo Domingo: Editora Amigo del Hogar, 1995. 230 p. (Novel)

Jakowska, Sophie. *Hijos de la tierra: Meditación para niños y adultos sobre la protección ambiental y la conservación de recursos*. Santo Domingo: Editora Taller, 1978. 38 p. (Prose)

_____. *Amigos del cocodrilo*. Santo Domingo: ZOODOM, 1979. 280 p. + il. (Prose)

Jerez Matos, Mary. *Memorias de una Maestra*. Santo Domingo: Editora Visión, 1982. 168 p. (Prose)

Jorge, Bernarda. *La música dominicana. Siglos XIX-XX*. Santo Domingo: Editora de la UASA, Colección Arte y Sociedad No. 10, 1982. 207 p. (Essay)

_____. *El canto de tradición oral de República Dominicana*. Santo Domingo: Editora Amigo del Hogar, Colección Banreservas, Serie Arte y Cultura No. 2, 1996. 297 p. (Essay)

Junta de la Acción Feminista Dominicana. *La Junta de la Acción Feminista Dominicana se dirige a todas las mujeres del país*. San Pedro de Macorís: Imprenta de P.A. Gómez, 1931. (Essay)

Junta Patriótica de Damas. *Manifiesto de la Junta Patriótica de Damas a raíz de la intervención norteamericana, con motivo de la Semana Patriótica*. n.p., 1922. (Essay)

Lamarche, Martha María. *Cauce hondo*. San Juan, P.R.: Editorial Roger, 1935. 75 p. (Poetry)

_____. *Retozos de luz*. Ciudad Trujillo: Editorial La Palabra de Santo Domingo, 1950. 93 p. Cover design by Celeste Woss y Gil. (Poetry)

Landestoy, Carmita. *Mis relaciones con el Presidente Trujillo*. Ciudad Trujillo: n.p., 1945. (Essay)

_____. *¡Yo también acuso!* 2nd. ed. La Habana: Editorial LEX, 1946. (Essay)

Lara Fernández, Carmen. *Cristales*. Santiago, Rep. Dom.: Editora El Diario, 1940. 114 p. (Poetry)

_____. *Resplandores de gloria*. Ciudad Trujillo: Editora Montalvo, 1945. 138 p. (Essay)

_____. *Historia del feminismo en la República Dominicana*. Ciudad Trujillo: Imprenta Arte y Ciencia, 1946. 191 p. (Essay)

_____. *Primera ciudad cristiana del nuevo mundo: La Isabela*. Ciudad Trujillo: Editora Montalvo, 1947. 160 p. (Essay)

_____. *La catedral primada de América*. Ciudad Trujillo: Imprenta Arte y Cine, 1950. (Essay)

_____. *Intima*. Santo Domingo: Ediciones ¡Hola!, 1983. n.p. + il. Prologue by Freddy Ginebra. (Poetry)

_____. *Cómo educar a sus hijos*. Santo Domingo: Editora Taller, 1989. 110 p. + il. (Essay)

_____. *Primacias del nuevo mundo*. Santo Domingo: Taller, 1989. (Essay)

Lara, Mencía. *Mi corazón se queja*. Santo Domingo: Editorial La Unión, 1982. 48 p. (Poetry)

_____. *El corazón no envejece*. Santo Domingo: Editora M & L, 1987. 46 p. (Poetry)

Lazala, Josefina B. et al. *El delito político y tiranicidio en la República Dominicana*. Santo Domingo: Editora Montalvo, 1962. (Essay)

Lebrón de Anico, Rosa. *Vocación y entrega: Doctora Consuelo Bernardino*. Santo Domingo: Editora Corripio, 1990. 169 p. (Essay)

_____. *Mujeres del mundo*. Santo Domingo: Editora Corripio, 1992. 168 p. (Essay)

Licairac, Julieta. *Album de composiciones para piano*. Santo Domingo: n.p., 1910. 65 p. (Musical Compositions)

Lil de Lapategui, Amparo. *Tributo de admiración: Una mujer dominicana al Jefe Ilustre Generalísimo Doctor Rafael L. Trujillo Molina*. Ciudad Trujillo: Editorial Caribe, 1939. (Essay)

Liriano, Alejandra. *Identidad nacional: Algunos elementos para su comprensión*. Santo Domingo: Centro Poveda, 1989. 57 p. (Essay)

López Baralt, Mercedes. *Mito taíno*. n.p.: Ediciones Huracán, 1977. n.p. (Essay)

Luciano, Margarita, *El día que llevaron la electricidad al paraje* La Ciénaga. Santo Domingo: Secretaría de Estado de Educación, 1988. 34 p. (Prose)

Luna de Espaillat, Margarita. *Por el mundo de la orquesta*. Santo Domingo: Editora Cultural Dominicana, 1973. 238 p. (Essay)

Madera, Teonilda. *Corazón de Jade con lágrimas de miel*. Santo Domingo: Editora Búho, 1995. 82 p. (Poetry)

Malagón de De Jesús, Jacqueline. *Objetivos y proyecciones de un estudio analítico de instituciones educativas norteamericanas: Experiencias de un viaje educativo*. Santo Domingo: APEC, 1978. 125 p. (Prose)

Marión Landais, Irma. *Recetas de arte culinario adoptadas para las alumnas de segundo curso de la Escuela Industrial de Señoritas*. Ciudad Trujillo: Impresora Roldán, 1942. 20 p. (Prose)

Martínez Almonte, Bibiana. *Máximo Gómez, perfiles humanistas*. Santo Domingo: Editorial Central del Libro, 1987. 81 p. (Essay)

Martínez-Bonilla, Carmen Natalia. [Carmen Natalia] *Alma adentro*. Santo Domingo: Editora Plus Ultra, 1939. 110 p. (Poetry)

_____. *Veinte actitudes y una epístola*. Ciudad Trujillo: Imprenta Rincón, 1945. 75 p. (Poetry)

_____. *Llanto sin término por el hijo nunca llegado*. San Juan (Puerto Rico): Ateneo Puertorriqueño, 1960. 35 p. First Prize, Festival de Navidad of 1959, Ateneo Puertorriqueño. (Poetry)

_____. *Alma adentro—obra poética completa 1939-1976*. Santiago: Universidad Católica Madre y Maestra, 1981. 349 p. Prologue by Pedro Mir. (Poetry)

_____. *La victoria*. Santo Domingo: Ce-Mujer, 1992. 171 p. Prologue by Manuel Matos Moquete. (Novel)

Martínez, Lusitania. *Palma Sola: Opresión y esperanza*. Santo Domingo: Editorial Central del Libro, 1987. 81 p. (Essay)

_____. *La teoría feminista y la investigación social*. Santo Domingo: Editora Tele-3, 1991. 15 p. (Essay)

_____. *Actitudes femeninas frente a los oficios tradicionales*. Santo Domingo: Editorial Palmas, Publicaciones del Centro de Solidaridad para el Desarrollo de la Mujer, 1994. 204 p. (Essay)

Martínez de Trujillo, María. *Meditaciones morales*. Santiago, Rep. Dom.: Editorial El Diario, 1945. 41 p. (Essay)

_____. *Falsa amistad: Argumento*. Ciudad Trujillo: Imprenta La Opinión, 1946. 16 p. (Essay)

_____. *Meditaciones morales*. Ciudad Trujillo: n.p., 1947. 121 p. (Essay)

_____. *Meditaciones morales*. México: Continente, 1948. 176 p. (Essay)

_____. *Meditaciones morales*. Barcelona: Gráficas Seix Barral Hnos., 1954. 167 p. + il. (Essay)

_____. *Por Francia*. Ciudad Trujillo: Imprenta Montalvo, n.d., n.p. (Essay)

Marra de Alvarez, Gilda. *Estatuario espiritual*. Santo Domingo: Editorial de la Salle, 1971. 106 p. Illustration by Thimo Pimentel. (Poetry)

_____. *Las auroras blancas: Poemas*. Santo Domingo: Taller del Directorio Comercial de la Rep. Dom., 1975. 28 p. (Poetry)

_____. *Paredes en el tiempo*. Santo Domingo: Taller, 1977. 94 p. (Poetry)

_____. *Las voces perdidas*. Santo Domingo: Taller, 1980. 88 p. (Poetry)

Marrero de Munné, Melba. *Alas abiertas*. Santiago de los Caballeros, Rep. Dom.: Editorial El Diario, 1950. 69 p. (Poetry)

_____. *Faena para Adán*. Ciudad Trujillo: Impresora Dominicana, 1952. 105 p. (Poetry)

_____. *Eva en extremaución*. Barcelona: Talleres de Filograf, 1953. 94 p. (Poetry)

_____. *Caña dulce: Novela criolla*. Ciudad Trujillo: Impresora Dominicana, 1954. 109 p. (Novel)

_____. *Estampas suecas*. Ciudad Trujillo: Impresora Dominicana, 1955. 60 p. (Prose)

_____. *Cáfila amarga: Romance cafetalero*. Santiago de los Caballeros, Rep. Dom.: Imprenta La Información, 1955. 47 p. (Prose)

_____. *El voto*. n.p.: n.p., 1956. 188 p. (Novel)

_____. *El banquete de las hadas*. San Francisco de Macorís: n.p., 1957. 59 p. (Poetry)

_____. *Tiempo para la muerte: Poema*. Barcelona: Talleres de Filograf, 1957. 38 p. (Poetry)

Matamoros, Mercedes. *Caonabo (Poema en verso)*. Santo Domingo: Imprenta El Eco de la Opinión, 1892. 12 p. (Poetry)

Matos, Esthervina. *Rapsodia épica (en el centenario de la República)*. Ciudad Trujillo: Editorial Cambier, 1944. 21 p. Obra premiada. (Poetry)

_____. *Estudios de la literatura dominicana.* Ciudad Trujillo: Pol Hermanos, 1955. 387 p. (Essay)

_____. *El genio de Beethoven y su música inmortal.* Santo Domingo: Editora Montalvo, Colección Rutas Estéticas, 1962. 32 p. (Essay)

_____. *Silogismo.* Santo Domingo: Editora Montalvo, 1963. 62 p. (Poetry)

_____. *Proyecciones en el tiempo.* Santo Domingo: Amigo del Hogar, 1972. 16 p. (Poetry)

_____. *Sócrates y Jesús.* Santo Domingo: Editora Montalvo, Colección Pensamiento Filosófico, No. 2, 1983. 29 p. (Essay)

Medrano, Marianela. *Oficio de vivir.* Santo Domingo: Impresora Isabel, 1986. 16 p. (Poetry)

_____. *Los alegres ojos de la tristeza.* Santo Domingo: Editora Búho, 1987. 72 p. (Poetry)

Mejía, Abigaíl. *Por entre frivolidades.* Barcelona: Hermenegildo Miralles, 1922. 232 p. (Novel)

_____. *Sueña, Pilarín.* Barcelona: Altés Impresor, 1925. 2nd. edición. Santo Domingo: Editora de Colores, Instituto del Libro, Librería La Trinitaria, 1992. 248 p. Introduction by Virgilio Díaz Grullón. (Novel)

_____. *Historia de la literatura castellana.* Barcelona: Imprenta Editorial Altés, 1929. 313 p. (Essay)

_____. *Ideario Feminista y algún apunte para la historia del feminismo dominicano.* Santo Domingo: Imprenta P. A. Gómez, "Nueva Edición", Vol. I, 1939. 53 p. (Essay)

_____. *Historia de la literatura dominicana,* Ciudad Trujillo: n.p., 1937. 146 p. 2nd. ed. revisada, 1939. 5ta. ed. Santiago, Dom. Rep.: Editorial el Diario, 1943. 7ma. ed. Santo Domingo: Impresora Dominicana, 1951. (Essay)

_____. *Ideario feminista.* Santo Domingo: Secretaría de Educación, 1975. 53 p. (Essay)

_____. *Obras escogidas.* Vols. I & II. Arístides Incháustegui y Blanca Delgado Malagón, compiladores. Santo Domingo: Secretaría de Bellas Artes y Cultos, 1995. 499 p. 514 p. (Essay and Novel)

Mejía B. de Espaillat, Gisela. *Figuras y retablos de ayer.* Santo Domingo: Editora del Caribe, 1964. (Essay)

Mejía, Rosalía. *Comunión de soledades.* Santo Domingo: Gráficas Rodi, 1990. (Poetry)

_____. *Música del agua.* Santo Domingo: Editora Corripio, 1995. 70 p. (Poetry)

Melo de Cardona, Ligia A. *Participación de la mujer en la educación sistemática en la República Dominicana.* Santo Domingo: Publicación de la Universidad Autónoma de Santo Domingo, Vol. 238, Colección Crítica No. 19, 1977. 15 p. (Essay)

Méndez, Ana Marina. *Bibliografía sobre energía y campos afines.* Santo Domingo: CDE, 1981. vii, 76 p. (Prose)

_____. *Palma Sola...desde el sol hasta el ocaso. Un aporte bibliográfico a su estudio.* Santo Domingo: Editora Artes Gráficos, Colección Orfeo, 1986. Prologue by Frank Moya Pons. (Prose)

Miguel, Aura Luz de. *Alas de mi conciencia*. Santo Domingo: Amigo del Hogar, 1982. 78 p. Prologue by Leo Beato. Portada e ilustraciones de Rafael Mercedes. (Poetry)

Milán Lugo, Gloria. *Manual consular*. Santo Domingo: n.p., 1971. 319 p. (Prose)

Miller, Jeannette. *Fórmulas para combatir el miedo: 1962-1970*. Santo Domingo: Biblioteca Taller No. 4, 1972. 59 p. (Poetry)

_____. *Historia de la pintura dominicana*. 2nd. ed. Santo Domingo: Amigo del Hogar, 1979. 106 p. (Essay)

_____. *Fichas de identidad/Estadías*. Santo Domingo: Editora Taller, 1985. 164 p. Prologue by Manuel Rueda. (Poetry)

Miró, Carmen A. *La influencia de los cambios de población*. Santo Domingo: Asociación Dominicana Probienestar de la Familia, 1970. 13 p. (Essay)

Montás, Argentina. *El arte de formular*. Ciudad Trujillo: Secretaría de Estado de Sanidad y Asistencia Social, 1947. 33 p. (Prose)

_____. *Drogas y soluciones y materia médica*. Ciudad Trujillo: Secretaría de Estado de Sanidad y Asistencia Social, 1947. 70 p. (Prose)

Montero, Jenny. *La cuentística dominicana*. Santo Domingo: Colección Orfeo, Biblioteca Nacional, 1979. 200 p. (Essay)

Moore Garrido, Carmen Eva. *¿A dónde se fue la educación?* Santo Domingo: Taller, 1978. 111 pp. + il. (Essay)

Mora Ramis, Tatiana. *Tiempos del olvido*. Santo Domingo: Editora Taller, 1980. 59 p. (Poetry)

Moreta Feliz, Altagracia. *Un poema para ti...es un poema para el mundo*. Santo Domingo: Editora Búho, 1988. 52 p. (Poetry)

_____. *El extraño fenómeno de los 500 años*. Santo Domingo: Impresión Grafideas, 1992. 176 p. 2nd. ed. 1994. (Prose)

Moreta de Perdomo, Octavia. *Intimidades*. Santo Domingo: Editorial Express Prints, 1980. 58 p. (Poetry)

Moya de Castellanos, Colombina. *Inquietud prenatal*. Santo Domingo: Médico Dominicano, 1970. 98 p. (Poetry)

_____. et al. *Dos cantos para una sola América*. Santo Domingo: Fondo de Cultura, 1971. 58 p. (Poetry)

Moya de Vásquez, Trina. *El día de las madres*. Santo Domingo: n.p., 1925, 4 p. (Himno a las madres, música de Manuel J. González).

_____. *Patria y hogar: Poesías*. Madrid: Editorial Saturnino Calleja. 1929. 78 p. Prologue by Fabio Fiallo. (Poetry)

Nacidit-Perdomo, Ylonka. *Contacto de una mirada*. Santo Domingo: Editora Búho, 1989. 69 p. (Poetry)

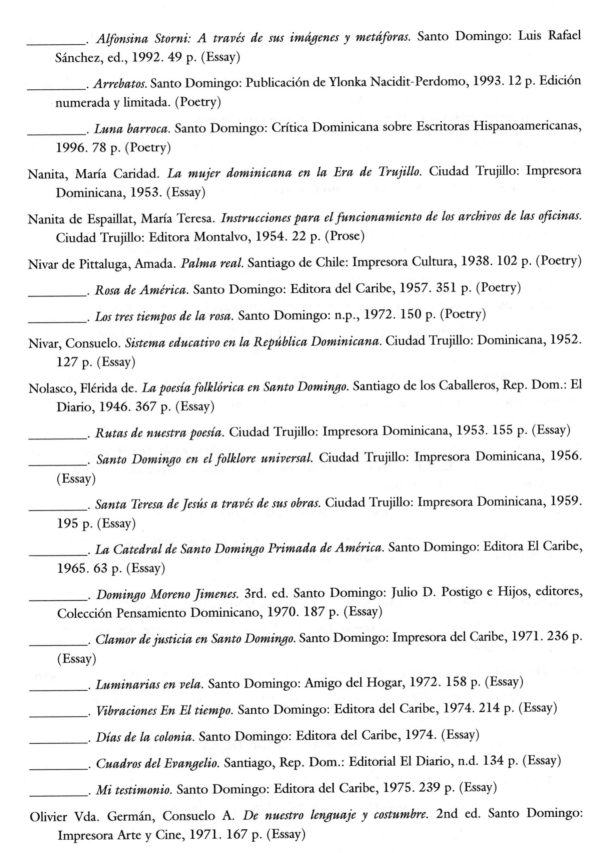

_____. *Alfonsina Storni: A través de sus imágenes y metáforas.* Santo Domingo: Luis Rafael Sánchez, ed., 1992. 49 p. (Essay)

_____. *Arrebatos.* Santo Domingo: Publicación de Ylonka Nacidit-Perdomo, 1993. 12 p. Edición numerada y limitada. (Poetry)

_____. *Luna barroca.* Santo Domingo: Crítica Dominicana sobre Escritoras Hispanoamericanas, 1996. 78 p. (Poetry)

Nanita, María Caridad. *La mujer dominicana en la Era de Trujillo.* Ciudad Trujillo: Impresora Dominicana, 1953. (Essay)

Nanita de Espaillat, María Teresa. *Instrucciones para el funcionamiento de los archivos de las oficinas.* Ciudad Trujillo: Editora Montalvo, 1954. 22 p. (Prose)

Nivar de Pittaluga, Amada. *Palma real.* Santiago de Chile: Impresora Cultura, 1938. 102 p. (Poetry)

_____. *Rosa de América.* Santo Domingo: Editora del Caribe, 1957. 351 p. (Poetry)

_____. *Los tres tiempos de la rosa.* Santo Domingo: n.p., 1972. 150 p. (Poetry)

Nivar, Consuelo. *Sistema educativo en la República Dominicana.* Ciudad Trujillo: Dominicana, 1952. 127 p. (Essay)

Nolasco, Flérida de. *La poesía folklórica en Santo Domingo.* Santiago de los Caballeros, Rep. Dom.: El Diario, 1946. 367 p. (Essay)

_____. *Rutas de nuestra poesía.* Ciudad Trujillo: Impresora Dominicana, 1953. 155 p. (Essay)

_____. *Santo Domingo en el folklore universal.* Ciudad Trujillo: Impresora Dominicana, 1956. (Essay)

_____. *Santa Teresa de Jesús a través de sus obras.* Ciudad Trujillo: Impresora Dominicana, 1959. 195 p. (Essay)

_____. *La Catedral de Santo Domingo Primada de América.* Santo Domingo: Editora El Caribe, 1965. 63 p. (Essay)

_____. *Domingo Moreno Jimenes.* 3rd. ed. Santo Domingo: Julio D. Postigo e Hijos, editores, Colección Pensamiento Dominicano, 1970. 187 p. (Essay)

_____. *Clamor de justicia en Santo Domingo.* Santo Domingo: Impresora del Caribe, 1971. 236 p. (Essay)

_____. *Luminarias en vela.* Santo Domingo: Amigo del Hogar, 1972. 158 p. (Essay)

_____. *Vibraciones En El tiempo.* Santo Domingo: Editora del Caribe, 1974. 214 p. (Essay)

_____. *Días de la colonia.* Santo Domingo: Editora del Caribe, 1974. (Essay)

_____. *Cuadros del Evangelio.* Santiago, Rep. Dom.: Editorial El Diario, n.d. 134 p. (Essay)

_____. *Mi testimonio.* Santo Domingo: Editora del Caribe, 1975. 239 p. (Essay)

Olivier Vda. Germán, Consuelo A. *De nuestro lenguaje y costumbre.* 2nd ed. Santo Domingo: Impresora Arte y Cine, 1971. 167 p. (Essay)

Olivier, Maritza, ed. *Cinco siglos con la mujer dominicana*. Santo Domingo: Amigo del Hogar, 1965. (Essay)

Ortea, Virginia Elena. *Risas y lágrimas*. Santo Domingo: n.p., 1901. vii + 219 p. Prologue by Américo Lugo. 2nd. ed. Santo Domingo: Alfa y Omega, Edición Cultural Puertoplateña, 1978. 171 p. Prologue by Sebastián Rodríguez Lora. (Short Story and Prose)

Paiewonsky, Denise. *El aborto en la República Dominicana*. Santo Domingo: CIPAF, 1988. 118 p. (Essay)

Paniagua, Hortencia. *Hasta luego, adiós*. Santo Domingo: Editora Tele-3, 1991. 57 p. (Short Story)

Pantaleón, Adalgisa. *Mi silencio roto*. Santo Domingo: Editora Centenario, 1995. 76 p. Introductory words by José Rafael Lantigua. (Poetry)

Paradas, Ana Teresa. *Efectos jurídicos del matrimonio putativo en caso de bigamia*. Santo Domingo: Imprenta La Cuna de América, 1913. (Essay)

Payano Tolentino, Carmen María. *Temas de amor*. (n.l.): Imprenta Quiñones, s.f n.p. (Poetry)

Peguero Calderón Vda. Michell, Celia. *Fidelidad*. Ciudad Trujillo: Editorial Arte y Cine, 1947. 38 p. (Poetry)

_____. *Luz y sombra*. Santo Domingo: Instituto Técnico Salesiano, 1973. 117 p. (Poetry)

Peguero, Valentina, et. al. *Visión general de la historia dominicana*. Santo Domingo: Taller, 1978. (Essay)

Pelaez Ortiz de Piña, Luz Bethania. *Estado de la profesión de abogado en la República Dominicana*. Valencia, Venezuela: Editora Nivar, Publicaciones del Colegio de Abogados de la República Dominicana, 1970. 8 p. (Essay)

Pellerano, Soucy de. *Resultante*. Caracas: Ateneo de Caracas, 1971. 6 p. (Essay)

Peña Cruz, Altagracia. *Biblioteca escolar dominicana: Un sistema para su organización*. Santiago de los Caballeros, Rep. Dom.: Universidad Católica Madre y Maestra, Colección Estudios, 1995. (Prose)

Peña, Angela. *Así era Duarte*. Santo Domingo: Editora de la Salle, 1976. (Essay)

_____. *Partidos políticos y presidentes dominicanos*. Santo Domingo: Editora Lozano, 1978. 132 p. 2d. ed. 1996. (Essay)

Peña, Octavia de. *Cantares a la Era Gloriosa de mi Patria*. Ciudad Trujillo: n.p., 1947. 30 p. (Poetry)

_____. *El premio de Dios: Cuento para niños*. Ciudad Trujillo: Tipografía Carrasquero, 1946. 5 p. (Short Story for children)

Peña de Bordas, Virginia. *Toeya: Fantasía indígena*. Ciudad Trujillo: Impresora Dominicana, 1949. 303 p. 2nd. ed. Posthumous offerings by Flérida de Nolasco. Santo Domingo: Editora Taller, 1978. viii- 355 p. illustrated. (Novel)

_____. *Seis novelas cortas*. Santo Domingo: Taller, 1978. 159 p. (Novel)

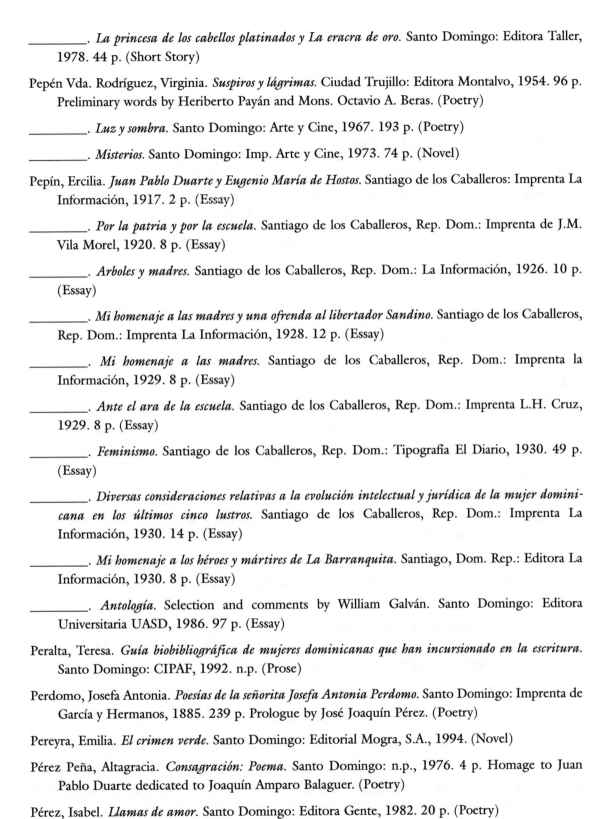

_____. *La princesa de los cabellos platinados y La eracra de oro.* Santo Domingo: Editora Taller, 1978. 44 p. (Short Story)

Pepén Vda. Rodríguez, Virginia. *Suspiros y lágrimas.* Ciudad Trujillo: Editora Montalvo, 1954. 96 p. Preliminary words by Heriberto Payán and Mons. Octavio A. Beras. (Poetry)

_____. *Luz y sombra.* Santo Domingo: Arte y Cine, 1967. 193 p. (Poetry)

_____. *Misterios.* Santo Domingo: Imp. Arte y Cine, 1973. 74 p. (Novel)

Pepín, Ercilia. *Juan Pablo Duarte y Eugenio María de Hostos.* Santiago de los Caballeros: Imprenta La Información, 1917. 2 p. (Essay)

_____. *Por la patria y por la escuela.* Santiago de los Caballeros, Rep. Dom.: Imprenta de J.M. Vila Morel, 1920. 8 p. (Essay)

_____. *Arboles y madres.* Santiago de los Caballeros, Rep. Dom.: La Información, 1926. 10 p. (Essay)

_____. *Mi homenaje a las madres y una ofrenda al libertador Sandino.* Santiago de los Caballeros, Rep. Dom.: Imprenta La Información, 1928. 12 p. (Essay)

_____. *Mi homenaje a las madres.* Santiago de los Caballeros, Rep. Dom.: Imprenta la Información, 1929. 8 p. (Essay)

_____. *Ante el ara de la escuela.* Santiago de los Caballeros, Rep. Dom.: Imprenta L.H. Cruz, 1929. 8 p. (Essay)

_____. *Feminismo.* Santiago de los Caballeros, Rep. Dom.: Tipografía El Diario, 1930. 49 p. (Essay)

_____. *Diversas consideraciones relativas a la evolución intelectual y jurídica de la mujer dominicana en los últimos cinco lustros.* Santiago de los Caballeros, Rep. Dom.: Imprenta La Información, 1930. 14 p. (Essay)

_____. *Mi homenaje a los héroes y mártires de La Barranquita.* Santiago, Dom. Rep.: Editora La Información, 1930. 8 p. (Essay)

_____. *Antología.* Selection and comments by William Galván. Santo Domingo: Editora Universitaria UASD, 1986. 97 p. (Essay)

Peralta, Teresa. *Guía biobibliográfica de mujeres dominicanas que han incursionado en la escritura.* Santo Domingo: CIPAF, 1992. n.p. (Prose)

Perdomo, Josefa Antonia. *Poesías de la señorita Josefa Antonia Perdomo.* Santo Domingo: Imprenta de García y Hermanos, 1885. 239 p. Prologue by José Joaquín Pérez. (Poetry)

Pereyra, Emilia. *El crimen verde.* Santo Domingo: Editorial Mogra, S.A., 1994. (Novel)

Pérez Peña, Altagracia. *Consagración: Poema.* Santo Domingo: n.p., 1976. 4 p. Homage to Juan Pablo Duarte dedicated to Joaquín Amparo Balaguer. (Poetry)

Pérez, Isabel. *Llamas de amor.* Santo Domingo: Editora Gente, 1982. 20 p. (Poetry)

_____. *Burócratas del polvo*. Santo Domingo: Editora Taller, Colección Montesinos No. 1, 1984. 65 p. (Poetry)

_____. *Poemas para amar*. La Romana, Rep. Dom.: Colección Vagón No. 15, 1988. 145 p. (Poetry)

_____. Compiler. *Antología de la poesía romanense*. La Romana: Editorial Buho, Colección Editorial Vagón, 1989. 262 p. (Poetry)

Pérez, Italia F. de. *Progreso y poesía*. Santo Domingo: n.p., 1969. 34 p. (Poetry)

Pérez Marrero, Josefina. *Investigaciones universitarias 1978-1983*. Santo Domingo: Editora de la UASD, Colección Educación y Sociedad, No. 23, 1984. (Essay)

Pérez-Kamber, Kelva. *Me gusta el verde de tus sueños*. New York: Ediciones Moria, 1991. 51 p. (Poetry)

Pichardo Lapeyretta, Lydia. *Ave, María*. Ciudad Trujillo: Editora Montalvo, 1955. (Essay)

Pichardo, Nina et al. *Tradiciones macorisanas*. La Romana: Imprenta de la Rosa, 1970. 58 p. (Prose)

Pineda, Magaly. *"...la vida mía no es fácil." La otra cara de la zona franca*. Santo Domingo: CIPAF, 1990. (Interviews-essay)

Polanco Castro, Marta. *¡El destino manda!* Ciudad Trujillo: Librería Dominicana, 1955. 97 p. Marta Polanco de León appears on the cover. (Novel)

Polanco de León, Marta. *El retrato del Maestro*. Santo Domingo: Imundeso, 1974. (Essay)

Porcella de Brea, Leonor. *Sed y hambre*. Santo Domingo: Editora Amigo del Hogar, 1970. 179 p. (Poetry)

Prats Ramírez de Pérez, Ivelisse. *Diagnóstico de la realidad educativa dominicana*. Santo Domingo: Publicación de la Universidad Autónoma de Santo Domingo, Vol. 171, Colección Conferencia No. 18, 1974. 24 p. (Essay)

_____. *Educación superior en la República Dominicana: Diagnóstico, prognóstico y estrategia*. Santo Domingo: Publicación de la Universidad Autónoma de Santo Domingo, Vol. 214, Colección Crítica No.5, 1976. 24 p. (Essay)

_____. *Por la educación: Ensayos y conferencias*. Santo Domingo: Publicación de la Universidad Autónoma de Santo Domingo, Vol. 292, Colección Educación y Sociedad No. 16, 1981. 192 p. 2nd. ed. Santo Domingo: Amigos del Hogar, 1981. 200 p. (Essay)

_____. *Los días difíciles*. Santo Domingo: Editora Méndez Abreu, 1982. 2 v. (Essay)

_____. *Necesaria existencia*. Santo Domingo: n.p., 1982. 192 p. (Poetry)

Polanco, Maruja. *Técnicas en el arte de coser*. Santo Domingo: Editora Cultural Dominicana, 1978. 115 p. + il. (Prose)

Primer Congreso Femenino Dominicano. *Reglamento, resoluciones y programa*. Ciudad Trujillo: Comisión Nacional Organizadora, 1943. (Essay)

Puente y Juliá, Rosario. *La guerra, mi hijo y yo*. México, D.F.: n.p., 1948. 408 p. (Novel)

Quidiello de Bosch, Carmen. *Desde mi orilla.* Santo Domingo: Editora Alfa y Omega, 1980. (Essay)

_____. *Pajaritas de papel.* Santo Domingo: Editora Corripio, 1982. 112 p. (Essay)

_____. *El peregrino.* Santo Domingo: Alfa y Omega, 1983. (Drama)

_____. *Alguien espera junto al puente.* Santo Domingo: Alfa y Omega, 1984. (Drama)

_____. *La eterna Eva y el insoportable Adán.* Santo Domingo: 1995. (Drama)

R. Vda. de Ulloa, Milagros. *Mi vieja lira: Poesía*s. Santo Domingo: Imp. Arte y Cine, 1969. (Poetry)

Ramírez Duval, Altagracia. *Técnicas de oficina y práctica secretarial.* Santo Domingo: ONAP, 1970. 102 p. (Prose)

Ramírez P., Martha. *Los principios cooperativos.* Santo Domingo: IDECOOP, 1975. 15 p. (Essay)

Ramos, Emelda. *El despojo o por los trillos de la leyenda.* Santo Domingo: Taller, 1983. 102 p. (Novel)

Rathe, Magdalena. *Impacto distributivo de la gestión fiscal.* Santo Domingo: Editora Taller, 1991. (Prose)

_____. et. al. *Reforma social: Una agenda para combatir la pobreza.* Santo Domingo: Alfa y Omega, 1993. (Prose)

Reynoso, Ana Silvia. *El despertar de las espigas.* Santo Domingo: Editora de la Universidad Autónoma de Santo Domingo, 1976. 109 p. Presentación de Abelardo Vicioso. (Poetry)

_____. *Pinceladas, memorias tempranas.* Santo Domingo: Editora Universitaria, 1989. 206 p. Drawings by Rosa Tavárez, Vladimir Velásquez, Ana Silvia Reynoso, Abraham Abud. (Poetic Prose)

Reynoso de Columna, Ana Silvia. *Intimismo.* Ciudad Trujillo: Librería Dominicana, 1960. 73 p. Prologue by Antonio Fenández Spencer. (Poetry)

Rivera, Martha. *20th Century* (aún sin nombre en español) *y otros poemas.* Santo Domingo: Ediciones Armario Urbano, 1985. n.p. (Poetry)

_____. *Transparencias de mi espejo.* Santo Domingo: Editora Búho, 1985. n.p. (Poetry)

_____. *Geometría del vértigo.* Santo Domingo: Editora el Nuevo Diario, 1995. 69 p. Cover and sketches by Desirée Domínguez. (Poetry)

_____. *He olvidado tu nombre.* Santo Domingo: Casa de Teatro, 1997. 139 p. Premio Internacional de Novela Casa de Teatro 1996. (Novel)

Rizik, Marisela. *El tiempo del olvido.* Santo Domingo: Editora Taller, 1996. (Poetry)

Rodríguez de Fernández, Aida. ed. *Poesías, adivinanzas y canciones para niños.* Santo Domingo: Producciones CENCAP, 1973. 57 p. il. Music by Luis Alberti. (Prose and poetry)

Rodríguez Cáceres, Amira. *Mi fuente cantarina.* Ciudad Trujillo: Editorial Montalvo, 1945. 140 p. (Poetry)

_____. *Hojas caídas.* Ciudad Trujillo: Editora Montalvo, 1952. 112 p. Critical commentary by Francisco R. Mejía and others. (Poetry)

Rodríguez Muñoz, Ana. *Cuando te encontré*. Santo Domingo: Editora Sante, S.A., 1989. n.p. (Poetry)

Rodríguez, Evangelina. *Granos de polen*. San Pedro de Macorís: n.p., 1915. 170 p. (Essay)

_____. *Le Guerisseur: Cuento chino biblíco filosófico de moral social*. La Vega: Tipografía El Progreso, 1927. 19 p. (Short Story)

Rodríguez, Natalia. *Sexismo y discriminación en la educación técnica en la República Dominicana*. Santo Domingo: Centro de Investigación para Acción Feminista, 1992. 126 p. (Essay)

Rodríguez, Sally. *Luz de los cuerpos*. Santo Domingo: Biblioteca Nacional, Colección Orfeo, 1985. 86 p. Prologue by the author. Epilogue by Manuel Mora Serrano. (Poetry)

Rodríguez Demorizi, Silveria R. *Salomé Ureña de Henríquez*. Washington: Boletín de la Unión Panamericana, 1942. Also expanded and with a biography in: Santo Domingo: "Cuadernos Dominicanos de Cultura," 1943 and in Buenos Aires: n.p., 1944. 45 p. (Essay)

Rodríguez Vélez, Wendalina. *El turbante blanco, muertos, santos y vivos en lucha política*. Santo Domingo: Museo del Hombre Dominicano, 1982. 289 p. (Essay)

Rojas de Sonni, María Candelaria. *Primicias*. Santo Domingo: Tipografía Guanateme, 1957. 16, 20 p. (Poetry)

_____. *Versos sencillos*. Santo Domingo: Tipografía Komar, No.3, 1969. n.p. (Poetry)

Roldán, Beatriz A. *A través de los años*. La Romona: Imprenta La Romana, 1945. 121 p. (Novel)

Román, Sabrina. *De un tiempo a otro tiempo*. Santo Domingo: Taller, 1978. 252 p. (Poetry)

_____. *Palabra rota*. Santo Domingo: Impresora Matos, 1984. 113 p. 2nd. ed. Santo Domingo: Editora Corripio, 1995. (Poetry)

_____. *Imágenes repetidas en múltiples septiembres*. Santo Domingo: Biblioteca Nacional, 1986. 102 p. (Poetry) Cover and text design by Charito Chávez.

_____. *Piedras, ríos y maderas encontradas*. Santo Domingo: Editora Búho, 1987. 108 p. Cover and text design by Charito Chávez. (Poetry)

_____. *Carrusel de mecedoras*. Santo Domingo: Centro Dominicano de Promoción de Exportaciones, 1989. 91 p. Cover and text design by Luis Arias Vera. (Poetry)

_____. *Carrusel de mecedoras, Fantasía teatral en un acto*. Santo Domingo: Editora de Colores, 1994. 72 p. (Drama)

Ruiz Vda. de Noboa, Altagracia. *Alma dice...* Santo Domingo: n.p., 1970. 73 p. (Poetry)

Sagredo, María Antonieta. *Florecillas del sendero*. Santiago de los Caballeros, Rep. Dom.: Imprenta La Información 1944. 18 p. (Poetry)

_____. *Nardos y rosas*. Santiago de los Caballeros, Rep. Dom.: Imprenta La Información, 1944. 9 p. (Poetry)

_____. *La serenata de los ángeles*. Santiago de los Caballeros, Rep. Dom.: Imprenta La Información, n.d., 7 p. (Poetry)

_____. *Páginas íntimas*. Santiago de los Caballeros, Rep. Dom.: Imprenta La Información, 1948. 42 p. (Prose and poetry)

Salado, Carlota. *La primera derrota*. Santo Domingo: Letras y Ciencias, 1894. n.p. (Short Story)

Salgado, Teresina. *De mi ayer romántico*. Ciudad Trujillo: Roques Hermanos, editores, 1928. 190 p. (Poetry)

Sánchez de Casado, Alma. *Niveles*. Santo Domingo: Taller, 1980. 124 p. (Poetry)

Sánchez, Ana Quisqueya. *Ofrendas líricas*. Ciudad Trujillo: Editorial La Nación, 1944. 154 p. Prólogos de Alberto E. Fiallo y Carmen Natalia Martínez. (Poetry)

_____. *Intensidad de abril*. Ciudad Trujillo: Imprenta Arte y Cine, 1946. 33 p. (Poetry)

Sánchez, Carmen. *Descalza entre piedras*. Santo Domingo: Alcance, 1984. 66 p. (Poetry)

_____. *Demando otro tiempo*. Santo Domingo: Offset Encuadernacipies, 1995. 91 p. Includes a prologue by the author. (Poetry)

Sánchez, María Luisa (María Serena). *País de vendimia*. Santo Domingo: Editora Búho, 1994. 58 p. Ilus. Tony Capellán, dis. Jorge Pineda, ed. Chiqui Vicioso, prologue by Bruno Rosario Candelier. (Poetry)

Sánchez, María Teresa de. *Historia de la civilización: Educación media*. Santo Domingo: Imprenta Amigo del Hogar, 1977. 115 p. (Essay)

Santos Noboa, Gladys E. de los. *Trébol patriótico*. Santo Domingo: Secretaría de Estado de Salud y Previsión Social, 1967. 13 p. (Poetry)

_____. *Manual de información sobre las actividades de asistencia social en la República Dominicana*. Santo Domingo: Impresora Arte y Cine, 1970. 103 p. (Prose)

Santos, Yrene. *Desnudez del silencio*. Santo Domingo: Editora Búho, 1988. 64 p. Prologue by Bruno Rosario Candelier. Ilustracion by Silvano Lora. (Poetry)

Sarlouis, Clara. *Chispas*. Santo Domingo: Editora del Caribe, 1969. 79 p. (Poetry)

Segundo Congreso Femenino Dominicano. *La mujer dominicana en pro de la reelección: Labores del Segundo Congreso Femenino Dominicano*. Ciudad Trujillo: Editorial La Nación, 1945. (Essay)

Selman, Aidita. *El tiempo de un cuarto: Cuentos*. Santo Domingo: Editora Internacional, 1979. 25 p. (Short Story for children)

_____. *Cuando la luna llega*. Santo Domingo: Editora Corripio, 1983. 46 p. Prologue by Josefina de la Cruz. (Short Story for children)

Serra, Nidia. *Arte infantil: Un siglo de luz*. Santo Domingo: Universidad Central del Este, 1982. 108 p. + il. (Essay)

Simó Delgado, Dulce María. *Catorce sonetos de amor*. Santo Domingo: Di-Do-Offset, 1966. 28 p. (Poetry)

Smester, Clementina. *Cuentos*. Santiago: n.p., 1959. 38 p. (Short Story)

Smester, Rosa. *Prosas.* Santiago de los Caballeros: Linotipografía El Diario, 1931. 75 p. 2nd. ed. Santo Domingo: Comisión Permanente de la Feria del Libro, 1987. (Prose)

Tavárez Belliard, Aurora. *Castilla Silabario.* 6ta. ed. (Santiago, Dom. Rep.: Impr. Muchas Gracias, 1942. 84 p. + ilus. (Prose)

_____. *En el sendero de Kempis.* Santiago de los Caballeros, Rep. Dom.: Imprenta La Información, 1944. (Essay)

Tavárez, Julia. *Guide to Caribbean Pre-History.* Santo Domingo: Editora Taller, Museo del Hombre Dominicano, Serie Catálogo y Memorias, 1978. 20 p. (Prose)

Tejada, Argelia. *Metodología de una experiencia en el sector rural.* Santo Domingo: Servicios Gráficos Diversos, 1978. 35 p. (Essay)

Tejada Rojas, Pura Dolores. *Cápsulas amargas.* México: Imprenta Grafos, 1950. 113 p. (Poetry)

_____. *Brizna o el mensaje de taurus.* Santo Domingo: n.p., 1982. 82 p. (Drama)

Terradas de Lamarche, Enriqueta. *Crisoles interiores.* Santo Domingo: Tipografía Cambier, 1933. 52 p. (Poetry)

Terrero, Viola Nuris. *La poesía va a la escuela: Versos, prosa y cuentos para niños.* Santo Domingo: Editora Taller, 1989. 96 p. (Poetry and prose)

Tolentino, Marianne de. *Balzac y García Márquez.* Santo Domingo: Taller, 1971. 39 p. (Essay)

_____. *Estudio crítico.* Santo Domingo: Biblioteca Taller No.60, 1975. xx,xxxii p. (Essay)

_____. *El árbol de los pájaros.* Santo Domingo: Editora Taller, 1983. 32 p. (Prose)

Tormes, María Nieves. *Cálices en flor.* Santo Domingo: Imp. Arte y Cine, 1969. 73 p. (Poetry)

Ugarte España, María. *Monumentos coloniales.* Santo Domingo: Museo de las Casas Reales, 1977. 291 p. (Essay)

_____. *La catedral de Santo Domingo, Primada de América.* Santo Domingo: Colección Quinto Centenario, 1992. 145 p. (Essay)

_____. *Iglesias, capillas y ermitas coloniales.* Santo Domingo: Colección Banreservas, Serie Historia, V. I, n.d. 237 p. (Essay)

Ulloa Vda Patria, Milagros R. *Tiempo y verso...* Santo Domingo: n.p., 1967. 112 p. (Poetry)

_____. *Mi vieja lira.* Santo Domingo: Impresora Arte y Cine, 1969. 125 p. il. (Poetry)

_____. *Porvenir: Versos didácticos.* Santo Domingo: Impresora Arte y Cine, 1970. 160 p. (Poetry)

Ureña, Dulce. *Preámbulo.* Santo Domingo: Editora Universitaria, 1988. 86 p. (Poetry)

_____. *Babonucos.* Santo Domingo: Editorial Gente, 1995. (Poetry)

Ureña de Henríquez, Salomé. *Poesía.* Santo Domingo: Imprenta de García Hermanos, Sociedad Literaria "Amigos del país", 1880. xv-214 p. Unsigned biography by José Lamarche and prologue by Fernando A. de Meriño. (Poetry)

_____. *Poesías.* Madrid: Tipografías Europa, 1920. 142 p. Selection and prologue by Pedro Henríquez Ureña. (Poetry)

_____. *Poesías completas.* Ciudad Trujillo: Secretaría de Estado y Bellas Artes, Colección Biblioteca Dominicana, vol. IV, serie I, 1950. 351 p. Prologue by Joaquín Balaguer; edition under the care of Manuel E. Suncar Chevalier. 5th. ed., Santo Domingo: Secretaría de Estado de Educación, Bellas Artes y Cultos, 1975. Foreword by Jorge Tena Reyes. 6th. ed., Santo Domingo: Publicación de la ONAP, 1985. Prologue by Jaime A. Viñas Román. 7th. ed., Santo Domingo: Publicaciones ONAP, Colección "Feria del Libro" 1988. Prologue by Margarita Vallejo de Paredes. 9th. ed., Santo Domingo: ONAP, 1992. 351 p. (Poetry)

_____. *Poesías escogidas.* Ciudad Trujillo: Librería Dominicana, Julio D. Postigo, Colección Pensamiento Dominicano No. 19, 1960. 188 p. (Poetry)

_____. *Cantos a la Patria.* Santo Domingo: Publicaciones América, n.d. n.p. (Poetry)

_____. *Poesías completas.* Santo Domingo: Fundación Corripio, Biblioteca de Clásicos Dominicanos VII, 1989. 299 p. Prologue and additional notes by Diógenes Céspedes. Original prologue by Mons. Fernando Arturo de Meriño. (Poetry)

_____. *Anacaona.* Santo Domingo: Publicaciones América, Colección Parnaso Dominicano, n.d. 94 p. (Poetry)

Valle, Luz del. *Flores de mi alma.* Ciudad Trujillo: s.n., 1959. 20 p. (Poetry)

Vallejo de García, Francisca. *La mano de la providencia.* San Pedro de Macorís, Rep. Dom.: Imprenta del Boletín Mercantil, 1905. n.p. (Novel)

Vallejo de Paredes, Margarita. *Historia de caracoles: Juguete cómico en un acto.* Ciudad Trujillo: Publicaciones de la Secretaría de Educación y Bellas Artes, 1957. 10 p. (Drama)

_____. ed. *Antología literaria dominicana,* 5 vols. Santo Domingo: Instituto Tecnológico de Santo Domingo, 1981. (Contiene 1. poesía; 2. cuento; 3. teatro; 4. discursos, semblanzas y ensayos; 5. folklore)

_____. *Vida y obra de Ercilia Pepín.* Santo Domingo: Publicaciones ONAP, 1994. 77 p. (Essay)

_____. *Apuntes biográficos y bibliográficos de algunos escritores dominicanos del siglo XIX.* Santo Domingo: Publicaciones de la ONAP, 1995. (Essay)

Vargas de Toyos, Altagracia. *Sueño de ideal.* Santo Domingo: Editora Montalvo, 1967. 84 p. (Novel)

_____. *Vana espera.* n.p.: Impresora Carolina, n.d. 63 p. (Prose)

Vargas Valente, Virginia. *El aporte de la rebeldía de las mujeres* Santo Domingo: Centro de Investigación para Acción Feminista, Colección Teoría, 1988. 47 p. (Essay)

Varias. *Ofrenda de la mujer vegana al Generalísimo Trujillo.* La Vega: manuscript, 1941. n.p. (Prose and poetry)

Vásquez, Cándida Anelsa. *Los últimos toques de la espuma.* Santo Domingo: Biblioteca Nacional, Colección Orfeo, 1986. 120 p. Prologue by Carlos Dobal. Cover designed by R. Canals. Photos by Vitico Cabrera. (Poetry)

Vega, Annelie et al. *Mariposa de colores*. Santo Domingo: Biblioteca Piloto Infantil, 1982. 20 p. (Poetic Prose)

Vega de Bonnelly, Vanessa. *Inquietudes en el tiempo*. Santiago de los Caballeros, Rep. Dom.: Imp. Teófilo, 1976. 41 p. (Poetry)

_____. *Otras inquietudes en el tiempo*. Santiago de los Caballeros, Rep. Dom.: Offset L.H. Cruz, C por A, 1989. 71 p. Introductory note by Carlos Dobal. (Poetry)

_____. *Cuentos en el camino*. Santiago de los Caballeros, Rep. Dom.: Editora Nani, 1995. 54 p. (Short Story)

Veloz, Livia. *Preludios sentimentales*. Santo Domingo. Imprenta La Cuna de América, 1929, 36 p. (Poetry)

_____. *Acordes*. Santo Domingo: Imprenta Gómez, 1936. 45 p. (Poetry)

_____. *Transparencias*. Madrid: Escuela Nueva, 1971. 79 p. Madrid Escuela Nueva. Premio Salomé Ureña 1964. (Poetry)

_____. *Historia del feminismo en la República Dominicana*. Santo Domingo: Secretaría de Estado de Educación, Bellas Artes y Cultos, 1977. 46 p. (Essay)

_____. *Ojos entreabiertos*. Santo Domingo: Publicación de la Biblioteca Nacional, 1992. 134 p. Foreword by Miguel Collado. Under the title *La más chiquita*, won Special Mention in a contest sponsored by Ateneo Dominicano in 1940. Posthumous publication (Novel)

Ventura Alvarez, Míriam. *Poemas de la noche*. Santo Domingo: Editora Weber, 1986. 24 p. (Poetry)

_____. *Trópico acerca del otoño*. Santo Domingo: Huellas, 1987. 67 p. (Poetry)

_____. *Claves para fantasmas*. Nueva York: Alcance, 1997. 90 p. (Poetry)

Vicente, María del Carmen. *Territorios verticales*. Santo Domingo: Talleres de Graficolor, 1983. n.p. (Poetry)

Vicioso, Sherezada (Chiqui). *Viaje desde el agua*. Santo Domingo: Visuarte, 1981. 71 p. Includes a letter by Mateo Morrison. (Poetry)

_____. *Un extraño ulular traía el viento*. Santo Domingo: Alfa y Omega, 1985. n.p. Illustrated by Tony Capellán. (Poetry)

_____. *Bolver a vivir, imágenes de Nicaragua*. Santo Domingo: Editora Búho, 1985. n.p. (Essay)

_____. *Julia de Burgos la nuestra*. Santo Domingo: Alfa y Omega, 1987. n.p. Illustrated by Belkis Ramírez. (Essay and poetry)

_____. *Algo que decir. Ensayos sobre literatura femenina. 1981-1991* Santo Domingo: Editora Búho, 1991. 143 p. Foreword by José Alcántara Almánzar. (Essay)

_____. *Internamiento*. Santo Domingo: Editora Búho, 1992. 60 p. Illustrated by Jorge Pineda. (Poetry)

_____. *Working with rather than for Women*. Haiti/Dominican Republic: UNICEF, 1995. 24 p. (Educational Module III)

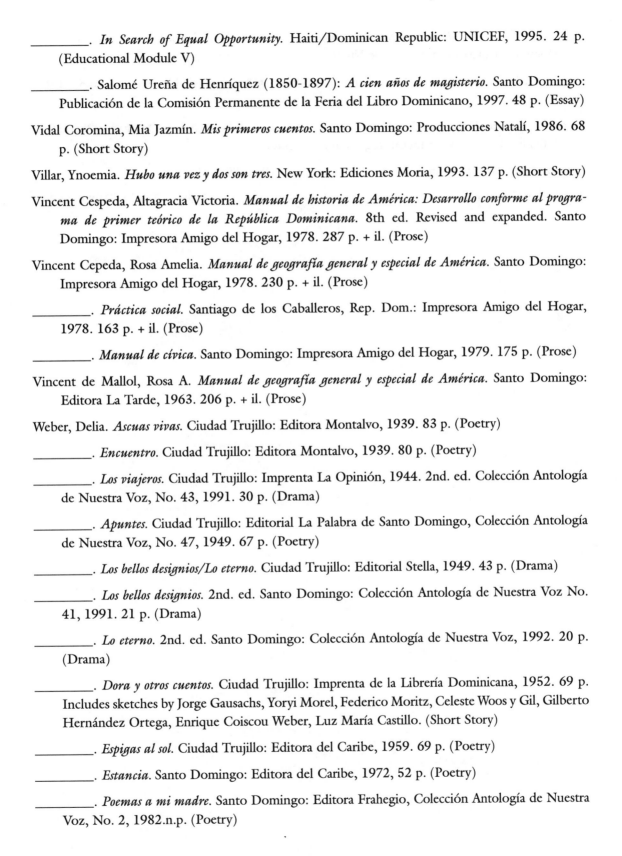

_____. *In Search of Equal Opportunity.* Haiti/Dominican Republic: UNICEF, 1995. 24 p. (Educational Module V)

_____. Salomé Ureña de Henríquez (1850-1897): *A cien años de magisterio.* Santo Domingo: Publicación de la Comisión Permanente de la Feria del Libro Dominicano, 1997. 48 p. (Essay)

Vidal Coromina, Mia Jazmín. *Mis primeros cuentos.* Santo Domingo: Producciones Natalí, 1986. 68 p. (Short Story)

Villar, Ynoemia. *Hubo una vez y dos son tres.* New York: Ediciones Moria, 1993. 137 p. (Short Story)

Vincent Cespeda, Altagracia Victoria. *Manual de historia de América: Desarrollo conforme al programa de primer teórico de la República Dominicana.* 8th ed. Revised and expanded. Santo Domingo: Impresora Amigo del Hogar, 1978. 287 p. + il. (Prose)

Vincent Cepeda, Rosa Amelia. *Manual de geografía general y especial de América.* Santo Domingo: Impresora Amigo del Hogar, 1978. 230 p. + il. (Prose)

_____. *Práctica social.* Santiago de los Caballeros, Rep. Dom.: Impresora Amigo del Hogar, 1978. 163 p. + il. (Prose)

_____. *Manual de cívica.* Santo Domingo: Impresora Amigo del Hogar, 1979. 175 p. (Prose)

Vincent de Mallol, Rosa A. *Manual de geografía general y especial de América.* Santo Domingo: Editora La Tarde, 1963. 206 p. + il. (Prose)

Weber, Delia. *Ascuas vivas.* Ciudad Trujillo: Editora Montalvo, 1939. 83 p. (Poetry)

_____. *Encuentro.* Ciudad Trujillo: Editora Montalvo, 1939. 80 p. (Poetry)

_____. *Los viajeros.* Ciudad Trujillo: Imprenta La Opinión, 1944. 2nd. ed. Colección Antología de Nuestra Voz, No. 43, 1991. 30 p. (Drama)

_____. *Apuntes.* Ciudad Trujillo: Editorial La Palabra de Santo Domingo, Colección Antología de Nuestra Voz, No. 47, 1949. 67 p. (Poetry)

_____. *Los bellos designios/Lo eterno.* Ciudad Trujillo: Editorial Stella, 1949. 43 p. (Drama)

_____. *Los bellos designios.* 2nd. ed. Santo Domingo: Colección Antología de Nuestra Voz No. 41, 1991. 21 p. (Drama)

_____. *Lo eterno.* 2nd. ed. Santo Domingo: Colección Antología de Nuestra Voz, 1992. 20 p. (Drama)

_____. *Dora y otros cuentos.* Ciudad Trujillo: Imprenta de la Librería Dominicana, 1952. 69 p. Includes sketches by Jorge Gausachs, Yoryi Morel, Federico Moritz, Celeste Woos y Gil, Gilberto Hernández Ortega, Enrique Coiscou Weber, Luz María Castillo. (Short Story)

_____. *Espigas al sol.* Ciudad Trujillo: Editora del Caribe, 1959. 69 p. (Poetry)

_____. *Estancia.* Santo Domingo: Editora del Caribe, 1972, 52 p. (Poetry)

_____. *Poemas a mi madre.* Santo Domingo: Editora Frahegio, Colección Antología de Nuestra Voz, No. 2, 1982.n.p. (Poetry)

_____. *La india: Renacimiento en Bengala/Personalidad de Rabindranath Tagore.* Santo Domingo: Colección Antología de Nuestra Voz., No. 13, 1987. n.p. (Essay)

_____. *Pensamiento inédito.* Santo Domingo: Colección Antología de Nuestra Voz No.32, 1987, 72 p. (Essay)

Yangüela, Violeta. *Esclava te doy*, 2nd ed. Santo Domingo: Editora Alfa y Omega, 1978. 235 p. Introduction by Héctor Incháustegui Cabral. (Essay)

Zouain, Zaidy. *Lilibeth.* Santo Domingo: Ediciones ZZ, 1979. 89 p. (Poetry)

Zouain de Castellanos, Yolanda. *La mesa árabe.* Santo Domingo: Editora Tele #., 1982. 369 p. (Prose)

Daisy Cocco De Filippis is a native of the Dominican Republic. As many other immigrants, Dr. Cocco De Filippis attended The City University of New York as she and her husband of thirty-three years, Nunzio De Filippis, raised their three sons. Dr. Cocco De Filippis received her B.A. Summa cum laude, in Spanish and English literatures in 1975, and an M.A. in Spanish Literature in 1978 from Queens College. In 1984, Dr. Cocco De Filippis received her Ph.D. in Caribbean and Latin American Literatures from the Graduate Center. Dr. Cocco De Filippis is Professor of Spanish and Chair of the Department of Foreign Languages, ESL and Humanities at York College where she has taught language and literature since 1978. A prolific writer, Professor Cocco De Filippis has devoted much of the past two decades to disseminate Dominican letters in the U.S. Her extensive bibliography is included in the bibliography of works written by Dominican women included in this publication. During academic year 1996-97, Professor Cocco De Filippis was a Rockefeller Foundation, Visiting Research Professor at the CUNY Dominican Studies Institute where this publication was written.

Raquel Paiewonsky is a native of the Dominican Republic. During the past decade, Paiewonsky has divided her time between New York City and the Dominican Republic. In 1993, she received her B.F.A. from Parsons School of Design in New York. From 1989-1991 she studied Fine Arts at the Altos de Chavón School in the Dominican Republic.

Raquel Paiewonsky has been recognized as one of the finest young talents in the Dominican Republic today. Paiewonsky has received much recognition as a plastic artist. Her paintings, installations and sculptures have been shown in collective as well as individual exhibits both in the Dominican Republic and the U.S. Paiewonsky has received the 1996 "Medalla de Oro" (Gold Medal), Bienal de Artes Visuales, Museo de Arte Moderno, Santo Domingo, Rep. Dom. Other recognitions include a 1989-1991 award from the Parsons School of Design, and a 1993 Bluhdom Award.